DERIVATIVE SECURITIES PRICING AND MODELLING

CONTEMPORARY STUDIES IN ECONOMIC AND FINANCIAL ANALYSIS

Series Editors: Robert Thornton and J. Richard Aronson

Recent Volumes:

Volume 83:	Foreign Direct Investment in the United States, Edited by W. L. Casey
Volume 84:	Colombia: An Opening Economy? Edited by C. M. Callahan and F. R. Gunter
Volume 85:	The Irish Economy in Transition: Success, Problems and Prospects, Edited by J. R. Aronson, V. Munley and R. J. Thornton
Volume 86:	Asia Pacific Financial Markets in Comparative Perspective: Issues and Implications for the 21st Century, Edited by J. A. Batten and T. A. Fetherston
Volume 87:	Developments in Litigation Economics, Edited by P. A. Gaughan and R. J. Thornton
Volume 88:	European Responses to Globalization: Resistance, Adaptation and Alternatives
Volume 89:	Globalization: Perspectives from Central and Eastern Europe, Edited by Katalin E. Fabian
Volume 90:	Privatization in Transition Economies: The Ongoing Story, Edited by Ira W. Lieberman and Daniel J. Kopf
Volume 91:	Personal Injury and Wrongful Death Damages Calculations: Transatlantic Dialogue, Edited by John O. Ward and Robert J. Thornton
Volume 92:	Moving Beyond Storytelling: Emerging Research in Microfinance, Edited by Todd A. Watkins and Karen Hicks
Volume 93:	The Impact of the Global Financial Crisis on Emerging Financial Markets, Edited by Jonathan A. Batten and Peter G. Szilagyi

CONTEMPORARY STUDIES IN ECONOMIC AND FINANCIAL ANALYSIS VOLUME 94

DERIVATIVE SECURITIES PRICING AND MODELLING

EDITED BY

JONATHAN A. BATTEN
Hong Kong University of Science & Technology, Hong Kong

NIKLAS WAGNER
University of Passau, Germany

Emerald

United Kingdom – North America – Japan
India – Malaysia – China

Emerald Group Publishing Limited
Howard House, Wagon Lane, Bingley BD16 1WA, UK

First edition 2012

British Library Cataloguing in Publication Data
A catalogue record for this book is available from the British Library

ISBN: 978-1-78052-616-4
ISSN: 1569-3759 (Series)

CONTENTS

PART II: DERIVATIVES PRICES AND RISK-NEUTRAL DISTRIBUTIONS

PART III: DERIVATIVES MODELS AND MODEL PERFORMANCE

PART IV: DERIVATIVES MODELS, RISK MANAGEMENT, CREDIT AND CORPORATE CONTROL

LIST OF CONTRIBUTORS

Kavous Ardalan	School of Management, Marist College, Poughkeepsie, NY, USA
A.S.M. Sohel Azad	School of Accounting, Economics and Finance, Deakin University, Victoria, Australia
Gaia Barone	Department of Economics, "Tor Vergata" University, Rome, Italy
Jonathan A. Batten	Department of Finance, Hong Kong University of Science and Technology, Hong Kong
David P. Brown	School of Business, University of Wisconsin–Madison, Madison, WI, USA
Axel Buchner	Department of Finance, University of Passau, Passau, Germany
John Cotter	School of Business, University College Dublin, Blackrock, Ireland
Victor Fang	School of Accounting, Economics and Finance, Deakin University, Victoria, Australia
Miguel Angel Fuentes	CONICET, Centro Atomico Bariloche, Bariloche, Black River, Argentina; School of Government, Universidad del Desarrollo, Santiago, Chile
Marco M. García-Alonso	BBVA Madrid, Madrid, Spain
Austin Gerig	CABDyN Complexity Centre, Saÿd Business School, University of Oxford, UK

Aleksandr V. Gevorkyan	Paul McGhee Division, SCPS, New York University, New York, NY, USA
Arkady Gevorkyan	Department of Economics, NSSR, The New School, New York, NY, USA
Jim Hanly	School of Business, Dublin Institute of Technology, Dublin, Ireland
Michael Herold	Chair of Banking and Financial Control, University of Bamberg, Bamberg, Germany
Michalis Ioannides	BNP Paribas, Fixed Income, Corporate and Investment Banking, London, UK
Jens Carsten Jackwerth	Department of Economics, Universität Konstanz, Konstanz, Germany
Ognyan Kounchev	Institute of Mathematics, Bulgarian Academy of Sciences, Sofia, Bulgaria
Delphine Lautier	DRM-Finance, University Paris Dauphine, Paris, France; Fime Laboratory, Paris, France; Cerna, Mines ParisTech, Paris, France
Chien-Ting Lin	School of Accounting, Economics and Finance, Deakin University, Victoria, Australia
Igor Loncarski	Faculty of Economics, University of Ljubljana, Slovenia
Krasimir Milanov	Institute of Mathematics and Informatics, Bulgarian Academy of Sciences, Sofia, Bulgaria
Abdulkadir Mohamed	Department of Economics, Finance and Accounting, Liverpool University, Liverpool, UK
Manuel Moreno	Department of Economic Analysis and Finance, University of Castilla La-Mancha, Toledo, Spain

Matthias Muck	Chair of Banking and Financial Control, University of Bamberg, Bamberg, Germany
Javier F. Navas	Department of Financial Economics and Accounting, Pablo de Olavide University, Seville, Spain
Franck Raynaud	Laboratory of Cell Biophysic, École Polytechnique Fédérale de Lausanne, Switzerland
Mark Rubinstein	Haas School of Business, University of California at Berkeley, Berkeley, CA, USA
Frank S. Skinner	Brunel University, Uxbridge, Middlesex, UK
Matevz Skocir	Faculty of Economics, University of Ljubljana, Slovenia
Ales Berk Skok	Faculty of Economics, University of Ljubljana, Slovenia
Javier Vicente	Department of Business Administration, Universidad Carlos III, Madrid, Spain
Niklas Wagner	Department of Finance, University of Passau, Passau, Germany
Lixin Wu	Department of Mathematics, Hong Kong University of Science and Technology, Hong Kong

PART I
ADVANCES IN DERIVATIVES AND ECONOMIC STABILITY

DERIVATIVES SECURITIES PRICING AND MODELLING

Jonathan A. Batten and Niklas Wagner

ABSTRACT

In terms of notional value outstanding, derivatives markets declined in both over-the-counter and exchange-traded transactions during the 2007–2009 global financial crisis (GFC) period, as counterparty and credit concerns became pre-eminent. However, during the 2010–2011 second stage of the GFC, markets rebounded and by June 2011 outstandings reached new levels which highlight the importance these contracts continue to play in the day-to-day risk management and trading activities of corporations and financial intermediaries. The bulk of the contracts traded are interest rate-related instruments and are denominated in either US dollars or Euro. Credit-related instruments remain an important market segment, although outstandings remain at pre-crisis period levels. Of particular concern for regulators is the role of non-bank financial intermediaries, which are the main counterparty to derivatives transactions. While their share of the market remains unchanged over the last decade, outstandings overall have increased more than fourfold. The present volume considers the issues that participants face in today's derivatives markets including the potential impact of derivatives on economic stability, pricing issues, modelling as well as model performance

Derivative Securities Pricing and Modelling
Contemporary Studies in Economic and Financial Analysis, Volume 94, 3–14

ISSN: 1569-3759/doi:10.1108/S1569-3759(2012)0000094003

and the application of derivatives for risk management and corporate control.

Keywords: Contingent capital securities; corporate control; derivatives and economic stability, modelling as well as model performance; risk management; risk-neutral distributions

Global corporations and financial intermediaries trade billions of dollars of derivative contracts on a daily basis across a range of products and markets. These instruments may be traded in both over-the-counter (OTC) or exchange-traded markets, although in terms of notional amounts outstanding, the amounts in OTC markets (US$707.6 trillion in June 2011) easily eclipse those in exchange-traded markets (US$26.3 trillion).[1] Fig. 1 plots the sevenfold increase in outstandings since 1998. The impact of the 2007–2009 global financial crisis (GFC) period is clearly evident by the reduction in outstandings in 2008. Importantly, this figure also reveals that after an increase of only 3% in the second half of 2010, total notional amounts outstanding of OTC derivatives rose by 18% in the first half of 2011, so that they now surpass those levels achieved prior to the 2007–2009 GFC period.

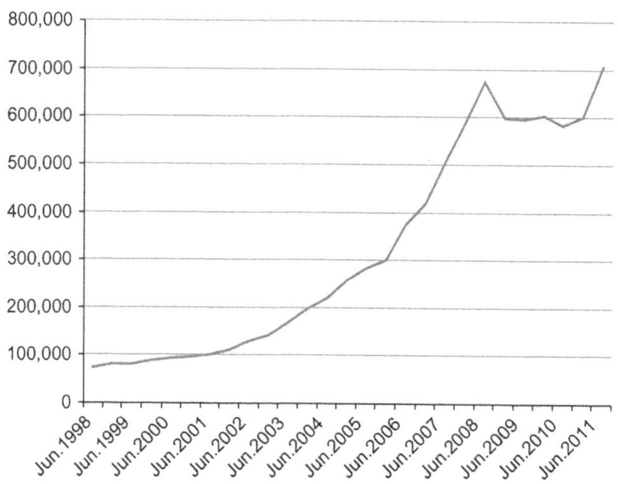

Fig. 1. Derivatives Contracts Outstanding in Billions of US Dollars from June 1998 to 2011. *Source*: BIS (2011, Table 19). *Notes*: The figure reports over-the-counter (OTC) derivatives markets statistics of notional amounts outstanding in billions of US dollars.

While there are many instruments traded, they may be grouped into four main categories: interest rate, foreign exchange, equity and commodity contracts. Davydoff and Naacke's (2009) investigation of the derivatives market illustrates that worldwide derivatives trading volumes increased across all products over the period from 1998 to 2008. During this period the smallest increase was for interest rate products with volumes increasing 3.6 times, while stock index options and futures showed the largest rise with volumes increasing 17-fold as these instruments gained popularity for portfolio hedging. Overall, the average increase in volumes was a factor of 7.8.

Fig. 2 shows that interest rate contracts are the main OTC contract traded accounting for 78.3% (US\$553.9 trillion) of the US\$707.6 trillion in outstandings in June 2011, while foreign exchange contracts account for only 9.1% (US\$553.9 trillion), equity contracts less than 1% (US\$6.9 trillion) and commodity contracts less than half a percent (US\$3.2 trillion). Fig. 3 demonstrates that in June 2011 the major form of interest rate contract traded is the interest rate swap (79.8% or US\$441.6 trillion), with interest rate options and forward rate agreements (FRAs) accounting for only 10.2% (US\$56.4 trillion) and 10.1% (US\$55.8 trillion), respectively. While

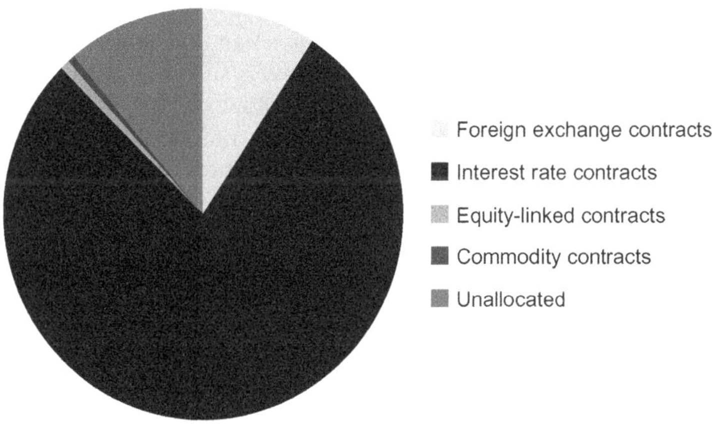

Fig. 2. Types of Derivatives Contracts Traded in June 2011. *Source*: BIS (2011, Table 19). *Notes*: From June 1998, the committee on the global financial system (CGFS) initiated the collection by the central banks of the G10 countries of statistics on forwards, swaps and options of foreign exchange, interest rate, equity and commodity derivatives. From December 2004, credit default swaps (CDSs) notional amounts outstanding and gross market values for single- and multi-name instruments were also collected.

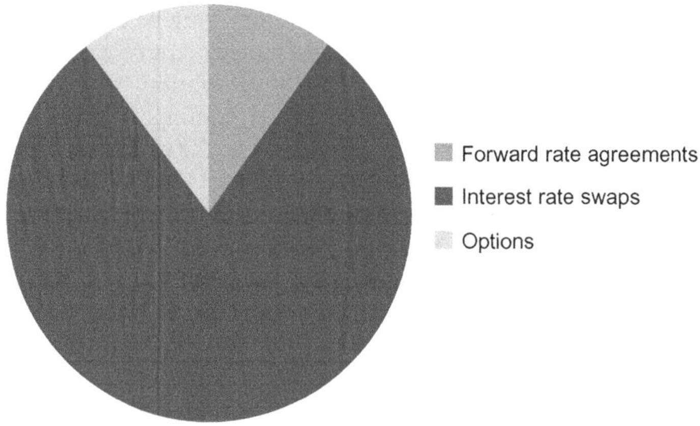

Fig. 3. Types of Interest Rate Contracts Traded in June 2011. *Source*: BIS (2011, Table 19). *Notes*: From June 1998, the committee on the global financial system (CGFS) initiated the collection by the central banks of the G10 countries of statistics on forwards, swaps and options of foreign exchange, interest rate, equity and commodity derivatives. From December 2004 credit default swaps (CDSs) notional amounts outstanding and gross market values for single- and multi-name instruments were also collected.

these latter amounts are still significant it is clear that interest rate swaps, which enable counterparties to switch between single currency fixed and floating rate exposures across multiple cash flow periods, is the preferred product for interest rate risk management and trading. Swap usage is also consistent with a proactive approach to balance sheet management which is evident from a number of industry surveys.[2]

While the scale and scope of derivatives trading worldwide is enormous, the interconnectedness of these products to other financial markets is of significant concern for regulators and policymakers. The link between derivatives trading in financial markets and broader questions of economic stability became a serious concern during the recent GFC, which comprised at least two separate stages: the 2007–2009 US subprime financial crisis and the subsequent 2010–2011 European sovereign debt crisis, both evolving along with ongoing corresponding global banking concerns.[3] One critical lesson from the GFC is the extent of financial market integration and the difficulty in diversifying those financial risks that arise in both the national and the international context.

A feature of derivatives markets that has been at the centre of regulatory attention is the role played by non-bank financial intermediaries, which in most developed financial markets are outside the direct control of banking regulators. For example, in the United States, these intermediaries have been traditionally supervised by the Securities and Exchange Commission[4] rather than the Federal Reserve Bank.[5] The potential scale of this problem is evident when one considers counterparties to derivatives trades in foreign exchange markets, which – while modest as compared to interest rate-related transactions – impose significant financial stability risks owing to their capital account impacts. In June 2011, 40.5% (US$26.2 trillion) of these transaction comprised trades between banks (termed reporting dealers by the BIS), while trades between banks and other financial institutions comprised the bulk of transactions (44.6%), while trades with non-financial customers comprised the least (14.9%). For example, the system-wide impact of a carry-trade-related currency purchase and subsequent sale between an investment bank, or a hedge fund, and a reporting bank may be difficult to track if it is undertaken across different reporting jurisdictions and time zones. Finally, it was OTC trading in credit derivatives which played a key role in the causes as well as in the transmission of crisis effects during the subprime financial crisis (see e.g. Breitenfellner & Wagner, 2010) such that both non-bank financial intermediaries and OTC trading became issues of increased concern for regulators.

Not surprisingly, the fragmented nature of domestic financial market supervision in many countries, in addition to the lack of co-ordination between national and international organisations has recently come under scrutiny, with many arguing that this policy environment encouraged risk-taking by intermediaries in the period prior to the GFC (see Pauget, 2009). In response, regulators and legislators worldwide are continuing to examine the role that derivatives played in the crisis and the appropriateness of new forms of regulation. However, of course, proposed regulations could adversely impact many techniques that corporations currently use to mitigate their financial and business risks (such as managing credit exposures using credit derivatives). Nonetheless, efforts to create a sounder financial system should enable regulation to improve safety and transparency in the derivatives market.

The primary objective of the present volume is to add to the exciting and relatively limited literature by providing new insights into the link between derivatives and the role they now play in managing risk in financial and broader economic systems. The volume considers many of the issues that market participants and regulators face, including the potential impact of derivatives on economic stability, pricing, modelling as well as model performance and the application of derivatives for risk management and corporate control. The volume contains 17 chapters, which are grouped into four parts: the first part deals with the relationship between derivatives and economic stability; the second addresses derivatives pricing and risk-neutral probabilities; the third investigates derivatives modelling and model performance and the final part provides insights into financial risk management, credit management and issues concerning corporate control.

PART I: ADVANCES IN DERIVATIVES AND ECONOMIC STABILITY

The first part of the volume, titled 'Advances in Derivatives and Economic Stability', offers five chapters, including this introduction to the volume. The chapters provide insights into the link between derivatives usage and economic stability and demonstrate the role options play in managing economic risk, risk management using contingent capital securities, and the final chapter which addresses the need to consider high dimensionality in the pricing of derivatives.

The second chapter in this part by Ardalan provides an extensive review of the financial option pricing literature and its applications to managing the underlying risks associated with corporate assets and liabilities. Ardalan's focus is on the direct relationship between the volatility of the underlying asset and the value of the option, which when combined is the cornerstone of a dynamic hedging strategy. Ardalan argues that this approach adopts a one-sided emphasis on the value-creating role of volatility and can promote excessive risk taking. He concludes that the value of real investments is underpinned by the highly volatile value of the real options embedded in such projects. Consequently, this can lead to severe cycles in real investment and the economy.

The third chapter by Gevorkyan and Gevorkyan argues that a more extensive understanding of the phenomena of asset price dynamics is necessary to link financial empirical analysis with modern socially responsible economic development. The authors cite recent trends in the commodity and financial futures contracts, which may inflict detrimental effects on global development efforts. They note that this is especially the case for emerging markets that face well-known fears of underlying inflation and speculative capital flows. In turn this may impose costs of social stability and inhibit sustained economic development. Nonetheless, surprisingly the regulatory reforms undertaken by many emerging economies since the last major crisis in 1997–1998 (termed the Asian financial crisis), which included opening up their financial markets and developing better risk management capability allowed them to better address the contagion from the GFC that originated in the developed world (Batten & Szilagyi, 2011).

The fourth chapter in this part by Ioannides and Skinner investigates the use of contingent capital securities (called contingent capital securities, CoCos). The authors believe that these securities should be designed to maintain confidence in a bank before a crisis begins because once a crisis commences it is difficult to see how a bank can assure the capital market without the support of state aid. The authors also find, after reviewing existing examples of these securities that currently trade in financial markets, that bank CoCos generally have the right design. They also point out that existing bank CoCos are unfunded since there is no need to structure these securities to provide additional liquidity. If a bank does face a liquidity crisis then the CoCos has already failed in its attempt to maintain confidence in the bank.

The final chapter by Lautier and Raynaud investigates the use of graph theory as a tool to investigate high dimensionality in finance, specifically analysing systemic risk in derivatives markets. Holtz (2008) refers to dimensionality as the property of derivative prices that allows them to be represented as expected values, which in turn can be transformed to high-dimensional integrals. These integrals cannot be calculated analytically and are larger the more random variables are involved. The novelty of the Lautier and Raynaud chapter is that their technique builds a graph, called a 'minimum spanning tree', which provides the series of connections based on the correlation matrix of price returns. Being filtered networks they enable the identification of the most probable and shortest path for the transmission of a price shocks across a complex network. This approach offers a valuable application to better understanding the complex transmission process across a series of assets trading in financial markets with different degrees of integration.

PART II: DERIVATIVES PRICES AND RISK-NEUTRAL DISTRIBUTIONS

The second part of the volume, titled 'Derivatives Prices and Risk Neutral Distributions', provides three chapters that relate to the recovery of stochastic processes from option prices including the implications of risk neutral densities for catastrophe events.

The first chapter in this part by Jackwerth and Rubinstein focuses on the recovery of the risk-neutral stochastic processes from index option prices. The authors compare the ability of nine different option pricing models, the naïve volatility smile predictions of traders, constant elasticity of variance, displaced diffusion, jump diffusion, stochastic volatility and implied binomial trees to explain otherwise identical observed option prices that differ by strike prices, times-to-expiration or times. Importantly, the authors find that the better performing models incorporate the negative correlation between the level of the index and volatility, while improvements require predicting the future at-the-money implied volatility. Importantly, the standard deviation of errors is large so that economically it is difficult to distinguish between the simple and more complex models.

The second chapter by Brown and Jackwerth addresses the pricing kernel puzzle of Jackwerth (2000). The pricing kernel is calculated as the ratio of the option implied state-price density and the historical smoothed return distribution. The pricing kernel puzzle concerns the observation that the pricing kernel implied from stock index options and index returns is not monotonically decreasing in wealth as suggested by standard asset-pricing theory. That is investors appear to be risk seeking, with respect to small changes in the stock index. In their chapter the authors address this concern by developing a representative agent model where volatility is a function of a state variable. The authors then apply this model to S&P 500 index options and index returns and are then able to generate the implied pricing kernels that were evident after the 1987 stock market crash.

The third and final chapter in this part by Herold and Muck considers the issue of catastrophe events on risk-neutral densities which can be implied from European option markets. The authors consider two events: the nuclear power plant at Fukushima and the downgrading of US sovereign debt in 2011. They apply a two-lognormal mixture approach to recover risk-neutral densities from European-style call and put options on the German blue chip index DAX. The authors find that the probability mass of risk-neutral density functions derived from long-term options is shifted towards the right, implying that very good states of the economy as well as deep out-of-the-money options become more expensive. On balance, their findings suggest that there was speculation on a recovery of the stock market after the shocks took place through investments in out-of-the-money call options.

PART III: DERIVATIVES MODELS AND MODEL PERFORMANCE

The third part of the volume, titled 'Derivatives Models and Model Performance', includes four chapters that investigate the application of derivatives models and their performance. The first two chapters consider the effects of non-Gaussian price distributions on derivatives prices, while the last two investigate hedging performance in the oil market and the use of binomial option pricing models for pricing convertible bonds.

The first chapter in this part by Fuentes, Gerig and Vicente focuses on the first of these issues: the presence of non-Gaussian features in the underlying asset returns underpinning an option. They propose that asset returns can be decomposed into two components: a Gaussian noise term and a volatility parameter. They allow volatility to be constant across a single day and driven by a mean-reverting process in the longer term. Applying these features to intraday data the authors are able to reproduce both the non-Gaussian shape (fat-tailed or leptokurtic) and apparent stability of the asset return distribution that is typical in financial markets.

This theme is continued in the chapter by García-Alonso, Moreno and Navas, who consider the effects of skewness and kurtosis on stochastic volatility models. This group of option pricing models attempt to address the unrealistic assumption of constant stock volatility over the life of the option contract, by introducing GARCH features, or introducing a continuous-time stochastic process for the asset volatility. The authors approach is to conduct a 'horse race' by determining whether option pricing models with stochastic volatility or non-normal distributions provide a better fit to S&P 500 index call options. A comparison is then made based on in-and out-of-sample pricing errors.

The next chapter in this part by Cotter and Hanly departs from many of the previous studies which focus on stock markets, by investigating the hedging performance of short and long hedgers using crude oil futures. The authors utilise a number of different approaches and find that hedging effectives is reduced by the presence of skewness in the distribution of oil returns. The authors conclude that one-sided hedging performance measures (such as value at risk and conditional value at risk) are recommended. Interestingly, they also find that simple least squares regression techniques provide the best hedging performance rather than more complex approaches that utilise GARCH techniques.

The final chapter in this part by Milanov and Kounchev investigates alternate approaches for the pricing and risk assessment of convertible bonds. Typically a binomial-tree approach is used as an approximation for the widely used Tsiveriotis–Fernandes model for pricing a convertible bond. This model divides the price of the convertible bond into a cash-only component, which is subject to credit risk, and an equity component, which is independent of the credit risk. The approach of the authors is to compare the pricing effectives of a number of alternate approaches. Importantly, the authors show that in many typical examples the binomial-tree technique is less effective than the finite-difference scheme.

PART IV: DERIVATIVES MODELS, RISK MANAGEMENT, CREDIT AND CORPORATE CONTROL

The final part of the volume, titled 'Derivatives Models, Risk Management, Credit and Corporate Control', offers five chapters that provide insights into the practical aspects of derivatives usage and modelling. The first chapter investigates the modelling of inflation derivatives; the second, management compensation; the third, credit risk; the fourth, swap spreads; and the final chapter, derivatives usage by non-financial firms.

The part starts with Wu's chapter on inflation derivatives modelling, which begins by defining the term structure of inflation rates and then uses this technology to price inflation caplets, floorlets and swaptions with the Black formula for displaced-diffusion processes. One benefit of this approach is that it enables these derivatives to be quoted using Black's implied volatilities, and also serves as a platform for managing volatility smile risk in inflation-rate derivatives.

The second chapter in this part by Buchner, Mohamed and Wagner provide an option-pricing framework for the modelling of fund management compensation and consider the case of private equity funds. Their numerical analysis shows that performance-related compensation only accounts for a relatively small portion of the total compensation paid. Importantly, their framework enables a detailed analysis of the determinants of private equity fund fee value. Their results have important corporate governance implications since fund managers may influence the value of their future fee payments by, for example, making riskier investments to increase the carried interest value. Thus, the fee structure of private equity funds gives rise to classical risk-shifting problems.

The third chapter by Barone considers an equity-based credit risk model where the key innovation in their chapter is by deriving new closed formulas for the pricing of credit default swaps (CDSs) within the Leland (1994) model. Therefore, the Leland model can be calibrated jointly to equity option and CDS quotes in order to identify trading opportunities across the two markets and/or to measure and manage equity and credit risk within a unified framework.

The next chapter by Fang, Azad, Batten and Lin provides Australian evidence on the impact of macroeconomic surprises and business cycle effects on the pricing of interest rate swaps. These authors find that the impact of news announcements on swap spreads depends on the state of the economy, with unexpected news on the inflation rate having a significant impact on swap spreads across all maturities. Interestingly, unanticipated unemployment rate news tends to be more relevant for the 10-year swap, while unanticipated changes in money supply tends to be more relevant for 4- and 7-year swaps, but only during periods of economic expansion. Another key finding is that macroeconomic shocks in general are negatively related to the conditional volatility of the swap spread.

The final chapter in the volume is the study by Skok, Loncarski and Skocir who provide a perspective on the derivative usage by Slovenian non-financial firms over the period 2004–2009. The expansion of the Slovenian economy during 2004–2008 could have led to the adoption of improved risk management practice. On the other hand, the adoption of the Euro in 2007 should have improved financial market stability. In fact their survey finds that firms decreased the use of derivatives for hedging foreign exchange risk and substantially increased use of interest rate and commodity derivatives, although larger firms used derivatives more intensely. Interestingly, the authors find that the use of derivatives in Slovenian non-financial firms is still much lower than in the majority of developed countries.

NOTES

1. BIS (2011).
2. See, for example AFP (2010).
3. Note that some commentators break the GFC into more than two stages. For example, Elliott (2011) considers five stages. See also, for example Sikorski (2011) for a detailed history of events.
4. The Securities and Exchange Commission's (SEC) 1 uniform net capital rule (15c3-1) and customer protection rule (15c3-3) form the foundation of the securities industry's financial responsibility framework (http://www.sec.gov/about/offices/oia/oia_market/key_rules.pdf. Accessed on 22 February 2012).
5. The Federal Reserve is the supervisor and regulator for US-based bank holding companies and their subsidiaries, member state banks and Edge Act Corporations, and shares responsibilities with the Office of the Comptroller of the Currency (OCC)

for foreign banks (see Table 5.1, Board of Governors of the Federal Reserve System, 2005).

REFERENCES

Association for Financial Professionals (AFP). (2010, April). *AFP financial risk survey*. Bethesda, MD.

Bank for International Settlements (BIS). (2011, December). *BIS quarterly review*. Basel, Switzerland.

Batten, J. A., & Szilagyi, P. G. (2011). The impact of the global financial crisis on emerging financial markets In J. A. Batten & P. G. Szilagyi (Eds.), *The impact of the global financial crisis on emerging financial markets* (Vol. 93, pp. 3–16). Contemporary Studies in Economic and Financial Analysis. Bingley, UK: Emerald Group Publishing Limited.

Board of Governors of the Federal Reserve System. (2005). *The federal reserve system: Purposes and functions* (9th ed.). Washington, DC: Board of Governors of the Federal Reserve System.

Breitenfellner, B., & Wagner, N. (2010). Government intervention in response to the subprime financial crisis: The good into the pot, the bad into the crop. *International Review of Financial Analysis*, *19*, 289–297.

Davydoff, D., & Naacke, G. (2009, May): *Derivative trading: Trends since 1998*. Amsterdam: International Options Market Association.

Elliott, L. (2011). Global financial crisis: Five key stages 2007–2011. *The Guardian*, 7 August. Retrieved from http://www.guardian.co.uk/business/2011/aug/07/global-financial-crisis-key-stages. Accessed on 9 March 2012.

Holtz, M. (2008): *Sparse grid quadrature in high dimensions with applications in finance and insurance*. Dissertation. Universität Bonn, Germany.

Jackwerth, J. C. (2000). Recovering risk aversion from option prices and realized returns. *Review of Financial Studies*, *13*(2), 433–451.

Leland, H. E. (1994). Corporate debt value, bond covenants, and optimal capital structure. *Journal of Finance*, *49*(4), 1213–1252.

Pauget, G. (2009, September). Regulation-supervision: The post-crisis outlook. In *The future of financial regulation*. Banque de France. *Financial Stability Review*, *13*, 117–122.

Sikorski, D. (2011). The global financial crisis. In J. A. Batten & P. G. Szilagyi (Eds.), *The impact of the global financial crisis on emerging financial markets* (Vol. 93, pp 17–90). Contemporary Studies in Economic and Financial Analysis. Bingley, UK: Emerald Group Publishing Limited.

ON THE ROLE OF OPTION APPLICATIONS IN ECONOMIC INSTABILITY

Kavous Ardalan

ABSTRACT

The purpose of this chapter is to discuss the potential contribution of the option applications to economic instability. To this end, the chapter briefly reviews the extant literature on financial option pricing and its applications to corporate assets and liabilities. It focuses on the direct relationship between the volatility of the underlying asset and the value of the option. It shows that the theory of option applications by its one-sided emphasis on the value-creating role of volatility promotes excessive risk-taking. Then the chapter discusses how the theory of option applications through the educational system encourages economic agents to make excessively risky decisions. Furthermore, the interactions among these risk-welcoming agents lead to an economic system which becomes increasingly risky. This risky economy, combined with the fact that more than half of the value of the option applications is constituted by the highly volatile value of the options embedded in such applications, translates into wide variations in real investments and the economy.

Keywords: Financial options; real options; equity as option; volatility; instability

Derivative Securities Pricing and Modelling
Contemporary Studies in Economic and Financial Analysis, Volume 94, 15–46

ISSN: 1569-3759/doi:10.1108/S1569-3759(2012)0000094004

INTRODUCTION

The theory of option pricing has been one of the most significant developments in financial economics. Although the history of this literature goes back to at least the beginning of the twentieth century, the major breakthrough came with a paper by Black and Scholes (1973). This is notable for two important reasons. First, option-pricing theory has had a considerable impact on practitioners as they have made widespread use of the option-pricing models in the valuation of traded options. Second, option-pricing theory has provided a distinct insight regarding corporate assets and liabilities. With respect to corporate assets, option-pricing theory is applied to the investment decision of the firm, which is referred to as "real options." These are related to the "option" aspects of investment projects such as project timing, the scale of the investments, and the right to abandon the project. Further, after a project is undertaken, there exist operating options in terms of the choice of inputs and outputs in the actual production process. As for corporate liabilities, they can be viewed as combinations of simple options contracts. For instance, the equity of a levered firm may be regarded as a European call option written on the firm's value, where the exercise price is the promised payment on the debt and the expiration date is the maturity date of the debt.

OPTIONS THEORY: BLACK–SCHOLES OPTION-PRICING MODEL

According to the option-pricing model of Black and Scholes (1973),[1] the value of a call option is determined as follows:

$$\begin{aligned} W(x,t) &= x\mathrm{N}(d_1) - ce^{r(t-t^*)}\mathrm{N}(d_2) \\ d_1 &= \frac{\ln(x/c) + [r + (v^2/2)](t^* - t)}{v(t^* - t)^{0.5}} \\ d_2 &= \frac{\ln(x/c) + [r - (v^2/2)](t^* - t)}{v(t^* - t)^{0.5}} \end{aligned} \tag{1}$$

where W(x,t) is the value of the option; x is the stock price; c is the exercise price; t^* is the maturity date; t is the current date; v^2 is the variance rate of the return on the stock; ln is the natural logarithm; and N(d) is the cumulative normal density function.

The value of the call option increases continuously as any one of the following factors increases: time to maturity, risk-free rate, and variance of the rate of return on the underlying asset. The latter two factors are of particular interest:

1. *The Variance in the Value of the Underlying Asset*: The holder of a call option has the right to buy the underlying asset at a predetermined price. The higher the variance in the value of the underlying asset is, the greater the value of the option would be. This is because the owners of options can never lose more than the price they pay for them; while they have the potential to earn significant return from large price increases.
2. *The Riskless Interest Rate Corresponding to the Life of the Option*: The riskless interest rate affects the value of an option mainly through the present value of the exercise price. Since the exercise price does not have to be paid until the call option is exercised, an increase in the interest rate increases the value of the call option.

OPTION APPLICATIONS TO CORPORATE ASSETS AND LIABILITIES

The option-pricing theory has been applied to corporate assets and liabilities. Subsection "Option Applications to Corporate Assets: Real Options" discusses the applications of option-pricing theory to corporate assets, that is, real options. Subsection "Option Applications to Corporate Liabilities: Equity in a Levered Firm" discusses the applications of option-pricing theory to corporate liabilities, for example, equity.

Option Applications to Corporate Assets: Real Options

The real options approach is the application of financial option-pricing models to the valuation of options on real (i.e., nonfinancial) assets. The real options approach to investments in real assets regards discounted cash flow (DCF) approaches to capital budgeting, including the net present value (NPV) rule, as inadequate. This is because the DCF-based approaches cannot properly account for management's flexibility to adapt and revise later decisions in response to changing market conditions. The NPV approach implicitly assumes that there is an "expected scenario" of cash flows and that management is passively committed to a certain "operating strategy," such as initiating the project immediately, and operating it continuously and uniformly till the end of its expected useful life.

The real options approach emphasizes that markets are characterized by change, uncertainty, and competitive interactions. With the arrival of new information, the uncertainty about market conditions and future cash flows is gradually resolved. As a result, management may have valuable flexibility to change its operating strategy in order to take advantage of favorable future opportunities or mitigate losses.

Such management flexibility expands an investment opportunity's value. This is because it improves the investment opportunity's upside potential while limiting its downside losses compared to the passive management of the investment opportunity. The managerial adaptability, therefore, results in an asymmetry that calls for an "expanded NPV" rule that reflects both: (1) the conventional (traditional, static, or passive) NPV of direct cash flows; and (2) the option value of operating and strategic adaptability. That is:

$$\text{Expanded NPV} = \text{Conventional NPV} + \text{Combined Real Options Value} \tag{2}$$

The value of options from active management is the total value of a collection of real (call or put) options embedded in capital investment opportunities. These options have as their underlying asset the gross project value of expected operating cash flows. Many of these real options occur naturally – for example, to defer, to contract, to shut down, or to abandon – while others may be costly – for example, to expand capacity or to build growth options, to default when the investment is staged sequentially, or to switch between alternative inputs and outputs. More specifically, real options are as follows:

1. *Option to defer*: The management holds a lease on (or holds an option to buy) valuable land or resources. The management can wait a certain number of years to see if output prices justify constructing a building or plant; or developing a field.
2. *Time to build option* (*staged investment*): The management stages investment as a series of outlays and creates the option to abandon the project midway if the arrival of new information makes the continuation of the project unfavorable. Each stage of the investment can be regarded as an option written on the value of subsequent stages, and valued as a compound option.
3. *Option to alter operating scale* (*e.g., to expand; to contract; to shut down and restart*): If market conditions are more favorable than expected, the

management can decide to expand the scale of production or accelerate resource utilization. Conversely, if market conditions are less favorable than expected, the management can decide to contract the scale of operations. Under extremely unfavorable market conditions, the management can decide to temporarily halt the production and start up again.
4. *Option to abandon*: If market conditions decline severely, management can decide to abandon project's operations permanently by selling the capital equipment and other assets in second-hand markets and obtaining the resale value.
5. *Options to switch (e.g., outputs or inputs)*: If prices or demand change, the management can decide to change the output mix of the production facility ("product" flexibility). Alternatively, the management can decide to use different types of inputs ("process" flexibility) in order to produce the same outputs.
6. *Growth options*: The management can decide to make an early investment (e.g., R&D, lease on undeveloped land or oil reserves, strategic acquisition, information network/infrastructure) which is a prerequisite or link in a chain of interrelated projects. This initial investment opens up future growth opportunities (e.g., new generation product or process, oil reserve, access to new market, strengthening of core capabilities). This process can be regarded as inter-project compound options.
7. *Multiple interacting options*: In practice, projects usually involve a "collection" of options. These options can be a combination of both upward-potential enhancing calls and downward-protection put options. The value of the combination of the options may differ from the sum of separate option values. This is because the options within the combination interact.

The standard NPV analysis is inadequate in capturing the value of the following two aspects of an investment project: first, the "operating flexibility" available within a single project which enables management to make or revise decisions at a future time (such as options to defer, expand, or abandon the project); and second, the "strategic" option value of a project resulting from its interdependence with future and follow-up investments.

Real options also include the maintenance of plant and equipment, advertising or other marketing expenses, expenditures on raw materials, labor, research and development, etc. Indeed, all variable costs are discretionary investments and can be treated as options.

Option Applications to Corporate Liabilities: Equity in a Levered Firm

As noted previously, Black and Scholes (1973) developed the following formula for the determination of the price of a call option:

$$\mathrm{W}(x, t) = x\mathrm{N}(d_1) - ce^{r(t-t^*)}\mathrm{N}(d_2) \tag{1}$$

They noted that the equity in a levered firm can be regarded as a call option, in the following way. Consider a company which is financed by common stocks and bonds and its only asset is the shares of common stock of another company. Suppose that the company's bonds are 10-year pure discount bonds that give the holder the right to a fixed sum of money, if the corporation is able to pay it. Further, suppose that the only restriction that the bonds place on the company is that the company cannot pay any dividends until after the bonds are paid off. Finally, suppose that the company will sell all the stocks it is holding at the end of 10 years, make full payment to the bond holders if possible, and pay any remaining money to the stockholders as a liquidating dividend.

Under these conditions, the stockholders have a call option on their company's assets. In effect, the bond holders own the company's assets, but they have given options to the stockholders to buy the company's assets back. Therefore, the value of the common stock at the end of 10 years will be equal to either the value of the company's assets minus the face value of the bonds, or zero, whichever is greater.

Thus, the value of the common stock is $\mathrm{W}(x,t)$, as given by Eq. (1), where v^2 is the variance rate of return on the shares held by the company, c is the total face value of the outstanding pure discount bonds, and x is the total value of the shares held by the company. The value of the bonds is $x - \mathrm{W}(x,t)$.

If the corporation's debt is increased, while the total value of the corporation is kept constant, the probability of corporation's default increases and the market value of each of the corporation's bonds decreases. Therefore, if the company changes its capital structure by issuing more bonds and using the proceeds to retire common stock, it will financially hurt the existing bond holders, and financially help the existing stockholders. That is, the corporation's bond price will fall, and the corporation's stock price will rise. To prevent this possibility, the existing bond holders, through the bond indenture, may prohibit the sale of additional debt of the same or higher priority in case the corporation decides to recapitalize.

The Black–Scholes option-pricing model expresses the value of a call option as an increasing function of the instantaneous variance of the underlying asset. Since equity in a levered firm can be regarded as a call option, shareholders have an incentive to substitute "risky" for "less risky" operating and investment policies.

OPTION APPLICATIONS PROMOTE EXCESSIVE RISK-TAKING

The theory of option applications places too much emphasis on risk-taking. The common and prominent theme in option applications is their emphasis on the direct relationship between the variance of the rate of return on the underlying asset and the value of the option. Subsection "Option Applications to Corporate Assets Promote Excessive Risk-Taking" discusses how the applications of option-pricing theory to corporate assets place too much emphasis on risk-taking. Subsection "Option Applications to Corporate Liabilities Promote Excessive Risk-Taking" discusses how the applications of option-pricing theory to corporate assets place too much emphasis on risk.

Option Applications to Corporate Assets Promote Excessive Risk-Taking

This subsection discusses how the applications of option-pricing theory to corporate assets place too much emphasis on risk-taking. The common and prominent theme in option applications to corporate assets, that is, real options, is their emphasis on the direct relationship between the volatility of the value of the underlying asset and the value of the real option.

In the rest of this subsection, it is shown that the emphasis that the applications of the option-pricing theory to corporate assets place on risk-taking is excessive. As was noted previously, real options imply that:

$$\text{Expanded NPV} = \text{Conventional NPV} + \text{Combined Real Options Value} \tag{2}$$

Real options applications place a great deal of emphasis on the idea that the greater is the uncertainty about the potential profitability of the investment, the greater will be the Combined Real Options Value, and therefore the greater will be the total or the Expanded NPV. However, this argument neglects the effect of the uncertainty on the value of the Conventional NPV. That is, uncertainty also plays a role in the determination of the magnitude of the Conventional NPV. This is because as a result of higher uncertainty there will be a larger discount rate to be used to compute present values of the expected cash flows from the project. This leads to a lower Conventional NPV such that the net effect of the increase in uncertainty on the Expanded NPV cannot be determined in advance.

This effect can be shown with respect to all previously discussed seven types of real options and as recalled in what follows:

1. *Option to defer*: The management holds a lease on (or holds an option to buy) valuable land or resources. The management can wait a certain number of years to see if output prices justify constructing a building or plant; or developing a field.

In this case, the higher uncertainty about the future course of events will increase the value of the real option. However, when the project will be undertaken at some point in the future, in effect, the management will have undertaken a project whose future is highly uncertain as well and therefore it will have a lower Conventional NPV. This is because the expected cash flows from the project are uncertain which would need to be discounted at a higher discount rate which would in turn result in a lower Conventional NPV. In other words, the management has had a valuable option of investing in a high-risk project.

In addition, for the management to initially obtain the lease on the project, it needs to buy the lease. However, the purchase price of the lease has already embodied the value of the option.[2] In this way, the management, in effect, has already paid for the value of the real option which it has obtained. This means that, in Eq. (2), the benefit and cost of the real option will cancel each other out and the Expanded NPV will be equal to the Conventional NPV.

2. *Time to build option (staged investment)*: The management stages investment as a series of outlays and creates the option to abandon the project midway if the arrival of new information makes the continuation of the project unfavorable. Each stage of the investment can be regarded as an option written on the value of subsequent stages, and valued as a compound option.

In this case, the higher uncertainty about the future course of events will increase the value of the real option. However, once the full project will be undertaken at some point in the future, in effect, the management will have undertaken a project whose future is highly uncertain as well and therefore will have a lower Conventional NPV. This is because the expected cash flows from the project are uncertain which would need to be discounted at a higher discount rate which would in turn result in a lower Conventional NPV. In other words, the management has had a valuable option of investing in a high-risk project.

In addition, when the arrival of new information makes the continuation of the project unfavorable and the management decides to abandon the project, it means that the management will sell the assets in the market. But at what price will the management be able to sell the assets for? Naturally, the arrival of unfavorable new information that has made the project undesirable and has forced the management to abandon the project will also depress the value of the project in the resale market, which would come as a great cost to the company. Indeed, in the final analysis, the management has paid a great deal to have had the real option.

Moreover, when the project is abandoned at any stage, in effect, the management will have lost all the investment which has been made in previous stages of the project investment.

3. *Option to alter operating scale (e.g., to expand; to contract; to shut down and restart)*: If market conditions are more favorable than expected, the management can decide to expand the scale of production or accelerate resource utilization. Conversely, if market conditions are less favorable than expected, the management can decide to contract the scale of operations. Under extremely unfavorable market conditions, the management can decide to temporarily halt the production and start up again.

In this case, the higher uncertainty about the future course of events will increase the value of the real option. However, once the full project will be undertaken at some point in the future, in effect, the management will have undertaken a project whose future is highly uncertain as well and therefore will have a lower Conventional NPV. This is because the expected cash flows from the project are uncertain which would need to be discounted at a higher discount rate which would in turn result in a lower Conventional NPV. In other words, the management has had a valuable option of investing in a high-risk project.

Moreover, there is a cost associated with the expansion, the contraction, and the shut down and restart of the project. The higher is the level of uncertainty, the higher will be the frequency that these costs will be incurred in practice. These costs counter the value of the real option.

In addition, for the management to initially invest in the project, it needs to pay for it. However, the payment for the investment has already embodied the value of the option.[3] In this way, the management, in effect, has already paid for the value of the real option which it has obtained. This means that, in Eq. (2), the benefit and cost of the real option will cancel each other out and the Expanded NPV will be equal to the Conventional NPV.

4. *Option to abandon*: If market conditions decline severely, management can decide to abandon project's operations permanently by selling the capital equipment and other assets in second-hand markets and obtaining the resale value.

In this case, the higher uncertainty about the future course of events will increase the value of the real option. However, at the time the project is undertaken, in effect, the management has undertaken a project whose future is highly uncertain as well and therefore has a lower Conventional NPV. This is because the expected cash flows from the project are uncertain which would need to be discounted at a higher discount rate which would in turn result in a lower Conventional NPV. In other words, the management has had a valuable option by investing in a high-risk project.

Moreover, when the arrival of new information makes the continuation of the project unfavorable and the management decides to abandon the project, it means that the management will sell the assets in the market. But at what price will the management be able to sell the assets for? Naturally, the arrival of unfavorable new information that has made the project undesirable and has forced the management to abandon the project will also depress the value of the project in the resale market, which would come as a great cost to the company. Indeed, in the final analysis, the management has paid a great deal to have had the real option.

5. *Options to switch* (*e.g., outputs or inputs*): If prices or demand change, the management can decide to change the output mix of the production facility ("product" flexibility). Alternatively, the management can decide to use different types of inputs ("process" flexibility) in order to produce the same outputs.

In this case, the higher uncertainty about the future course of events will increase the value of the real option. However, at the time the project is undertaken, in effect, the management has undertaken a project whose future is highly uncertain as well and therefore has a lower Conventional

NPV. This is because the expected cash flows from the project are uncertain which would need to be discounted at a higher discount rate which would in turn result in a lower Conventional NPV. In other words, the management has had a valuable option by investing in a high-risk project.

Moreover, there is a cost associated with switching the outputs or the inputs of the project. The higher is the level of uncertainty, the higher will be the frequency that these costs will be incurred in practice. These costs counter the value of the real option.

In addition, for the management to initially invest in the project, it needs to pay for it. However, the payment for the investment has already embodied the value of the option.[4] In this way, the management, in effect, has already paid for the value of the real option which it has obtained. This means that, in Eq. (2), the benefit and cost of the real option will cancel each other out and the Expanded NPV will be equal to the Conventional NPV.

6. *Growth options*: The management can decide to make an early investment (e.g., R&D, lease on undeveloped land or oil reserves, strategic acquisition, information network/infrastructure) which is a prerequisite or link in a chain of interrelated projects. This initial investment opens up future growth opportunities (e.g., new generation product or process, oil reserve, access to new market, strengthening of core capabilities). This process can be regarded as inter-project compound options.

In this case, the higher uncertainty about the future course of events will increase the value of the real option. However, once one of the projects in the chain will be undertaken at some point in the future, in effect, the management will have undertaken a project whose future is highly uncertainty as well and therefore will have a lower Conventional NPV. This is because the expected cash flows from the project are uncertain which would need to be discounted at a higher discount rate which would in turn result in a lower Conventional NPV.

7. *Multiple interacting options*: In practice, projects usually involve a "collection" of options. These options can be a combination of both upward-potential enhancing calls and downward-protection put options. The value of the combination of the options may differ from the sum of separate option values. This is because the options within the combination interact.

In this case, the higher uncertainty about the future course of events will increase the value of the real option. However, a combination of the negative effects offered in the previous six real options types would apply.

Similarly, the real options literature overestimates the effect of an increase in the risk-free rate on the Expanded NPV. This is because a higher risk-free rate while increasing the value of the real option, it reduces the Conventional NPV by increasing the discount rate which is used to discount the expected future cash flows of the project.

Option Applications to Corporate Liabilities Promote Excessive Risk-Taking

This subsection discusses how the applications of option-pricing theory to corporate liabilities place too much emphasis on risk-taking. The common and prominent theme in option applications to corporate liabilities, for example, equity, is their emphasis on the direct relationship between the variance of the value of the firm and the value of the equity. In the rest of this subsection, it is shown that the emphasis that the applications of the option-pricing theory to corporate liabilities place on risk-taking is excessive.

Real options applications place a great deal of emphasis on the idea that the greater is the volatility of the value of the firm, the greater will be the value of the equity. Such argument is based on the idea that shareholders gain when the value of the firm increases while their losses are truncated when the value of the firm decreases. This leads to the conclusion that equity holders prefer to substitute riskier for less risky operational and investment activities because this substitution increases the value of their equity in the firm.[5]

However, the insight gained from the real options literature can be applied to the equity of a firm so that the value of the equity can be expressed as the sum of the DCF value of equity and the value of equity holders' options:

$$\text{Value of Equity} = \text{DCF Value of Equity} + \text{Value of Equity Holders Options} \tag{3}$$

where the value of equity holders' options includes the equity holders' option to substitute riskier for less risky operational and investment activities.

More specifically, there are essential elements which must be considered in identifying the value of a company's stocks. First, there are the physical assets of the company that generate cash flows. Second, share values are often substantially greater than the amount related to the present value of the expected cash flows from existing operations.[6] Typically, the major portion of share value is accounted for by the Value of Equity Holders' Options, that is, the present value of growth opportunities, the option to substitute riskier for less risky operational and investment activities, other real options, the hope of receiving a premium price in an acquisition, etc.[7]

In Eq. (3), then, the higher volatility that increases the Value of Equity Holders' Options, at the same time reduces the DCF Value of Equity. This is because a riskier asset leads to a higher discount rate which is to be used in the present value calculation of the expected future dividends. Overall, the net effect of a higher volatility on the value of equity is indeterminate.

Intuitively speaking, shareholders may not want to substitute riskier for less risky operational and investment activities because in making such substitution they are risking their equity. In other words, equity holders may not want to undertake riskier projects or riskier financing alternatives because although such actions would increase their potential gains, they would place at risk the value of the equity which they are currently holding. That is, equity holders may not want to gamble their currently held equity for potential future gain.

In the Black–Scholes option-pricing model, the option is written on an underlying asset such that the value of the option depends on the value of the underlying asset, but not conversely. However, this unidirectional relationship is violated in the option applications to corporate liabilities.[8] More specifically, when the equity of a levered firm is regarded as a call option written on the value of the firm,[9] then not only the value of the equity depends on the value of the firm, but also the value of the firm depends on the value of the equity through the balance-sheet identity, as follows:

$$\text{Firm Value} = \text{Equity Value} + \text{Debt Value}$$

Whereas the holders of a financial option will benefit from an increase in the volatility of the underlying asset, the holders of the equity of a firm will benefit from an increase in the volatility of the underlying asset but at the risk of losing the value of the equity which the equity holders are currently holding. Therefore, the equity holders may not prefer to raise the upward potential of their equity investment at the risk of losing the value of their current equity holding. Indeed, only very highly levered firms select very risky projects while the opposite statement applies to low-levered firms. According to the explanation provided here, the equity holders in a very highly levered firm do not have much to lose in terms of the value of their equity and therefore they stand ready to gamble their equity for the upward potential. By the same reasoning, the equity holders in a low-levered firm would prefer not to do so.[10]

Similarly, the literature on option applications to corporate liabilities overestimates the effect of an increase in the risk-free rate on the Value of Equity. This is because a higher risk-free rate while increasing the value of equity holders' options, it reduces the DCF Value of Equity by increasing the discount rate which is used to find the present values of dividends.

FROM THEORY TO PRACTICE

Knowledge of theory conditions human beings' beliefs, attitudes, and behavior. These, in turn, contribute to the formation of the qualities of the reality which the human beings accordingly construct. Subsection "From Theory to Practice: In General" discusses, in general, how knowledge influences the formation of reality. Subsection "From Theory to Practice: In Finance" discuses, in particular, how knowledge of finance influences financial reality; and by implication how the knowledge of option theory and option applications – that promote excessive risk-taking – influences the formation of the risky economic reality.

From Theory to Practice: In General

Knowledge structures shape social life in important ways. The way that people know their world has significant implications for the way people construct their world. Any form of concrete reality occurs in major part because of certain powerful patterns of social consciousness.[11]

In the current era, rationalism as a general configuration of knowledge has greatly promoted the current way of thinking and, through it, the formation of the current concrete reality. This framework of knowledge has four main features. First, rationalism is secularist: it equates reality with the physical world, with no reference to transcendent and divine forces. Second, rationalism is anthropocentric: it analyzes reality primarily in terms of human interests (in contrast to, for instance, ecological integrity). Third, rationalism is "scientist" in character: it understands phenomena in terms of single incontrovertible truths which are discoverable by rigorous application of objective research methods. Fourth, rationalism is instrumental: it searches for most efficient ways to solve immediate problems.

When rationalism reigns as a predominant social structure, it subordinates other kinds of knowledge. It singles out its own way of "making sense" with the exclusion of all others. Rationalists dismiss aesthetics, spirituality, emotion, and fantasy. Rationalists only accept these and other "irrationalities" to the extent that they complement and advance rational knowledge. Rationalists do not see "Irrationalities" as containing any primary truth in their own right.

Rationalism is a secular faith. According to rationalists, science enables human beings to discover the single, definitive, objective, cumulative truths about phenomena. People can then use this knowledge to control natural and social forces in order to improve the welfare of human beings. Accordingly, techno-scientific rationality enables people to prevent disease, hunger, poverty, war, etc. Consequently, the potentials of human life will be maximized.

Rationalist knowledge is manifest in all which is regarded as "reasonable" in modern society. For instance, rationalism has guided people to separate "society" from "nature" and to use scientific and technical means to control natural forces for instrumental human purposes. Secular, anthropocentric, instrumental calculations have resulted in the emphasis on the efficiency of the capitalist production. A rationalist mindset underlies the power of "objective" secular law in modern social relations and the prevalence of bureaucracy in modern organizations – governments, firms, civic associations, schools, hospitals, and so on. Rationalism has expanded the production of "scientific" knowledge through universities and think tanks.

Rationalism, as any other social structure, is a historical phenomenon. It has come about at particular times and places under particular conditions. Of course, one can find instances of secular, anthropocentric, scientific, instrumental thinking in various historical contexts. However, a rationalist social structure – that systematically marginalizes other forms of knowing – is a distinctive character of the modern era. Rationalism first consolidated during the eighteenth century "Enlightenment" in the North Atlantic area. Enlightenment thought excluded myth, faith, and other "traditional" ways of understanding from "knowledge." Subsequently rationalism has been spread to all corners of the earth.

From Theory to Practice: In Finance

The difference between the natural and social sciences is rooted in their respective relationships to the phenomena they study.[12] In the social sciences, research changes the phenomena under investigation more than does research in the natural sciences. Social behavior is shaped by culturally shared frameworks of conceptual understanding, which is the chief product of social science. Therefore, as the concepts and theories are communicated and filtered into daily life, they reconstitute the reality. This is especially true in sciences of business administration, including finance, where theories function as instruments of managerial control. These practically oriented sciences provide advice regarding potential interventions in daily affairs of businesses. The relationship between finance theory and managerial practice is a dialectical one, whereby theory not only reflects but also structures its own subject matter.

Examination of theories, Ph.D. programs, journals, and conferences in academic finance shows that they adhere, almost exclusively, to the "scientific" paradigm. Finance students who graduate from academia receive special training. This training helps to shape graduates' perception, attitude, beliefs, and behavior in a special way. Students will carry these traits with them to their professional careers. These careers are mostly in universities, corporations, and financial institutions. The increasing number of finance graduates who work for universities, corporations, and financial institutions, which play an increasing role in financial markets, will help to create the reality of finance.

The practice of financial management shows that modern analytical models and techniques being taught in universities are finding their way into relatively widespread use among large U.S. corporations. Indeed, corporations in general have noticeably increased their use of sophisticated financial management techniques.

For instance, in 1961, a total of 82% of firms used criteria that ignore time value of money, such as payback method and accounting rate of return. However, due to the continuous emphasis of financial education on the importance of the concept of time value of money, such concepts over time have been increasingly applied in practice by financially trained corporate managers. This is evidenced by the surveys of corporate practices, as follows:

1. In 1959, only 19% of large industrial companies used DCF techniques to evaluate and rank projects; and in 1970, that percentage increased to 57%.
2. In 1981, that percentage increased to 76%.
3. In 1989, both the majority of Fortune 500 large firms and the majority of Forbes 200 best small companies used DCF techniques.

4. In 1992, about 99% of the 100 largest Fortune 500 companies used IRR or NPV as either the primary or secondary evaluation measure.
5. The use of non-DCF techniques, such as payback, as the primary evaluation measure has declined.

Despite their mathematical complexity, the models of finance theory have nevertheless had a direct and significant influence on finance practice. This is a prevailing theme in modern finance. In this way, the reality of finance comes to be formed, among other things, by the theory of finance.

The theory of option applications is following the same pattern as has been observed in the case of the concept of the time value of money: from academic scholarship; to academic textbooks and programs; to the practice of finance and the creation of financial reality. The theory of option applications – compared to the concept of the time value of money – has been more recently analyzed by finance scholars; has been more recently incorporated into the advanced undergraduate, MBA, Ph.D. textbooks and programs, and practitioners training; and has more recently started, to a large extent, to be intuitively practiced by financially trained corporate managers, who accordingly create the financial reality.

Since the publication of Myers (1977), in which corporate investment opportunities were viewed as real options, the idea has had a huge impact on academic research. Triantis (2005) estimates that there are nearly 1,000 research papers on real options. Real options concepts and techniques have not only been prevalent in research in finance and economics, but have also influenced research in other business disciplines, including strategy, organizations, management science, operations management, information systems, accounting, and marketing. Real options have thus become a cross-disciplinary area of research, with great potential to improve corporate practice.

The core of the academic literature on real options applications is as follows: Baldwin and Ruback (1986), Brealey and Myers (1991), Brealey, Myers, and Allen (2008), Brennan (1990), Brennan and Schwartz (1985), Carr (1988), Chung and Charoenwong (1991), Gibson and Schwartz (1990), Ingersoll and Ross (1992), Jacoby and Laughton (1992), Kasanen (1993), Kensinger (1987), Kester (1984, 1986, 1993), Kulatilaka (1988, 1993a, 1993b), Kulatilaka and Marcus (1988), Kulatilaka and Trigeorgis (1993), Laughton and Jacoby (1993), Majd and Pindyck (1987), Margrabe (1978), McDonald and Siegel (1985, 1986), Morck, Schwartz, and Stangeland (1989), Myers (1977), Myers and Majd (1990), Ott (2002), Paddock, Siegel, and Smith (1988), Pindyck (1988, 1991), Siegel, Smith, and Paddock (1987),

Smit and Ankum (1993), Stulz (1982), Titman (1985), Tourinho (1979), Triantis and Hodder (1990), Trigeorgis (1988, 1993b), Trigeorgis and Mason (1987), and Williams (1991).

These authors have analyzed all the seven types of real options discussed previously in Subsection "Option Applications to Corporate Assets: Real Options," that is, (1) Option to defer; (2) Time to build option (staged investment); (3) Option to alter operating scale (e.g., to expand; to contract; to shut down and restart); (4) Option to abandon; (5) Options to switch (e.g., outputs or inputs); (6) Growth options; and (7) Multiple interacting options.

Furthermore, these authors have analyzed the above real options in the context of various industries. More specifically, the industries are: All natural resource extraction industries; real estate development; farming; paper products; all R&D intensive industries, especially pharmaceuticals; long-development capital intensive projects, for example, large-scale construction or energy-generating plants; start-up ventures; natural resource industries such as mine operations; facilities planning and construction in cyclical industries; fashion apparel; consumer goods; commercial real estate; capital intensive industries, such as airlines and railroads; financial services; new product introductions in uncertain markets; output shifts: any good sought in small batches or subject to volatile demand, for example, consumer electronics; toys; specialty paper; machine parts; autos; input shifts: all feedstock-dependent facilities, for example, oil; electric power; chemicals; crop switching; sourcing; all infrastructure-based or strategic industries, especially high tech, R&D, or industries with multiple product generations or applications (e.g., computers, pharmaceuticals); multinational operations; strategic acquisitions; and real-life projects in most industries discussed above.

The notion of real options has earned chapters in standard finance textbooks, and is now taught in most, if not all, MBA programs, Ph.D. programs, and professional training programs. In addition, it is an interdisciplinary subject, discussed not only in finance but also in strategy and information-systems courses.[13]

The basic introductory articles are: Amram and Kulatilaka (1999a, 2000), Barwise, March, and Wensley (1989), Chen, Conover, and Kensinger (2002), Copeland (2001), Copeland and Tufano (2004), Copeland and Weiner (1990), Damodaran (2000), Dixit and Pindyck (1995), Glassman, Amram, and Baldwin (2000), Hayes and Garvin (1982), Hodder and Riggs (1985), Kemna (1993), Kensinger (1987), Kester (1984), Kulatilaka and Marcus (1992), Leslie and Michaels (1997), Luehrman (1998, 2009),

Mason and Merton (1985), Myers (1987), Ross (1995), Sick (1989), Teach (2003), Trigeorgis (1988, 1993a), Trigeorgis and Kasanen (1991), Trigeorgis and Mason (1987), and Van Putten and MacMillan (2004).

The fundamental books on real options are: Amram and Kulatilaka (1999b), Copeland and Antikarov (2001), Dixit and Pindyck (1994), Schwartz and Trigeorgis (2001), and Trigeorgis (1995, 2000).

In practice, many corporate managers go beyond passive NPV analysis and use intuition and executive judgment to value future managerial flexibility. Surveys, however, show that at least two-thirds of firms do not explicitly incorporate real options into their evaluations of long-term projects.[14] It should be noted, however, that in the same way that it took decades for NPV to become widely accepted in practice, real options, which is an even more sophisticated tool, will also take a few decades to be well integrated into corporate practice. Nevertheless, the majority of corporate managers intuitively apply the concept of real options. Actually, there is a large body of literature on the intuitive use of the real options by managers: Arnold and Hatzopoulos (2000), Barwise et al. (1989), Benaroch, Jeffrey, Kauffman, and Shah (2007), Benaroch, Lichtenstein, and Robinson (2006), Bernstein, Chesney, and Wang (2011), Bowman and Hurry (1993), Busby and Pitts (1997), Copeland and Weiner (1990), Denison, Farrell, and Jackson (2010), Dixit and Pindyck (1994), Dunbar (2000), Fichman, Keil, and Tiwana (2005), Howell and Jagle (1997), Kasanen (1993), Kemna (1993), Kogut and Kulatilaka (1994), Lankton and Luft (2008), Leslie and Michaels (1997), Luehrman (1998), McDonald (2000), McGrath (1997, 1999), Miller and Arikan (2004), Miller and Shapira (2004), Quigg (1993), Ryan and Ryan (2002), Tallon, Kauffman, Lucas, Whinston, and Zhu (2002), Teach (2003), Tiwana, Keil, and Fichman (2006), Tiwana, Wang, Keil, and Ahluwalia (2007), Triantis (2005), Trigeorgis (1993b), van Putten and MacMillan (2004), and Yavas and Sirmans (2005).

THE CONTRIBUTION OF OPTION APPLICATIONS TO ECONOMIC INSTABILITY

Previously, Section "Option Applications Promote Excessive Risk-Taking" discussed how the theory of option applications promotes excessive risk-taking and Section "From Theory to Practice" discussed how theory influences practice. Therefore, it can be concluded that the theory of option applications leads to excessive risk-taking in financial practice.

The interactions among these risky agents create more risk and uncertainty, which is more welcomed by these real-options-trained agents. This is because they value highly the upward potential of options. The interactions among risky agents create more risk because each time an agent either does or does not exercise one of his/her options sends a signal to its competitors and changes the environment in which all agents are competing.[15] In the new riskier and more uncertain environment, the real-options-trained agents will be encouraged to undertake more risky project, because the new environment increases the value of the real options of new investment projects, and so on. In other words, in an economy where there are lots of players who prefer and create more volatility, then such volatility will cause all of them to act and re-act to volatilities and create more volatility and risk.

In addition, more than half of the investment value is constituted by real options.[16] But, the values of these real options are highly volatile and quickly and drastically change with changing economic and market conditions.[17] This particularly applies to companies in highly volatile and unpredictable industries, such as electronics, telecommunications, and biotechnology. This means that in good economic times the values of these real options will be substantially higher and conversely in bad economic times the value of these real options will be substantially lower. These would make actual investments too volatile. That is, real-options-trained professionals by their welcoming emphasis on risk-taking would help aggravate the economic cycle and the economic crisis.

In order to see how this risky behavior would contribute to economic crisis it helps if the list of the causes of the recent financial crisis[18] is reviewed, as follows[19]:

Imprudent Mortgage Lending: When credit was abundant, interest rates were low, and house prices were rising, lending standards were relaxed such that many people bought houses which they could not really afford. As house prices started falling and loans began going bad, the financial system was hit by a severe shock.

Housing Bubble: The Federal Reserve followed expansionary monetary policies that allowed housing prices to rise to unsustainable levels. Finally, the burst of the housing bubble triggered the crisis.

Global Imbalances: Some countries (such as China, Japan, and Germany) ran large surpluses every year, while others (such as the United States and United Kingdom) ran deficits. The U.S. external deficits were compounded by internal deficits, for example, the household and government sectors. The U.S. borrowing accumulated over time and placed severe stress on the system that finally resulted in financial disruptions.

Securitization: Securitization reduced lenders' incentives to be prudent. It internationally spread the "originate-to-distribute" model, especially when there was a vast investor demand for subprime loans packaged as AAA bonds. This wide ownership of mortgage-backed securities had repercussions throughout the global system when subprime loans went bad in 2007.

Lack of Transparency and Accountability in Mortgage Finance: Throughout the housing finance industry, many participants contributed to the creation and sale of bad mortgages and bad securities. Lenders sold exotic mortgages to home-owners and traders sold toxic securities to investors, apparently without fear of bearing personal responsibility in case those contracts failed. It was due to the lack of participant accountability that the originate-to-distribute model of mortgage finance, with its great promise of managing risk, became a massive generator of risk.

Rating Agencies: The credit rating agencies incorrectly assigned AAA ratings to various issues of subprime mortgage-backed securities, of which many were subsequently downgraded to junk grade. The reasons for the rating agencies' failure have been: use of poor economic models, conflicts of interest, and lack of effective regulation. Another reason is the market's excessive use of ratings, which has been promoted by numerous laws and regulations that necessitate the use of ratings in determining permissible investments or required capital levels.

Mark-to-Market Accounting: FASB standards require financial institutions to report on their financial statements the fair (i.e., current market) value of their financial assets. According to this requirement, banks have to recognize losses based on "fire sale" prices, which prevail in distressed markets and are known to be below long-run fundamental values. These losses deteriorate market confidence and amplify banking system problems.

Deregulatory Legislation: The Gramm–Leach–Bliley Act (GLBA) and the Commodity Futures Modernization Act (CFMA) allowed financial institutions to engage in unregulated risky transactions on a large scale. Unfortunately, the laws were based on faith in self-regulating markets.

Shadow Banking System: Risky financial activities – such as the use of leverage, borrowing short-term to lend long, etc. – which were limited to regulated-banks moved outside the explicit government safety net which was provided by deposit insurance and safety and soundness regulation. In particular, mortgage lending migrated from banks to unregulated institutions. This unsupervised risk-taking led to the financial crisis.

Nonbank Runs: When nonbank financial institutions – that is, financial institutions outside the banking system – took financial positions based on borrowing short-term and lending long-term, they exposed themselves to liquidity risk in the form of nonbank runs, as happened to Bear Stearns, etc.

Off-Balance Sheet Finance: Many banks established off-the-books special-purpose entities – such as structured investment vehicles, or SIVs – in order to engage in risky speculative investments. These enabled banks to hold less capital reserves against potential losses. Consequently, with the onset of the crisis, it drastically reduced market confidence in banks' creditworthiness.

Government-Mandated Subprime Lending: To help low-income borrowers – for example, the Community Reinvestment Act (CRA) and Fannie Mae and Freddie Mac's affordable housing goals – federal mandates forced banks to engage in risky mortgage lending.

Failure of Risk Management Systems: Some firms compartmentalized the analysis of market risk and credit risk. Such dichotomy did not work for complex structured products, for which those risks were indistinguishable.

Financial Innovation: New instruments in structured finance developed so rapidly that market infrastructure and systems were not yet properly in place when those instruments came under stress. That is, accountants, regulators, ratings agencies, and settlement systems were not given time to catch up.

Complexity: Certain financial instruments were complex in three respects: (1) investors were unable to properly judge the merits of investments, (2) risks of market transactions were unknown, and (3) regulators were confused. The complexity of these financial instruments was at the heart of the crisis.

Human Frailty: Behavioral finance emphasizes that investors do not always make optimal decisions due to "bounded rationality" and limited self-control. Therefore, in complex financial situations, regulators should help them by better disclosure and through reinforcing financial prudence.

Bad Computer Models: Expectations of the performance of complex structured products linked to mortgages were formed based on only a few decades of data. For subprime loans, only a few years of data were used. Complex systems can go beyond historical experience.

Excessive Leverage: In the years prior to the crisis, interest rates were low and capital was abundant, and the yield on fixed income securities was low. To enhance the rate of return on their capital, many investors used borrowed funds in their investments. This excessive leverage magnified the impact of the housing downturn. The consequent deleveraging caused the interbank credit market to tighten.

Relaxed Regulation of Leverage: The Securities and Exchange Commission (SEC) by liberalizing its net capital rule in 2004 allowed investment bank holding companies to increase their leverage ratios to very high levels. In addition, its Consolidated Supervised Entities program, which applied to the largest investment banks, was voluntary and ineffective.

Credit Default Swaps (CDS): Initially, credit derivatives developed for risk management. Then, they continued to grow and became more sophisticated with the help of financial engineering. Later, they became an instrument for speculative transactions, such that credit derivatives increased, rather than decreased, risk.

Over-the-Counter Derivatives: The OTC derivatives – including credit swaps – are largely unregulated. A dealer's default could not only impose substantial losses to counterparties, but also trigger panic because of the uncertainty about the extent and distribution of those losses.

Fragmented Regulation: The regulation of U.S. financial system is dispersed among various agencies. Consequently, no single agency is capable of monitoring emerging system-wide problems.

No Systemic Risk Regulator: No single regulator, in the United States, had jurisdiction over all systemically important financial institutions. Even the Federal Reserve, which had the role of systemic risk regulator, lacked authority over investment banks, hedge funds, nonbank derivatives dealers, etc.

Short-Term Incentives: Traders and managers at many financial institutions receive an annual bonus, which constitutes a large portion of their compensation. Therefore, they lack incentives to avoid risky strategies which might fail drastically every 5 or 10 years.

Tail Risk: Many investors and risk managers tried to increase their returns by providing insurance or writing options against low-probability financial events. A good example is CDS. When market participants are aware that many such potential losses are distributed throughout the financial system, but do not know exactly where or how large they are, uncertainty and fear are magnified when markets come under stress.

As can be noted, the common theme among all the above causes of the recent financial crisis has been the excessive risky behavior by some economic agents. It can, therefore, be concluded that: the theory of option applications promotes risk-taking, and this in turn will lead to risky behavior in the economy, the interactions among risky agents would make the economy more risky which is more welcomed by the risky agent and so on, and this in turn will aggravate the economic cycle and the economic crisis.

CONCLUSION

The purpose of this chapter has been to discuss the potential contribution of the theory of option applications to economic instability. To this end, the chapter took the following steps: (1) reviewed the extant literature on financial option pricing and its applications to corporate assets and liabilities; (2) focused on the emphasis of this literature on the direct relationship between the volatility of the underlying asset and the value of the option; (3) showed that the theory of option applications by its one-sided emphasis on the value-creating role of volatility promotes excessive risk-taking; (4) reviewed the extensive academic research that has recognized various real options and their applications to very many industries; (5) discussed that the academic research on real options has gone far beyond the field of Finance and into other areas of business research; (6) added that the concepts of real options have been included in the introductory, intermediate, and advanced textbooks and curricula, as well as in the practitioners-training programs; (7) discussed how the theory of option applications through the educational system encourages economic agents to make excessive risky decisions; (8) showed that, indeed, in practice, the majority of corporate managers intuitively apply the concepts of real options; (9) discussed that the interactions among all these risk-welcoming agents create an increasingly risky financial and economic system; (10) concluded that this risky economy, combined with the fact that more than half of the value of real investments is constituted by the highly volatile value of the real options embedded in these projects, translates into wider cycles in real investments and the economy.

NOTES

1. See Black and Scholes (1973), Elettra and Rossella (2003), Galai and Masulis (1976), Geske (1977, 1979), Merton (1973, 1974), and Myers (1977).
2. For the effect of competitive behavior and bidding see Akdogu (2011), Amram and Kulatilaka (1999a), Copeland and Weiner (1990), Damodaran (2000), Glassman et al. (2000), Ott (2002), Paddock, Siegel, and Smith (1988), Quigg (1993), Siegel et al. (1987), and Yavas and Sirmans (2005).
3. See Note 2.
4. See Note 2.
5. See, for example, Fernandez (2005), Frydenberg (2011), and Kester (1986).
6. See Copeland et al. (2006), Dixit and Pindyck (1995), Kester (1984), Pindyck (1988), and Woolridge (1995).
7. This formulation is consistent with Ardalan (1997), Chen et al. (2002), Miller and Modigliani (1961), and Myers (1987).
8. It seems that they used the "analogy" to provide the insight for better understanding, but they fell into the trap that all aspects of the two domains correspond to each other. But, in an "analogy" only certain relationships are the same and transferrable between domains. In this sense, their analogy is not quite valid.
9. See Copeland et al. (2006), Green (1984), Jensen and Meckling (1976), Mason and Merton (1985), Mello and Parsons (1992), Merton (1974), and Smith and Warner (1979).
10. For evidence, see Chesney and Gibson (1999).
11. See Kupperman (2010) and Stevenson and Haberman (2008). This subsection is based on Scholte (2000).
12. The first five paragraphs of this subsection are based on Ardalan (2004). See also Hodgson (2009).
13. See Busby and Pitts (1997), Copeland and Tufano (2004), Luehrman (1998, 2009), Ott (2002), Reuer and Tong (2007), and Teach (2003).
14. For the evidence on actual use of the real options in practice by managers see Copeland and Tufano (2004), Denison et al. (2009), Dunbar (2000), Graham and Harvey (2001), Ryan and Ryan (2002), Teach (2003), and Triantis (2005).
15. See Copeland and Weiner (1990), Fernandez (2005), Grenadier (1999), and Mittendorf (2004).
16. See Dixit and Pindyck (1995), Kester (1984), Pindyck (1988), and Woolridge (1995).
17. See Dixit and Pindyck (1995).
18. This list is based on Jickling (2009).
19. See also Babus, Carletti, and Allen (2009), Bhattacharya and Yu (2008), Brunner (2009), Caprio, Demirguc-Kunt, and Kane (2010), Diamond and Rajan (2009), Gorton (2010), Marsh and Pfleiderer (2010), Obstfeld and Rogoff (2009), and Reihnart and Rogoff (2010). This section is based on Jickling (2009).

REFERENCES

Akdogu, E. (2011). Value-maximizing managers, value-increasing mergers, and overbidding. *Journal of Financial and Quantitative Analysis*, *46*(1), 83–110.

Amram, M., & Kulatilaka, N. (1999a). Disciplined decisions: Aligning strategy with the financial markets. *Harvard Business Review* (January–February), 95–105.

Amram, M., & Kulatilaka, N. (1999b). *Real options: Managing strategic investment in an uncertain world*. Boston, MA: Harvard Business School Press.

Amram, M., & Kulatilaka, N. (2000). Strategy and shareholder value creation: The real options frontier. *Journal of Applied Corporate Finance*, *13*(2), 15–28.

Ardalan, K. (1997). Textbook treatment of volatility in valuing options and corporate liabilities. *Financial Practice and Education* (Spring/Summer), 103–112.

Ardalan, K. (2004). On the theory and practice of finance. *International Journal of Social Economics*, *31*(7), 684–705.

Arnold, G. C., & Hatzopoulos, P. D. (2000). The theory–practice gap in capital budgeting: Evidence from the United Kingdom. *Journal of Business Finance & Accounting*, *27*(5), 603–626.

Babus, A., Carletti, E., & Allen, F. (2009). *Financial crises: Theory and evidence*. University of Pennsylvania – Finance Department, European Corporate Governance Institute (ECGI).

Baldwin, C. Y., & Ruback, R. (1986). Inflation, uncertainty, and investment. *Journal of Finance*, *41*(July), 657–669.

Barwise, P., March, P. R., & Wensley, R. (1989). Must finance and strategy clash? *Harvard Business Review*, *67*(5), 85–90.

Benaroch, M., Jeffrey, M., Kauffman, R. J., & Shah, S. (2007). Option-based risk management: A field study of sequential information technology investment decisions. *Journal of Management Information Systems*, *24*(2), 103–140.

Benaroch, M., Lichtenstein, Y., & Robinson, K. (2006). Real options in IT risk management: An empirical validation of risk-option relationship. *MIS Quarterly*, *30*(4), 827–864.

Bernstein, A., Chesney, M., & Wang, M. (2011). *An experimental study on real option strategies*. Research Paper No. 09-50. Swiss Finance Institute, University of Zurich, Zurich, Switzerland.

Bhattacharya, U., & Yu, X. (2008). The causes and consequences of recent financial market bubbles: An introduction. *Review of Financial Studies*, *21*(1), 3–10.

Black, F., & Scholes, M. (1973). The pricing of options and corporate liabilities. *Journal of Political Economy* (May–June), 637–654.

Bowman, E. H., & Hurry, D. (1993). Strategy through the option lens: An integrated view of resource investments and the incremental-choice process. *Academy of Management Review*, *18*(4), 760–782.

Brealey, R. A., & Myers, S. C. (1991). *Principles of corporate finance* (4th ed.). New York, NY: McGraw-Hill.

Brealey, R. A., Myers, S. C., & Allen, F. (2008). Brealey, Myers and Allen on real options. *Journal of Applied Corporate Finance*, *20*(4), 58–71.

Brennan, M. J. (1990). Latent assets. *Journal of Finance*, *45*, 709–730.

Brennan, M. J., & Schwartz, E. S. (1985). Evaluating natural resource investments. *Journal of Business*, *58*(2), 135–157.

Brunner, R. F. (2009). *The dynamics of a financial crisis: The panic of 1907 and the subprime crisis*. Working Paper Series No. 1434714. University of Virginia, Darden Graduate School of Business Administration, Charlottsville, Virginia.

Busby, J. S., & Pitts, C. G. C. (1997). Real options in practice: An exploratory survey of how finance officers deal with flexibility in capital appraisal. *Management Accounting Research*, *8*(2), 169–186.

Caprio, G., Demirguc-Kunt, A., & Kane, E. J. (2010). The 2007 meltdown in structured securitization: Searching for lessons, not scapegoats. *World Bank Research Observer*, *25*(1), 125–155.

Carr, P. (1988). The valuation of sequential exchange opportunities. *Journal of Finance* (December), 1235–1256.

Chen, A. H., Conover, J. A., & Kensinger, J. W. (2002). Proven ways to increase share value. *Journal of Applied Finance*, *12*(1), 89–97.

Chesney, M., & Gibson, R. (1999). The investment policy and the pricing of equity in a levered firm: A reexamination of the contingent claims' valuation approach. *European Journal of Finance*, *5*(2), 95–107.

Chung, K. H., & Charoenwong, C. (1991). Investment options, assets in place, and the risk of stocks. *Financial Management*, *20*(3), 21–33.

Copeland, T. (2001). The real-options approach to capital allocation. *Strategic Finance*, *83*(4), 33–40.

Copeland, T., & Antikarov, V. (2001). *Real options: A practitioner's guide*. New York, NY: Texere LLC.

Copeland, T., Stewart, B., Harris, T. S., O'Byrne, S. F., Pettit, J., Wessels, D., & Chew, D. (2006). Financial management association roundtable on stock market pricing and value-based management. *Journal of Applied Corporate Finance*, *18*(2), 56–81.

Copeland, T., & Tufano, P. (2004). A real-world way to manage real options. *Harvard Business Review* (March), 1–12.

Copeland, T., & Weiner, J. (1990). Proactive management of uncertainty. *McKinsey Quarterly*, *4*, 133–152.

Damodaran, A. (2000). The promise of real options. *Journal of Applied Corporate Finance*, *13*(2), 29–44.

Denison, C., Farrell, A. M., & Jackson, K. E. (2010, April). *Managers' incorporation of the value of real options into their long-term investment decisions: An experimental investigation*. Working Paper No. 2010-15. Iowa State University, Ames, Iowa.

Diamond, D. W., & Rajan, R. G. (2009). *The credit crisis: Conjectures about causes and remedies*. NBER Working Paper No. W14739. National Bureau of Economic Research, Cambridge, MA.

Dixit, A. K., & Pindyck, R. S. (1994). *Investment under uncertainty*. Princeton, NJ: Princeton University Press.

Dixit, A. K., & Pindyck, R. S. (1995). The options approach to capital investment. *Harvard Business Review*, *73*(3), 105–115.

Dunbar, N. (2000). The power of real options. *Risk*, *13*(8), 20–22.

Elettra, A., & Rossella, A. (2003). A generalization of the Geske formula for compound options. *Mathematical Social Science*, *45*(1), 75–82.

Fernandez, P. (2005). Valuing real options: Frequently made errors. *Journal of Financial Transformation*, *13*(April), 77–81.

Fichman, R. G., Keil, M., & Tiwana, A. (2005). Beyond valuation: Real options thinking in IT project management. *California Management Review*, *47*(2), 74–96.
Frydenberg, S. (2011). Theory of capital structure – A review. In G. Arntzen, L. Fallan & O. Gustafsson (Eds.), *FrihetogMangfold, FestsskriffTil Odd.* Trondheim, Norway: Tapir/TØH, Tapir Academic Press.
Galai, D., & Masulis, R. W. (1976). The option pricing model and the risk factor of stock. *Journal of Financial Economics*, *3*(January–March), 53–81.
Geske, R. (1977). The valuation of corporate liabilities as compound options. *Journal of Financial and Quantitative Analysis* (November), 541–552.
Geske, R. (1979). The valuation of compound options. *Journal of Financial Economics*, *7*(1), 63–81.
Gibson, R., & Schwartz, E. S. (1990). Stochastic convenience yield and the pricing of oil contingent claims. *Journal of Finance*, *45*, 959–976.
Glassman, D., Amram, M., & Baldwin, C. (2000). Bank of America roundtable on: The real options approach to creating value in the new economy. *Journal of Applied Corporate Finance*, *13*(2), 45–63.
Gorton, G. B. (2010). *Questions and answers about the financial crisis*. NBER Working Paper No. W15787. National Bureau of Economic Research, Cambridge, MA.
Graham, J., & Harvey, C. (2001). The theory and practice of corporate finance: Evidence from the field. *Journal of Financial Economics*, *60*(May), 187–243.
Green, R. C. (1984). Investment incentives, debt, and warrants. *Journal of Financial Economics*, *13*, 115–136.
Grenadier, S. R. (1999). Information revelation through option exercise. *Review of Financial Studies*, *12*, 95–129.
Hayes, H., & Garvin, G. (1982). Managing as if tomorrow mattered. *Harvard Business Review* (May–June), 71–79.
Hodder, J. E., & Riggs, H. E. (1985). Pitfalls in evaluating risky projects. *Harvard Business Review*, *1*, 128–135.
Hodgson, G. M. (2009). The great crash of 2008 and the reform of economics. *Cambridge Journal of Economics*, *33*(August), 1205–1221.
Howell, S. D., & Jagle, A. J. (1997). Laboratory evidence on how managers intuitively value real growth options. *Journal of Business Finance and Accounting*, *24*(7&8), 915–935.
Ingersoll, J. E., & Ross, S. (1992). Waiting to invest: Investment and uncertainty. *Journal of Business* (January), 1–29.
Jacoby, H. D., & Laughton, D. G. (1992). Project evaluation: A practical asset pricing method. *Energy Journal*, *13*(2), 19–29.
Jensen, M. C., & Meckling, W. H. (1976). Theory of the firm: Managerial behavior, agency costs and ownership structure. *Journal of Financial Economics*, *3*(4), 305–360.
Jickling, M. (2009). Causes of the financial crisis. Congressional Research Service, 7-5700, R40173.
Kasanen, E. (1993). Creating value by spawning investment opportunities. *Financial Management*, *22*(3), 251–258.
Kemna, A. G. Z. (1993). Case studies on real options. *Financial Management*, *22*(3), 259–270.
Kensinger, J. W. (1987). Adding the value of active management into the capital budgeting equation. *Midland Corporate Finance Journal*, *5*(1), 31–42.
Kester, W. C. (1984). Today's options for tomorrow's growth. *Harvard Business Review*, *62*(2), 153–160.

Kester, W. C. (1986). An options approach to corporate finance. In E. Altman (Ed.), *Handbook of corporate finance* (2nd ed.). New York, NY: Wiley.

Kester, W. C. (1993). Turning growth options into real assets. In R. Aggarwal (Ed.), *Capital budgeting under uncertainty* (pp. 187–207). Englewood Cliffs, NJ: Prentice Hall.

Kogut, B., & Kulatilaka, N. (1994). Option thinking and platform investments: Investing in opportunities. *California Management Review*, *36*(4), 52–71.

Kulatilaka, N. (1988). Valuing the flexibility of flexible manufacturing systems. *IEEE Transactions on Engineering Management*, *35*(4), 250–257.

Kulatilaka, N. (1993a). The value of flexibility: The case of a dual-fuel industrial steam boiler. *Financial Management*, *22*(3), 271–280.

Kulatilaka, N. (1993b). Operating flexibilities in capital budgeting: Substitutability and complementarity in real options. In L. Trigeorgis (Ed.), *Real options in capital investments: New contributions*. New York, NY: Praeger.

Kulatilaka, N., & Marcus, A. J. (1988). General formulation of corporate real options. *Research in Finance*, *7*, 183–199.

Kulatilaka, N., & Marcus, A. J. (1992). Project valuation under uncertainty: When does DCF fail? *Journal of Applied Corporate Finance* (Fall), 92–100.

Kulatilaka, N., & Trigeorgis, L. (1993). The general flexibility to switch: Real options revisited. *International Journal of Finance*, *5*, 179–198.

Kupperman, J. J. (2010). *Theories of human nature*. Indianapolis, IN: Hackett Publishing Company, Inc.

Lankton, N., & Luft, J. (2008). Uncertainty and industry structure effects on managerial intuition about information technology real options. *Journal of Management Information Systems*, *25*(2), 203–240.

Laughton, D. G., & Jacoby, H. D. (1993). Reversion, timing options, and long-term decision-making. *Financial Management*, *22*(3), 225–240.

Leslie, K. J., & Michaels, M. P. (1997). The real power of real options. *McKinsey Quarterly*, *33*(Summer), 4–19.

Luehrman, T. A. (1998). Investment opportunities as real options: Getting started on the numbers. *Harvard Business Review* (July–August), 51–67.

Luehrman, T. A. (2009). Strategy as a portfolio of real options. *Harvard Business Review*, March.

Majd, S., & Pindyck, R. S. (1987). Time to build, option value, and investment decisions. *Journal of Financial Economics*, *18*(1), 7–27.

Margrabe, W. (1978). The value of an option to exchange one asset for another. *Journal of Finance*, *33*(March), 177–186.

Marsh, T., & Pfleiderer, P. C. (2010). *The 2008–2009 financial crisis: Risk model transparency and incentives*. Working Paper No. 72. Rock Center for Corporate Governance at Stanford University, Stanford, CA.

Mason, S. P., & Merton, R. C. (1985). The role of contingent claims analysis in corporate finance. In E. I. Altman & M. G. Subrahmanyam (Eds.), *Recent advances in corporate finance* (pp. 7–54). Homewood, IL: Richard D. Irwin.

McDonald, R. L. (2000). Real options and rules of thumb in capital budgeting. In M. J. Brennan & L. Trigeorgis (Eds.), *Project flexibility, agency, and competition* (pp. 13–33). Oxford, England: Oxford University Press.

McDonald, R. L., & Siegel, D. R. (1985). Investment and the valuation of firms when there is an option to shut down. *International Economic Review*, *26*(2), 331–349.

McDonald, R. L., & Siegel, D. R. (1986). The value of waiting to invest. *Quarterly Journal of Economics*, *101*(4), 707–727.
McGrath, R. G. (1997). A real options logic for initiating technology positioning investments. *Academy of Management Review*, *22*(4), 974–996.
McGrath, R. G. (1999). Falling forward: Real options reasoning and entrepreneurial failure. *Academy of Management Review*, *24*(1), 13–30.
Mello, A. S., & Parsons, J. E. (1992). Measuring the agency cost of debt. *Journal of Finance*, *XLVII*(5), 1887–1904.
Merton, R. C. (1973). The theory of rational option pricing. *Bell Journal of Economics and Management Science*, *4*(Spring), 141–183.
Merton, R. C. (1974). On the pricing of corporate debt: The risk structure of interest rates. *Journal of Finance*, *29*, 449–470.
Miller, K. D., & Arikan, A. T. (2004). Technology search investments: Evolutionary, option reasoning, and option pricing approaches. *Strategic Management Journal*, *25*(5), 473–485.
Miller, K. D., & Shapira, Z. (2004). An empirical test of heuristics and biases affecting real option valuation. *Strategic Management Journal*, *25*(3), 269–284.
Miller, M., & Modigliani, F. (1961). Dividend policy, growth, and the valuation of shares. *Journal of Business*, *34*(4), 411–433.
Mittendorf, B. (2004). Information revelation, incentives, and the value of a real option. *Management Science*, *50*(12), 1638–1645.
Morck, R., Schwartz, E., & Stangeland, D. (1989). The valuation of forestry resources under stochastic prices and inventories. *Journal of Financial and Quantitative Analysis*, *24*, 473–488.
Myers, S. C. (1977). Determinants of corporate borrowing. *Journal of Financial Economics*, *5*(2), 147–175.
Myers, S. C. (1987). Finance theory and financial strategy. *Midland Corporate Finance Journal*, *5*(1), 6–13.
Myers, S. C., & Majd, S. (1990). Abandonment value and project life. *Advances in Futures and Options Research*, *4*, 1–21.
Obstfeld, M., & Rogoff, K. (2009). *Global imbalances and the financial crisis: Products of common causes.* Discussion Paper No. DP7606. Center for Economic Policy Research (CERP), Washington, DC.
Ott, S. H. (2002). Real options and real estate: A review and valuation illustration. In K. Wang & M. L. Wolverton (Eds.), *Real estate valuation theory* (Chapter 18, pp. 411–423), Boston, MA: Kluwer Academic Publishers.
Paddock, J. L., Siegel, D. R., & Smith, J. L. (1988). Option valuation of claims on real assets: The case of offshore petroleum leases. *Quarterly Journal of Economics*, *103*(3), 479–508.
Pindyck, R. S. (1988). Irreversible investments, capacity choice, and the value of the firm. *American Economic Review*, *78*(5), 969–985.
Pindyck, R. S. (1991). Irreversibility, uncertainty, and investment. *Journal of Economic Literature*, *XXIX*(September), 1110–1148.
Quigg, L. (1993). Empirical testing of real option-pricing models. *Journal of Finance*, *XLVIII*(2), 621–640.
Reihnart, C. M., & Rogoff, K. (2010). *From financial crash to debt crisis.* NBER Working Paper No. W15795. National Bureau of Economic Research, Cambridge, MA.

Reuer, J. J., & Tong, T. W. (2007). *Advances in strategic management: Real options theory*. New York, NY: Elsevier.

Ross, S. A. (1995). Uses, abuses, and alternatives to the net-present-value rule. *Financial Management, 24*(3), 96–102.

Ryan, P. A., & Ryan, G. P. (2002). Capital budgeting practices of the Fortune 1000: How have things changed? *Journal of Business and Management, 8*(4).

Scholte, J. A. (2000). *Globalization: A critical introduction*. New York, NY: Palgrave MacMillan.

Schwartz, E. S., & Trigeorgis, L. (Eds.). (2001). *Real options and investment under uncertainty*. Boston, MA: MIT Press.

Sick, G. (1989). *Capital budgeting with real options*. Monograph Series in Finance and Economics. University of Calgary, Canada.

Siegel, D. R., Smith, J. L., & Paddock, J. L. (1987). Valuing offshore oil properties with option pricing models. *Midland Corporate Finance Journal, 5*(1), 22–30.

Smit, H. T. J., & Ankum, L. A. (1993). A real options and game-theoretic approach to corporate investment strategy under competition. *Financial Management, 22*(3), 241–250.

Smith, C. W., & Warner, J. B. (1979). On financial contracting: An analysis of bond covenants. *Journal of Financial Economics, 7*(2), 117–161.

Stevenson, L., & Haberman, D. L. (2008). *Ten theories of human nature*. Oxford, England: Oxford University Press.

Stulz, R. (1982). Options on the minimum or maximum of two risky assets: Analysis and applications. *Journal of Financial Economics, 10*(July), 161–185.

Tallon, P. P., Kauffman, R. J., Lucas, H. C., Whinston, A. B., & Zhu, K. (2002). Using real options analysis for evaluating uncertain investment in information technology: Insights from the ICIS 2001 debate. *Communications of the AIS, 9*(September), 136–167.

Teach, E. (2003). Will real options take root? *CFO Magazine*, July.

Titman, S. (1985). Urban land prices under uncertainty. *American Economic Review, 75*, 505–514.

Tiwana, A., Keil, M., & Fichman, R. G. (2006). Information systems project continuation in escalation situations: A real options model. *Decision Sciences, 37*(3), 357–391.

Tiwana, A., Wang, J., Keil, M., & Ahluwalia, P. (2007). The bounded rationality bias in managerial valuation of real options: Theory and evidence from IT projects. *Decision Sciences, 38*(1), 157–181.

Tourinho, O. (1979). *The option value of reserves of natural resources*. Working Paper No. 94. University of California, Berkeley, CA.

Triantis, A. J. (2005). Realizing the potential of real options: Does theory meet practice? *Journal of Applied Corporate Finance, 17*(2), 8–16.

Triantis, A. J., & Hodder, J. E. (1990). Valuing flexibility as a complex option. *Journal of Finance, 45*, 549–566.

Trigeorgis, L. (1988). A conceptual options framework for capital budgeting. *Advances in Futures and Options Research, 3*, 145–167.

Trigeorgis, L. (1993a). Real options and interactions with financial flexibility. *Financial Management, 22*(3), 202–224.

Trigeorgis, L. (1993b). The nature of option interactions and the valuation of investments with multiple real options. *Journal of Financial and Quantitative Analysis, 28*(1), 1–20.

Trigeorgis, L. (Ed.). (1995). *Real options in capital investment: Models, strategies, and applications*. Westport, CT: Praeger.

Trigeorgis, L. (2000). *Real options: Managerial flexibility and strategy in resource allocation*. Cambridge, MA: MIT Press.

Trigeorgis, L., & Kasanen, E. (1991). An integrated options-based strategic planning and control model. *Managerial Finance*, *17*(2/3), 16–28.

Trigeorgis, L., & Mason, S. P. (1987). Valuing managerial flexibility. *Midland Corporate Finance Journal*, *5*(1), 14–21.

Van Putten, A. B., & MacMillan, I. (2004). Making real options really work. *Harvard Business Review*, *82*(12), 134–141.

Williams, J. T. (1991). Real estate development as an option. *Journal of Real State Finance and Economics*, *4*, 191–208.

Woolridge, J. R. (1995). Do stock prices reflect fundamental values? *Journal of Applied Corporate Finance*, *8*(1), 64–69.

Yavas, A., & Sirmans, C. F. (2005). Real options: Experimental evidence. *Journal of Real Estate Finance and Economics*, *31*(1), 27–52.

DERIVATIVES, COMMODITIES, AND SOCIAL COSTS: EXPLORING CORRELATION IN ECONOMIC UNCERTAINTY

Aleksandr V. Gevorkyan and Arkady Gevorkyan

ABSTRACT

Derivatives market has been epitomized with gross evil in the wake of the global economic crisis that ensued in 2008. This study argues for more extensive understanding of the phenomena as dynamics previously viewed unrelated now exhibit correlation. As empirical reference, this research relies on recent trends in the commodity futures contracts with analytical relation to the currency exchange rate and by extension the financial and real sectors. With varying intensity often speculative sporadic trading in crude oil, coffee, wheat, rice, sugar, and gold benchmark futures may inflict detrimental effects on the global development efforts. The issue is most acute in the emerging markets facing inflation fears, speculative movements of foreign currency-denominated funds, and underlying domestic currency value. This dynamic reasserts the concept of fundamental uncertainty allowing us to connect the typical risk-return stand with a dialectical unity of the financial, real sector, and social costs. Ultimately, issues raised in this study relate to the problems of social

Derivative Securities Pricing and Modelling
Contemporary Studies in Economic and Financial Analysis, Volume 94, 47–70

ISSN: 1569-3759/doi:10.1108/S1569-3759(2012)0000094005

stability and sustained economic development in the postcrisis environment given high frequency and volatility of capital flows. As such, this chapter contributes to the literature that bridges financial empirical analysis with modern socially responsible economic development.

Keywords: Commodity derivatives; fundamental uncertainty; emerging markets; exchange rate; international reserves; sovereign debt

INTRODUCTION

Active derivatives trading has been epitomized with gross evil in the wake of the global economic crisis of late 2000s. Insightful commentary has ranged from outright rejection to cardinal regulatory reorganization of the entire financial industry. This chapter calls for more extensive analysis of the phenomena as dynamics previously viewed unrelated now exhibit correlation. As an installment in a larger research effort, we attempt to link commodity derivatives volatility to problems of economic and social development. In recent years, this has manifested in globally spread shortages, food and energy prices inflation, especially in net commodities importer nations (e.g., Ahmed, 2008).

Many emerging markets, pursuing tactically diverse economic policies, act as the world's main exporters of specific commodities. This leads to existence of more complex linkages between commodity derivatives trading and social development. In most simplest form, three such links, bearing social costs and fundamental uncertainty, can be identified: (1) downward trending of commodity derivative prices and subsequent exporting nations' terms of trade deterioration, (2) drastic short-term volatility in commodity contracts and immediate financial corrections by risk-hedging investors leading to speculative capital flows in and out exporting economy, and finally (3) commodity derivatives dynamics exerting pressures on exporting economy's currency and ultimately macroeconomy. From the empirical standpoint, this chapter tackles, what appears, the most obscure third linkage.

Over the past decade, commodity derivatives, traded in US dollars, have evolved to become one of the most significant categories in modern derivatives trade (Basu & Gavin, 2011). Producers and speculative investors alike hedging their risks are actively engaged in these trades. At the same time, many emerging economies that are major commodities exporters rely on foreign exchange for their economic stability. Hence, rising frequency in commodity contracts trading and implied underlying commodity price volatility feed into problems of terms of trade via exchange rate affecting also internal effective demand.

Among empirical commentary, recent work by Chen, Yu-Chin, Rogoff, and Rossi (2008) stands out for its comprehensive dealing with the problem. The authors define "commodity currency" exchange rates based on a selected group of five relatively advanced economies in consideration. As a result, they find support for predictive capacity of the currency exchange rates over commodity prices, yet effectively no support for reverse relationship. This limited predictive power is due to the forward looking tendency of the currency exchange rates, while commodity prices carry strong sensitivity to short-term variations. In what follows, we analyze commodity specific trends based on individual prices (vs. combined indices as in Chen et al.) and center around the issue of short-term sensitivity, looking at a larger group of emerging markets.

Partially related to the first of the above three links, additional insights are found in close consideration of the Prebisch–Singer hypothesis of downward trending commodity prices in relation to the prices of the manufactured goods. The concept takes its name from the influential work by Prebisch (1950) and Singer (1950). Looking at price variations earlier, both Kondratieff (1922, 1935) and Kuznets (e.g., 1930, 1949, 1971, 1973) analyzed similar dynamics in a more inclusive context of long wave cycles in economic development (for a detailed survey, see Bernard, Gevorkyan, Palley, & Semmler, 2011). More recently, Harvey, Kellard, Madsen, and Wohar (2010) find empirical evidence in support of the Prebisch–Singer hypothesis for some (but not all) commodity groups studied. The implication is of a negative dynamic for economies for which commodities represent significant proportion of their exports. Clearly, countries that have underdeveloped industrial base and that rely on primary exports revenues to fund imports of manufactured goods are the most affected.

With the above considerations in mind, the remainder of this chapter is organized as follows. The second section offers a brief macroeconomic rationale of commodity derivatives and currency exchange rates linkage. Importantly, this section discusses the core commodities group and target countries based on significance in international trade. The main theoretical model and data description are developed in the third section with discussion of relevant literature. The fourth section summarizes main empirical results with related policy analysis. Summary of findings and key analytical observations are finalized in the concluding section.

COMMODITY DERIVATIVES, EMERGING MARKETS, AND EXCHANGE RATES

Commodities trade is not a recent phenomenon. The markets have evolved from the earliest agricultural exchanges of the Near East, more complex financial agreements of Medieval Europe, to modern fast pace futures contracts trading (for a brief overview, see German, 2005). Producers and end users of the physical primary commodities have relied on the evolved commodities markets to hedge their risk exposure to unexpected falls in extraction (e.g., oil, coal, and metals) or production (e.g., agricultural staples like wheat and rice). The essence remains the same, being an advance agreement on the tangible commodity's delivery price. All key commodities that today are taken as indicators of global economy's health are traded primarily in US dollars – hard currency for majority of the core primary commodities producing and exporting nations. Therefore, revenues generated from volume sales may significantly affect the seller's foreign exchange balances.

This leads to a more recent phenomenon of increased securitization of the commodities trading and, as a result, the added complexity of modern international trade and financial flows. Today, commodity derivatives are futures and options traded on exchanges and forward and option contracts traded over the counter (OTC). The trend is seen in Fig. 1 that compares equity derivatives to commodity contracts through the end of 2010 traded OTC.

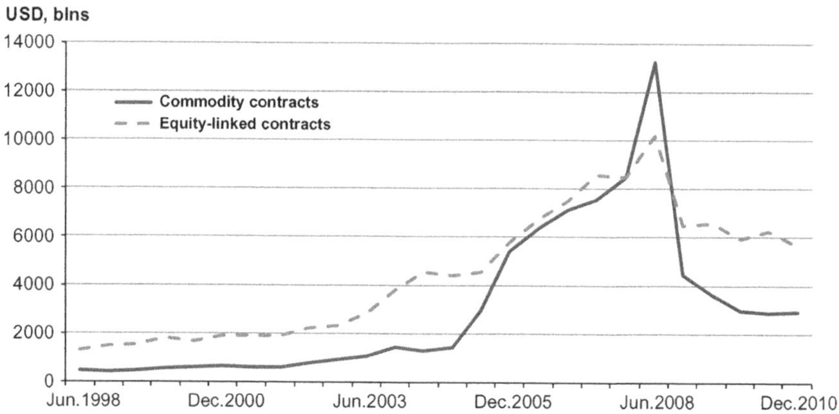

Fig. 1. Commodity and Equity Linked Derivative Contracts. *Source*: BIS (2011).

Overall, interest rate and foreign exchange contracts are the largest in US dollar volumes, or 83% of all OTC contracts between 2000 and 2010, and have trended similar to the contracts in Fig. 1 according to the latest Bank for International Settlements (BIS) data. Emerging markets have kept up with the rest of the world introducing new instruments and actively engaging in foreign exchange and interest rate contracts (for an overview, see Mihaljek & Packer, 2010).

As has been mentioned, for every commodity there is a benchmark contract followed by variations of similar contracts. For example, the main oil contract is crude light oil, West Texas Intermediate that serves the purpose of the global benchmark (Brent contract, with production/shipment originating from Northern Europe, is another benchmark but with 10% share is quite small in the overall trade). Despite the fact that securitization may offer directional guidance to a short-term investor in a volatile market, given the role benchmark contracts play, there often may be a negative "domino" effect beyond financial markets.

For commodity derivatives markets, changes in benchmark contracts have direct impacts on less traded, or of other variety, yet equally relevant, contracts contributing to physical commodity price instability. Such short-term volatility, combined with high securitization, increases artificial correlation between commodities contracts trading, not necessarily supported by the actual production. For example, Basu and Gavin (2011) show that growth in commodity derivatives trading far outstrips the growth in the commodity production and the need for derivatives to hedge risk by commodity users and commercial producers. One of the reasons for this growth (a second link identified by us earlier) is associated with investors looking for higher yields, when return on more traditional assets is lower. On sidelines it should be noted that, Basu and Gavin (2011) conclude that even if US stock market and futures commodities were negatively correlated, it is likely that such correlation would be an equilibrium arbitrage phenomenon applicable to an environment of no unexploited hedging profit opportunity. Hence, the rise in commodity derivative trading poses a dominant challenge to a standard well-articulated rational asset pricing model.

A clarification of commodities derivatives market is overdue. Conceptually, the value of the underlying (primary) asset drives the frequency and volumes of trading of these financial instruments, which, in turn, determines a defined contract's price per unit (e.g., 5,000 bushels per contract for wheat or 1,000 US barrels for crude oil contract). We defer the reader to a more definitive categorization and risk management techniques in other studies (e.g., Clubley, 2000; Pilipovic, 2007; Schofield, 2008; Spurga, 2006; and others). In our study, we look at the world's six key traded commodities in the energy, agriculture, and precious metals sectors: coffee, crude oil, gold, rice, sugar, and wheat.

Unsurprisingly, and consistent with some economic literature (e.g., Harvey et al., 2010; Rada & Taylor, 2006; and others) outside of the developed economies of North America and Western Europe (also excluding Australia and New Zealand), major primary commodity exporters are the emerging markets. Table 1 shows the top 10 exporters (excluding advanced economies) with corresponding percentage of exports in relation to total world exports for each commodity as of 2010. Significantly, the first three economies dominate in each grouping in terms of individual export proportions on the global scale. Within each of these individual economies' international trade structure, exports of the respective primary commodities are significant (e.g., in 2010, Russia's oil exports accounted for 35% of the economy's total exports, Brazil's 10% or gold exports of 22% in Peru's total exports, etc.), according to the latest United Nations Conference on Trade and Development (UNCTAD, 2011) data.

Relying on the foreign exchange flows from export revenues, these economies are directly affected by short-term volatility on commodities markets (also valid for the net importers but depending on actual price fluctuation). A quick glance at historical futures (traded on the organized exchange vs. OTC) settlement prices for the chosen commodities confirms this view (see Fig. 2) also echoed in the study of derivatives markets in LiPuma and Lee (2004). Clearly, heavy dependence on the "right" US dollar price of the primary commodity in their net exports contributes significantly to financial and macroeconomic instability.

In other words, proliferation of different types of derivative contracts and ease of making short-term investments may lead to a situation when a risk-hedging investor quickly enters or leaves domestic market (including, alternative to commodities, equity, and debt obligations) in correlation with (or in response to) the derivative contracts prices of underlying export commodity. Such instability, a feature of modern financial markets, gradually affects economic and social indicators feeding fundamental uncertainty (Flaschel & Semmler, 2003; Gevorkyan & Gevorkyan, 2011).

For the emerging markets, possible macroeconomic indicators may include targeted inflation levels, income growth, but most likely exchange rate – our third link. Related to these is the concept of foreign currency-denominated debt obligations at public and private levels. In emerging markets, these obligations are usually short-term, subject to immediate revisions, and may run at higher yields (Gevorkyan, 2011). Today, emerging

Table 1. Primary Commodities and Emerging Markets' Exporters, Percentage of Global Exports in 2010.

Coffee	Percentage	Wheat	Percentage	Oil	Percentage	Rice	Percentage	Gold	Percentage	Sugar	Percentage
Brazil	18.2	Russia	6.1	Saudi Arabia	15.5	Thailand	25.4	Peru	5.1	Brazil	26.2
Vietnam	8.4	Argentina	5.8	Russia	10.5	India	15.2	Thailand	4.3	Thailand	5.1
Colombia	6.8	Kazakhstan	2.7	Nigeria	5.4	Vietnam	11.4	Mexico	3.8	India	3.9
Indonesia	3.1	Ukraine	2.7	Angola	3.7	Uruguay	2.0	Colombia	1.4	Mexico	2.7
Peru	2.8	Romania	1.5	Kazakhstan	3.0	Egypt	1.7	Brazil	1.2	Guatemala	1.7
Guatemala	2.5	Hungary	1.3	Mexico	2.9	Argentina	1.3	South Africa	0.9	Argentina	1.5
Ethiopia	2.4	Bulgaria	1.3	Brazil	1.3	Brazil	0.8	Indonesia	0.8	Colombia	1.4
India	2.4	Poland	0.8	Colombia	1.1	Russia	0.4	Vietnam	0.7	Poland	1.3
Honduras	2.2	Paraguay	0.7	Indonesia	0.8	Paraguay	0.3	Chile	0.7	Egypt	1.0
Mexico	1.6	Brazil	0.7	Malaysia	0.8	Tajikistan	0.3	Egypt	0.7	Czech Republic	0.8

Source: Own calculations based on data from UNCTAD (2011).

markets gauging greater effectiveness in their net exports composition rely on a competitive currency exchange rate taken as a nominal anchor in the overall macroeconomic model. In turn, that policy is supported via active use of international reserves that are accumulated due to extra revenues from commodities exports. This works fine provided predictability or, more aptly, lack of short-term drastic variations in underlying export commodity's prices, that in turn are driven by commodity derivatives trading (Semmler & Gevorkyan, 2011).

In fact, LiPuma and Lee (2004) suggest derivatives markets (and commodities portion especially) with their size could influence exchange rate between hard and soft currencies and thus the purchasing power of a country's currency. Such relation becomes especially crucial when economy

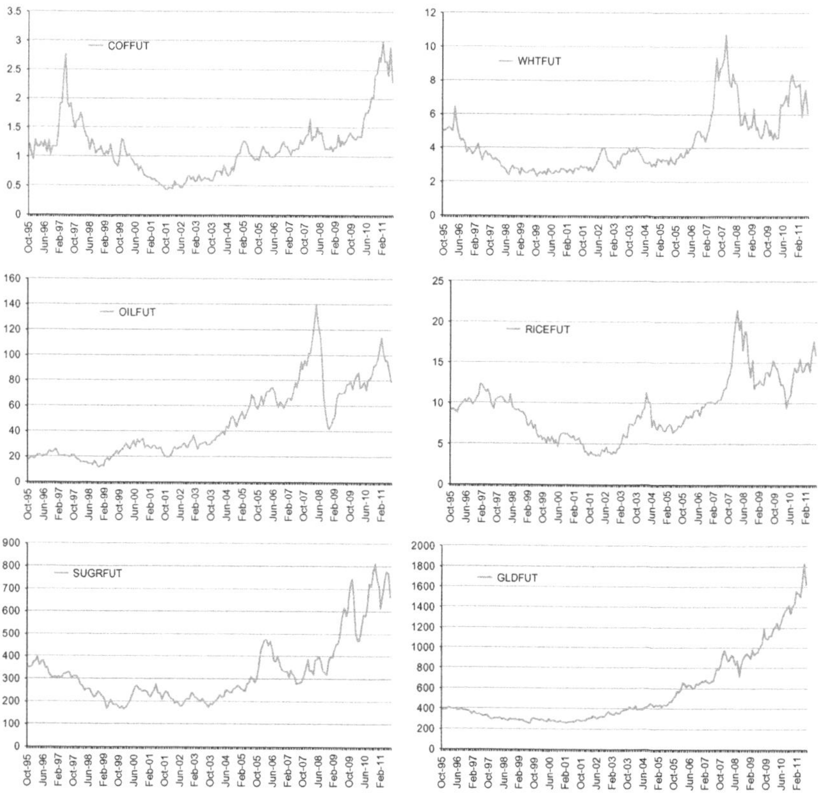

Fig. 2. Commodities Futures Contracts Volatility. *Source*: Bloomberg (2011).

is struggling and the state is weakened. This consideration is of immediate concern for the countries mentioned in Table 1, emerging markets laden with a range of socioeconomic issues high on the agenda. For many of these economies, including the largest in the group, bigger issues are at stake than simply hedging financial risks. Namely, short-term commodity derivatives price variations, via the mechanism described above, coupled with global demand fluctuations, may have a strong impact on these markets' ultimate development direction resulting from lacking foreign exchange reserves, assuming activist monetary and fiscal policies, as is the case in most cases discussed here. In what follows, we attempt to empirically test the relationship between currency exchange rates and commodity derivatives volatility.

STRUCTURAL METHODOLOGY DISCUSSION AND DATA SPECIFICATION

Building on the conceptual framework of commodity derivatives and social costs, by way of exchange rate influence, we seek to structure a methodological approach to examine this relationship empirically. In addition to the already mentioned studies by Chen et al. (2008) and Harvey et al. (2008), we pull useful insights from several other sources. Overall, majority of empirical work attempts to find definitive determinants of the commodity prices, as early as Gilbert (1989).

For example, Akram (2009) considers movements in the real interest rates and US dollar impacts on commodity prices utilizing structural VAR models based on quarterly data. Empirical results suggest negative relation between real interest rates, as commodity prices increase in response to declines in the real interest rates. Likewise, commodity prices appear to be higher in response to weaker dollar. In the context of our analysis, these findings suggest that increased availability of credit in the financial markets and lower transaction costs in conducting trades denominated in US dollars lead to speculative bid-up of commodity prices seen in the mid-2006 (e.g., oil price spiking $150 level, as in Fig. 2) and greater futures contract volatility.

In another study, Chinn, LeBlanc, and Coibion (2005) compare between spot and futures prices on energy commodities. The authors find weak support for futures as predictors of the spot prices. In a follow-up study, Chinn and Coibion (2010) reinforce the initial finding, but with a reference to the depth of the market in recent years (read: increased volatility trading). Hong and Yogo (2011) develop a forecasting model indicating procyclical relationship between open interest (contracts outstanding in futures market) and asset price fluctuations, including commodity derivatives. Finally, Chen et al. (2008) determine not only selected economies currency exchange rates predictive power over commodity prices, but also the weak reverse relationship. The latter may be due to the authors' choice of countries with hard currencies in their sample, in addition to the complexity of the macroeconomic determinants of the currency exchange rate. Nevertheless, these studies are quite insightful in serving as foundation for our methodological approach.

Common to the above, and other studies surveyed during our background review, is the focus on commodity prices as the dependent variables as the bulk of the effort goes on uncovering their precise determinants. That has a direct value for speculative capital movements. But while successful attempts, some cited above, would suggest more informed investor decisions, this somewhat leaves out the other side of the transaction: the seller of the underlying commodity, which, in our case, are the emerging economies dependent on hard currency revenues.

In looking at exchange rate dynamics, an analogy with the J-curve concept (from a larger scope of balance of payments) may be appropriate. Some relevant empirical and methodological studies are by Magee (1973), Meade (1988), Bahmani-Oskooee (1985, 1989), Backus, Kehoe, and Kydland (1994), Gevorkyan (2011), and others. In essence, the work on J-curve suggests existence of a lag in economy's current account response to changes in the exchange rate. Other macroeconomic parameters notwithstanding, the relationship is important uncovering structural dynamics, in particular for the developing economies. The lag is usually minimal measured in months, but is due to either delayed net exports prices pass-through or contractual obligations.

Within the context of our analysis, we note the forward looking currency exchange rate determinations and a more short-term shocks susceptible commodity futures price fluctuation. Adopting the insights from the above and other studies, including the relevant gist of the J-curve hypothesis, we propose to test for the reverse relationship: commodity futures – to currency exchange rates assuming lagged pass-through of information from prices into exporting economies' exchange rates.

That is not to suggest, however, that commodity futures fully determine currency values. Rather there may exist a strong relationship that translates commodity derivatives volatility into exchange rate adjustments with implications for macroeconomic policy. The model is a version of the autoregressive conditional heteroskedastic model (ARCH) (e.g., see Engle, 1982 or Bollerslev, 1987). Formally, our base model assumes the following specification:

$$ER_{i,t} = \alpha + \beta_1 F_{i,t} + \beta_2 F_{i,t-1} + \varepsilon_i \quad (1)$$

where $ER_{i,t}$ is the exporter currency index at time t (defined properly below) for commodity group i, $F_{i,t}$ is the respective commodity futures price in the corresponding period t, and $F_{i,t-1}$ is the price with one period lag. α, β_1, β_2, and ε_i are the corresponding constant term, coefficients, and error terms.

Perhaps a more insightful analysis due to the complexity and not always direct link between the *ER* and *F* is an analysis that studies the variation between periods in each variable and their correlation to each other. Consequently, we adjust the base model in Eq. (1) to the following form:

$$\Delta ER_{i,t} = \alpha + \beta_1 \Delta F_{i,t} + \beta_2 \Delta F_{i,t-1} + \varepsilon_i \quad (2)$$

The new model in Eq. (2) now compares one period change in the exchange rate index to a monthly change in the commodity futures price. Such specification of the model captures the dynamic between dependent and independent variables. Here, $\Delta F_{i,t}$ is the change in commodity futures between periods t and $(t-1)$, and $\Delta F_{i,t-1}$ refers to the change between periods $(t-1)$ and $(t-2)$, that is, effectively adding two lags to the analysis.

Consistent with Eq. (2), one may reasonably expect a positive relation between lagged futures and exchange rate index parameters (assuming positive coefficient results). This would indicate some exchange rate reaction for emerging markets in response to volatility in commodity futures. Furthermore, in cases where exchange rates are actively managed by the monetary authorities (as in the core group of emerging markets), a positive correlation would suggest proactive measures of the authorities to maintain competitive currency conversion. However, country-specific result may not be immediately evident due to the exchange rate index construction in this model.

Next, we provide exchange rate specification by defining a *commodity currency exchange rate index*. We rely on the monthly data between October 1995 and September 2011 derived from Capital IQ expressed for each country in Table 1 as domestic currency per one US dollar. We limit the number of countries in each category for our review to five per each commodity group. This achieves a manageable sample size and will help with results interpretation. Therefore, an unweighted average *ER* index (in relation to US dollar) for commodity group *i*, comprised of five countries' exchange rates *j*, would be:

$$ER_i = \frac{1}{j}\sum_{j=1}^{5} ER_{i,j} \tag{3}$$

with all variables defined consistently per above, and group *i* ranging from 1 to 6 for the six commodity contracts in review: coffee, wheat, crude oil, rice, gold, and sugar. We rely on monthly futures contract prices for each commodity as reported by Bloomberg (2011). According to Eq. (3), increase in the *ER* index corresponds to currency appreciation for each commodity grouping.

Our intention is to capture individual shocks to emerging markets' currencies. In some cases (as in the recent case of Russia, see Gevorkyan, 2011), a mix of monetary and fiscal policies resulted in proactive use of currency reserves in sustaining competitive exchange rates. Layering the actual (levels) observations on the monthly commodity futures prices (see Fig. A1) reveals initial pattern that raises more questions than immediate answers.

With exception of fluctuations of the past 2–3 years (roughly the period between 2009 and 2011), there does not seem to be any strong correlation, except for the unprecedented growth in commodity prices. Some currency indices (e.g., sugar) have followed the pattern appreciating over the past two periods. Nevertheless, it is premature to call the final results and we revisit this question in the discussion section below. A more intriguing revelation comes from the analysis of lagged and variance results, which we conduct in the following section.

RESULTS DISCUSSION AND ECONOMIC POLICY IMPLICATIONS

As empirical test, we estimate the time series analysis model in Eq. (2). Our sample included data for the first five countries from Table 1 that we identify as the world's leading exporters of the respective commodity within the emerging markets group. Estimation results are presented in Table 2.

Working initially with levels data, we observe positive correlation for all six commodities futures contracts to exchange rate dynamics in the first lag, but with two commodities outliers (oil and rice results are not statistically

Table 2. Estimation Results Based on Levels Lags.

	Coffee	Wheat	Oil	Rice	Gold	Sugar
Constant	−0.002	−0.011	−0.015	−0.004	−0.003	−0.003
First lag $\Delta F_{i,t}$	0.065 (0.041)***	0.078 (0.044)***	0.015 (0.067)	0.033 (0.044)	0.167 (0.074)**	0.055 (0.049)***
Second lag $\Delta F_{i,t-1}$	−0.038 (0.026)***	−0.035 (0.029)***	−0.045 (0.050)	0.0026 (0.028)	−0.104 (0.049)**	0.012 (0.039)

Note: Standard errors in parenthesis. **, ***Indicate significance at 1%, 5%, and 10%.

significant). At the same time, the second lag results are less consistent with all negative trends, with exception of rice and sugar (see Table 2). Aside from statistical formalities, which we acknowledge in our model, these variations are most likely due to the varying currency regimes pursued in each of the commodity exporting country groups and individual countries.

A more complete theoretical model of exchange rate would necessarily link the real interest rate (or a proxy, e.g., LIBOR or domestic intrabank borrowing rate, also known as federal funds rate in the United States). Analytically, such model would be an extension of the base formulation in Eq. (1):

$$ER_{i,t} = \alpha + \beta_1 F_{i,t} + \beta_2 F_{i,t-1} + \beta_3 I_{i,t} + \beta_4 R_{i,t} + \varepsilon_i \tag{4}$$

Essentially, Eq. (4) adds a more complete dimension to exchange rate determination by incorporating the interest rate I and foreign exchange reserves balances R, consistent with model descriptions above. The latter have become an important component of modern day monetary and fiscal policy coordination in the emerging markets (e.g., Semmler & Gevorkyan, 2011). Pinning down precise currency exchange rate model is beyond the scope of the present research and we leave this as an option for a follow-up complex work.

However, Eq. (4) specification prompts a modification of our base model in Eq. (2), suggesting levels-based analysis is not entirely insightful due to possible scale variations. Namely, we modify Eq. (2) to accommodate data analysis based on growth rates instead of levels as done above. This does not alter the model statement significantly. Instead, we convert core data into simple growth rates from one period to another.

New estimation results in Table 3 lend more support to our hypothesis of positive correlation between commodity futures and currency exchange rates for respective commodity exporter country groups. Results are statistically significant in the case of coffee and wheat (one lag), and rice (second lag). We find weak support for the main supposition in gold and sugar. This implies that direction of currency exchange rate (*ER* index here) directly follows with lag corresponding commodity futures dynamic.

Perhaps a more puzzling result is the negative correlation in the first and second lags for oil futures to exchange rates. Intuitively, consistent with the above discussion (recall the three links mechanism reviewed in the introductory section and the Prebisch–Singer hypothesis), rising oil prices as have been seen in recent years should be contributing to the corresponding domestic currency appreciation. The connection is rather simple: higher oil

Table 3. Estimation Results Based on Growth Rates.

	Coffee	Wheat	Oil	Rice	Gold	Sugar
Constant	−0.001	0.000	0.000	−0.001	−0.001	−0.002
First lag $\Delta F_{i,t}$	0.066 (0.028)**	0.049 (0.027)***	−0.001 (0.051)	−0.024 (0.018)***	0.038 (0.055)	0.021 (0.041)
Second lag $\Delta F_{i,t-1}$	−0.034 (0.015)**	−0.026 (0.015)***	−0.025 (0.029)	0.021 (0.010)**	0.006 (0.032)	−0.003 (0.025)

Note: Standard errors in parenthesis. **, ***Indicate significance at 1%, 5%, and 10%.

futures prices mean higher revenues earned in hard currency for such exporters as Saudi Arabia, Russia, Nigeria, Angola, Kazakhstan, and other comprising the group, per Table 1).

The negative correlation (though of weak significance, most likely due to our simple model specification) of growth rates suggests quite the opposite. In our view, this is a result of proactive exchange rate maintenance policies pursued by the monetary authorities (mixed with fiscal agent participation, by country) in the economies comprising the ER_{oil} index. In this case, a rising oil futures price pushes US dollar-denominated export revenues higher. In a free float regime, this would immediately lead to domestic currency appreciation, via simple foreign currency supply and demand frameset. This would work in a hypothetical case of immediate foreign currency pass-through into the domestic financial system.

However, if the exchange rate is maintained within a currency corridor (as in most of these countries, especially Russia and Kazakhstan), central bank will actively intervene and remove from the market extra foreign currency via open market operations and domestic currency inflows. As a result, domestic currency is pushed to artificially undervalued levels and extra foreign exchange may be stashed in state coffers or as foreign exchange reserves with the aim of using as a cushion in crisis times (exactly what happened in Russia and other Commonwealth of Independent States net exporters in 2008 and 2009, see Gevorkyan, 2011, for a complete analysis). The negative correlation found in our growth rates analysis confirms this analytical proposition.

Managed float, as exchange rate policy, may well be justified (and is actively pursued by a number of countries, including all of the primary oil exporters in Table 3 as well as the largest emerging market, China). The benefits of such proactive terms of trade management are obvious, achieving competitive price in the international market for primary exports. The costs are equally high, and in today's volatile financial markets, there persists a risk of currency runs. Given the role of foreign exchange reserves balances in this scheme, short-term volatility of commodity futures is significant for countries relying on continuous supply of hard currency, via extra US dollar-denominated profits, to maintain competitive exchange rate policy (Semmler & Gevorkyan, 2011).

More concretely, volatility of the ER_i and commodity futures growth rates is clearly depicted in the panels of Fig. 3 for the three selected commodities with weak correlation to exchange rates: oil, gold, and sugar. The panels plot currency exchange rate index volatility against commodity futures contracts' growth rates.

Looking at the absolute amplitude in each case, we note a constrained behavior of the oil currency index post-2000 (suggesting the beginning of the managed float regimes) with increased volatility in the oil futures trading and coinciding upward trend in benchmark commodity price (see charts in Fig. A1). Note the greater amplitude in oil futures volatility, suggesting a speculative and hedging trader activity. Similar pattern evolves in the case of gold and sugar as evident in Fig. 3. Incidentally, gold currency index's volatility is somewhat comparable (conscious of minor scale adjustment) in amplitude to the futures contract's volatility, suggesting a possibly direct link.

All in all, empirical results seem to suggest that exchange rates do react to changes in the commodity derivatives trading. For economic policy considerations, the perceived lag is incredibly small (measured in months), which implies immediate adjustments in the monetary sector and real economy. In this, real social costs in the emerging markets are a step away.

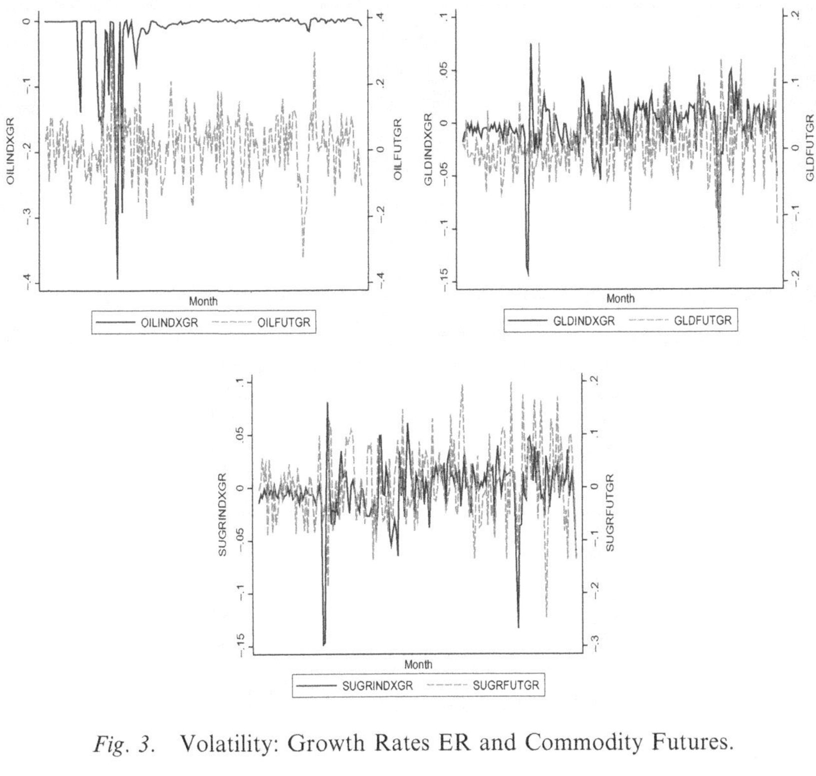

Fig. 3. Volatility: Growth Rates ER and Commodity Futures.

One manifestation of that has been food prices inflation in the countries relying on agricultural staples imports. This happens even despite possible leading position in exports of some agricultural commodities. Commodity derivatives linked inflation is one of the real social cost factors affecting emerging economies. On average, consumer price inflation has gone up for the group of emerging markets listed in Table 1 from 6.8% to 11% and predicted 8% in 2011, according to the latest IMF World Economic Outlook (2011) data.

More costly imports (manufactured goods and some raw materials not produced locally) combined with shortages, as futures trading outstrips actual production (e.g., food crises of 2008), lead to the same. Other contributing factors may be oil price increase and consequently escalating transportation costs. Additional insights, specifically on food price inflation, may be found in Ahmed (2008), Eckaus (2008), Jones and Kwiecinski (2010), Loening et al. (2009), to name a few.

In fact, commodities-driven inflation may easily be triggered by amalgamation of complex processes in an economy, including rundown on foreign exchange reserves, and eventual currency depreciation as a particular economy's export commodities futures contracts bid downward in speculative trading. This becomes evident in the monetary authorities' effective inability to catch up with the primary determinants of the domestic currency rate. As the markets determine exchange rate via some type of interest parity rule, short-term fluctuations in commodity prices and resulting changes in the international reserves balances complicate accurate forward looking exchange rate setting.

Other manifestations come in disproportionate income distributions, for example, by way of state subsidies to the exporting sector at the expense of domestic consumer market and household disposable income; or concentration of market share within closed circle of few exporter/importer entities. However, these macroeconomic parameters cannot be claimed to be directly influenced by the commodity derivatives volatility without consideration of more structural problems of economic capacity and financial system functioning in any given country. Rather commodity derivatives volatility assumes a contributing factor role, yet again via demand pressures for physical production levels and unstable exchange rate.

For a large majority (if not all) of emerging markets, currency exchange rate variation defines a broad spectrum of economic activities. In most abstract sense, these allude to maintaining average consumer's purchasing power from one period to another. On a more concrete scale, to expand on earlier statement, that includes public and private sector decisions on consumption of imported manufactured goods (final or intermediate), access and use of credit in financing either consumer or investment projects, and ability to sustain interest payments on debt denominated in foreign currency.

For example, in earlier work, Semmler and Gevorkyan (2011) develop a monetary policy model with foreign exchange reserves targets showing how exchange rate variations lead to unsustainable foreign currency-denominated debt accumulation in the relatively insulated net exporting economies. Deferring the details and some definitions to the original work, the result is evident from the following solutions:

$$b = \frac{m - \varepsilon e^{e}}{y(g_y - \gamma)} \tag{5}$$

$$d_{\text{prv}} = \frac{\Lambda - sp}{g_y + su} \tag{6}$$

$$d_{\text{pub}} = \frac{g - t}{g_y - z} \tag{7}$$

$$h = \frac{w - c}{(g_y - \theta)y} \tag{8}$$

$$k = \frac{X^{f}}{V(g_v + \varsigma - \phi)} \tag{9}$$

Eqs. (5)–(6), where y is the national income and g_y is the growth rate of income, represent higher order solutions in the open economy for net foreign assets (sovereign debt) to income ratio, b; private debt to income ratio, d_{prv}; public debt to income ratio, d_{pub}; a share of required investment to income ratio, Λ; a positive constant share, s; profits to income ratio, p; interest rate determined by sum of domestic interest rate and country specific risk premium, u; domestic households demand for foreign currency-denominated assets ratio to national income h; and finally financial institutions' effective leverage as a ratio of loans in foreign currency (or foreign currency on hand, or, which is the same, as foreigners' holdings of domestic financial institutions' bonds) to the present value of the domestic financial institutions' cash flows: k. In all cases, among other factors, domestic interest rate and specific risk premiums have a strong effect on the debt ratios, via γ, u, z, θ, ς, ϕ as defined in the original model. Exchange rate is derived from a more encompassing central bank function with target international reserves and enters in each factor either as net exports, foreign currency-denominated earnings, investment, securities holdings, or expenditure by each sector.

Eventually, the implied volatility and instability in foreign exchange flows, compounded by accumulation of foreign currency-denominated debt of all categories, has a potential of pushing an economy to a crisis-like situation. This scenario is prone with credit contraction, investment scale-down, and subsequent output gaps and unemployment. Hence, emerging markets relying on undiversified pool of primary commodities exports amplify the risk of facing fundamental uncertainty problems sooner or later (for more details on the concept of fundamental uncertainty, see Gevorkyan & Gevorkyan, 2011). At this point, problems in macroeconomy spill into real social costs instantaneously exacerbating unequal income distribution and social exclusion.

The question of "what can be done to avoid such situation?" is quite broad and is not entirely within the scope of the present research. Briefly, though it is evident that due to their undiversified structural economic base, the emerging economies relying on export revenues from primary commodities must cease the moment of the high historical commodities prices. At this point, it would matter not if the futures contracts are driven by direct derivatives trading or secondary, an index, or speculative risk hedging.

From the somewhat selfish position of the exporter, the higher than usual profit margin should be associated with added funding toward economic policy improvements and proactive development of the high-tech manufacturing sectors in tandem with solid financial system. This, however, requires a proactive fiscal and monetary authorities' actions: the first in devising and implementing the operational plan and the second in maintaining the balance in the financial system and shielding domestic currency exchange rate from drastic short-term volatility in the respective commodity derivatives markets.

CONCLUSION

In this chapter, we attempted to link analytically and empirically currency exchange rate dynamics to volatility in the commodity derivatives trading, as that relates to the social costs of development in the emerging markets.

In doing so, we identified four core links in the system: (1) primary commodities shortages and food and energy prices inflation, (2) downward trending of commodity derivative prices and subsequent exporting nations' terms of trade deterioration (Prebisch–Singer hypothesis), (3) drastic short-term volatility in commodity contracts and immediate financial corrections by risk-hedging investors leading to speculative capital flows in and out exporting economy, and finally (4) commodity derivatives dynamics exerting pressures on exporting economy's currency and ultimately macroeconomy.

Further, we identified specific lead emerging markets exporters in relation to world exports for each commodity group and related their currency exchange rate index to the traded commodity futures contracts. Our empirical results seem to indicate a lagged response in the currency index to the commodities futures, which is explainable given exchange rate's forward looking and more complex composition, via international reserves policies and interest rate parity relation.

It is evident that economies heavily attached to certain primary commodities could face extremely negative consequences as commodities prices, determined in the derivatives markets, fluctuate. Open emerging markets economies are prone to financial instability (especially in managed float or fixed exchange rate regime) and fundamental uncertainty given poorly diversified economic structure. Social costs (i.e., problems of social development) build on this foundation and resurface full force in times of crisis, as may be anticipated. Finally, fundamental uncertainty implies systemic crisis possibility that is difficult to time due to speculative capital's quick entry and exit of developing financial markets.

Derivative financial instruments are not new and are not about to cease to exist despite heavy criticism and complex regulation measures. Yet, the relations between different markets must be properly understood as such insightful information helps gauge effective economic policy. We invite additional research within the conceptual framework laid in this study as more complex and realistic modeling assumes the leading role in the postcrisis financial economics.

REFERENCES

Ahmed, S. (2008). *Global food price inflation. Implications for South Asia, policy reactions, and future challenges*. World Bank Policy Research Paper No. 4796.

Akram, F. (2009). Commodity prices, interest rates and the dollar. *Energy Economics*, *31*, 838–851.

Backus, D., Kehoe, P., & Kydland, F. (1994). Dynamics of the trade balance and the terms of trade: The J-curve?. *The American Economic Review*, *84*(1), 84–103.

Bahmani-Oskooee, M. (1985). Devaluation and the J-curve: Some evidence from LDCs. *The Review of Economics and Statistics*, *67*(3), 500–504.

Bahmani-Oskooee, M. (1989). Devaluation and the J-curve: Some evidence from LDCs: Errata. *The Review of Economics and Statistics*, *71*(3), 553–554.

Bank for International Settlements (BIS). (2011). *Detailed tables on semiannual OTC derivatives statistics*. Retrieved from http://www.bis.org/statistics/derdetailed.htm

Basu, P., & Gavin, W. T. (2011). What explains the growth in commodity derivatives? *Federal Reserve Bank of St. Louis Review* (January/February), 37–48.

Bernard, L., Gevorkyan, A. V., Palley, T., & Semmler, W. (2011). *Time scales and economic cycles: The contributions of Kondratieff, Kuznets, Schumpeter, Goodwin, Kaldor and Minsky*. Working Paper No. 2011-11. Schwartz Center for Economic Policy Analysis. Available online at http://www.economicpolicyresearch.org/working-papers.html

Bloomberg. (2011). *Electronic database*. Retrieved from http://www.bloomberg.com

Bollerslev, T. (1987). A conditionally heteroskedastic time series model for speculative prices and rates of return. *The Review of Economics and Statistics*, *69*(3), 542–547.

Chen, Yu-Chin, Rogoff, K., & Rossi, B. (2008). *Can exchange rates forecast commodity prices?* NBER Working Paper No. 13901.

Chinn, M., & Coibion, O. (2010). *The predictive content of commodity futures*. NBER Working Paper No. 15830.

Chinn, M., LeBlanc, M., & Coibion, O. (2005). *The predictive content of energy futures: An update on petroleum, natural gas, heating oil and gasoline*. NBER Working Paper No. 11033.

Clubley, S. (2000). *Trading in oil futures and options*. Cambridge: Woodhead Publishing Ltd.

Eckaus, R. (2008). *The oil price really is a speculative bubble*. Center for Energy and Environmental Policy Research, MIT Energy Initiative. Available online at http://web.mit.edu/ceepr/www/publications/workingpapers/2008-007.pdf

Engle, R. F. (1982). Autoregressive conditional heteroscedasticity with estimates of the variance of U.K. inflation. *Econometrica*, *50*, 987–1008.

Flaschel, P., & Semmler, W. (2003). *Currency crisis, financial crisis, and large output loss*. CEM Bielefeld University Working Paper No. 52. Bielefeld University, Germany.

German, H. (2005). *Commodities and commodity derivatives: Modeling and pricing for agriculturals, metals, and energy*. Chichester: Wiley.

Gevorkyan, A. V. (2011). *Innovative fiscal policy and economic development in transition economies*. Oxford: Routledge.

Gevorkyan, A. V., & Gevorkyan, Ar. (2011). *Fundamental uncertainty, reserves funds, and fiscal policy rules in emerging financial markets*. Unpublished draft, available upon request.

Gilbert, C. (1989). The impact of exchange rates and developing country debt on commodity prices. *The Economic Journal*, *99*(397), 773–784.

Harvey, D., Kellard, N., Madsen, J., & Wohar, M. (2010). The Prebisch-Singer hypothesis: Four centuries of evidence. *The Review of Economics and Statistics*, *92*(2), 367–377.

Hong, H., & Yogo, M. (2011). *What does futures market interest tell us about the macroeconomy and asset prices?* NBER Working Paper No. 16712.

IMF World Economic Outlook. (2011). *September 2011 release*. Washington, DC: IMF.

Jones, D., & Kwiecinski, A. (2010). *Policy responses in emerging economies to international agricultural commodity price surges*. OECD Food, Agriculture and Fisheries. Working Paper No. 34, OECD Publishing, Paris, France.

Kondratieff, N. (1922). *The world economy and its conjunctures during and after the war* (in Russian). Vologda.

Kondratieff, N. (1935). The long waves in economic life. *The Review of Economic Statistics*, *18*(6), 105–115.

Kuznets, S. (1930). *Secular movements in production and prices. Their nature and their bearing upon cyclical fluctuations*. Boston, MA: Houghton Mifflin.

Kuznets, S. (1949). National income and industrial structure. *Econometrica*, *17*, 205–241.

Kuznets, S. (1971). *Economic growth of nations: Total output and production structure*. Cambridge: Belknap Press of Harvard University Press.

Kuznets, S. (1973). Modern economic growth: Findings and reflections. *The American Economic Review*, *63*(3), 247–258.

LiPuma, E., & Lee, B. (2004). *Financial derivatives and the globalization of risk*. New York, NY: Duke University Press.

Loening, J. L., Durevall, D., & Birru, Yohannes, A. (2009). *Inflation dynamics and food prices in an agricultural economy: The case of Ethiopia*. Working Papers in Economics No. 347, University of Gothenburg, Sweden.

Magee, S. (1973). Currency contracts, pass-through, and devaluation. *Brookings Papers on Economic Activity*, *4*(1), 303–325.

Meade, E. (1988). Exchange rates, adjustment, and the J-curve. *Federal Reserve Bulletin*, *74*(10), 633–644.

Mihaljek, D., & Packer, F. (2010). Derivatives and emerging markets. *BIS Quarterly Review* (December), 43–58.

Pilipovic, D. (2007). *Energy risk: Valuing and managing energy derivatives* (2nd ed.). New York, NY: McGraw-Hill.

Prebisch, R. (1950). The economic development of Latin America and its principal problems. *Economic Bulletin for Latin America*, *7*, 1–12.

Rada, C., & Taylor, L. (2006). *Empty sources of growth accounting, and empirical replacements a la Kaldor and Goodwin with some beef*. UNDESA and BSCEPA Working Paper 2004-5. Retrieved from www.newschool.edu/cepa

S&P Capital IQ. (2011). *Global market data*. Retrieved from https://www.capitaliq.com

Schofield, N. C. (2008). *Commodity derivatives: Markets and applications*. Chichester: Wiley.

Semmler, W., & Gevorkyan, A. V. (2011). Sailing out of crisis emerging markets style: Blending fiscal-monetary rules, nominal targets, and debt dynamics in some transition economies. In J. A. Batten & P. G. Szilagyi (Eds.), *The impact of the global financial crisis on emerging financial markets* (pp. 155–195). Bingley, UK: Emerald Group Publishing Limited. doi:10.1108/S1569-3759(2011)0000093007. [Contemporary Studies in Economic and Financial Analysis, Volume 93].

Singer, H. (1950). Comments to the terms of trade and economic development. *Review of Economics and Statistics*, *40*, 84–89.

Spurga, R. (2006). *Commodity fundamentals: How to trade the precious metals, energy, grain, and tropical commodity markets*. Hoboken, NJ: Wiley.

UNCTAD. (2011). *UNCTADstat*. Retrieved from http://www.unctad.org

APPENDIX

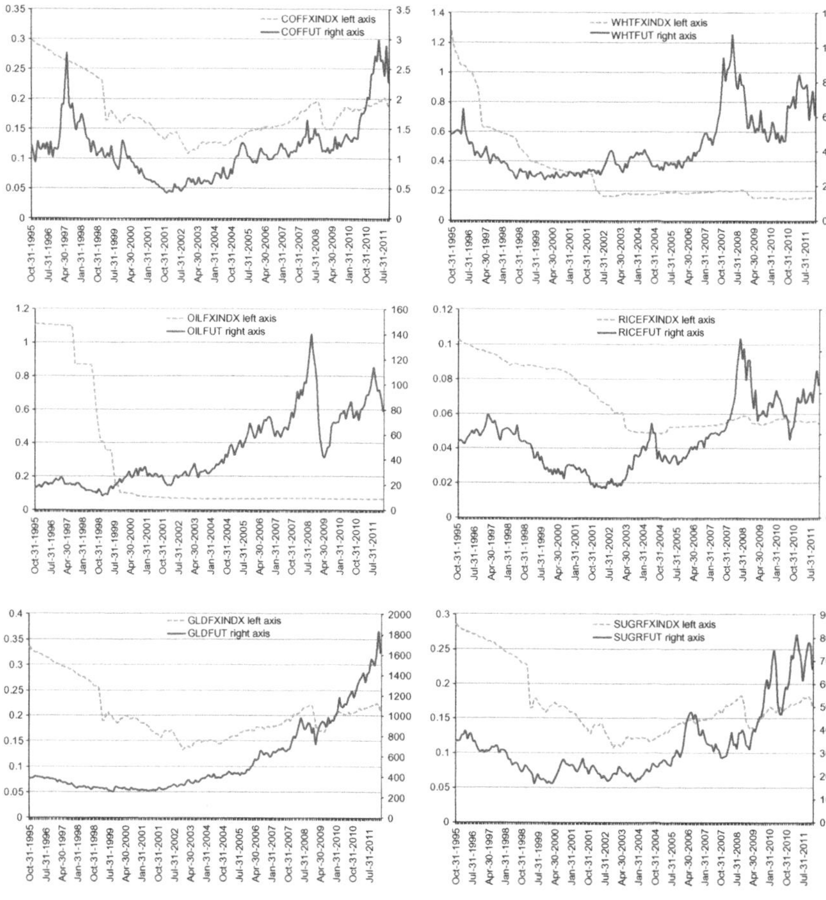

Fig. A1. Commodity Futures and Respective Exchange Rate Index. *Source*: Own calculations based on data from Bloomberg (2011) and S&P Capital IQ (2011).

CONTINGENT CAPITAL SECURITIES: PROBLEMS AND SOLUTIONS

Michalis Ioannides and Frank S. Skinner

ABSTRACT

We describe some recent contingent capital securities (CoCos) and explore the issues that confront their development. We take the view that bank CoCos should be designed to maintain confidence in a bank before a crisis begins because once a crisis commences it is difficult to see how a bank can assure the capital market without the support of state aid. With this overriding objective in mind we find that, in at least some respects, existing examples of bank CoCos have got the 'right' design. Existing bank CoCos are unfunded as they should be as there is no need to structure these securities to provide additional liquidity. If funding turns out to be necessary then a liquidity crisis is already underway and the CoCo has already failed in its attempt to maintain confidence in the bank. Moreover, existing CoCos use the simpler single trigger that we favour rather than dual trigger structure recommended by some.

The financial crisis of 2008 necessitated the bailout of numerous financial institutions worldwide as the financial system's liquidity dried up. These bailouts involved enormous sums, hundreds of billions of dollars, and were

Derivative Securities Pricing and Modelling
Contemporary Studies in Economic and Financial Analysis, Volume 94, 71–92

ISSN: 1569-3759/doi:10.1108/S1569-3759(2012)0000094006

used to support financial institutions that evidently were in rude financial health. Yet these institutions were unable to raise significant new equity from capital market investors other than from sovereign wealth funds and governments. To deal with issues that raised these conditions, European and US banking regulators are coming to terms with the idea of contingent capital securities (hereafter CoCos). Contingent capital is a form of committed financing that is negotiated in advance to ensure that a company's balance sheet and capital resources are not unduly strained should significant and unexpected losses occur. Both the FSA and US treasury have talked about the desirability of these instruments. For example, Ben Bernake, the chairman of the Federal Reserve has stated that '... systemically important institutions could be required to issue contingent capital, such as debt-like securities that convert to common equity in times of macroeconomic stress or when losses erode the institution's capital base ...'.

In general, these instruments should enhance confidence in the viability of the distressed institution and enable them to raise new funds to alleviate liquidity problems. The promise held out by these securities is that should a financial crisis occur, distressed financial institutions will automatically be bailed out by the private sector without the involvement of government funds.

CoCos should be built around three key components: (i) the host instrument, (ii) the trigger upon which the CoCo will convert into equity and (iii) the trigger mechanism. In addition, the design of these securities needs to account for the interests of the investor and the issuer of CoCos. These interests are not always aligned, especially at the critical conversion point. Moreover, the success of the CoCo innovation will be influenced by the views of regulatory authorities and rating agencies. As a result, the design of the CoCo security is a critical issue that is fraught with difficulties.

We will first discuss the current funding practice of banks, looking at the typical capital structure of banks, examining where CoCos will likely fit within this structure and giving examples of recently issued CoCos. We will then take a step back and explore the key design choices of bank CoCos analysing the potential problems that each present. We will then review the insurance CoCo market to look for solutions to these problems. Based on this analysis we make our recommendations.

CURRENT FUNDING PRACTICE AND USE OF COCOS

The main securities issued by banks and insurance companies to date are common equity, senior debt, subordinated debt, preferred stock and hybrid instruments (i.e. convertibles, adjustable-rate preferred securities and trust-preferred stock) (Fig. 1).

Tier 1 capital is meant to be fully loss absorbing while the bank is a going concern, whereas Tier 2 capital is fully loss absorbing only when the bank is declared bankrupt. For example, common equity is Tier 1 because it is fully loss absorbing while the bank is a going concern, whereas senior debt is Tier 2 as it is loss-absorbing only after the bank or insurance company has failed. Other examples of Tier 2 capital include preferred stock and hybrids that are loss-absorbing in the event of insolvency but they can be partially included in Tier 1 if they are designed to provide partial loss-absorbency through the cancellation or deferral of dividends or coupons while the firm is still a going concern.

CoCos could form part of the capital structure and sit between equity, subordinated debt and hybrids depending upon the degree of loss absorption. Initially, CoCos can be issued as a debt security that would pay interest to capital market investors and then automatically convert into

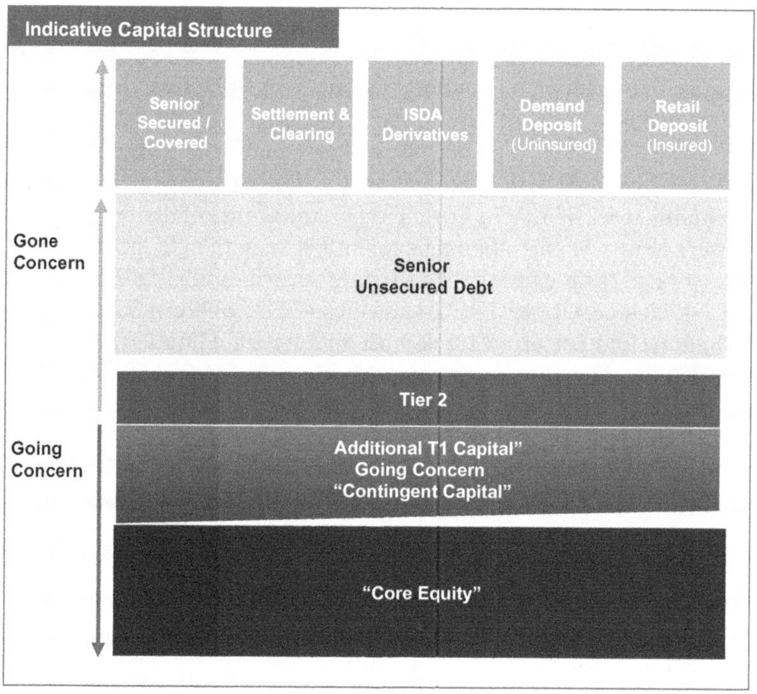

Fig. 1. Current Funding Practice and Use of CoCos. *Source*: BNP Paribas.

Tier 1 equity at times of extreme financial stress. Otherwise, the CoCo could mature at some predefined date (unless the CoCo is a perpetual) and presumably be replaced with another CoCo issue.

Regulatory thinking on the use and structure CoCos are in a state of flux. Current Basel III – that is pre-systemic buffers – leaves little room for contingent instruments as only equity can be used to meet Tier 1 capital requirements. In contrast, the UK Independent Commission on Banking recommends that Bail In bonds (CoCos) could form a percentage of the primary loss absorbing capacity of retail and investment banks. Moreover, on the one hand, the Basel committee is worried about backward looking triggers, which could prevent loss absorption at a time of need. On the other hand, the Swiss banking regulator, FINMA, is not worried that a solvency-based trigger could be backward looking. FINMA asserts its beliefs by proposing to set the triggers to a level high enough that CoCos are closer to core equity. In a recent consultation paper, FINMA has announced that at minimum Swiss banking institutions would be expected to have 19% of their total available capital in core equity out of which 9% could be represented by CoCos.

Prior to financial crisis, the issuance of contingent capital has been non-existent by banks. Below, we tabulate the latest issued CoCos from banking institutions. The Lloyd's Banking Group's (LBG) CoCo has initiated interest in this new form of capital securities, which Lloyd's calls Enhanced Capital Notes (ECNs). The ECNs will originally be subordinated debt (Lower Tier 2 capital) with a fixed maturity. They are convertible by Lloyds into common stock if LBG's core Tier 1 capital ratio falls below 5%. The ECNs were issued as part of an agreement between the UK government and Lloyd's to raise fresh capital. The existing securities eligible for conversion into ECNs include Upper Tier 2 securities (£2.52 billion), Tier 1 securities (£7.68 billion) and preferred stock with an aggregate liquidation preference of £4.09 billion. In return for giving up more senior for more subordinated claims, investors in ECNs will reportedly receive between 1.5% and 2.5% in additional coupon income vis-à-vis the existing securities. Although, the intention is that Lloyd's will be recapitalised with a larger equity cushion to absorb further losses at a time of financial distress, we believe that this trigger is set to low, and it may not provide enough cushion to protect LBG from significant losses.

Nevertheless, this transaction is a landmark deal. While we appreciate it is executed in a specific context and through an exchange, we believe it served as a blueprint transaction for Rabobank's newly issued Senior Contingent Note (SCN) and its 8.375% Tier 1 Perpetual issue and for the Credit Suisse

Table 1. Example Contingent Capital Securities from Banking Institutions.

Issuer	Lloyds	Rabobank	Rabobank	Credit Suisse
Market	Institutional	Institutional	Retail	Retail
Coupon	9.125	6.875	8.375	7.875
Amount	€710.5 million	€1.25 billion	$2 billion	$2 billion
Launch	03/11/09	12/03/10	19/01/11	17/02/11
Maturity	15/07/20	19/03/20	Perpetual	24/02/41
Call date	–	–	26/07/16	24/08/16
Issue rating	Ba2/BB/BB	–	–/–/A	–/–/BBB+
Senior debt rating	A1/A/A	Aaa/AAA/AA+	Aaa/AAA/AA+	Aa2/A/AA–
Type	LT2 (ECN)	Senior (SCN)	Tier 1	LT2 (BCN)
Regulatory call	Yes	No	Yes prior to first call date	Yes
Trigger	Core Tier 1/RWA <5%	Equity capital/RWA <7%	Equity capital/RWA <8%	Core T1 or common equity ratio <7%
Equity conversion/write-down	Conversion	Write-down	Write-down	Conversion
Relevant ratio at YE2010	10.2%	14.2%	14.2%	13%
YTC/YTM	8.9	6.8	6.4	7.4
Spread vs. MS	588	377	466	558

Source: BNP Paribas.

deal. Table 1 describes the main features of each bond. Rabobank's senior note is dated and matures in 2020, whilst the trigger is exercised if the Tier 1 ratio of the bank falls below 7%. Meanwhile, Rabobank's Tier 1 instrument is undated or perpetual and bears a trigger which is set at 8%.

The two charts (Fig. 2) illustrate the pricing of Lloyd's ECN (left-hand side) and Rabobank's Senior Note and Tier 1 Perp (right-hand side). For the purposes of this comparison, the illustrated quotes are in terms of basis points priced off the mid-swap spread, which is the usual convention when dealing and/or issuing instruments in the capital markets. Capital market investors perceive the riskiness in the ECN and reflect their expectations directly in the pricing, as the ECN is trading wider than Lloyds senior (Sen) and Lower Tier 2 (LT2) securities. Initially, investors have made a similar distinction between Rabobank's SCN and Tier 1 Perpetual issue. However, the spread between the two Rabobanks' instruments have collapsed by the end of the first quarter of 2011.

Insurers have been using traditional reinsurance agreements to pass insurance risk to reinsurance companies. Contingent capital is a positive sign that additional resources could be made available to complement traditional reinsurance agreements and the growing catastrophe bond market. For insurance and reinsurance companies, the underlying purpose of issuing contingent capital remains the same as for reinsurance agreements that is access to a pool of capital that lies off balance sheet until required.[1]

Some recent examples of CoCos illustrating the variety of contract structures that exist in the insurance industry include the Farmers Group and the SCOR issues. In July 2007, Zurich Financial Services' US affiliate, Farmers Group, issued $500 million in contingent capital which can be best described as a committed capital line. This structure enables the US insurer to issue 10-year surplus loan notes to a syndicate of major commercial banks any time within the next 5 years of the issue date at a predetermined price. This is structured to compliment Farmers' existing reinsurance programme, the trigger is a Texas windstorm loss of at least $1.5 billion. This structure is a seminal-landmark deal in the insurance space, which much like the LBG's ECNs set up an unexplored part of the capital market for further issues.

More recently, SCOR, the French reinsurance company, has issued contingent capital in the form of warrants to UBS. Each warrant gives UBS the right to subscribe to two new SCOR shares. The SCOR CoCo or committed equity line (CEL) is a €150 million facility which is made available in two tranches of €75 million each. An individual tranche of €75m would be drawn down in order to ensure the availability of financial cover in case of the occurrence of a natural catastrophic event. The drawdown on the

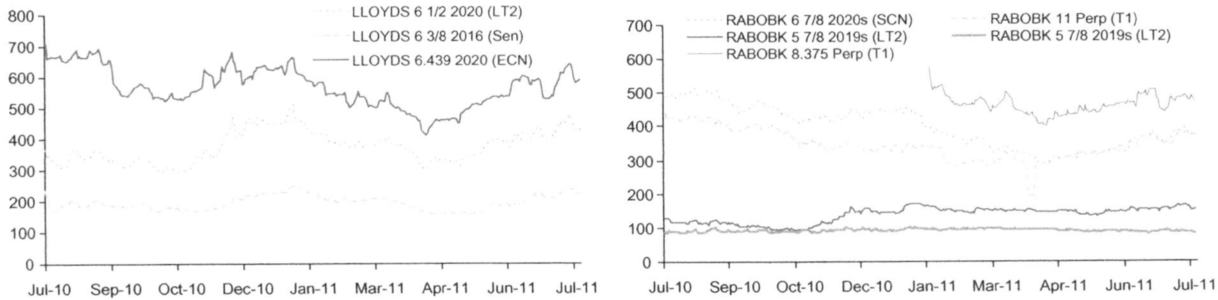

Fig. 2. Pricing of Lloyd's ECN and Rabobank's Senior Note and Tier 1 Perp. *Source*: BNP Paribas.

facility occurs upon the breach of one of two triggers. The first drawdown could occur when the amount of the estimated ultimate net loss incurred by the group in reference to a number of natural catastrophic events reached predefined thresholds. Unlike the Farmers trigger which was only linked to Texas windstorm, SCOR tied this facility to losses occurred by 27 natural catastrophic events including earthquakes, seaquakes, tidal waves, tsunami, floods, hurricanes, landslips, landslides, forest fires and meteor/asteroid impacts. The second drawdown could occur if the daily volume weighted average price of the SCOR shares on the Euronext Paris falls below €10. The second trigger is conditional upon no drawdown having been made under the facility.

DESIGN ISSUES – WHAT ARE THE PROBLEMS TO BE RESOLVED BY BANK COCOS?

CoCos are not meant to resolve a 'liquidity crisis' because once a 'liquidity crisis' begins, depositors, money market lenders and derivative counterparties will shun the target bank so that any amount of liquidity it has on hand or any liquidity it raises subsequently will drain away. A good case in point is covered in Halsworth and Skinner (2008) where they describe how no amount of assurance from the UK government, short of a public takeover, could resolve the liquidity crisis for Northern Rock, a medium-sized UK commercial bank.

Moreover, CoCos will not prevent a 'credit crunch'. Restoring capital levels will not eliminate a flow of credit losses from lending that in the current market conditions turns out to be 'lax'. All banks will be reluctant to extend anything but loans to strong credits in fears of picking up poor credits irrespective of their capital position.

Instead, CoCos are meant to reduce the likelihood of a crisis in confidence by restoring the capital cushion in the event of adverse market conditions. A bank that has successfully recapitalised via a CoCo and so has maintained the confidence of the market should be able to access liquidity from more traditional sources. This means they will at least continue to have the *ability* to loan to good credits and so reduce the severity of a credit crunch. Consequently, the design of a CoCo must anticipate the conditions that can lead to a 'crisis in confidence'.

With this objective in mind we now turn to a discussion of three critical design issues, specifically, conversion triggers, conversion price mechanisms and agency problems.

CONVERSION TRIGGERS

According to the above analysis, the conversion trigger should be pulled before the market anticipates a crisis in confidence. There are two aspects that need to be considered here. The first is how the trigger should be measured, the three choices being accounting, market and regulatory judgment based triggers. The second issue is whether to use a single or a dual trigger.

Accounting, Market or Regulatory Triggers?

Triggers are the events that determine whether a CoCo will be converted into equity capital. Accounting triggers would be based on definitions of bank capital. For example, one such rule might be that conversion is required should Tier 1 capital fall below a threshold of say 5%. A regulatory trigger could take the form of declaration by the monetary authorities that extra capital is required. Finally, a market trigger could be say a trailing average decrease in share price of 50% over the last 20 trading days.

The key practical issue here is the choice between errors caused by pulling the trigger when it is unnecessary (type I error) and errors caused by not pulling the trigger when it is necessary (type II errors).[2] The consequence of a type I error is that banks will become overcapitalised and inefficient in creating value for shareholders. For type II errors the consequence is a crisis in confidence in the bank and the awkward choice for regulators to either let the bank fail or bail the bank out. Although the costs of type I errors are not trivial, given the objectives as set out above, type II errors are more serious. Resolving type II errors must be given priority in CoCo contract design. Based on these criteria alone, one would favour market-based triggers over accounting and regulatory triggers.

Regulatory triggers have the disadvantage that regulators could delay making a decision until it is too late. McDonald (2010) observes that during adverse market conditions the situation will always appear uncertain so the temptation to wait for further developments can be overwhelming. This can cause delays just when more prompt action is needed. Moreover, political interference could be another source of delay. Perhaps even worse are fears that the declaration of a crisis could actually worsen the situation. This would create a conflict for regulators responsible for maintaining confidence in the financial situation.

By that as it may, under the Basel III contingent capital requirement, the home country supervisor of an internationally active bank would have the authority to trigger a write-off or a conversion of non-common Tier 1 and Tier 2 instruments issued by the bank. A trigger event may be declared as deemed necessary to help prevent the issuer from becoming insolvent.

It is innocuous to have such a requirement in banking regulations if the regulatory trigger is not the sole trigger for conversion. In fact, a regulatory trigger could be useful as a 'trigger of last resort' where if, for example, an accounting or market trigger fails to perform as expected the regulator could then intervene. Of course, this is likely to occur once a crisis has actually begun and the CoCo provision has already failed in its' objective of anticipating a crisis.

There is a strong view in the literature (see Duffie, 2009; Flannery, 2009; Martino, Libertucci, Marangoni, & Quagliariello, 2010, amongst others) that accounting-based measures do not work because they are backward looking and lag current market condition. For example, Duffie (2009) reports that CitiBank received a substantial bailout yet it never reported a capital ratio less than 7% throughout the 2008 financial crisis. The temptation by banks to manipulate accounting measures during adverse market conditions can be overwhelming just when accuracy, transparency and consistency are paramount. Moreover, accounting triggers are calculated infrequently and so are often stale. During adverse market conditions, a lead or coincident indicator is needed. The clinching argument, however, is provided by Martino et al. (2010). They conduct a back test over the 1994–2009 time period for the top 15 banks of eight countries (Canada, France, Germany, Italy, Spain, Japan, United Kingdom and United States). They use a variety of double triggers finding that accounting-based triggers have excessive type II errors while market triggers tend to have more type I errors.

In contrast, market-based triggers are forward looking and can objectively forewarn an impending crisis in confidence. They are transparent, not being dependent on private information by banks or regulators and so are not subject to manipulation by banks or delays by regulators. Martino et al. (2010) note that market-based triggers are less prone to type II errors. However, market-based triggers are prone to type I errors. Moreover, stock market manipulation is another concern and later we will discuss this issue in detail. For now, we conclude that market-based triggers have the greatest potential to resolve the critical problem of anticipating and avoiding a crisis in confidence in the banking system. Meanwhile, the Basel III regulatory trigger can be seen as a 'fail safe' option that regulators can rely on if for some unforeseen reason the market trigger fails to perform as expected.

Single or Dual Triggers?

A single trigger is one where a single bank related condition need be met before the CoCo conversion clause is invoked. Therefore, whether the CoCo is converted or not depends upon the financial condition of the bank in question. A dual trigger is one where two sets of conditions needs to be met before the CoCo conversion clause is invoked. McDonald (2010) envisions one where a market-level trigger is pulled when there is a potential systemic banking problem and a bank-level trigger is pulled when there is a potential individual bank problem. For example, the market trigger could be say a decrease of 25% in the bank stock index and the individual trigger could be say a decrease of 50% in the bank's stock price averaged over the last 20 trading days.

The intention of a dual trigger is to separate systemic from idiosyncratic risk. If an individual bank finds itself in trouble so the individual trigger is pulled yet the problem is not systemic so the market-level trigger is not pulled then the CoCo conversion clause is not invoked. The bank is on its' own to resolve its' financial problems and could conceivably fail. If there is a systemic problem so the market-level trigger is pulled but an individual bank is not in trouble then the bank is not forced to raise unneeded capital through conversion of the CoCo. Presumably this will reward a conservative bank for not following the herd in seeking additional risk. Only when both triggers are pulled will the CoCo be converted into equity capital.

The great advantage of this dual trigger is that Tier 2 capital investors such as subordinate debt holders, Tier 1 capital investors such as shareholders and CoCo investors are all motivated to monitor the risk-taking activities of the bank. Tier 2 investors have the incentive to monitor the bank because they can experience credit losses when the bank trigger alone is pulled. Clearly, a bank-level trigger alone is pulled when the distressed bank is not too large to trigger a wider market-level trigger. In this case, the CoCo is not converted, the bank is allowed to fail and losses are absorbed by the subordinate debt holders. Similarly, shareholders have the incentive to monitor the bank mangers as they too will experience losses when the bank trigger alone is pulled. Meanwhile the contingent capital security holders are motivated to monitor the bank as they can experience losses in the case of a dual trigger event.

The critical choice here is whether the CoCo should be designed to prevent a crisis in confidence of the entire banking system or that of a single bank. Flannery (2009) does not distinguish between a systemic crisis and a crisis in confidence of an individual bank because he examines systemically important ‘too big to fail’ TBTF banks where a failure of one of these individual banks sparks a crisis in confidence of the entire banking system. In contrast Martino et al. (2010) does make this distinction as they are concerned with the health of a banking system composed of a variety of banks ranging in size from large TBTF to small local banks. So the choice between single and dual triggers can be dictated by the structure of the domestic banking industry.

It is tempting to suggest a compromise where TBTF banks are subject to a single trigger whereas all other banks are subject to dual triggers. This can be problematic because a bank thought to be a small bank could turn out to be a TBTF bank once a crisis actually starts. Moreover failures of small banks could foreshadow bigger things to come. An excellent example of this is Northern Rock, a UK medium-sized commercial bank. Once Northern Rock was understood to be failing, the UK government was forced to take over the bank partly because Northern Rock turned out to have a disproportionate presence in the systemically important home mortgage market and partly because it became the focal point of widespread fears of a systemic failure in the UK financial system. We do not think anyone could have foreseen these events.

Therefore, the distinction between a TBTF and a non-TBTF bank can be surprisingly difficult to make in practice because it appears that the distinction among them is dependent upon market sentiment as well as market presence. Moreover, the hope that subordinate shareholders will monitor managements’ risk-taking activities in the fear that a bank-level trigger alone is pulled appears dependent on whether they judge the bank to be TBTF. If the bank is TBTF then they will rely on the implicit guarantee that the bank will be bailed out and will not be motivated to monitor, otherwise they will monitor the risk-taking activities of bank management. Subordinate shareholders themselves are in a better position to judge these matters and will behave accordingly irrespective of whether we have a dual or single market-level trigger. Therefore, it appears that a dual trigger will not make much difference in the monitoring behaviour of subordinate shareholders. Also, allowing a non-TBTF bank to fail can turn a minor market problem into a systemic one. Since a dual trigger does not appear to accomplish anything that a single trigger cannot, prevention of systemic risks is paramount and simplicity is a virtue, we conclude that the simpler single trigger will be best.

In other words, we are suggesting that Basil III compliant banks will have two triggers, a market-based trigger and a Basil III compliant regulatory trigger. However, this would not be a dual trigger as such because conversion can occur when either of the two triggers is pulled. Our thinking is that the regulatory trigger will be pulled only under circumstances where the market-based trigger should have been pulled but for some reason was not.

CONVERSION PRICE MECHANISMS

The conversion price is a critical design variable because if it is set too high, stockholders can actually benefit ex post by expropriating wealth from the CoCo holders so stockholders can have the incentive to force conversion. If it is set too low, CoCo holders have the incentive to manipulate stock prices in an attempt to force conversion on favourable terms. Meanwhile, the likelihood that the conversion price is set too high or too low will affect burden sharing between shareholders and CoCo holders and the interest rate that CoCo holders will need to compensate them for potential loses that can occur upon conversion. Equitable burden sharing of the expected losses among shareholders and CoCo holders is a desirable goal as regulators believe that holders of risk capital should participate in loses. If shareholders and CoCo holders both share the burden of potential credit losses then they each have the incentive to monitor the risk-taking behaviour of bank management. Effectively, the conversion price mechanism comes down to a choice of a fixed or a variable number of shares upon conversion.

Fixed Number of Shares upon Conversion

A fixed number of shares can influence the amount of dilution and the amount of burden sharing and consequently, the interest rate CoCo holders require. To illustrate, if the share trigger price is say $20, one scheme would convert every $1,000 CoCo into 50 shares implying a nominal par conversion. Then no loss is experienced by the CoCo holders upon conversion so the CoCo interest rate is likely to be modest. However, there is little burden sharing as shareholders bear all losses up to the trigger point of $20. Another scheme could adjust burden sharing by converting each $1,000 CoCo into 40 shares, implying a nominal share price for conversion of $25, once the $20 share price trigger is encountered. Therefore, upon conversion CoCo holders receive a value of $800 in shares of a claim originally worth $1,000. Clearly then the CoCo holders will require a larger interest rate in the later case to compensate them for potential losses upon conversion.

One problem with a fixed conversion price is that if the nominal conversion price turns out to be too high, stockholders have the incentive to force conversion and vice versa the CoCo holders can have the incentive to manipulate stock prices to force conversion on favourable terms. For example, if we chose a $20 nominal conversion price (1,000/50) and if the stock price is currently $21, CoCo holders would be tempted to manipulate the share price to say $19 to force conversion at $20. Once the stock price returns to $21 each CoCo holder receives a profit of $50.

It is controversial whether CoCo holders can actually manipulate share prices in this way but this possibility can be reduced if instead the nominal conversion price is chosen to ensure CoCo holders burden share. For example, if the share price trigger is $20, but the nominal conversion is $25 (1,000/40), it is certainly less likely that CoCo holders will be able to depress share prices from above $25 to less than $20 to recapture the conversion loss and make a profit as the share price rebounds to above the $25 conversion price. Instead, shareholders have the incentive to depress share prices below the trigger point to impose losses through conversion upon the CoCo holders. For example, again imagine the stock price is $21 and the trigger is $20. Now shareholders have the incentive to depress share prices below $20 to force conversion at a much higher conversion price of $25 and impose losses on the CoCo holders. Clearly then the nominal conversion price implied by the fixed number of shares each CoCo bond receives upon conversion is fraught with the risk of stock price manipulation. Moreover to the extent that the value actually received by CoCo holders upon conversion is uncertain we can anticipate that CoCo holders will require a large interest payment as compensation.

Variable Number of Shares upon Conversion

Instead of fixing the number of shares upon conversion, the CoCo can fix the dollar value of equity received upon conversion but the share price and the number of shares given to CoCo holders upon conversion will be determined at the point of conversion. For example, if burden sharing is desirable, then upon conversion say $800 worth of shares is given for each $1,000 par value CoCo security. If the share price is say $20 when the conversion trigger is encountered, then each CoCo bond will receive 40 shares, if the share price is $2 when the conversion trigger is encountered, then each CoCo bond receives 400 shares.

Under this approach, CoCo holders are assured that they will receive a pre-specified value for their claim upon conversion and so will likely reduce the required CoCo interest payment because they will have a clear idea of the losses they can expect upon conversion. Stockholders face serious dilution problems so they are motivated to monitor management. However, the incentive to manipulate stock prices by CoCo holders can be higher than for a fixed number of shares upon conversion. For example, imagine the conversion trigger is $20 when the market price is currently $21 and the CoCo holder is to receive shares valued at $1,000 upon conversion. If the CoCo holder depresses the stock price to 19, then they will receive 52.63 shares but if they are able to depress the share price even further to 18, they will receive 55.55 shares, 5% more than they would receive if the stock price was $19 at conversion.

Moreover, variable share conversion with the conversion price determined at the date of conversion encounters additional problems. As the number of shares that are issued upon conversion are unlimited, one can encounter sever dilution to the point where control of the bank can change hands. Public policy consideration can be paramount here. For example, imagine a foreign entity purchasing CoCos of financially distressed banks at bargain prices. Upon conversion, the foreign entity could then be in control of the bank. Also, variable share conversion can be subject to death spirals. The risk of dilution of the existing shareholders can lead to a depressed share price which in turn increases the risk of dilution leading to a repeat of the cycle. Some observers suggest ways out if this problem such as to cap the number of shares that can be obtained via variable share conversion (Martino et al., 2010) or base the conversion price on a trailing average of the share price say over the last 20 trading days (Duffie, 2009).

Relating the Trigger Price to the Conversion Price

As discussed above, the conversion price based on a fixed or a variable number of shares upon conversion are both problematic. This is the reason why some authors, McDonald (2010) for example, prefer a conversion price based on a fixed number of shares upon conversion while others, Martino et al. (2010) for example, prefer a conversion price based on a variable number of shares upon conversion. An alternative proposed by Henriques and Doctor (2011) that seems to break this deadlock is to have a variable number of shares tied to a variable solvency trigger.

For example, imagine a trigger of say a 50% reduction of the bank's share price based on a trailing average of the last 20 days closing price where the conversion trigger is defined the same way. Unlike previous proposals, this implies that the conversion price is tied to the trigger price. For example, if it turns out that a 50% reduction in the share price over the last 20 days is say \$10 the conversion price is also \$10. If CoCo bond holders are to burden share and receive only \$800 worth of shares upon the conversion of each \$1,000 par value then the CoCo holders will receive 80 shares. Similarly, if the trigger actually turns out to be \$5, the CoCo holders will receive 160 shares.

The above has the advantage of predefining the amount of exposure CoCo holders face upon conversion and so reduces uncertainty when compared to the fixed number of shares upon conversion. This should reduce the required CoCo interest rate, an important consideration for stockholders seeking a reasonable cost of CoCo funding. The above also provides a formula for determining the conversion price at the date of conversion and so provides a formula for shareholders to work out the expected amount of dilution upon conversion. This should reduce the uncertainty concerning the amount of dilution shareholders can expect and so reduce the likelihood of death spirals. While there can be incentives for stockholders and CoCo holders to manipulate market prices to force conversion on favourable terms, at least using a trailing average definition for the share price trigger and the conversion price can mitigate this possibility. Moreover, there is no reason why the number of shares received upon conversion can be subject to a cap to avoid takeover dilution and to further reduce the possibility of death spirals. Pricing is not an issue as modern derivative pricing techniques are robust enough to obtain accurate prices for the CoCo given the choice of burden sharing. Effectively, valuing a CoCo with a market conversion price (variable number of shares) tied to a solvency trigger based on a trailing average of the bank's share price is equivalent to valuing a path dependent out of the money American put option.

Overall, we favour the Henriques and Doctor's (2011) proposal to tie the solvency trigger to a variable number of shares upon CoCo conversion, as this proposal promises to obtain a workable contract that controls burden sharing and CoCo interest costs. It does so because a solvency trigger tied to the conversion price reduces the uncertainty of the CoCo holders concerning the value they will receive upon conversion and the uncertainty of shareholders concerning the amount of dilution they face upon conversion. While the trigger tied to the conversion price proposal does not completely resolve issues of a potential change in control, death spirals and market manipulations, neither do the alternative fixed or variable number of shares upon conversion. Meanwhile, ad hoc adjustments to alleviate these problems, placing a cap on the number of shares that can be issued upon conversion to avoid takeover dilution for example, or basing the trigger upon an average of past share prices to reduce the likelihood of stock price manipulations as another example, can be incorporated into the Henriques and Doctor's (2011) proposal.

AGENCY ISSUES

There appears to be two main agency issues related to CoCos, those related to implementation effects and moral hazard. While some agency problems like debt overhang are one-off implementation issues, the moral hazard problem is likely to be an ongoing problem requiring careful consideration in the design of the CoCo contract.

Implementation Effects

It is possible that banks will be reluctant to issue CoCos for the first time because CoCos could well cause a one-off decrease in the value of shares. The clearest way to see this is to consider a bank that is TBTF. Share prices in part reflect the high likelihood that, should the bank run into difficulty, the government will bail them out. Similarly, the firm's debt will reflect their near default risk free status. Once a TBTF firm issues CoCos the value of the shares will fall as they now pay for something they got for free before. The prices of the firm's existing debt will not likely change since debt holders do not pay for the near default free status of the bank in either case.

For a non-TBTF bank, introducing a CoCo in the bank's capital structure could well create a classic debt overhang problem where there is a one-off transfer of wealth from shareholders to existing debt holders. For a non-TBTF bank, there is a possibility that the bank might fail so adding CoCo reduces this likelihood. Presumably, the value of the bank will not change because any value created by reducing the default risk of the bank will be captured in the cost of funding the CoCo. The introduction of CoCos will raise the value of existing debt as now the likelihood of default is lower. Since in the absence of tax effects and other market frictions, the value of the bank will remain the same then the increase in the value of debt results in a one-off decrease in the value of the shares.

It is difficult to see how one can overcome these implementation issues by adjusting the CoCo contract. The only obvious solution is for the regulatory authorities to find ways of encouraging banks to issue CoCos. Indeed this seems to be evolving for nations that intend to adhere to the new Basel III accord are expected to include a 'non-viability' requirement in their national banking regulations for internationally active banks by 1 January 2013. While different nations are likely to have variations in how they implement the non-viability requirement, it is expected that all will require Tier 1 capital other than common stock and Tier 2 capital include a provision for write-off or conversion into common stock.

Moral Hazard

Once a CoCo is included in the bank's capital structure, the risk-taking activities of a bank can change. Specifically once a CoCo is in place, the bank has a guaranteed bailout package. The temptation is for the bank to make more risky loans charging commiserate higher interest rates in the hope of increasing profits. If a large number of these riskier loans fail, the bank can recapitalise via CoCo conversion. In other words, rather than reduce the likelihood of financial distress, CoCos can actually increase the likelihood of financial distress by perversely creating incentives that encourage precisely the behaviour that leads to financial difficulty. This is a classic problem faced by the insurance industry, so we now turn to insurance CoCos to determine if any solutions can be found there.

INSURANCE COCOS

By its' nature, the insurance business face the possibility of catastrophic claims that can impair the capital of insurance companies. Consequently, the insurance industry is at the forefront of developing and issuing CoCos. However, it is important to recognise one key difference among the risks faced by insurance as opposed to banking. Most of the risks involved in insurance are uncorrelated whereas most risks involved in banking are correlated. For example, the likelihood of a Texas windstorm causing a loss of at least $1.5 billion as in the case of the Farmers CoCo discussed earlier is unrelated to the possibility of an earthquake in California, but the possibility of a slowdown in the housing market in Texas can possibly be correlated with a slowdown in the housing market in California. Therefore, what works for the insurance industry may not work for the banking industry. Still, a careful review of some of the features of CoCos issued by the insurance industry can shed light on features that can be usefully employed by bank CoCos.

Funded versus Unfunded CoCos

So far we have considered only funded CoCos in the sense that the buyer of the CoCo provides funds to the bank at the date of issue. If the CoCo is triggered, the CoCo converts to equity and no new funds are provided to the bank. In contrast, many insurance CoCos such as the Farmers CoCo and the SCOR CoCo discussed earlier are unfunded in the sense that the buyer is only committed to provide equity funds if and when the CoCo is triggered. If counterparty risk is a problem, then the buyer of the CoCo could be required to collateralise their contingent obligation so that a special purpose vehicle that holds the collateral could purchase equity when the CoCo is triggered.

The advantage of an unfunded CoCo is that liquidity is provided along with an equity infusion. However, we must bear in mind that the banking CoCo is not meant to resolve liquidity problems. As we have argued above, if liquidity is needed then the CoCo has already failed in its key objective to maintain confidence in the bank in the face of adverse market conditions well before any problems of confidence or liquidity emerges. Therefore, it is difficult to see what an unfunded CoCo will do for the banking industry that a funded CoCo already does. As simplicity is a virtue we continue to consider only funded CoCos for banks.

Moral Hazard Solutions

Moral hazard is a classic risk faced by insurance companies for once insurance is granted, the insured party has a lower incentive to behave in a prudent way with regard to insured risks. Traditionally insurance companies have mitigated moral hazard by requiring deductibles and by screening (Culp, 2009). Deductibles encourage the insured to remain prudent as they will bear some part of the losses incurred should the insured event occur. This feature is easily incorporated into a bank CoCo through share price dilution in the event of conversion.

Screening is in part achieved by insurance companies by offering customers a variety of contract terms that encourages the insured party to reveal their risk class. Insurance premiums would then be assessed according to the revealed risk class. For example, the insured can chose the amount of insurance and the amount of the deductible. We anticipate that the CoCo underwriting process will mimic the insurance industry in this regard by offering different levels of burden sharing and shareholder dilution.

Therefore, it is important to develop a pricing model that is sensitive to a variety of target conversion levels. A Merton default risk type structural model that values the whole firm recognising the possibility of 'default' is a likely candidate here where one can substitute the definition of default with the CoCo conversion terms.

Exposure Control

Insurance companies control their exposure to risks by agreeing to short term, typically one year, insurance terms. This allows the insurance company to re-price the insurance contract to incorporate new information that has occurred in the previous year. This is done because with time new information concerning the behaviour or circumstances of the insured can reveal that the original insurance contract is wrong. For example, what appears to be an unlikely event can with time be revealed to be more likely or costly than anticipated. Additionally, annual re-pricing encourages insured parties to remain prudent to qualify for a lower insurance premium upon renewal.

Essentially this form of exposure control is more about an adjustable premium rather than a control of the time frame of the exposure. In fact, we see this kind of adjustable fee in the insurance CoCo market for some kinds of unfunded CoCos backed up by a collateralised trust fund. Here the CoCo coupon is adjusted periodically through an auction remarketing process. Investors bid on the coupon they are willing to receive for investing in the adjustable coupon CoCo bearing in mind the latest information concerning the exposure of the CoCo trust to conversion. In the event of a failure of the auction the coupon is set at a default maximum level.

We can incorporate an adjustable coupon payment to bank CoCos by making the coupon payment dependent upon market conditions, say the CDS spread of the bank. This feature will create an incentive for bank management to lend prudently as the cost of the CoCo will directly vary with the risk-seeking behaviour of the bank.

SUMMARY AND CONCLUSIONS

We have described some recent CoCo securities and have explored the issues that confront the developing concept of CoCos. We take the view that bank

CoCos should be designed to maintain confidence in a bank before a crisis begins because once a crisis commences it is difficult to see how a bank can assure the capital market without the support of state aid. With this overriding objective in mind we find that, in at least some respects, existing examples of bank CoCos have got the 'right' design. Existing bank CoCos are unfunded as they should be as there is no need to structure these securities to provide additional liquidity. If funding turns out to be necessary then a liquidity crisis is already underway and the CoCo has already failed in its attempt to maintain confidence in the bank. Moreover, existing CoCos use the simpler single trigger that we favour rather than dual trigger structure recommended by some.

However, in all other respects we find that existing practice is not ideal. Lloyds, Rabobank and Credit Suisse have all issued CoCos with a backward looking accounting-based trigger whereas we recommend a forward looking market-based trigger because a market-based trigger is more likely to detect an evolving crisis. Moreover, we suggest that the market-based trigger be based on a trailing average of the bank's stock price to reduce the likelihood of stock market manipulation by shareholders and by CoCo holders alike. We also favour a conversion mechanism that relates the trigger price to the conversion price as this mechanism will reduce the uncertainty for CoCo holders and shareholders alike as well as providing a method to control burden sharing. Specifically, CoCo holders have a clear idea of the amount of their exposure and so will be able to specify a CoCo interest rate that compensates them for their exposure. Meanwhile shareholders have a formula that will enable them to calculate the degree of dilution they can expect upon conversion. Other problems can be alleviated by adjusting this conversion mechanism slightly. Specifically, a cap on the number of shares that can be issued upon conversion can reduce the likelihood of a death spiral and an undesirable change of ownership upon conversion. Finally, we recommend that the CoCo coupon rate be made adjustable in some way so that the coupon rate can reflect the changing market conditions. This will incentivise the bank to control its risk-seeking activities as continued prudent exposure management will be rewarded by moderate CoCo interest costs.

NOTES

1. This is one of the ways insurance CoCos can be structured and has the advantage of providing new funds once the CoCo trigger is pulled. In contrast, once the trigger is pulled the typical bank CoCo converts Tier 2 debt securities into Tier 1

equity thereby enhancing loss absorption capacity but not providing new funds. The next two paragraphs describe two example of how insurance CoCos can provide additional funding.

2. Any trigger can fail in two ways, it can be pulled when it should not be and it fails to be pulled when it should be pulled. A type I error is a 'false positive' which in this case is when a CoCo is converted when it should not be converted. A type II error is a 'false negative', which in this case, is when a CoCo should be converted but was not.

REFERENCES

Culp, C. L. (2009). Contingent capital vs. contingent reverse convertibles for banks and insurance companies. *Journal of Applied Corporate Finance*, *21*, 17–21.

Duffie, D. (2009, November 9). *Contractual methods for out-of-court restructuring of systemically important financial institutions*. Submission requested by the U.S. Treasury working group on bank capital. Graduate School of Business, Stanford University.

Flannery, M. J. (2009, October 6). *Stabilizing large financial institutions with contingent capital certificates*. University of Florida. Retrieved from SSRN, http://dx.doi.org/10.2139/ssrn.1485689

Halsworth, A., & Skinner, F. S. (2008). Visibly in trouble: Northern Rock, a post-mortem on a financial crisis. *Area*, *40*(2), 278–283.

Henriques, R., & Doctor, S. (2011, February 15). *Making CoCos work: Structural and pricing considerations for contingent capital securities*. European Credit Research, J.P. Morgan, London.

Independent Commission on Banking. (2011, September). *Final Report: Recommendations*. Victoria House, Southampton Row, London.

Martino, G., Libertucci, M., Marangoni, M., & Quagliariello, M. (2010, September). *Countercyclical contingent capital (CCC): Possible use and ideal design*. Rome: Bank of Italy.

McDonald, R. L. (2010, February 15). *Contingent capital with a dual price trigger*. Kellogg School, Northwestern University. Retrieved from SSRN, http://dx.doi.org/10.2139/ssrn.1553430

HIGH DIMENSIONALITY IN FINANCE: A GRAPH-THEORY ANALYSIS☆

Delphine Lautier[1] and Franck Raynaud

ABSTRACT

In this chapter, we propose a nonconventional methodology, the graph theory, which is especially relevant for the study of high-dimensional financial data. We illustrate the advantages of this method in the context of systemic risk in derivative markets, a main subject nowadays in finance. A key issue is that this methodology can be used in various areas. Numerous applications have now to face the challenge of analyzing gigantic financial data sets, which are more and more frequent. We offer a pedagogical introduction to the use of the graph theory in finance and to some tools provided by this method. As we focus on systemic risk, we first examine correlation-based graphs in order to investigate markets integration and inter/cross-market linkages. We then restrain the analysis to a subset of these graphs, the so-called "minimum spanning trees." We study their topological and dynamic properties and discuss the relevance of these tools as well as the robustness of the empirical results relying on them.

☆This chapter is an adapted version of Lautier and Raynaud (2012).

Derivative Securities Pricing and Modelling
Contemporary Studies in Economic and Financial Analysis, Volume 94, 93–119

ISSN: 1569-3759/doi:10.1108/S1569-3759(2012)0000094007

INTRODUCTION

In this chapter, we propose a method, which is especially well suited to high-dimensional problems in finance: the graph theory. With such a method, any application requiring the exhaustive investigation of a large number of data, in a dynamic setting, can be fruitfully tackled: this is the case, for example, when one tries to analyze high-frequency trading strategies, or when one is in the quest for the optimal diversification of a portfolio in a high-dimensional universe. Other applications, naturally, can be found.

To illustrate the advantages of the graph theory, and to offer a pedagogical introduction to the tools provided by this method,[2] we apply it to the analysis of systemic risk in derivative markets, a main subject nowadays in finance. Meanwhile, we discuss the relevance of these tools as well as the robustness of the empirical results relying on them.

As a means to fully understand systemic risk in derivative markets, there is a need to comprehend the phenomenon through a three-dimensional (3-D) approach: observation time, space, and the maturity of the futures contracts. Only such an approach gives the possibility to investigate prices shocks appearing and propagating in the physical as well as in the paper markets. Taking into account three dimensions, however, requires the analysis of a huge volume of data. This is why, considering our data as a complex evolving system, we rely on recent methods originated from statistical physics.[3] Many theoretical and numerical advances have been made recently in order to investigate the behavior of dynamic complex systems (Holland, 2006; Strogatz, 2001). Among these works, complex networks and the graph theory have been used to study the interconnections between a wide variety of entities, such as social networks or electricity networks. For example, Albert, Jeong, and Barabasi (2000) examine the tolerance of complex systems to errors and attacks. More recently, Buldyrev, Parshani, Paul, Stanley, and Havlin (2010) studied catastrophic cascade of failures in interdependent networks. Since the pioneer work of Mantegna (1999), physicists also started to apply the graph theory to financial markets.

In this literature, we choose several measures, which are relevant for studying systemic risk. First of all, we build a graph representing all the existing connections in our systems, namely, a full connected graph. As we are focusing on systemic risk, this graph is based on the correlation matrix of price returns. We then restrain the analysis to a subset of this graph and examine what is called a "minimum spanning tree" (MST).

This chapter is organized as follows. The second section is devoted to the empirical framework of the study. In the third section, we explain how to construct financial networks on the basis of cross correlations, discuss the dynamical properties of the correlations investigated, and show what kind of information can be extracted from the full connected graph. We then expose in the fourth section the method of the MST, which is used to filter the information embedded in the graph. We describe the topological and dynamical properties of these trees, as well as their stability, when applied to the analysis of systemic risk in derivative markets.

THE EMPIRICAL FRAMEWORK OF THE STUDY

As stated in the first section, we apply the graph theory to the analysis of systemic risk in organized derivative markets. In such a context, we think about systemic risk as the possibility that a prices shock occurring on a specific asset's physical market can spread, not only through its own futures markets, but also onto other physical and/or paper markets, and vice versa. More precisely, we focus on integration, as it is a favorable condition in order for systemic risk to appear.

Concerns about such risk have recently grown in financial markets, notably in commodity derivative markets. The latter are supposed to be more and more integrated, both as regards each other and as regards other markets. For some months, fluctuations in the prices of energy commodities have often been invoked to explain those of soft commodities like soy, corn, or wheat. Moreover, since commodities are nowadays considered as a new class of assets, they are used by portfolio managers for diversification purposes. Part of the price fluctuations recorded in commodity markets might therefore be explained by external events, like the fall in stock prices or interest rates.

Financial literature has looked into such questions in various ways: herding behavior, cointegration techniques, spatial integration, etc.[4] These studies only take into account two dimensions of integration: space and observation time, or maturity and observation time. While these studies confirm that it is highly likely that integration is progressing, none of them tried to study spatial, temporal, and maturity evolutions simultaneously. Such an analysis is, however, crucial as it gives a complete understanding of systemic risk.

Our study fills this gap. We selected 14 futures markets corresponding to three sectors, namely, energy, agriculture, and financial assets.[5] We collected settlement prices for all available maturities (up to 120 months in the case of the Eurodollar contract) on a daily basis, over a 10-year period (from 2000 to 2009). This left us with more than 650,000 futures prices. Table 1 summarizes the main characteristics of our database.

Table 1. Main Characteristics of the Collected Data: Nature of the Assets, Trading Location, Time Period, Longest Maturity (in Months).

Underlying Asset	Exchange Zone	Period	Maturities	Records
Light crude oil	CME-US	1998–2009	Up to 84	2,965
Brent crude	ICE-EU	2000–2009	Up to 18	2,523
Heating oil	CME-US	1998–2009	Up to 18	2,835
Gas oil	ICE-EU	2000–2009	Up to 12	2,546
Natural gas (United States)	CME-US	1998–2009	Up to 36	3,140
Natural gas (Europe)	ICE-EU	1997–2009	Up to 9	3,055
Wheat	CME-US	1998–2009	Up to 15	3,026
Soy bean	CME-US	1998–2009	Up to 14	2,977
Soy oil	CME-US	1998–2009	Up to 15	3,056
Corn	CME-US	1998–2009	Up to 25	2,569
Eurodollar	CME-US	1997–2009	Up to 120	3,056
Gold	CME-US	1998–2009	Up to 60	2,877
Exchange rate €/$	CME-US	1999–2009	Up to 12	2,864
Mini SP500	CME-US	1997–2009	Up to 6	3,011

CME stands for Chicago Mercantile Exchange, ICE for Intercontinental Exchange, NYSE LIFFE for New York Stock Exchange – London International Financial and Futures Exchange.

When one has to face such a huge amount of data, the major obstacle is to provide oneself with a tool that allows to consider the system as a whole and to extract the financial information from numerous time series. In this context, the graph theory is a powerful framework.

BUILDING A GRAPH

In this section, we explain how to build a graph on the basis of financial data. For the moment, we consider a graph where all possible connections are taken into account. We define its nodes and explain how to describe, through the links, the relationships between these nodes. We then analyze the behavior of our data in a "traditional" way. Finally, we use the graph in order to give evidence of the connectivity of the different nodes.

The Nodes of the Graph

A graph, or network, gives a representation of pairwise relationships within a collection of discrete entities. It can be defined as a triple, consisting of a node (or vertex), a link (or edge), and the relation associating vertices and edges (West, 2001). The links of the graph describe the relationships between the nodes. More precisely, the graph can be weighted in order to take into account the intensities of the connections.

In this chapter, as we apply the graph theory to the analysis of systemic risk, the economic entity under scrutiny is a derivative market and/or a futures contract. Thus, each node of the graph corresponds to the time series of prices returns of a futures contract,[6] defined as the daily logarithm price differential r_i:

$$r_i = \frac{\ln F_i(t) - \ln F_i(t - \Delta t)}{\Delta t} \tag{1}$$

where $F_i(t)$ is the price of the futures contract at t and Δt is the time lag between two consecutive prices.

A Correlation-Based Analysis

In this study, we focus on market integration and comovement. The easiest way to study simultaneously the behavior of several time series is to compute the synchronous correlations of price returns, defined as follows:

$$\rho_{ij}(t) = \frac{\langle r_i r_j \rangle - \langle r_i \rangle \langle r_j \rangle}{\sqrt{\left(\langle r_i^2 \rangle - \langle r_i \rangle^2\right)\left(\langle r_j^2 \rangle - \langle r_j \rangle^2\right)}} \tag{2}$$

where $\langle \cdot \rangle$ denotes the statistical average performed over a time window of 500 trading days. With daily prices, such a window ensures a good compromise between the financial timescale and the question of statistical robustness. In Eq. (2), i and j correspond to two different time series of futures returns.

For a given time window and set of data, we thus computed the matrix of $(N \times N)$ correlation coefficients C, for all the pairs ij. C is symmetric with $\rho_{ij} = 1$ when $i = j$. Thus, it is characterized by $N((N-1)/2)$ coefficients.

The Evolution of the Correlation Coefficients and Their Variances

Before relying on a graph, it is interesting to examine the time evolution of our system through a "traditional" analysis on the basis of the correlation coefficients. In what follows, we present the mean correlations of the returns and their variances (Sieczka & Holyst, 2009).

The mean correlation $C^T(t)$ computed on the basis of the coefficients ρ_{ij}^T over the time window $[t - \Delta T, t]$ can be defined as follows:

$$C^T(t) = \frac{2}{N(N-1)} \sum_{i<j} \rho_{ij}^T(t) \tag{3}$$

The variance $\sigma_C^2(t)$ of the mean correlation is given by

$$\sigma_C^2(t) = \frac{2}{N(N-1)} \sum_{i<j} (\rho_{ij}^T(t) - C^T(t))^2 \tag{4}$$

with $\Delta T = 500$ trading days, where i and j stand for two different time series.

Fig. 1 represents the mean correlation of the futures prices returns, and its variance, in the spatial dimension (in such a case, we retain the nearby futures prices of each derivative market). It shows that the mean correlation increases over time, with a huge rise from 2007 to the end of 2008. The variance is characterized by a peak in 2007–2009, and reaches its maximum in the end of September 2008, just after the Lehman Brothers' bankruptcy.

Let us now examine the maturity dimension, that is to say, the prices correlation in a futures market. In Fig. 2, we exhibit, as an example, the statistical properties of the correlation coefficients of two futures contracts: the Eurodollar and the Brent crude oil. The latter behaves quite differently:

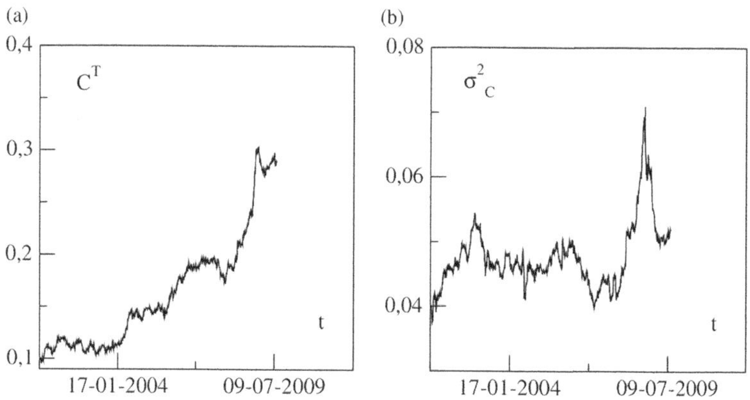

Fig. 1. Correlation Coefficients of the Price Returns in the Spatial Dimension, for All Markets 2001–2009. (a) Mean and (b) Variance.

Table 2. Characteristics of the Correlation Coefficients of the Price Returns in the Maturity Dimension.

Underlying Asset	Mean	Min	Max	Variance	$\rho_{mean-variance}$
Light crude	0.941	0.863	0.979	0.94×10^{-3}	–0.98
Brent crude	0.952	0.859	0.99	0.17×10^{-2}	–0.966
Heating oil	0.949	0.875	0.992	0.23×10^{-2}	–0.953
Gas oil	0.956	0.891	0.991	0.65×10^{-3}	–0.943
Natural gas (United States)	0.629	0.393	0.855	0.0255	–0.964
Natural gas (Europe)	0.289	-0.169×10^{-3}	0.769	0.097	–0.916
Wheat	0.926	0.814	0.993	0.21×10^{-2}	–0.943
Soy bean	0.913	0.769	0.974	0.37×10^{-2}	–0.794
Soy oil	0.948	0.826	0.997	0.23×10^{-2}	0.963
Corn	0.85	0.709	0.902	0.34×10^{-2}	–0.96
Eurodollar	0.803	0.705	0.878	0.69×10^{-2}	–0.826
Gold	0.984	0.939	0.996	0.13×10^{-3}	–0.883

Mean correlation, min and max, variance and correlation between mean and variance.

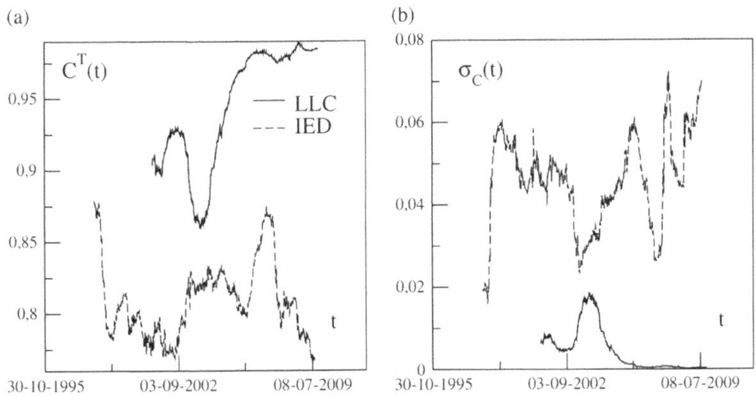

Fig. 2. Correlation Coefficients of the Price Returns in the Maturity Dimension for the Eurodollar (Dashed Line) and the Brent Crude (Back Lines) 1998–2009. (a) Mean and (b) Variance.

although the maturities of the Brent are more and more integrated over time (at the end of the period, the mean correlation is close to 1), the same is not true for the Eurodollar.

Table 2 summarizes the statistical properties of the mean correlations and variances for the 14 markets, in the maturity dimension. It confirms that, for almost every contract, the mean correlation is very high and anticorrelated with the mean variance. The two natural gases, however, exhibit more specific figures. Their correlation level is quite low compared with other markets, especially for the London Natural Gas. Meanwhile, the linear relationship holds for these markets and confirms the robustness of this result.

Merging space and maturity, we also observe an important rise in the mean correlations and variances, as shown by Fig. 3(a) and (b). Moreover, these values are positively correlated, with a maximal correlation and variance, respectively, at the end of 2008 (followed by a decrease in the mean correlation). So our prices system becomes more and more integrated; meanwhile, it is less stable.

Up to now, we have worked with cross-correlations between derivatives prices. Besides the new universal behavior of the cross-maturity correlations, we are still in the field of traditional financial analysis. Let us turn our attention to an alternative tool to deal with high-dimensional financial data and its use to study systemic risk in derivative markets. To attain such an objective, there is a need to construct the links of the graph.

The Links of the Graph: From Correlations to Distances

There are several ways to enrich the information contained in a graph through its links. In finance, for example, the connections between the nodes

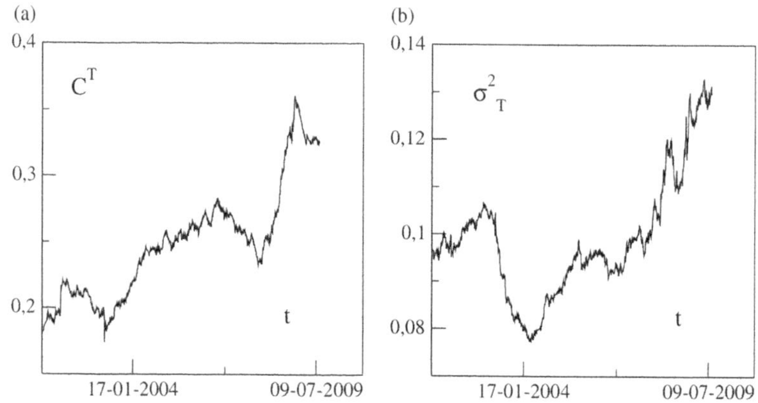

Fig. 3. Correlation Coefficients of the Price Returns in 3-D 2001–2009. (a) Mean and (b) Variance.

can be associated to the correlations of price returns, or to the positions of the operators. In what follows, as explained previously, we retain the synchronous correlations of price returns.

The trouble is, by definition, the correlation coefficients ρ_{ij} range between –1 (for perfectly anticorrelated pair of assets) and 1 (for fully correlated pair of assets). To use the graph theory and to study the spatial organization of the markets within the networks, we need to introduce an appropriate quantity that weights the edges. In our case, this quantity is the distance between the nodes: the more closer (respectively distant) the nodes, the more correlated (respectively anticorrelated) the assets. The correlation coefficients cannot be directly used to represent such distances, first because they can be negative, and second because they do not fulfill the three axioms that define a distance d_{ij} (or a metric) between the nodes i and j. These axioms, defined by Gower (1966), are the following: (1) $d_{ij}=0$, if and only if $i=j$; (2) $d_{ij}=d_{ji}$; and (3) $d_{ij}<d_{ik}= +d_{kj}$.

To explain how we transform the correlations into distances, let us rely on a geometric interpretation. In this context, we can represent the correlation coefficients by two unitary vectors $\vec{u}$ and $\vec{v}$. The level of correlation between the two assets can be seen as the similarity between the two vectors, that is to say, the modulus of the vector $\vec{w}=\vec{u}-\vec{v}$, linking the extremities of $\vec{u}$ and $\vec{v}$. Fig. 4(a) illustrates the cases of correlated and anticorrelated vectors. In the first case, the distance between the two extremities is very low, whereas in the second case it is much higher.

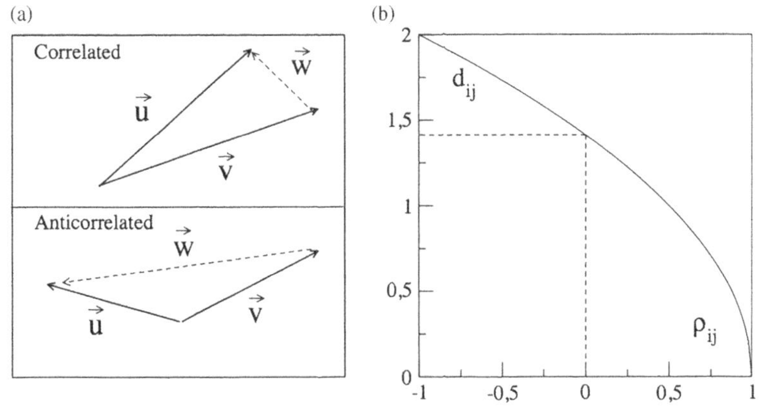

Fig. 4. (a) Geometric Representation of the Metric and (b) Value of the Distance as Function of the Correlation Coefficient.

Lastly, we choose unitary vectors because in our case their directions are more relevant than their lengths. The metric is obtained as follows:

$$\left|\overrightarrow{w^2}\right| = \left(\vec{u} - \vec{v}\right)\left(\vec{u} - \vec{v}\right) = \left|\overrightarrow{u^2}\right| + \left|\overrightarrow{v^2}\right| - 2\,\vec{u}\cdot\vec{v} \tag{5}$$

$$\text{Since } \vec{u} \text{ and } \vec{v} \text{ are unitary vectors :} \quad \left|\overrightarrow{u^2}\right| = \left|\overrightarrow{v^2}\right| = 1 \tag{6}$$

$$\text{we find :} \quad \left|\overrightarrow{w^2}\right| = 2 - 2\,\cos\left(\vec{u}, \vec{v}\right) = 2\left(1 - \cos\left(\vec{u}, \vec{v}\right)\right) \tag{7}$$

Finally, the metric is obtained by identifying the correlation coefficient ρ_{ij} and the cosine in Eq. (7):

$$\sqrt{\left|\overrightarrow{w^2}\right|} = d_{ij} = \sqrt{2 - (1 - \rho_{ij})} \tag{8}$$

A distance matrix D can thus be extracted from the correlation matrix C according to Eq. (8). C and D are both $(N \times N)$ dimensional. Although the coefficients ρ_{ij} can be positive or negative, the distance d_{ij} is always positive and ranges between 0 and 2, as illustrated by Fig. 4(b). Moreover, we can see that the distance is minimal (respectively maximal) when the correlation reaches its highest (respectively lowest) level.

The Full Connected Graph

With the distance matrix, we are now able to construct the full connected graph, which depicts all the possible connections in the prices system. An example of such a graph, in the maturity dimension, is exhibited by Fig. 5. It is the graph of the Light crude oil, extracted from the distance matrix and computed over the whole period.

The information provided by such graphs is, for instance, given by the spatial organization of the nodes, or its center, as in Cohen-Cole, Kirilenko, and Patacchini (2011) and Bech, Chapman, & Garratt (2010). In our case, we are more interested in the dynamical evolution of the connectivity of the nodes. Besides, we are dealing with a high-dimensional network whose

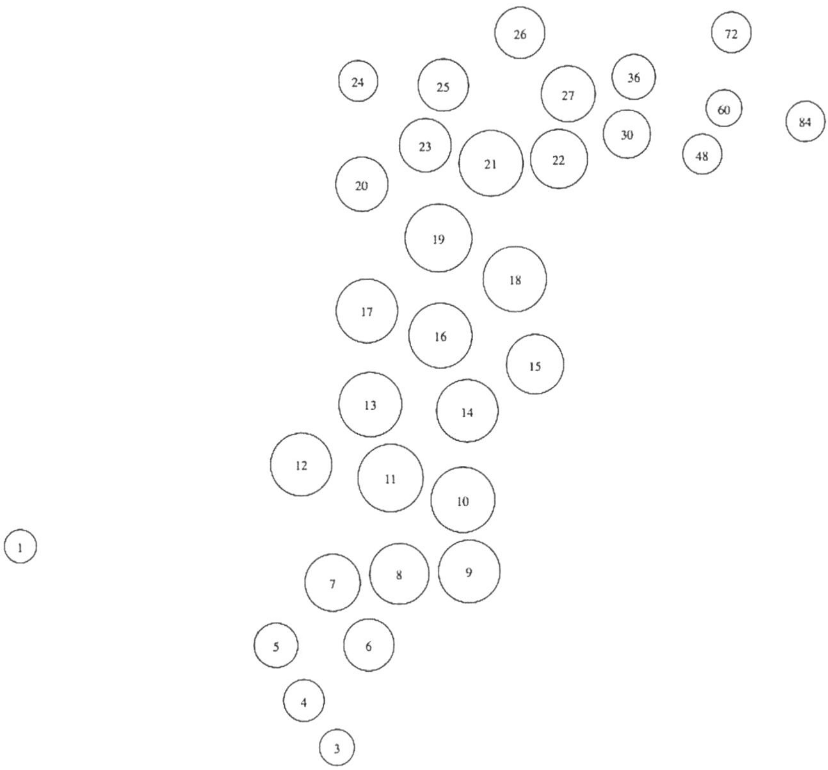

Fig. 5. Static Full Connected Graph of the Light Crude Oil.

spatial organization is difficult to analyze. This is why, in a first step, we rather compute the node's strength. This quantity provides information on how close a given node is from all others. It is defined as follows:

$$S_i = \sum_{i \neq j} \frac{1}{d_{ij}} \tag{9}$$

when S_i is high, the node i is close to the others; otherwise, it stands at the fringe of the network. In a second step, we will filter the information contained in the graph.

This measure provides information on the intensity of the correlations linking a given node to the others. In the case of correlation-based networks, it is more appropriate than the total correlation of a node.

Indeed, the total correlation of two anticorrelated assets would be the same as the one of two uncorrelated assets. These results, however, call for totally different interpretations. Such a difficulty could not appear with the node's strength.

Illustration

In what follows, for the sake of simplicity and robustness, we compute the node's strength in the spatial dimension.[7]

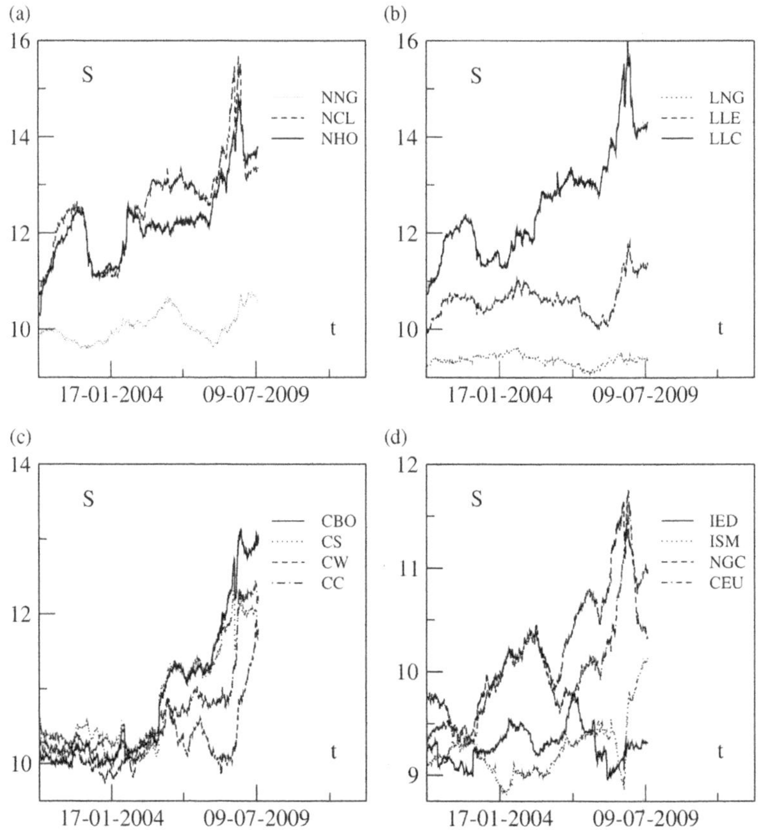

Fig. 6. Nodes Strength of the Markets in the Spatial Dimension. (a) American Energy Products; (b) European Energy Products; (c) Agricultural Products; (d) Financial Assets.

Fig. 6 represents the time evolution of the node's strength in the spatial dimension. The figure has been separated into four panels: the energy sector is at the top, with American products on the left and European ones on the right; the agricultural sector is at the bottom left and financial assets are at the bottom right.

Fig. 6 prompts the following remarks: at the end of the period, out of all the assets studied, the two crude oils and Heating oil show the greatest node's strength. They are followed by soy oil, other agricultural assets, the S&P500 contract, gold, the exchange rate USD/EUR, and the gas oil. The more distant nodes are those representing the Eurodollar and the two natural gases.

As far as the time evolution of this measure is concerned, the sector exhibits different patterns: the integration movement, characterized by an

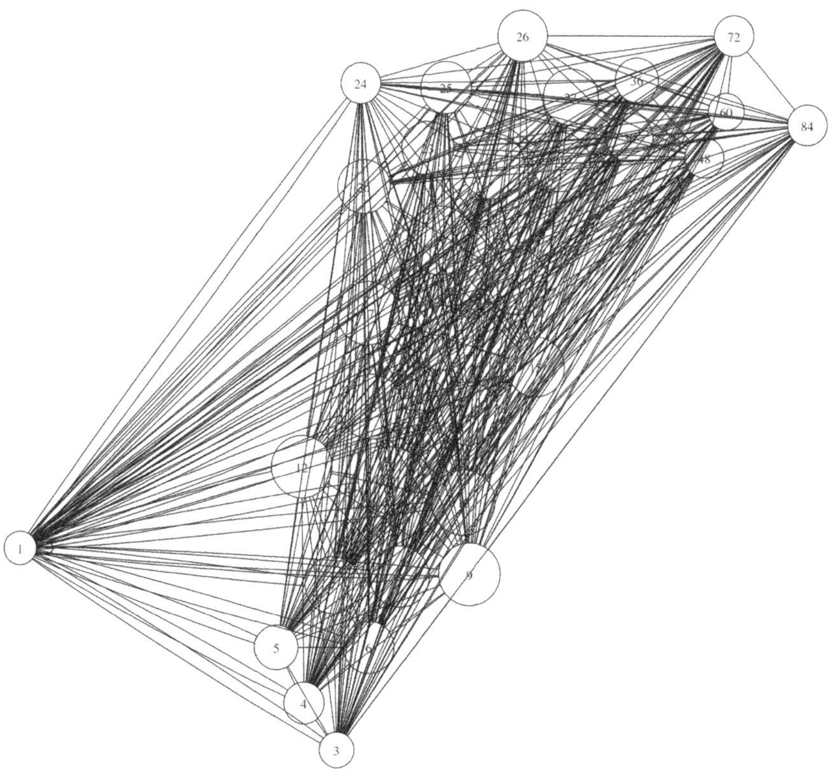

Fig. 7. Same as Fig. 6 with All the Edges of the Graph.

increase in the node's strength, emerges earlier for the energy sector than for the agricultural sector. Last, but not least, most of the products exhibit a strong increase, except for natural gases and interest rate contracts.

Although the nodes' strength is a relevant quantity to analyze the dynamical properties of the full connected networks, the visualization of the networks could also provide very useful information. Nonetheless, as depicted in Fig. 7, in the case of large networks, the visualization of the graph and the analysis of the properties of the links between the nodes become tricky. Fig. 7 is the same as Fig. 6, with all the links between the nodes. Remember that we are focusing on the maturity dimension only, and figuring out what would happen if we extend the analysis to all markets and maturities, in three dimensions.

In the face of a high-dimensional network, it is always possible, and often relevant, to focus on a subset of the full connected graph. In the next section, we restrain our analysis to such a subset and examine what is called an MST. We then study the organization, or topology, of the trees computed on our data.

INFORMATION FILTERING: THE MINIMUM SPANNING TREE

When there is too much information in a graph, there is a need to filter it. This is the reason why we restrain our analysis to a subset of the full connected graph, the MST. In what follows, we first explain what an MST is, and how to obtain it. We then analyze the organization of these specific networks. Finally, we examine their dynamic behavior.

Minimum Spanning Trees: The Method

Let us remember that whereas the full connected graph represents all the possible connections between N points, a tree is a subset of such a graph. A tree can be defined as a graph where any two nodes are connected by one and only one simple path; there are no cycles in such graphs.

Now, what we need is to reduce the dimensionality of the full connected graph, while keeping all relevant information. We have thus to span the graph: all its nodes need to be traversed. There are, however, a lot of paths spanning a graph. In our case, we are looking for the path that would always retain the most important correlations in prices returns. In other words, we are looking for the tree that minimizes the total distance between the nodes: the MST.

Through a filtering procedure (the information space is reduced from $(N(N-1)/2)$ links to $(N-1)$), the MST highlights the most relevant connections in the system. In our case, it represents the strongest links in terms of the correlations of price returns. Thus, as such a tree is unique, it can be considered as the easiest path for the transmission of a prices shock.[8]

The Topology of the Trees

The first information given by an MST is the kind of arrangement found between the vertices: its topology. The latter can be seen as the shape or the structure of a network. The visualization of the trees is a very important step, as it addresses the meaningfulness of the taxonomy that emerges from the system. As traditional measures of statistical significance are not suitable with our methodology, the economic meaning of the trees, and their robustness, becomes very important.

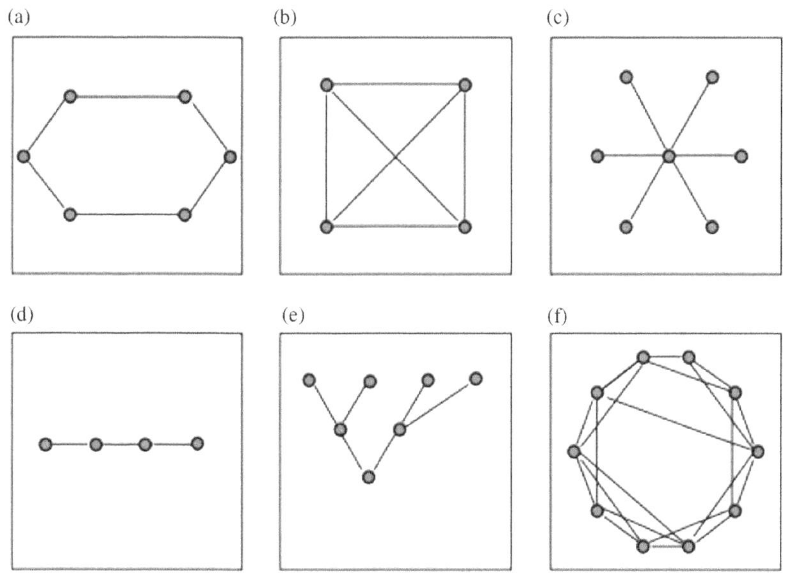

Fig. 8. Examples of Different Topologies. (a) Ring; (b) Full Connected Graph; (c) Star; (d) Chain; (e) Tree; (f) Small-World Network.

We display in Fig. 8 some examples of characteristic topologies. Fig. 8(a) describes a ring topology. In such a case, the information transmits between the nodes in a circular fashion and each node is supposed to receive and transmit some information. Fig. 8(b) represents a full connected graph. This type of network contains all the possible connections. The main disadvantage, with such a graph, is that the number of edges grows as the square of the node's number. Fig. 8(c) is a star-like tree. All the nodes are connected to a central node. This topology is particularly efficient in terms of information transfer, but the central node is a weak point. We will discuss this point a bit further in the next paragraph. Fig. 8(d) is a chain-like tree. Such a configuration reveals a strong organization between the nodes. Fig. 8(e) is another example of a tree, which can be seen as the so-called "family tree," with an "ancestor," the root, connected to one or more descendants. The latter are connected to their descendants and so on. The last graph, depicted in Fig. 8(f), corresponds to the so-called small-world network. The latter is defined as a network where the distance between two randomly chosen nodes grows as the logarithm of the total number of nodes.

Let us now give examples based on real data, and discuss the consequences of such results for systemic risk.

Fig. 9 presents the MST obtained for the spatial and maturity dimensions.[9] In Fig. 9(a), three sectors can be identified. The energy sector gathers American as well as European markets. It is situated between agriculture (on the top) and financial assets (on the bottom). The most connected node in the graph is the Brent crude, which makes it the best candidate for the transmission of price fluctuations.[10] Last but not least, the energy sector seems the most integrated, as the distances between the nodes are short. The link between the energy and agricultural products passes through soy oil. This is interesting, as the latter can be used for fuel. The link between commodities and financial assets passes through gold, which is also meaningful, as gold can be seen not only as a commodity but also as a reserve of value. The only surprise comes from the S&P500, which is more correlated to soy oil than to financial assets.

Such a star-like organization leads to specific conclusions regarding systemic risk. A prices move appearing in the energy markets, situated at the heart of the price system, will have more impact than a fluctuation affecting peripheral markets such as interest rates or wheat.

Things are totally different in the maturity dimension. The results are illustrated by the case of the Brent crude, depicted by Fig. 9(b) (as it was not possible to give an illustration for each of the 14 contracts under examination, we retained a representative one). Here, the MSTs are linear and the maturities, for all contracts, are always regularly ordered from the first to the last delivery dates. This result gives rise to three remarks.

First, this linear topology is meaningful on an economic point of view, as it reflects the presence of the Samuelson effect. In derivative markets, the movements in the prices of the prompt contracts are larger than the other ones. This results in a decreasing pattern of volatilities along the prices curve and leads to higher correlations between the maturities that are the closest to each other. Second, this type of organization impacts the possible transmission of prices shocks. The most likely path for a shock is indeed unique and passes through each maturity, one after the other. Third, the short parts of the curves are found to be less correlated with the others. This can result from prices shocks emerging in the physical market, with the nearby price being the most affected; it could also reflect noises introduced by investors on the first maturity.

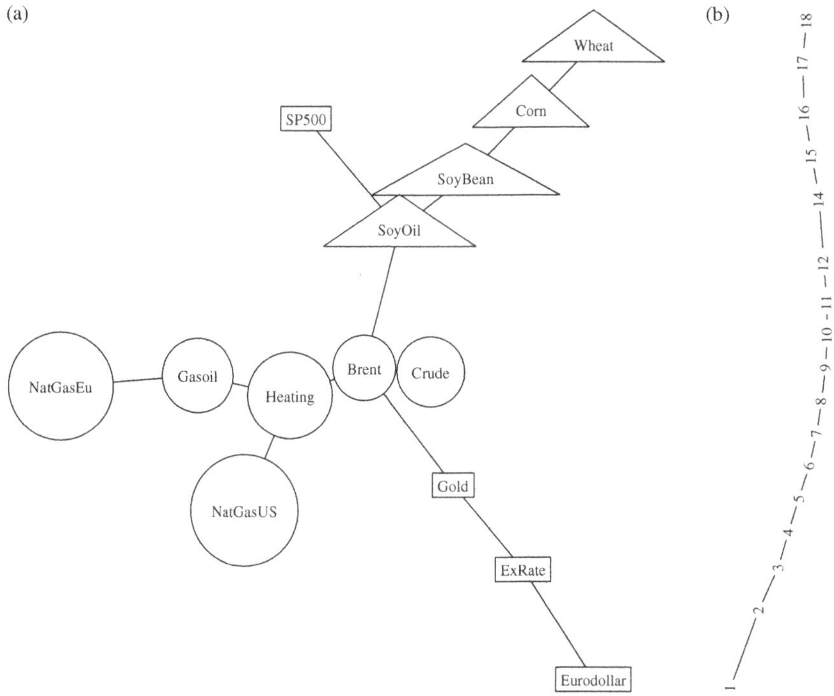

Fig. 9. Static Minimum Spanning Tree. (a) Spatial Dimension 2000–2009. (b) Brent Crude Oil in the Maturity Dimension, Maturities Increase from the Bottom to the Top.

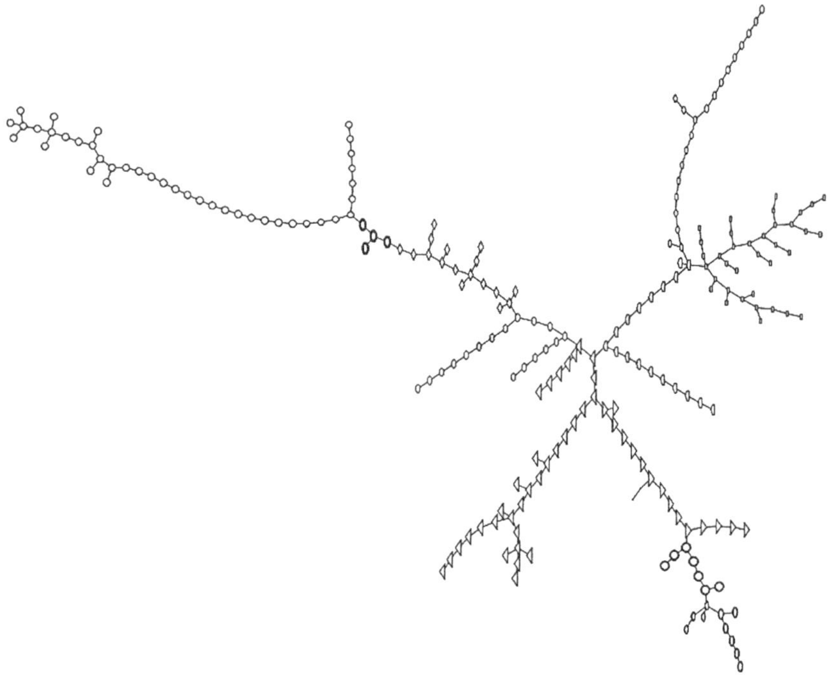

Fig. 10. Static Minimum Spanning Tree for the Three-Dimensional Analysis, 2000–2009. *Note*: The different futures contracts are represented by the following symbols: empty circle: Eurodollar; point: S&P 500; octagon: European natural gas; ellipse: gasoil; box: American natural gas; hexagon: Brent crude oil; triangle: light crude oil; house: heating oil; diamond: gold; inverted triangle: soy oil; triple octagon: exchange rate; double circle: soy bean; double octagon: wheat; egg: corn. For a given futures contract, all maturities are represented with the same symbol. The distance between the nodes is set to unity.

Let us now turn to the 3-D analysis depicted by Fig. 10. The shape of the 3-D MST brings to mind that observed in the spatial dimension. However, it is enhanced by the presence of the different maturities available for each market. The latter are clearly linearly organized. As previously mentioned, the tree shows a clear separation between the sectors, which are organized in the same way than before.

Although the visualization of the networks is very useful, this information remains mainly qualitative. It does not tell us, for instance, how to make a difference between the topologies of the MST in the spatial and the three dimensions. To get a deeper insight of the topological properties, there is a need to introduce a quantitative measurement: the allometric coefficients.

Quantifying the Topology of the MST: The Allometric Coefficients

The allometric coefficients provide a means of quantifying where a tree stands between two asymptotic topologies: star-like trees (as depicted in Fig. 8(c)), which are symptomatic of MST spanning uncorrelated entities, and chain-like trees (Fig. 8(e)), which reveal a strong ordering in the underlying structure.

The first model of the allometric scaling on a spanning tree was developed by Banavar, Maritan, and Rinaldo (1999). The first step of the procedure consists in initializing each node of the tree with the value 1. Then the root or central vertex of the tree must be identified. According to the nature of the network under scrutiny, the definition of the root can change. In the case of undirected trees, like ours, the choice of the root is arbitrary.[11] In what follows, we define it as the node connected with the highest number of other nodes. Starting from this root, the method consists in assigning two coefficients A_i and B_i to each node i:

$$A_i = \sum_j A_j + 1 \quad \text{and} \quad B_i = \sum_j B_j + A_i \tag{10}$$

where j stands for all the nodes connected to i. The allometric scaling relation is defined as the relationship between A_i and B_i:

$$B \sim A^{\eta} \tag{11}$$

The allometric exponent η is very important to characterize the structure of the trees and, consequently, the properties of the trees as regards as the propagations of price fluctuations. The transmission is far more efficient for star-like trees ($\eta = 1^+$) than for chain-like trees ($\eta = 2^-$). In the first case, indeed, a fluctuation can reach all the nodes in one step, whereas in a chain-like tree the nodes are reached one by one.

Table 3 summarizes the allometric properties of the MST computed on our data, for each dimension under consideration (spatial, maturity, and 3-D). The allometric coefficients have been computed in a static and a dynamic way. The static analysis refers to a study performed over a time window corresponding to the entire time period, whereas the dynamic one corresponds to a time window of 500 consecutive trading days. The first

Table 3. Allometric Properties of the Trees.

	Static	Dynamic
Crude	1.994 ± 0.045	1.906 ± 0.013
Brent	1.889 ± 0.003	1.904 ± 0.095
Heating	1.889 ± 0.004	1.917 ± 0.001
Gas oil	1.88 ± 0.003	1.943 ± 0.018
Natural gas (United States)	1.75 ± 0.037	1.74 ± 0.018
Natural gas (Europe)	1.874 ± 0.002	1.886 ± 0.059
Wheat	1.864 ± 0.13	1.761 ± 0.125
Soy bean	1.848 ± 0.095	1.822 ± 0.095
Soy oil	1.889 ± 0.003	1.886 ± 0.032
Corn	1.88 ± 0.003	1.834 ± 0.024
Eurodollar	1.927 ± 0.056	1.913 ± 0.011
Gold	1.732 ± 0.092	1.908 ± 0.013
Spatial	1.493 ± 0.056	1.621 ± 0.024
3D	1.757 ± 0.023	1.85 ± 0.09

Static and dynamic exponents for each futures contract in the maturity dimension as well as spatial and 3D.

lines of Table 3 are devoted to the maturity dimension, and information on the spatial and 3-D analyses is at the bottom. In each case, we reproduce the exponents and the standard errors resulting from a nonlinear regression.

Table 3 raises several comments. First, the error values are small, which confirms the robustness of the topologies of the trees: the economic meaningfulness is found when visualizing the shape of the trees is stable. Moreover, the dynamic allometric exponents are consistent with the static ones. Second, within the maturity dimension, the coefficients tend toward their asymptotic value[12] $\eta = 2^{-}$. Such a result is probably due to arbitrage operations. When performed on the basis of contracts having the same underlying asset, such operations are easy and rapidly undertaken, thus resulting in a perfect ordering of the maturities. Third, as far as the spatial dimension is concerned, the exponents indicate that the shape of the MST stands exactly between the two asymptotic topologies. Finally, even if the topologies of the spatial and 3-D trees seem similar, they are quantitatively different. The allometric exponent for the 3-D tree is higher. This tree merges the organization in sectors induced by the spatial dimension and the chain-like organization arising from the maturity dimension.

Given the time dependency of correlation measures, it is now important to focus on the dynamic behavior of the trees.

Dynamical Properties of the Filtered Information

Two measures can be used in order to examine the dynamical properties of the filtered information. We first focus on the average tree length. This quantity is a strongly reduced representation of the whole distance matrix, and bears the essential information about asset correlations. We then rely on survival ratios in order to study the fraction of edges, which survive between two consecutive time steps. The advantage of such a measure is twofold. First, it allows for identifying, over time, strong networks reconfigurations; second, it gives information on the robustness of the trees.

The Length of the Minimum Spanning Trees

The normalized tree's length can be defined as the sum of the lengths of the edges belonging to the MST:

$$L(t) = \frac{1}{N-1} \sum_{(i,i) \in MST} d_{ij} \tag{12}$$

where t denotes the date of the construction of the tree and $(N-1)$ is the number of edges. The length of a tree is thus longer when the distances between the nodes increase, and consequently when correlations are low. The more the length shortens, the more integration increases. On the contrary, where the tree characterized by random comovements, its length would be equal to $\sqrt{2}$.

Fig. 11 represents the dynamic behavior of the normalized length of the MST in its spatial dimension. The general pattern is that the length decreases, which reflects the integration of the prices system. This information confirms what was observed on the basis of the node's strengths. However, we are now analyzing a filtered network. Thus, what we see in Fig. 11 is that the most efficient transmission path for price fluctuations becomes shorter as time goes on. A more in-depth examination of the graph also shows a very important decrease between October 2006 and October 2008, as well as significant fluctuations in September and October 2008.

In the maturity dimension, as integration increases, the normalized tree's length also diminishes. This phenomenon is illustrated by Fig. 12(a) and (b), which represent the evolutions recorded for the Eurodollar contract and the Brent crude. The tree's length of interest rate contract first increases, then in mid-2001 it drops sharply and remains fairly stable after that date. For crude oil, the decrease is constant and steady, except for a few surges.

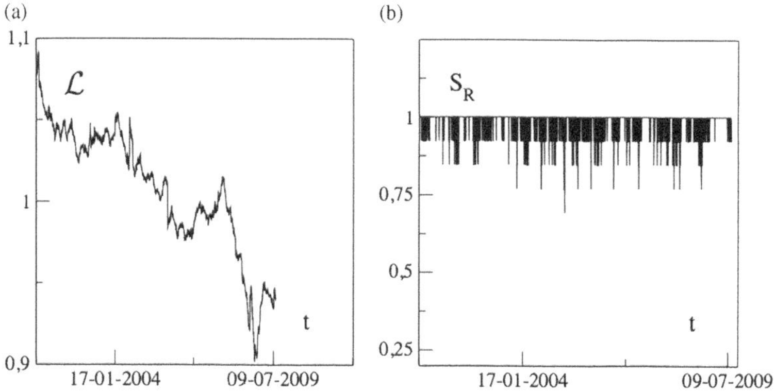

Fig. 11. MST Properties in the Spatial Dimension. (a) Normalized Tree Length and (b) Survival Ratio.

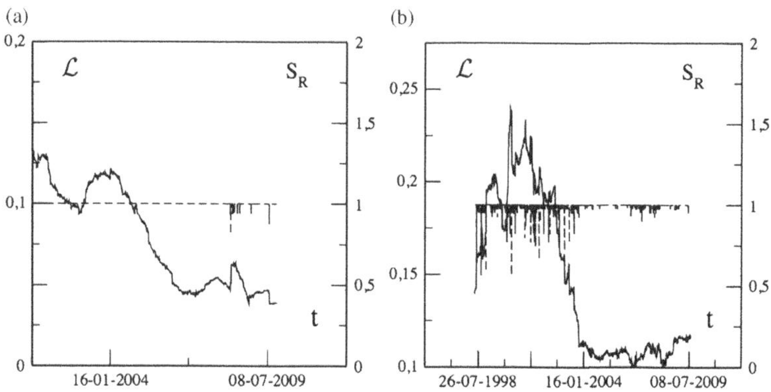

Fig. 12. MST Properties in the Maturity Dimension. (a) Brent Crude, Tree Length (Black Line), Survival Ratio (Dashed Line). (b) Eurodollar, Tree Length (Black Line), Survival Ratio (Dashed Line).

Survival Ratios

The robustness of the MST over time can be examined by computing the single-step survival ratio of the links. This quantity refers to the fraction of edges, in the MST, that survives between two consecutive trading days (Onnela, 2003). Fig. 13 explains how this quantity is found: Fig. 13(a) and (b) represent the same network at two different time steps. This network is characterized by 9 nodes and 8 edges. In the second time step, three new

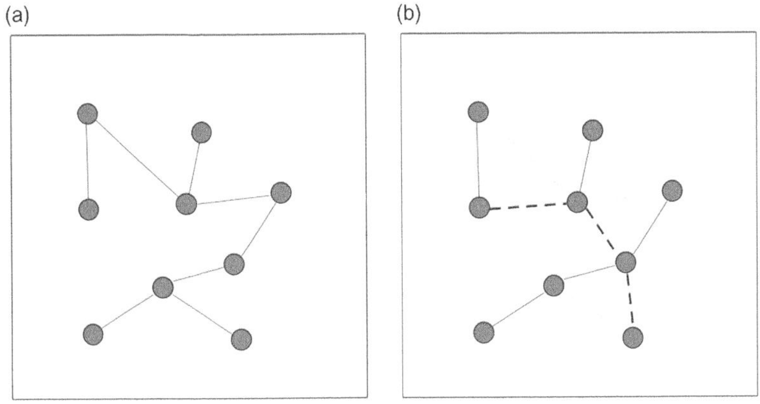

Fig. 13. Determination of the Survival Ratio.

links appear in the tree (they are represented by a dashed bold line) while three others disappear (thin gray line). Hence, the fraction of unchanged links between these two time steps, or the survival ratio of the tree, is 5/8.

More formally, the survival ratio is defined as:

$$S_R(t) = \frac{1}{N-1}\left|E(t) \cap E(t-1)\right| \tag{13}$$

where $E(t)$ refers to the set of the tree's edges at date t, $\cap$ is the intersection operator, and $|\cdot|$ denotes the number of elements contained in the set. The survival ratios are very important for our study. Under normal circumstances, the topology of the trees should be very stable, around 1.

Fig. 11(b) represents the evolution of the survival ratios in the spatial dimension. Most of the time, they remain constant, with a value greater than 0.9 in more than 96% of the cases. Thus, the topology of the tree is very stable: the shape of the most efficient path for the transmission of prices shocks does not change much over time. It is however possible to identify two events where 30% of the edges have been shuffled. As illustrated by Fig. 14, a focus on these two dates shows that the trees are totally rearranged. In 2004, the MST becomes highly linear, the financial sector stands at the center of the graph, and commodities appear mainly at the periphery of the system. Conversely, in 2008, the tree has a typical star-like shape, showing an organization based on the different sectors under examination.

Fig. 12(a) and (b) represents the survival ratios and the length of the MST for two representative contracts in the maturity dimension: the Brent crude

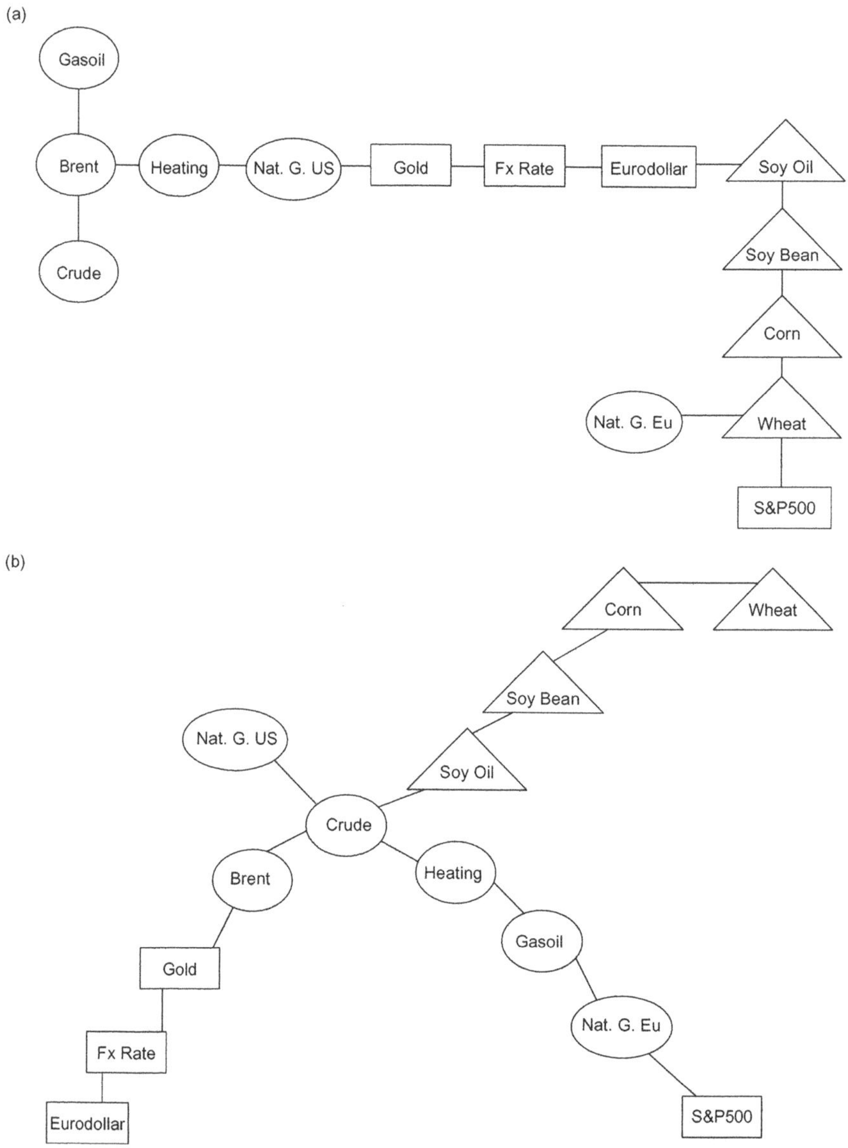

Fig. 14. Prunned MST. (a, top) February 9, 2004. (b, bottom) September 16, 2008.

and the Eurodollar. The organization of the former is very stable: the survival ratio is most of the time equal to 1, with few exceptions since the end of 2008. Again, what happens with the latter is very different. In 2000–2001, around the period of the Internet crisis, when the length of the tree increases, the tree becomes more spaced out. This sparseness comes with an important amount of reorganizations, and fluctuations in the survival ratios are greater as the length increases.

CONCLUSION

In this chapter, we proposed a nonconventional methodology, graph theory, which is especially relevant for the study of high-dimensional financial data, and we illustrate d the advantages of this method in the context of systemic risk. A key issue of the proposed tools, however, is that they can be used in various areas in finance; numerous applications, indeed, must now face the challenge of analyzing gigantic financial data sets. The latter are becoming more and more frequent.

Traditional financial analysis often relies on the study of cross-correlations between assets. Such a study allows for investigating dynamical synchronization between pair of assets and is often relevant for financial modeling. Nevertheless, the number of correlation coefficients scales as N^2 for N assets. Hence, it becomes quickly tedious to screen these coefficients over time. They are also numerically expensive to store and manage. In this context, the graph theory can play a crucial role.

In this chapter, as an illustration, we first focused on market integration by the mean of correlation-based networks. Second, based on the fact that previous studies mainly focused solely on the spatiotemporal dimension of integration, we introduced the maturity dimension and performed a 3-D analysis. In the context of an empirical study, which aims to understand the organization and the dynamic behavior of a high-dimensional prices system, our methodology proves very useful. Needless to say, it could also be used for higher systems, or for smaller ones. In our framework, MSTs are particularly interesting because they are filtered networks enabling us to identify the most probable and the shortest path for the transmission of a prices shock.

We show that the topology of the MST tends toward a star-like organization in the spatial dimension, whereas the maturity dimension is characterized by chain-like trees. These two topologies merge in the 3-D analysis, and all of them are very stable. The star-like organization reproduces the three different sectors studied (energy, agriculture, and finance), and the chain-like structure reflects the presence of a Samuelson effect. These findings are very important. The intuitive dimension of these results and the stability of the topologies are crucial for the robustness of the results.

NOTES

1. Delphine Lautier is also a member of the Fime Laboratory.
2. For an extensive introduction of the graph theory, see, for example, West (2001).
3. For an introduction to the interplay between statistical physics and finance, see, for instance, Mantegna and Stanley (2000), Bouchaud and Potters (2003), and Roehner (2002).
4. For a review of the literature on that point, see, for example, Lautier and Raynaud (2012).
5. We retained those contracts characterized by the largest transaction volumes over a long time period.
6. Other studies could naturally be performed on the basis of another construction: The nodes indeed could correspond to economic entities such as banks, hedge funds, and companies, as studied by Cossin and Schellhorn (2007). They could also figure out the holding account of such entities, or even individual traders.
7. As far as the maturity dimension is concerned, it was indeed not easy to represent the node's strength for all futures contracts. Furthermore, since in this case the level of correlation may be close to 1 (and thus the distance close to 0), the nodes' strength can lead to spurious results. A small fluctuation (a few percents) in the close-to-1 correlations can lead to huge variations in the nodes' strength: more than 50%.
8. Minimum spanning trees could naturally be used in other frameworks. For example, in Bonanno et al. (2004), the authors use this method to examine stocks portfolios and financial indexes. Miceli and Susinno (2003) rely on it to construct a correlation-based classification of banks and hedge funds.
9. Before going further, let us remind that we are now focusing on filtered information. Thus, when a link between two markets or maturities does not appear, this does not mean that it does not exist, but rather that it does not correspond to a minimal distance (maximal correlation).
10. Actually, the same could have been said for the Light crude, as the distance between the two crudes is very short.
11. For directed trees, the root is defined as the node without any predecessor.
12. They are however a bit smaller than 2 due to finite size effects (there is a finite number of maturities).

ACKNOWLEDGMENTS

Financial support of the French Energy Council and of the Chair Finance and Sustainable Development is gratefully acknowledged.

REFERENCES

Albert, R., Jeong, H., & Barabasi, A.-L. (2000). Error and attack tolerance of complex networks. *Nature*, *406*, 378–482.

Banavar, J. R., Maritan, A., & Rinaldo, A. (1999). Size and form in efficient transportation networks. *Nature*, *399*, 130–132.

Bech, M., Chapman, J., & Garratt, R. (2010). Which bank is the "central" bank? *Journal of Monetary Economics*, *57*, 352–363.

Bonanno, G., Caldarelli, G., Lillo, F., Miccichè, S., Vandewalle, N., & Mantegna, R. N. (2004). Networks of equities in financial markets. *The European Physical Journal B*, *38*, 363–371.

Bouchaud, J.-P., & Potters, M. (2003). *Theory of financial risk and derivative pricing* (2nd ed.). Cambridge: Cambridge University Press.

Buldyrev, S. V., Parshani, R., Paul, P., Stanley, H. E., & Havlin, S. (2010). Catastrophic cascade of failures in interdependent networks. *Nature*, *464*, 1025–1028.

Cohen-Cole, E., Kirilenko, A., & Patacchini, E. (2011). *Are networks priced? Network topology and systemic risk in high liquidity markets*. EIEF Working Papers Series 1011, Einaudi Institute for Economic and Finance (EIEF), Roma.

Cossin, D., & Schellhorn, H. (2007). Credit risk in a network economy. *Management Science*, *53*(10), 1604–1617.

Gower, J. (1966). Some distance properties of latent root and vector methods used in multivariate analysis. *Biometrika*, *53*(3/4), 325–338.

Holland, J. H. (2006). Studying complex adaptive systems. *Journal of Systems Science and Complexity*, *19*(1), 1–8.

Lautier, D., & Raynaud, F. (2012). Systemic risk in energy derivative markets: A graph-theory analysis. *The Energy Journal*, *33*(3), 217–242.

Mantegna, R. N. (1999). Hierarchical structure in financial markets. *European Physical Journal B*, *11*, 193–197.

Mantegna, R. N., & Stanley, H. E. (2000). *An introduction to econophysics: Correlations and complexity in finance*. Cambridge: Cambridge University Press.

Miceli, M., & Susinno, G. (2003). *Risk*, *16*, 11.

Onnela, J.-P. (2003). Dynamics of market correlations: Taxonomy and portfolio analysis. *Physical Review E*, *68*(5), 056110.

Roehner, B. M. (2002). *Patterns of speculation. A study in observational econophysics*. Cambridge: Cambridge University Press.

Sieczka, P., & Holyst, J. A. (2009). Correlations in commodity markets. *Physica A*, *388*, 1621–1630.

Strogatz, S. H. (2001). Exploring complex networks. *Nature*, *410*, 268–276.

West, D. B. (2001). *Introduction to graph theory*. Upper Saddle River, NJ: Prentice-Hall.

PART II
DERIVATIVES PRICES AND RISK-NEUTRAL DISTRIBUTIONS

RECOVERING STOCHASTIC PROCESSES FROM OPTION PRICES

Jens Carsten Jackwerth and Mark Rubinstein

ABSTRACT

How do stock prices evolve over time? The standard assumption of geometric Brownian motion, questionable as it has been right along, is even more doubtful in light of the recent stock market crash and the subsequent prices of U.S. index options. With the development of rich and deep markets in these options, it is now possible to use options prices to make inferences about the risk-neutral stochastic process governing the underlying index. We compare the ability of models including Black–Scholes, naïve volatility smile predictions of traders, constant elasticity of variance, displaced diffusion, jump diffusion, stochastic volatility, and implied binomial trees to explain otherwise identical observed option prices that differ by strike prices, times-to-expiration, or times. The latter amounts to examining predictions of future implied volatilities.

Certain naïve predictive models used by traders seem to perform best, although some academic models are not far behind. We find that the better-performing models all incorporate the negative correlation between index level and volatility. Further improvements to the models seem to require predicting the future at-the-money implied volatility. However, an "efficient markets result" makes these forecasts difficult, and improvements to the option-pricing models might then be limited.

Derivative Securities Pricing and Modelling
Contemporary Studies in Economic and Financial Analysis, Volume 94, 123–153

ISSN: 1569-3759/doi:10.1108/S1569-3759(2012)0000094008

How do stock prices evolve over time?[1] Ever since Osborne (1959), the standard view has been that stock prices follow a geometric Brownian motion. Merton (1973) uses this assumption as the basis for an intertemporal model of market equilibrium, and Black and Scholes (1973) uses it as the basis for their option-pricing model. Tests of options on stock in the early years of exchange-traded options more or less supported the implications of Brownian motion, see, for example, Rubinstein (1985). While it has long been well known that empirical return distributions exhibit fatter tails than implied by Brownian motion, evidence that something is not all right with this world is that S&P 500 index options since the crash of 1987 exhibit pronounced volatility smiles, see Jackwerth and Rubinstein (1996). A volatility smile describes implied volatilities that are largely convex and monotonically decreasing functions of strike prices.[2] Such volatilities contradict the assumptions of geometric Brownian motion and perfect markets, which would imply a flat line. Another way to describe this is that the implied risk-neutral probability densities are heavily skewed to the left and highly leptokurtic, unlike the lognormal assumption in Black–Scholes. Like the equity premium puzzle, this option-pricing puzzle may ultimately lead us to a better understanding of the determinants of security prices.

There are three possibilities why option prices can spuriously exhibit volatility smiles. First, there are market imperfections, and observed option prices are always different from the true option prices at any time. The S&P 500 index option market is a rather deep and liquid market with rather unfettered access. Its daily notional volume is sizable, as reported in Table 1 for longer-term options. Even as the daily notional volume increased sixfold

Table 1. Daily Notional Volume.

Year	Moneyness							
	Less than 0.91		0.91–0.97		0.97–1.03		More than 1.03	
	Calls	Puts	Calls	Puts	Calls	Puts	Calls	Puts
1986–1987	84	247	53	152	78	76	93	44
1988–1989	16	433	29	231	118	296	284	85
1990–1991	32	942	41	877	637	700	829	345
1992–1993	20	1,534	73	1,113	495	629	999	103
1994–1995	53	2,242	109	1,937	613	1,954	1,401	233

Note: Daily notional volume (in million $) across moneyness and time, based on 252 trading days per year. Time-to-expiration is 135–225 days.

from $1.5 billion in 1989 to $8.5 billion in 1995, the volatility smile did not change. Most of our results are based on longer-term options, which account for about 4% of the total daily notional volume in all maturities. However, our results do not seem to be sensitive to our focus on the longer-term options.

Since the S&P 500 index is rather high (370 dollars on average from 1986 through 1995), the value of an option is high compared to the bid/ask spread, which for at-the-money options is only some 42 cents, decreasing to 33 cents for out-of-the-money options. Moreover, we expect the true option price to be close to the midpoint quote for most of the time. Thus, market imperfections are not likely candidates to explain the volatility smile.

The second possibility is that option prices are measured correctly but that the implied probabilities are calculated incorrectly. For example, the wrong interpolation or extrapolation method is used to obtain a dense set of option prices across strike prices. Jackwerth and Rubinstein (1996) show, however, that the choice of method does not really matter much because most methods back out virtually the same risk-neutral distribution, as long as there are a sufficient number of strike prices, say, about 15.[3]

The third possibility is that the observed option prices are systematically distorted, and that one can make money in the options market by exploiting such mispricing. Jackwerth (2000) takes this view to some extent.

We assume instead that we see correctly measured option prices that yield meaningful implied risk-neutral probability distributions. The volatility smile is then a way of describing the relation of option prices at the same time, with the same underlying asset and the same time-to-expiration, but with different strike prices. Option prices also provide three other types of comparisons that can be windows into an understanding of the stochastic process of the underlying assets:

(1) Option prices at the same time, with the same underlying asset, and the same strike price, but with *different times-to-expiration*.
(2) Option prices with the same underlying asset, the same expiration date, and the same strike price, but observed at *different times*.
(3) Option prices at the same time, with the same time-to-expiration and with the same strike price, but with *different underlying assets*.

Jackwerth and Rubinstein (1996) consider relationships among option prices at the same time and with the same underlying and time-to-expiration, but with different strike prices. The ultimate objective is to discover a single model that can explain all four relations simultaneously. For example, the postcrash smile of index options and the implied binomial tree model of Rubinstein (1994) strongly suggest that a key aspect of the "correct" model will be one that builds in a negative correlation between index level and at-the-money implied volatility. This can explain the relation in Jackwerth and Rubinstein (1996) and turns out in the postcrash period to be an empirical regularity of relation (2).

While we focus here on the smile in the S&P 500 data for the United States, Tompkins (2001) documents that similar smiles, albeit not as steep as the U.S. smile, are seen in the United Kingdom, Japan, and Germany. In addition, Dennis and Mayhew (2000) show that individual option smiles in the United States are not as steep as the index smile, a finding that likely holds for the other markets as well but that has not been documented.

There are several rational economic reasons why the postcrash smile effect might obtain. First, corporate leverage effects imply that as stock prices fall, debt–equity ratios (in market values) rise, causing stock volatility to increase. Second, Kelly (1994) notes that equity prices have become more highly correlated in down markets, again causing an increase in volatility. Third, risk aversion effects can cause investors who are poorer after a downturn in the market to react more dramatically to news events. This would lead to increased volatility after a downturn. Fourth, the market could be more likely to jump down rather than up. Indeed, since the stock market crash period of 1987 until the end of 1998, the five greatest moves in the S&P 500 index have been down. Finally, as the volatility of the market increases, the required risk premium rises, too. A higher risk premium will in turn depress stock prices. We do not try to provide an economic explanation for observed smile patterns, but rather have the more limited objective of comparing alternative models that purport to explain relations (1) and (2). We leave to subsequent research an investigation of relation (3). A comparison of smile patterns for index options and individual stock options, as in Dennis and Mayhew (2000), provides a way to distinguish between leverage and wealth effects as explanations of the inverse correlation between at-the-money option implied volatilities and index levels. If leverage is the force behind the scenes, the downward slope of the smiles for index and stock options should be about the same. If the wealth effect is predominant, the downward slope of the smile would be highest for index options and become less sloped the lower the ratio of a stock's systematic variance to its total variance.

To investigate the empirical problems, we suggest two main tests. Our first test investigates relation (1), using options prices at the same time and with the same underlying and strike price, but with different times-to-expiration. Here we find out how well different option-pricing models are capable of simultaneously explaining option prices of different times-to-expiration. For this, we deduce shorter-term option prices from longer-term option prices. The volatility smile for the longer-term options is assumed known, and the volatility smile for the shorter-term options is unknown. The problem of relation (1) is to fit alternative option-pricing models to the longer-term option prices. We can then compare the model values with the observed market prices for the shorter-term options and calculate pricing errors. To help understand the source of remaining errors, we also conduct a related experiment. We assume in addition that we also know the at-the-money implied volatility of the shorter-term options.

The second test investigates relation (2), using option prices with the same underlying asset, expiration date, and strike price, but observed at different times. In this case, we use option valuation models to forecast future option prices conditional on the future underlying asset price. We calibrate alternative models on current longer-term option prices. Then, we wait 10 and 30 days, observe the underlying asset price, and assess the errors in our forecasts. A related test extends the forecasting procedure by incorporating information from both current longer-term and current shorter-term option prices. Again, to decompose the source of any remaining errors, we also assume in addition that we know in advance the future at-the-money option price.

For all tests, we evaluate five kinds of option valuation models (nine models altogether). We compare deterministic models and stochastic models and naïve trader rules. Related empirical work is in Dumas, Fleming, and Whaley (1998), Bates (2000), and Bakshi, Cao, and Chen (1997). The first paper investigates only different deterministic volatility models while the other two compare only different stochastic models.

The five categories of models are: first, mostly for reference, the Black–Scholes formula; second, two naïve smile-based predictions that use today's observed smile directly for prediction; third, two versions of Cox's (1996) constant elasticity of variance (CEV) formula; fourth, an implied binomial tree model; fifth, three parametric models that specify the stochastic process of the underlying, namely, displaced diffusion, jump diffusion, and stochastic volatility.

The naïve predictions do not rely on any solid theoretical basis, but we examine them because they are very simple and widely used by professionals. We show that they perform surprisingly well compared to the more rigorous academic models. We use the CEV model because it explicitly builds in an assumption that local volatility is negatively correlated with the underlying asset price and is therefore a natural candidate, given our observations.

Implied binomial trees, which are nonparametric, have been proposed by Rubinstein (1994), Derman and Kani (1994), and Dupire (1994). Work on implied risk-neutral distributions that is closely related has been conducted by Jackwerth and Rubinstein (1996) and Aït-Sahalia and Lo (1998).[4] We focus here on the implied binomial trees in Rubinstein (1994) and the generalizations in Jackwerth (1997). The generalizations allow us to incorporate information from times other than the end of the tree. We rely solely on the observed option prices in the market, and thus avoid having to specify a stochastic process a priori.

Next, we introduce the data. Then we conduct our two tests. Sections "Looking Backward (Unknown Term Structure of Volatilities)" and "Looking Backward (Known Term Structure of At-the-Money Volatilities)" are concerned with inferring shorter-term option prices from concurrent longer-term option prices (relation (1)), with an unknown and known term structure of volatilities respectively. Sections "Looking Forward (Unknown Term Structure of Volatilities)" and "Looking Forward (Known Term Structure of At-the-Money Volatilities)" are concerned with forecasting future smiles using current longer-term option prices (relation (2)), with an unknown and known term structure of future volatilities respectively. We conclude with our surprising result that the naïve trader rules work as well as the more rigorous academic models.

DATA

The database includes minute-by-minute trades and quotes covering S&P 500 European index options, S&P 500 index futures, and S&P 500 index levels from April 2, 1986, through December 29, 1995.

All option models are parameterized to price the observed longer-term options best, those with times-to-expiration of between 135 and 225 days. In the first test, the models are then used to price shorter-term options with 45 to 134 days to expiration.

To obtain sets of option prices across several strike prices for the two times-to-expiration, we aggregate all daily quotes into two volatility smiles, one for the shorter- and one for the longer-term options. Throughout each day, we calculate the implied volatilities for all options with the same strike price and time-to-expiration. We compute the median implied volatilities for each strike price and treat this set as our representative daily volatility smile for a given time-to-expiration.

Interestingly, the number of available options quotes during the day does not influence the results very much. As in Jackwerth and Rubinstein (1996), we use only strike prices with strike price/index level ratios (moneyness) between 0.79 and 1.16 because of the lack of liquidity for the further away options.

The dividend yield is based on the actual payments throughout the life of the option. The interest rate is the average of the median implied borrowing and lending rates assuming put-call parity of all feasible pairs of options for a given time-to-expiration on a given day. The index level for our representative daily sets of option prices is the average of the daily high and low of a futures-based index. The futures-based index is obtained by deflating all futures quotes and trades by the median daily implied repo rate corresponding to the time-to-maturity of the future. For each minute, the median of all deflated quotes and trades is computed and used as the futures-based index for that minute.[5]

There are 2,074 days in the almost ten years elapsed time for which we have a sufficient number of longer-term options. We specify two subperiods: a precrash period from April 2, 1986, through October 16, 1987, and a postcrash period from June 1, 1988, through December 29, 1995. We avoid the period right after the crash, which is often difficult to interpret empirically, as the market took about half a year to get settled again. The sample size is 1,953 days: 386 days for the precrash period, and 1,567 days for the postcrash period. For the empirical studies, where we need both shorter-term and longer-term options, there are 1,639 days: 372 days for the precrash period, and 1,267 days for the postcrash period. For the smile forecasts, we shorten the precrash period so that it ends September 16, 1987. This avoids forecasting across the crash with associated large errors.

To obtain the implied probability distributions as inputs for the implied binomial trees, we use the maximum smoothness method proposed in Jackwerth and Rubinstein (1996). As Fig. 1 shows, even though the smoothness criterion does not rely on a lognormal prior distribution, the implied probability distribution calculated from option prices that are based on a lognormal distribution is very close to the underlying lognormal distribution.

Since we use the method of Jackwerth and Rubinstein (1996) for finding implied probability distributions, we sample the implied distributions on equal dollar-spaced asset values. Implied binomial trees are generally sensitive to the spacing at the end of the tree and do not work well with equal spacing. Thus, we have to resample the implied probability distributions onto equally *log-spaced* asset values that are given by a standard binomial tree with the same number of steps. To construct the

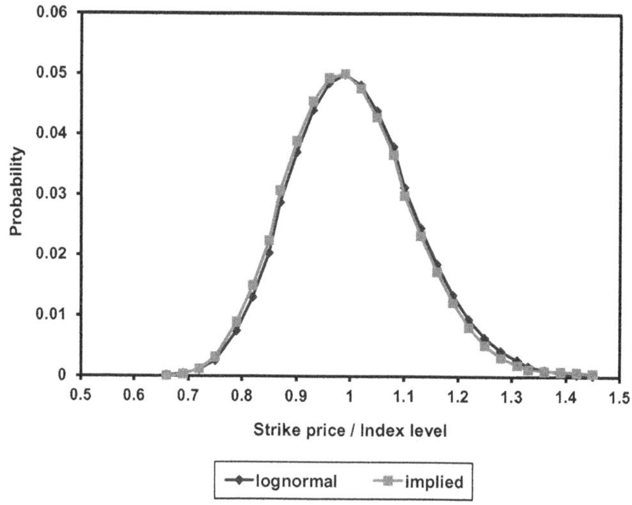

Fig. 1. Lognormal and Implied Probability Distributions. *Notes*: In this figure, we graph a lognormal distribution with an annualized volatility of 0.1602, which perfectly prices a set of 15 hypothetical options with strike prices in the range from 0.86 to 1.08. Given those option prices, we can derive the corresponding implied probability distribution according to the maximum smoothness criterion, graphed as well. The interest rate and dividend yield are chosen to match the observed options with 189 days-to-expiration on March 16, 1990.

standard binomial tree, we have to specify the volatility parameter, which we set equal to the implied volatility of the longer-term at-the-money option. For the resampling, we use piecewise-linear interpolation in the cumulative probabilities. The use of cubic splines improves performance only marginally but at a significantly higher computational cost.

The resulting probability distribution overprices options only slightly, with a median absolute error of about 3 cents for a test of 23 semiannual observations, even if the log spacing spans as few as 80 values. We could detect no pricing bias across strike prices.

Each model used to derive the shorter-term options is calibrated on the same set of longer-term options, although the different models imply different (risk-neutral) probability distributions for the longer-term options. Fig. 2 depicts these distributions for the implied binomial tree, the Black–Scholes model, and the CEV model for a representative day after the crash. The implied binomial tree and the CEV models show rather similar implied distributions, but the implied binomial tree is more flexible.

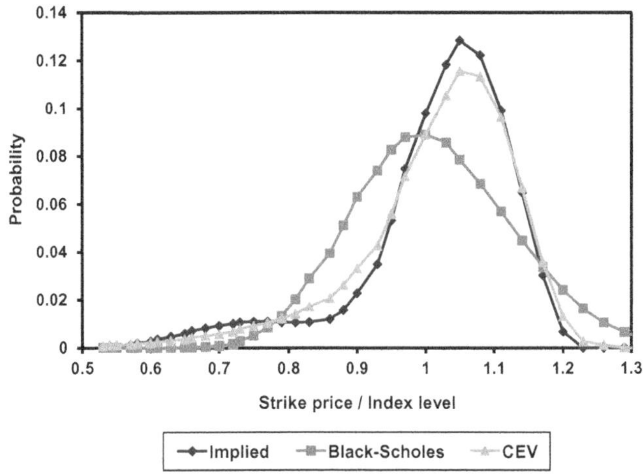

Fig. 2. Implied, Lognormal, and CEV Probability Distributions. *Notes*: For the options with time-to-expiration of 189 days on March 16, 1990, we graph the implied probability distribution, the lognormal distribution based on the volatility of the at-the-money option, and the CEV model implied distribution where the (unrestricted) CEV parameters are chosen to fit the observed option prices best.

LOOKING BACKWARD (UNKNOWN TERM STRUCTURE OF VOLATILITIES)

The first test investigates otherwise similar options but with different times-to-expiration (relation (1)). We look backward in that we fit the models to concurrent longer-term option prices. Then, we price the shorter-term options using the fitted models.

Alternative Option-Pricing Models

The simplest model is Black–Scholes, which suggests that the volatility smile is truly flat ("flat smile" model). That is, we price shorter-term options according to a flat smile, which is determined by the at-the-money implied volatility of the concurrent longer-term options. We repeat this calibration each day for all models. Note that the resulting parameters will vary from day to day. Such recalibrations are typical for how practitioners use the models and take account of the fact that the volatility smile moves from day to day.

Two other models, the displaced diffusion model of Rubinstein (1983) and the jump diffusion of Merton (1976), produce empirical results very similar to the Black–Scholes model in all tests, so we do not report these results separately. Neither of these models is flexible enough to generate volatility smile patterns that are sufficiently different from the flat smile of the Black–Scholes model.

The second set of predictions is often used by traders to accommodate observed non-flat smile patterns. These assume that the longer-term smile is the best guess for the shorter-term smile. There are two different versions depending on if the smile is defined across "moneyness" or strike price. One version is the "relative smile" prediction, which traders call the "sticky delta" method.[6] Here we assume that each shorter-term option with a given *moneyness* has an implied volatility equal to the corresponding longer-term option with the same moneyness. In a second version, we consider the "absolute smile" prediction, which traders call the "sticky vol" method. Here we assume that a shorter-term option with a given *strike price* has an implied volatility equal to the corresponding longer-term option with the same strike price.

For the relative and absolute smiles, we need to interpolate the longer-term implied volatilities to arrive at the corresponding implied volatilities for the shorter-term options. We use piecewise-linear interpolation since it gives very similar results to more sophisticated methods such as cubic spline or polynomial interpolation. We extrapolate for values (of moneyness or strike prices) outside the longer-term smile by assuming that all lower values have the same implied volatility as the lowest observable value and all higher values those of the highest observable value.[7]

Next, we examine two versions of the CEV model. The formula is based on a diffusion process specifying the instantaneous volatility $\sigma(S,t)$ as:

$$\sigma(S,t) = \sigma' S^{\rho-1} \tag{1}$$

where σ' = volatility parameter; S = index level; and $\rho = 1 +$ elasticity of variance with respect to index level.

Several well-known processes are nested in the CEV such as the absolute process ($\rho = 0$), the square-root process ($\rho = 0.5$), and the standard process underlying the Black–Scholes formula ($\rho = 1$). If the parameter ρ is less than one, then the index level and the instantaneous volatility are inversely related, consistent with empirical findings. We measure a correlation between S&P 500 index level and at-the-money implied volatility of −0.72 for the 1,880 observations from June 6, 1988, through December 28, 1995, so we impose an upper bound on ρ at 1. Options priced under this parameterization will exhibit a downward-sloping volatility smile.

We allow for two different lower bounds on ρ. In the restricted version, a lower bound of zero is chosen, corresponding to the absolute process. This limits the chance of bankruptcy to plausible levels. In a second version, we leave the ρ parameter unrestricted. Although this is mathematically legitimate, it may have undesirable economic implications (which we discuss later).

The CEV model has two additional parameters that need to be specified, the elasticity ρ–1 and the volatility σ'. We choose both parameters in an optimal fashion by minimizing the pricing error of the longer-term options. We then price the shorter-term options while using these two optimal parameters.

For the implied binomial tree model (Rubinstein, 1994), the natural starting point is the end of the tree, where we assume that all ending probabilities and asset nodal values are known from the method of Jackwerth and Rubinstein (1996).[8] In order to allow for subsequent generalizations, we use the notation of Jackwerth (1997). Let $S_{i,j}$ be the nodal asset value at step $i=0, \ldots, n$ and at level $j=0, \ldots, i$. Let $P_{i,j}$ be the corresponding nodal probability. The recursive method is then, starting at the end of the tree:

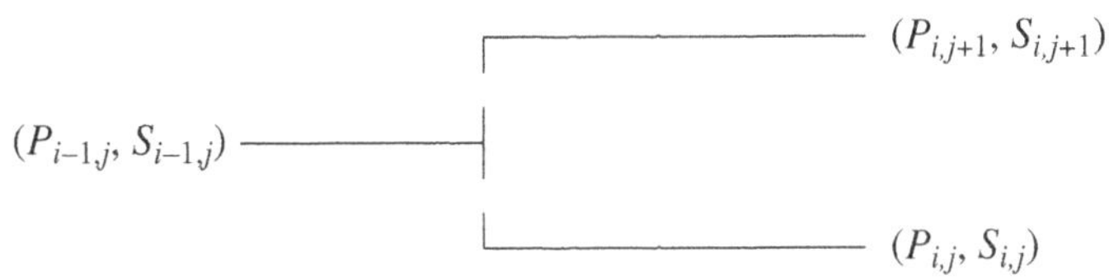

$$\text{Step One:} \qquad P_{i-1,j} = (1 - w_{i,j})P_{i,j} + w_{i,j+1}P_{i,j+1} \tag{2}$$

$$\text{Step Two:} \qquad p_{i-1,j} = w_{i,j+1}\frac{P_{i,j+1}}{P_{i-1,j}} \tag{3}$$

$$\text{Step Three:} \qquad S_{i-1,j} = \frac{(1 - p_{i-1,j})S_{i,j} + p_{i-1,j}S_{i,j+1}}{(r/\delta)^{t/n}} \tag{4}$$

where $w_{i,j}=(j/i)$ is the transition probability weight of going down as we move to the prior step; $r=1+$annualized interest rate; $\delta=1+$annualized dividend yield; $t=$time-to-expiration in years; and $n=$number of steps.

To price shorter-term options, we find the step i^* of the implied binomial tree corresponding in time:

$$i^* = \text{integer}\left[0.5 + \frac{t_s}{t}n\right] \tag{5}$$

where t_s = time-to-expiration of the shorter-term options and t = time-to-expiration of the longer-term options.

We can now price all shorter-term options using the formula:

$$C(K_m) = \frac{\sum_{j=0}^{i^*} P_{i^*,j} \max[0; S_{i^*,j} - K_m]}{r^{t_s}} \tag{6}$$

where K_m = strike price of the shorter-term option m.

We use implied binomial trees with 200 steps. Binomial trees are rather insensitive to the number of steps used. Even trees with as few as 80 steps yield pricing errors that are only 4 cents worse than the errors for 200 step trees which vary from 24 to 83 cents across different tests. Increasing the number of steps beyond 200 does not improve the fit of the trees significantly.

The last model is the stochastic volatility model of Heston (1993). Volatility is modeled as a mean-reverting square-root process. In his exact notation for the risk-neutral process:[9]

$$\begin{aligned} dS(t) &= rSdt + \sqrt{v(t)}Sdz_1(t) \\ dv(t) &= \kappa^*[\theta^* - v(t)]dt + \sigma\sqrt{v(t)}dz_2(t) \end{aligned} \tag{7}$$

where κ^* = mean reversion; θ^* = long-run variance; $v(t)$ = current variance; ρ = correlation of $z_1(t)$ and $z_2(t)$; σ = volatility of volatility parameter; and r = interest rate.

Again, we fit the first five parameters by minimizing the error of the longer-term options and then keep the parameters to price the shorter-term options.

More complex models incorporate stochastic interest rates and stochastic jumps in addition to stochastic volatility. Evidence in Bakshi et al. (1997), however, suggests that adding jumps only slightly improves on the stochastic volatility model for short-term options. Adding stochastic interest rates only slightly improves on the stochastic volatility model for long-term options. In both cases, there is no difference for hedging performance. Bates (2000) finds that adding jumps slightly improves performance over the stochastic volatility model, but that the implied probability distributions are inconsistent. Thus, we focus on the simpler stochastic volatility model since it seems to account for the lion's-share of performance improvement over the Black–Scholes model.

One model we do not include is the GARCH option-pricing model of Duan (1995). Since some GARCH models converge to stochastic volatility models as the discrete time steps grow small (Heston & Nandi, 2000), we believe that we capture much of the effect by investigating the stochastic volatility model.

Empirical Results

Our empirical results are stated in terms of pricing errors. To evaluate the performance of the alternative option models we use the root mean squared error in cents:

$$\text{RMSE} = \sqrt{\frac{1}{m}\sum_{i=1}^{m}[C_{\text{observed}}(K_i) - C_{\text{model}}(K_i)]^2} \tag{8}$$

where C_{observed} = midpoint option price observed in the market; K_i = strike price for the observed option i; and C_{model} = option price derived from an option valuation model.

Thus, the pricing error is an aggregate measure across all strike prices for options of a given time-to-expiration. Expressed in cents, the relative impact is less for a call option with a low strike price than for a call option with a high strike price. Choosing March 16, 1990, as an example, a typical day for the postcrash period, the at-the-money option (strike price = 34,500 cents) is worth 975 cents. A low pricing error of 20 cents corresponds to 2%, and a high pricing error of 100 cents corresponds to 10%. The corresponding percentages for the 6%-in-the-money call (strike price = 32,500) with price 2,442 are 1% and 4%. The corresponding percentages for the 6%-out-of-the-money call (strike price = 36,500) with price 148 are 14% and 68%.

There are two reasons we use cent errors. First, because we translate all puts into calls through put-call parity, we are concerned that expressing relative errors in terms of call prices might have adverse consequences for the corresponding put prices. The cent errors are unaffected; however, if the put is over-priced by a cent, then the put-call-parity implied call is also over-priced by a cent. Second, the alternative of expressing errors in terms of implied volatilities means that for in-the-money calls small cent errors translate into large volatility errors.

Table 2. Pricing Errors for Precrash Period (Unknown Term Structure of Volatilities).

Pricing Method	Cent Error		
	Mean	Median	SD
Black–Scholes formula	27	21	21
Relative smile prediction	27	21	21
Absolute smile prediction	28	22	21
CEV restricted formula	26	20	21
CEV unrestricted formula	26	20	21
Implied binomial tree	29	22	21
Stochastic volatility	27	21	22

Notes: This table uses seven methods to price shorter-term options, given concurrent longer-term option prices. The sample covers the pre-crash period from April 2, 1986, through October 16, 1987, where there are 360 observations.

Table 3. Pricing Errors for Postcrash Period (Unknown Term Structure of Volatilities).

Pricing Method	Cent Error		
	Mean	Median	SD
Black–Scholes formula	126	125	40
Relative smile prediction	54	51	24
Absolute smile prediction	57	54	24
CEV restricted formula	110	110	41
CEV unrestricted formula	75	57	57
Implied binomial tree	82	78	37
Stochastic volatility	78	73	61

Notes: This table uses seven methods to price shorter-term options, given concurrent longer-term option prices. The sample covers the post-crash period from June 1, 1988, through December 31, 1994, where there are 1,278 observations.

Tables 2 and 3 exhibit the pricing errors for the alternative models.[10] Table 2 reports the precrash errors and Table 3 the postcrash pricing errors.

Discussion

In the precrash period, assuming an unknown term structure of implied volatilities, the Black–Scholes formula yields median errors of 21 cents

(Table 2). These errors compare quite favorably with typical bid/ask spreads of 40 cents. Since precrash smiles are almost flat, there is no benefit to using the relative or absolute smile predictions.

The CEV model yields marginally lower errors because of the greater flexibility in choosing the ρ parameter, but it converges to the Black–Scholes formula as the parameter ρ takes on an optimal value of 1. This occurs for most days in the precrash period since the observed option prices imply probability distributions that are about lognormal. Moreover, the bound on ρ at zero for the restricted CEV model is almost never binding. This means that the two versions of the CEV model are virtually indistinguishable.

Implied binomial trees do slightly worse, with a median error of 22 cents. This is surprising, because the implied binomial tree nests the Black–Scholes formula if the ending probability distribution is lognormal. The implied probability distributions are not perfectly lognormal, however. The method used to derive them fits the implied probability distribution to match midpoint option prices that do not necessarily observe a flat smile, even in the precrash period. Although a flat smile usually prices all options within their bid/ask spreads, Jackwerth and Rubinstein (1996) argue in favor of using midpoints for numerical reasons in deriving the implied distributions.[11] Finally, the implied distribution has to be resampled onto a log spacing that introduces a small error in the order of a few cents.[12]

Similarly, the stochastic volatility model also converges to the Black–Scholes model in the precrash period.

The postcrash period produces more interesting results. Black–Scholes does the worst, with a median error of 125 cents. The relative and absolute smile predictions are best, with median errors of 51 and 54 cents, respectively. The implied binomial tree holds the middle ground with a median error of 78 cents.

The performance of the CEV depends strongly on restriction in the choice of the ρ parameter, with median errors of 110 (restricted) and 57 cents (unrestricted). Limiting ρ to values between 0 and 1 causes the CEV to come in second-to-last, while the unrestricted version is a relatively good model apart from its high standard deviation. The unrestricted version of the CEV model is questionable on economic grounds, however.

Three lines of argument support a restriction on the parameter ρ. First, several empirical studies using S&P 500 index returns find that estimates of ρ are mostly confined to the interval between 0 and 1.[13] We note that such estimates stem from the actual return process and not the risk-neutral process, which we use in our option-pricing model.[14]

Second, Bates (1996) argues that for stock market indices it is inconceivable that there is a significant probability of bankruptcy; with ρ sufficiently negative, however, this is possible. Let us consider $\rho = -4$, which is the closest integer to the mean optimal unrestricted CEV coefficient in the postcrash period. For three scenarios of interest rates, dividend yields, volatilities, and times-to-expiration that are typical for that period, the CEV model suggests a probability of bankruptcy for the S&P 500 (index = 0) over the next 4–7 months of between 2 and 304 out of 10,000. Typical values tend to lie in the center of this range and seem rather high, given the implication that the whole U.S. economy would be destroyed.

Third, He and Leland (1993) derive a condition that any stochastic diffusion process of asset prices has to meet for the economy to be in equilibrium. They assume a pure exchange economy with dynamically complete asset markets where investors maximize their expected utility of future consumption and have nonrandom exogenous income. This condition will hold if $\rho = 1$, which corresponds to the Black–Scholes process. The condition will also hold if, unrealistically, the expected return of the market equals plus or minus the risk-free return. If we accept this as a viable approximation of the U.S. economy, we must conclude that the CEV process is not compatible with that economy in general.

LOOKING BACKWARD (KNOWN TERM STRUCTURE OF AT-THE-MONEY VOLATILITIES)

Continuing the test of relation (1), we still investigate otherwise similar options but with different times-to-expiration. We again look backward in that we price shorter-term options using several methods based on concurrent longer-term option prices. In this case, we want to incorporate a known term structure of at-the-money volatilities. We can then assess how much failure of the models to incorporate the term structure of implied volatilities contributes to overall pricing errors. To do this, we need generalized versions of the models.

Alternative Option-Pricing Models

We generalize the Black–Scholes model by assuming a flat volatility smile that is determined solely by the at-the-money implied volatility of the shorter-term options, which we assume is known. For the relative smile prediction, we again assume that the implied volatility for identical levels of moneyness remains the same as for the longer-term options, but we also shift the smile vertically by a constant amount so that we match the implied volatility of the shorter-term at-the-money option. For the absolute smile prediction, we shift the smile vertically by a constant amount in a similar way.

To generalize use of the CEV model, we keep the shape parameter ρ constant, as determined by the best fit of the longer-term options, but allow the volatility parameter σ' to be chosen optimally so as to fit the shorter-term at-the-money option. Then we price the other shorter-term options using the adjusted parameters.

In order to incorporate a known term structure of volatilities into an implied binomial tree, we use the generalized binomial tree as described in Jackwerth (1997). We can use the same three-step algorithm used for the implied binomial tree, but a generalized binomial tree allows for arbitrary weight functions (instead of the linear weight function associated with a standard implied binomial tree) while preserving no-arbitrage in the interior of the tree. Matching of the volatility term structure is achieved by choosing

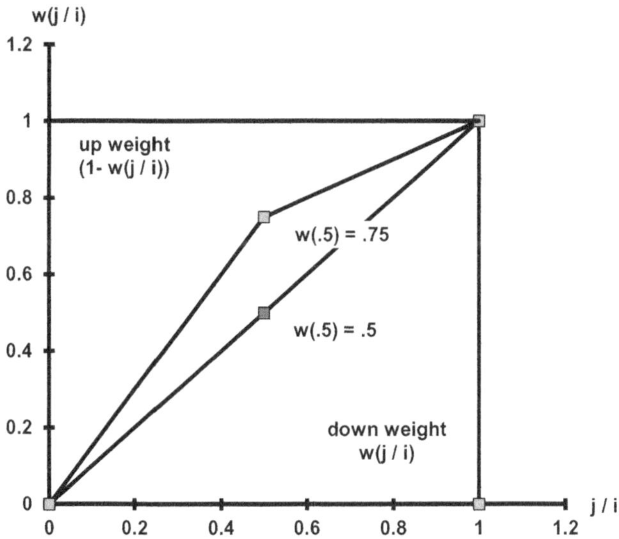

Fig. 3. Piecewise Linear Weight Function for a Generalized Binomial Tree. *Notes*: In a standard binomial tree, the weight function is the diagonal of the unit square. A generalized binomial is parameterized by any continuous function across the corners. Here, we use a piecewise linear specification that is determined by the weight at the halfway point.

a weight $w(0.5)$ between 0 and 1. We know that $w(0)=0$ and $w(1)=1$. We then use a piecewise-linear function to fit through the three points. This is illustrated for $w(0.5)=0.75$ in Fig. 3.

We can now select a weight $w(0.5)$ that causes the at-the-money shorter-term option value to equal its observed market price. Then, all other shorter-term options are priced using this optimal $w(0.5)$.

Finally, for the stochastic volatility model, we calibrate the parameters to the longer-term options, and then reset the parameter for the current volatility of the stock price $v(t)$ to fit the shorter-term at-the-money option.

Empirical Results and Discussion

Tables 4 and 5 show the pricing errors for the alternative models: Table 4 the precrash pricing errors and Table 5 the postcrash pricing errors.

Assuming a known term structure of at-the-money volatilities now means that the at-the-money shorter-term option is properly priced. The median error for the Black–Scholes formula improves to 13 cents. The relative and absolute smile predictions perform nearly as well, with median errors of 15 and 16 cents, respectively. For the CEV model, the ρ parameter is 1 for most days, again. Both the restricted and the unrestricted CEV model therefore converge to the Black–Scholes formula.

Table 4. Pricing Errors for Precrash Period (Known Term Structure of At-the-Money Volatilities).

Pricing Method	Cent Error		
	Mean	Median	SD
Black–Scholes formula	16	13	12
Relative smile prediction	17	15	12
Absolute smile prediction	18	16	12
CEV restricted formula	15	12	11
CEV unrestricted formula	15	12	11
Generalized binomial tree	28	21	21
Stochastic volatility	17	15	14

Notes: This table uses seven methods to price shorter-term options, given concurrent longer-term option prices. The sample covers the pre-crash period from April 2, 1986, through October 16, 1987, where there are 360 observations.

Table 5. Pricing Errors for Postcrash Period (Known Term Structure of At-the-Money Volatilities).

Pricing Method	Cent Error		
	Mean	Median	SD
Black–Scholes formula	124	121	40
Relative smile prediction	43	42	17
Absolute smile prediction	43	42	17
CEV restricted formula	102	101	38
CEV unrestricted formula	43	40	26
Generalized binomial tree	42	38	27
Stochastic volatility	51	43	58

Notes: This table uses seven methods to price shorter-term options, given concurrent longer-term option prices. The sample covers the post-crash period from June 1, 1988, through December 31, 1994, where there are 1,278 observations.

The generalized binomial tree produces a negligible improvement in the median error compared to the unknown term structure of volatilities. The reason for this disappointing performance in the precrash period is closely related to the problem of fitting the longer-term options too well, and thus implying distributions that are not perfectly lognormal. Adjusting the trees according to these distributions to match the shorter-term at-the-money option can result in excessive adjustments that improve the fit for some of the shorter-term options (particularly the at-the-money and near-the-money options) and harm the fit of other options. Thus, the overall effect is either no improvement or even worse performance compared to the assumption of an unknown term structure of volatilities.

The stochastic volatility model also converges to the Black–Scholes model and performs almost as well. In the precrash period overall, where the implied probability distributions are about lognormal and the volatility smiles almost flat, using the Black–Scholes formula remains the superior method.

In the postcrash period, assuming a known term structure of at-the-money volatilities, the Black–Scholes formula is again the worst-performing model, with a median error of 121 cents. The relative and absolute smile predictions again do well, with median errors of 42 cents in both cases.

Again, the restricted CEV does almost as poorly as the Black–Scholes model with 101 cents. The unrestricted CEV does much better, with a median error of 40 cents, but the objections to a negative parameter ρ still apply. Generalized binomial trees do very well, with median error 38 cents, and so does the stochastic volatility model with 43 cents.

Note that the better models now perform very similarly to one another. This is an indication that, after adjusting for the level of the shorter-term smile, there is little advantage in one model over the others.

We conclude that the observed term structure of volatilities is more complex than the models allow. From the present research, it is not clear if a better model of the term structure of volatility can remain deterministic, or if extension to a stochastic volatility structure is needed.

LOOKING FORWARD (UNKNOWN TERM STRUCTURE OF VOLATILITIES)

The second empirical test investigates the same options but at different times (relation (2)). Here, we evaluate forecasts of smiles 10 or 30 days in the future. We focus first on incorporating information from the current longer-term option prices. The results from incorporating the shorter-term options turn out to be very similar.

Alternative Option-Pricing Models

For the purpose of forecasting, we use the flat, relative, and absolute smiles as first defined. All smile predictions are based on the current longer-term options, and after waiting for 10 and 30 days we then measure the prediction errors. For the CEV models, we use the first approach again. After estimating the parameters ρ and σ' from the longer-term options, and potentially restricting ρ, we use these estimates for our smile forecasts.

We build the implied binomial trees based on the longer-term options. We then wait 10 or 30 days, and we assess which node (i, j) in the tree is closest to the index level on that future day. If we can now determine the risk-neutral probability distribution, conditional on being at node (i, j), then we can price options expiring at the end of the remaining tree.

There is an easy way to obtain the conditional probabilities. First, we go out for, say, 10 days into the future, and find the closest underlying asset value on the step of the tree closest in time to the observed asset value. The corresponding node (i, j) is the future node. Due to coarseness of the tree, the time and asset value at node (i, j) are likely to be a bit off the observed values. To correct for this, we update the observed option prices by assuming that the implied volatilities remain constant for small changes in the asset value and time. Then we choose the asset value to be exactly the one at node (i, j) in the tree and the time to be exactly the one of the selected step i. In addition, we use the interest rate and dividend yield that we use for the original tree. Given all this information and the implied volatilities of the observed options, we now calculate hypothetical option prices (with slightly different time-to-expiration and stock price), which replace the observed options.

The final step is to evaluate the options according to the tree. Here we need conditional probabilities (P') which we obtain by setting $P'_{i,j} = 1$ since we know with probability one that in 10 days we arrived at that node (i, j). We can easily calculate the probability of an up-move and down-move from node (i, j) as:

$$p_{i,j} = w_{i+1,j+1} \frac{P_{i+1,j+1}}{P_{i,j}} \tag{9}$$

where $P_{i,j}$ = probability of moving up from node (i, j) and $(1 - P'_{i,j})$ = probability of moving down from node (i, j).

We can then recursively develop a tree of the conditional probabilities P'as we go forward from node (i, j):

$$P'_{k,l} = P'_{k-1,l}(1 - p_{k-1,l}) \quad \text{for } k = 0 \tag{10}$$

$$P'_{k,l} = P'_{k-1,l}(1 - p_{k-1,l}) + P'_{k-1,l-1} p_{k-1,l-1} \quad \text{for } k = 1, \ldots, l-1 \tag{11}$$

$$P'_{k,l} = P'_{k-1,l-1} p_{k-1,l-1} \quad \text{for } k = l \tag{12}$$

The conditional probabilities at the end of the tree $(= P'_{n,1})$ are then used to price the set of observed options through:

$$C(K_m) = \frac{\sum_{l=0}^{n} P'_{n,l} \max[0; S_{n,l} - K_m]}{r^{t(n-i)/n}} \tag{13}$$

where K_m = strike price of the observed option m; $r = 1 +$ interest rate; t = time-to-expiration of the original tree; and i = step corresponding to the forecasting node (i, j).

Note that this procedure can adjust properly for small deviations in time, especially since a 200-step tree corresponds to about one day per step. The change in the index from one level to the next, even in a 200-step tree, however, can be coarse enough to affect the results when we update the observed smile by setting the index to its closest match observed in the tree.

There is an elegant way around this problem. Rather than building a tree of conditional probabilities starting at the closest index level, we start the tree of conditional probabilities at two nodes simultaneously. We choose the nodes just above and below the observed index level. Next we assign conditional probabilities $P'_{i,j+1}$ and $P'_{i,j}$ to the upper and lower node (summing to one), which causes the expected index level to coincide with the observed index level. At this point we unravel the conditional probability tree to the end. This method proves to be much more stable than the original version.

For the stochastic volatility model, we again calibrate the parameters κ^*, θ^*, $v(t)$, ρ, and σ to the longer-term options. We then wait for 10 or 30 days and use those parameters to forecast the option prices at those times.

Empirical Results and Discussion

Sometimes it is not possible to wait for 10 or 30 days because there are no data available. In this case, for the shorter wait we search for the closest wait to 10 days between 7 and 13 days; for the longer wait we search for the closest wait to 30 days between 20 and 40 days. Tables 6 and 7 exhibit the precrash and postcrash pricing errors for the various models based on knowing current longer-term option prices only.

Table 6 confirms the result that in the precrash world with about flat smiles, the lognormal Black–Scholes model performs well, with a 38 cent error for 10 day predictions and with a 72 cent error for 30 day predictions. All other models collapse into the nested special case of the Black–Scholes model.

In the postcrash period in Table 7, the Black–Scholes model and the restricted CEV model perform worst, with 172 and 136 cent errors for 10 day predictions and 172 and 145 cent errors for 30 day predictions. The implied trees trail the relative smile, the unrestricted CEV, and the stochastic volatility models, which perform equally well. The best model is the absolute smile, with a 44 cent error for 10 day predictions and a 63 error for 30 day predictions. To investigate this rather surprising result, we graph results for four models in Fig. 4.

We can see that the absolute smile model incorporates the fact that index level and implied volatility are negatively correlated. Thus, as the index goes up over the next 30 days, the absolute smile updates the future at-the-money volatility with the current volatility of an option with the same strike

Table 6. Pricing Errors for Precrash Period (Unknown Term Structure of Volatilities).

Forecasting Method	Cent Error		
	Mean	Median	SD
Black–Scholes formula	50 (81)	38 (72)	36 (54)
Relative smile prediction	51 (82)	42 (71)	34 (52)
Absolute smile prediction	52 (84)	42 (73)	35 (54)
CEV restricted formula	49 (80)	40 (71)	35 (53)
CEV unrestricted formula	50 (80)	40 (72)	35 (53)
Implied binomial tree	54 (87)	44 (69)	40 (64)
Stochastic volatility	50 (81)	40 (71)	34 (54)

Notes: This table uses seven methods to predict future option prices, given current longer-term option prices and the future underlying asset price. The cent errors correspond to evaluations of options closest to 10 (+/−3) days into the future, the cent errors in parentheses to evaluations of options closest to 30 (+/−10) days into the future. The sample period covers the pre-crash period from April 2, 1986, through September 16, 1987, where there are 363 (363) observations.

Table 7. Pricing Errors for Postcrash Period (Unknown Term Structure of Volatilities).

Forecasting Method	Cent Error		
	Mean	Median	SD
Black–Scholes formula	175 (181)	172 (172)	58 (71)
Relative smile prediction	73 (102)	56 (78)	61 (83)
Absolute smile prediction	56 (76)	44 (63)	43 (55)
CEV restricted formula	139 (154)	136 (145)	54 (68)
CEV unrestricted formula	74 (102)	56 (77)	60 (83)
Implied binomial tree	83 (116)	67 (97)	62 (79)
Stochastic volatility	75 (111)	57 (83)	66 (132)

Notes: This table uses seven methods to predict future option prices, given the current longer-term option prices and the future underlying asset price. The cent errors correspond to evaluations of options closest to 10 (+/−3) days into the future, the cent errors in parentheses to evaluations of options closest to 30 (+/−10) days into the future. The sample period covers the post-crash period from June 1, 1988, through November 30, 1994, where there are 1,553 (1,553) observations.

price as the future stock price. Such an option is currently an out-of-the-money call option. Its implied volatility tends to be lower than the current at-the-money volatility because of the negative slope of the typical post-crash smile.

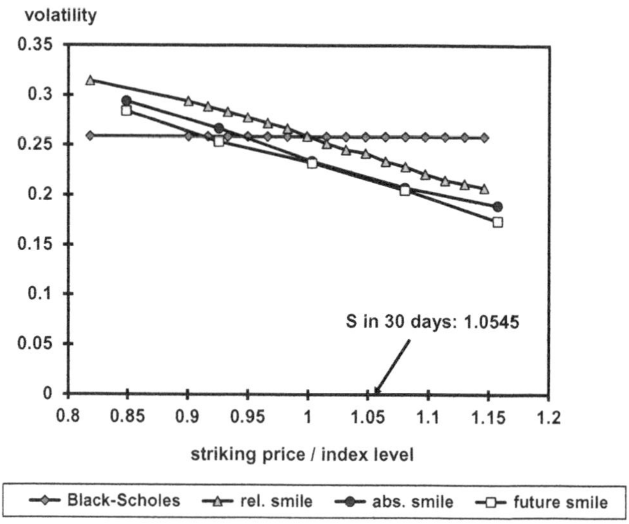

Fig. 4. Observed Future Smile and Predictions – Black–Scholes, Relative Smile, and Absolute Smile Models. *Notes*: For options with time-to-expiration of 150 days on October 16, 1990, we graph the predicted future smiles on November 15, 1990, 30 days into the future. The predictions are based on the Black–Scholes, the relative smile, and the absolute smile model. We also graph the future smile as we observe it 30 days later.

We can tie the CEV model nicely into this framework. We have established already that the restricted CEV model yields (and predicts) smiles similar to the Black–Scholes model. In addition, regressing the error on the unrestricted CEV forecasts against the relative smile model yields a correlation of 0.997. Thus, those two models behave almost identically.

Incorporating Known Current Shorter-Term Option Prices

The initial notion was that we could improve our forecasts of option prices by extending the models to incorporate both current shorter-term and longer-term option prices. For the Black–Scholes formula and the relative and absolute smile models, we combine the shorter-term and longer-term implied volatilities in order to find the forward term structure of implied volatilities, and we base our forecasts on this term structure. For the CEV and the stochastic volatility models, the parameters are chosen so as to minimize the pricing error of the shorter-term and longer-term options simultaneously. These optimal parameters are then used for the forecasts.

We again use the generalized binomial tree, where we match the shorter-term options by minimizing the pricing error through choosing a weight $w(0.5)$ between 0 and 1.[15] We can then use the conditional probability tree to forecast option prices and measure the pricing error.

It turns out that adding the information incorporated in shorter-term options does not help us in forecasting future option prices. The results are 1–4 cents worse than the pricing errors reported in Tables 6 and 7, where we use only the longer-term options. The only model that uses the additional information in a meaningful way is the generalized binomial tree in the postcrash period, which drops from an error of 67 cents for 10-day predictions to an error of 59 cents.

LOOKING FORWARD (KNOWN TERM STRUCTURE OF AT-THE-MONEY VOLATILITIES)

To continue the test of relation (2), we investigate again the same options but at different times. We then incorporate a known term structure of at-the-money future volatilities. This allows us to untangle the pricing errors related to the models from the impact of the shift in future at-the-money implied volatility. We use a simple vertical shift to each model's forecasted volatility smile to fit the future at-the-money implied volatility correctly.

Tables 8 and 9 present the pricing errors for the alternative models: Table 8 the precrash pricing errors and Table 9 the postcrash pricing errors.

For the precrash period reported in Table 8, assuming a known term structure of future at-the-money volatilities, all methods perform very similarly. Pricing errors are around 21 cents for 10-day and 30-day predictions.

More interesting is the postcrash period reported in Table 9. The Black–Scholes and the restricted CEV model are predictably the worst-performing models. All other models, except for the generalized binomial tree, perform similarly well, with 22–27 cent errors for the 10-day predictions and 30–33 cent errors for the 30-day predictions.

We also investigate the median pricing error outside the bid/ask spread, where we still assume that we know the future at-the-money implied volatility. We do not report the details, as all these errors are rather small: 7 cents precrash and 12 cents postcrash for the better-performing models. This is again an indication that, after incorporating the level of the future

Table 8. Pricing Errors for Precrash Period (Known Term Structure of Future At-the-Money Volatilities).

Forecasting Method	Cent Error		
	Mean	Median	SD
Black–Scholes formula	21 (20)	19 (18)	11 (10)
Relative smile prediction	26 (26)	22 (23)	14 (14)
Absolute smile prediction	27 (28)	23 (24)	15 (16)
CEV restricted formula	22 (21)	19 (19)	12 (11)
CEV unrestricted formula	22 (21)	19 (19)	13 (11)
Generalized binomial tree	24 (24)	21 (21)	13 (13)
Stochastic volatility	24 (23)	20 (20)	13 (13)

Notes: This table uses seven methods to predict future option prices, given current longer-term option prices, the future at-the-money volatility, and the future underlying asset price. The cent errors correspond to evaluations of options closest to 10 (+/−3) days into the future, the cent errors in parentheses to evaluations of options closest to 30 (+/−10) days into the future. The sample period covers the pre-crash period from April 2, 1986, through September 16, 1987, where there are 353 (353) observations.

Table 9. Pricing Errors for Postcrash Period (Known Term Structure of Future At-the-Money Volatilities).

Forecasting Method	Cent Error		
	Mean	Median	SD
Black–Scholes formula	163 (156)	167 (159)	45 (43)
Relative smile prediction	30 (37)	23 (31)	24 (23)
Absolute smile prediction	30 (37)	23 (31)	24 (23)
CEV restricted formula	125 (122)	131 (128)	41 (39)
CEV unrestricted formula	32 (37)	27 (33)	21 (19)
Generalized binomial tree	34 (53)	28 (51)	24 (27)
Stochastic volatility	32 (38)	22 (30)	31 (49)

Notes: This table uses seven methods to predict future option prices, given current longer-term option prices, the future at-the-money volatility, and the future underlying asset price. The cent errors correspond to evaluations of options closest to 10 (+/−3) days into the future, the cent errors in parentheses to evaluations of options closest to 30 (+/−10) days into the future. The sample period covers the post-crash period from June 1, 1988, through November 30, 1994, where there are 1,267 (1,267) observations.

smile, there is little advantage in one model over another. It seems that most models can generate the general shape of the smiles equally well, except for the rigid Black–Scholes and the restricted CEV models. All models seem to struggle with getting the level of the smile right, however.

This work suggests that we could improve the performance of all option-pricing models if we were able to develop good forecasts of future implied volatility. Some preliminary studies reveal several problems.

Implied volatilities are very persistent, so we investigate models in levels and in differences of implied volatilities. The most important effect is the negative relation to log returns, but this effect is already captured in the better-performing models; they all build in the negative correlation between the stock price and volatility.

We also investigate the explanatory power of various macroeconomic factors such as default risk (credit spread), change in the term structure of interest rates, inflation, industrial production, and consumption growth. None of these factors has explanatory power. Nor do NYSE trading volume or interest rates.

Finally, we use time-to-expiration, past index levels (1, 30, and 60 days), past implied volatility levels (1, 30, and 60 days), past log returns (30 and 60 days), and day-of-the-week dummies. Again, none of these variables has explanatory power. Neither does it help to take logarithms of times-to-expiration, index levels, or implied volatilities.

This suggests an "efficient markets results" for implied volatilities. Today's implied volatility seems to incorporate all the information publicly available at that time. Such result, while making it difficult to improve on option-pricing models, does make sense economically; implied volatilities are nothing but scaled option prices, and option prices should not be predictable in efficient markets.

CONCLUSION

We have asked what we can learn from option prices about the risk-neutral stochastic process of the S&P 500 index. This question has been partially addressed by others, but we believe we are the first to compare implied tree models with parametric models and naïve trader rules and for pre- and postcrash subperiods.

In our first test, we choose the parameters of nine different option valuation models to best fit the observed market prices of longer-term options. We then price shorter-term options using those parameters, assuming the term structure of at-the-money volatilities is unknown. If the term structure of volatilities is known, we allow one parameter to be chosen so that the at-the-money shorter-term option is priced properly. In a second test, we calibrate our models to the longer-term options and predict 10- and 30-day future volatility smiles. We rerun the test where we assume that we know the future at-the-money implied volatility.

First, in the precrash period, all models match the performance of the Black–Scholes model. The reason is that the volatility smiles were almost flat pre-crash, and the additional flexibility of the more complex models is not needed.

Second, in the postcrash period, the naïve trader rules perform best. In the backward-looking test the relative smile model has a median error of 51 cents, and the absolute smile model an error of 54 cents. In the forward-looking test, the absolute smile model has a median error of 44 cents. As the standard deviation of these errors is rather large, it is difficult to distinguish the different models economically. This could well be why options traders use the naïve methods instead of the more complicated academic models.

Third, all models, except the Black–Scholes and the restricted CEV model, perform very similarly. The incorporation of the inverse relation between index level and volatility achieves this superior performance. Beyond the models, however, there is considerable information incorporated in the level of the smile, as all models improve significantly when we add information about the at-the-money implied volatility of the shorter-term or the future option. It would seem fruitful to devote more research to incorporation of future at-the-money implied volatility into option-pricing models. Our attempts at modeling future at-the-money implied volatility suggest an "efficient markets result" which could make it impossible to forecast these future volatilities. Such result fundamentally limits the possibilities to improve on option-pricing models.

NOTES

1. Li and Pearson (2008) repeated the here presented research very faithfully while updating some of the option pricing models.

2. The implied volatility (σ^*) causes the Black–Scholes formula to accurately price the option in the market: $C = Sd^{-t}N(x) - Kr^{-t}N(x - \sigma^*\sqrt{t})$, where S is the index level, d the dividend yield, t the time, $N(\bullet)$ the cumulative normal distribution, $x = (\ln(Sd^{-t}/Kr^{-t})/\sigma^*\sqrt{t}) + \frac{1}{2}\sigma^*\sqrt{t}$, and K the strike price.

3. The methods differ most in the tails, where they tend to agree on the *total* tail probability but distribute this probability differently. We avoid this difficulty by focusing on the center of the distribution and not using far-away-from-the-money

option prices. Further evidence on the performance of different methods is surveyed in Jackwerth (1999).

4. A survey is in Jackwerth (1999).

5. See Jackwerth and Rubinstein (1996) for a more detailed description of the data.

6. See Reiner (1998) who analyzes single-factor models that exhibit such "sticky delta" or "sticky vol" behavior. He finds that such processes would not be diffusion processes, which could cause problems in hedging such options.

7. The typical smile is u-shaped, so we will introduce some bias in the far-away-from-the-money options which will be undervalued. While the effect should not be too large as those options have low option premia, it stacks the tests somewhat against the naïve methods.

8. We prefer the implied binomial tree of Rubinstein (1994) to the Derman and Kani (1994) tree because it is less susceptible to numerical instabilities resulting from negative probabilities within the tree. Even the improvements by Barle and Cakici (1998) do not eliminate all the instabilities of the Derman–Kani tree.

9. Some of the variable names are used in other models too, but we wanted to keep them as in the original model.

10. If any model cannot be evaluated on a given date, that date is eliminated from the sample. Thus, the number of observations for the two periods varies from table to table.

11. Since we are fitting midpoints, we have to be concerned about overfitting. Therefore, we also use implied probability distributions with a lower penalty parameter that produces smoother distributions with less fit. Finally, we use the (very smooth and unimodal) probability distribution implied in the CEV model after fitting the CEV model to observed option prices. The errors do not change significantly with the degree of smoothness in the probability distributions, so we use the original implied probability distributions throughout.

12. One further concern is that the number of known options could influence the error since each incremental option embodies some additional information that could be used in implying option prices. Empirically, we find that the error is virtually uncorrelated with the number of known options.

13. Beckers (1980), Gibbons and Jacklin (1988), and Christie (1982).

14. See Jackwerth (2000) for more empirical evidence that the risk-neutral process can be quite different from the actual process.

15. An extension to this method is to choose two points on the weight function, say, $w(0.33)$ and $w(0.66)$, and again get the best fit with the shorter-term options. This additional complexity of the weight function does not improve the performance of the binomial trees, so we use the simple adjustment $w(0.5)$ throughout.

ACKNOWLEDGMENTS

The authors gratefully acknowledge a research grant from the Q-Group. For helpful comments the authors would like to thank an anonymous referee, David Brown, Jim Hodder, David Modest and seminar participants at the AFA meetings 1996, Berkeley Program in Finance 1998, and at Erasmus, Konstanz, Warwick, Dartmouth, Iowa, UBC, Madison, and Oxford.

REFERENCES

Aït-Sahalia, Y., & Lo, A. W. (1998). Nonparametric estimation of state-price densities implied in financial asset prices. *Journal of Finance*, *53*(2), 499–547.

Bakshi, G., Cao, C., & Chen, Z. (1997). Empirical performance of alternative option pricing models. *Journal of Finance*, *52*(5), 2003–2049.

Barle, S., & Cakici, N. (1998). How to grow a smiling tree. *Journal of Financial Engineering*, *7*(2), 127–146.

Bates, D. S. (1996). Testing option pricing models. In G. S. Maddala & C. R. Rao (Eds.), *Handbook of statistics*. Statistical Methods in Finance (Vol. 15, pp. 567–611). Amsterdam: North Holland.

Bates, D. S. (2000). Post-'87 crash fears in the S&P 500 futures option market. *Journal of Econometrics*, *94*(1–2), 181–238.

Beckers, S. (1980). The constant elasticity of variance model and its implications for option pricing. *Journal of Finance*, *35*(3), 661–673.

Black, F., & Scholes, M. (1973). Pricing of options and corporate liabilities. *Journal of Political Economy*, *81*(3), 637–659.

Christie, A. A. (1982). The stochastic behavior of common stock variances. *Journal of Financial Economics*, *10*(4), 407–432.

Cox, J. C. (1996). The constant elasticity of variance option pricing model. *Journal of Portfolio Management*, *23*(Special Issue), 15–17.

Dennis, P., & Mayhew, S. (2000). *Implied volatility smiles: Evidence from options on individual equities*. Working Paper. University of Virginia, Charlotteville, VA.

Derman, E., & Kani, I. (1994). Riding on a smile. *Risk*, *7*(2), 32–39.

Duan, J.-C. (1995). The GARCH option pricing model. *Mathematical Finance*, *5*(1), 13–32.

Dumas, B., Fleming, J., & Whaley, R. E. (1998). Implied volatility functions: Empirical tests. *Journal of Finance*, *53*(6), 2059–2106.

Dupire, B. (1994). Pricing with a smile. *Risk*, *7*(1), 18–20.

Gibbons, M., & Jacklin, C. (1988). *CEV diffusion estimation*. Working Paper. Stanford University, Stanford, CA.

He, H., & Leland, H. (1993). On equilibrium asset price processes. *The Review of Financial Studies*, *6*(3), 593–619.

Heston, S. L. (1993). A closed-form solution for options with stochastic volatility with applications to bond and currency options. *Review of Financial Studies*, *6*(2), 327–343.

Heston, S. L., & Nandi, S. (2000). A closed-form GARCH option valuation model. *Review of Financial Studies*, *13*(3), 585–625.

Jackwerth, J. C. (1997). Generalized binomial trees. *Journal of Derivatives*, *5*(2), 7–17.

Jackwerth, J. C. (1999). Option implied risk-neutral distributions and implied binomial trees: A literature review. *Journal of Derivatives*, *7*(2), 66–82.

Jackwerth, J. C. (2000). Recovering risk aversion from option prices and realized returns. *Review of Financial Studies*, *13*(2), 433–451.

Jackwerth, J. C., & Rubinstein, M. (1996). Recovering probability distributions from option prices. *Journal of Finance*, *51*(5), 1611–1631.

Kelly, M. A. (1994). *The U.S. equity market has become more diversified*. New York, NY: J. P. Morgan Equity Derivative Strategies.

Li, M., & Pearson, N. D. (2008). A horse race among competing option pricing models using S&P 500 index options. Working Paper, Georgia Institute of Technology and University of Illinois at Urbana-Champaign, IL.

Merton, R. C. (1973). An intertemporal capital asset pricing model. *Econometrica*, *41*(5), 867–887.

Merton, R. C. (1976). Option pricing when underlying stock returns are discontinuous. *Journal of Financial Economics*, *3*(1–2), 125–144.

Osborne, M. F. M. (1959). Brownian motion in the stock market. *Operations Research*, *7*(2), 145–173.

Reiner, E. (1998). Volatility rules and implied processes. Paper presented at the RISK conference on New Advances in Derivatives Modelling and Analysis. Warburg Dillon Read LLC, UBC, Equity Structured Products, New York, NY.

Rubinstein, M. (1983). Displaced diffusion option pricing. *Journal of Finance*, *38*(1), 213–217.

Rubinstein, M. (1985). Nonparametric tests of alternative option pricing models using all reported trades and quotes on the 30 most active CBOE option classes from August 23, 1976 through August 31, 1978. *Journal of Finance*, *40*(2), 455–480.

Rubinstein, M. (1994). Implied binomial trees. *Journal of Finance*, *49*(3), 771–818.

Tompkins, R. G. (2001). Implied volatility surfaces: Uncovering the regularities for options on financial futures. *The European Journal of Finance*, *7*(3), 198–230.

THE PRICING KERNEL PUZZLE: RECONCILING INDEX OPTION DATA AND ECONOMIC THEORY

David P. Brown and Jens Carsten Jackwerth

ABSTRACT

The pricing kernel puzzle of Jackwerth (2000) concerns the fact that the empirical pricing kernel implied in S&P 500 index options and index returns is not monotonically decreasing in wealth as standard economic theory would suggest. Thus, those options are currently priced in a way such that any risk-averse investor would increase his/her utility by trading in them. We provide a representative agent model where volatility is a function of a second momentum state variable. This model is capable of generating the empirical patterns in the pricing kernel, albeit only for parameter constellations that are not typically observed in the real world.

The Capital Asset Pricing Model (CAPM) of William Sharpe and the option-pricing models of Fisher Black, Robert Merton, and Myron Scholes were seminal in developing our understanding of the pricing of financial assets; these works sparked a firestorm of research by economic theorists and empiricists. Despite the fact that the CAPM was developed to price equity shares while the option-pricing models were developed for options, these two sets of models share a common feature, namely a state-price

Derivative Securities Pricing and Modelling
Contemporary Studies in Economic and Financial Analysis, Volume 94, 155–183

ISSN: 1569-3759/doi:10.1108/S1569-3759(2012)0000094009

density (SPD), which allows us to price all securities. Early researchers understood the original works as distinct theories. The authors of the option models employed different assumptions and logic than Sharpe, and explained their results using a disparate set of arguments. However, it is now understood that asset-pricing models generally – a set that includes the CAPM, option-pricing models, and the work of Debreu (1972), Rubinstein (1976), and Cox, Ingersoll, and Ross (1985) – can be interpreted using a single, simple calculation. An asset price is equivalent to an expectation based on an SPD.[1]

Because of its central role in pricing assets, the SPD now has many uses. For example, Campa and Chang (1998) describe how central banks use estimates of SPDs to measure the credibility of exchange rate commitments and Jackwerth (1999) lists numerous other applications. Further use for SPDs is in risk management by banks, trading firms, and portfolio managers. Because an appropriate hedge position – say a position in an option – requires an assessment of the random changes in the value of the option, risk managers often rely on pricing models to evaluate the hedge. In turn, accurate valuation of the hedge requires precise estimates of the SPD.

Not surprisingly, researchers have taken great interest in estimating SPDs. An often-used approach relies on a model of a representative agent, and requires an estimate of the parameters of the agent's utility function. This is typically accomplished by fitting the optimality conditions of the agent's utility maximization to a set of asset returns and other data, for example, per capita consumption. Two of many examples are Brown and Gibbons (1985) and Hansen and Singleton (1983). An alternative method is the subject of this research. This method draws on a cross-section of options with different strike prices and does not impose strong assumptions on the utility of a representative agent. In fact, this method does not even require that a representative agent exists.

Breeden and Litzenberger (1978) first showed within a theoretical setting, given a set of options on aggregate consumption dense in the set of possible strike prices, that an SPD could be calculated exactly from the option prices. As Cox et al. (1985) demonstrate, this SPD may be used to price all securities. Rubinstein (1994) and Jackwerth and Rubinstein (1996) provide empirical procedures for estimating an SPD when a finite number of options exist instead of a dense set. They also extend the interpretations of Breeden and Litzenberger to the case where options are written on securities or security indices, and not on aggregate consumption. In this case, the SPD estimate is a projection; for example, the SPD obtained from options on an equity index is an empirical projection of the general consumption-based

SPD (discussed by Cox et al., 1985) onto the space of payoffs defined by the index. This implies that the SPD estimated from index option prices cannot be used to price all securities, but it can be used to price all securities in a large and important subset, namely the set of options and other securities derived from the index payoffs.

There is now a large literature documenting estimates of SPDs derived from various options markets, for example, foreign exchange, interest rates, equities, and equity indices. Some 100 papers on this topic are surveyed in Jackwerth (1999). As the evidence regarding the SPDs has been collected, a puzzle has arisen and was first documented in Ait-Sahalia and Lo (2000), Jackwerth (2000), and Rosenberg and Engle (2002). Estimates of the SPD derived from index options, which are written on the S&P 500 index and comprise the second largest options market in the world, appear to be inconsistent with fundamental assumptions about investor behavior. Specifically, when recent estimates are viewed through the lens of existing asset-pricing theory, they imply that investors behave as if they are risk seeking (and not risk averse) with respect to the risk inherent in the index. This conclusion is inconsistent with one of the fundamental assumptions of the economic theory. The empirical research suggests that the marginal utility of investors trading S&P 500 index portfolios is increasing over an important range of wealth levels and not decreasing in wealth, as economic theory would suggest. We seek to understand this puzzle.

There are several reasons to investigate this puzzle, and to investigate more generally the SPDs for equity indices. A first is that indices such as the S&P 500, DAX, FTSE, Nikkei, and those published by the Center for Research in Security Prices (CRSP) of the University of Chicago represent the large majority of the public equity capital in their respective nations. The S&P 500 index represents roughly 50% of public US equity capital.

Second, the very large market capitalization of broad equity indices has led to a long line of research on their distributional properties. For example, research into the random walk theory of equity price changes has asked if the S&P index returns are predictable. Also, early tests of the CAPM were carried out under the assumption that the value-weighted CRSP index was a good proxy for the entire capital of the US investors. More recent works, for example, by Fama and French (1988) and Poterba and Summers (1988), examine the predictability of a number of stock market indices. By their very nature, SPDs provide information regarding the statistical distribution of index returns.

In the following section, we describe the pricing kernel puzzle in more detail, see also Jackwerth (2004). In the second section, we discuss the literature and find that not many papers address the pricing kernel puzzle at all. Moreover, the few that do also have problems that we detail. We therefore suggest in the third section a novel model based on a representative investor who is faced with a second momentum state variable. The last section concludes. Information concerning the data is contained in the appendix.

FUNDAMENTAL DETERMINANTS OF STATE PRICES

We introduce the SPD by calculating the price of a European option. The option price C is the expectation of the random payoffs received at the option's expiration. Write C as a sum across states,

$$C = \sum_{s} q_s F_s \tag{1}$$

where F_s is the option payoff and q_s is the current Arrow–Debreu state price of a dollar paid in the future state s.[2,3] The sum of the q_s across states is equal to one, so the set of q_s represents a distribution analogous to, but distinct from a market participant's subjective distribution of probabilities of the states. Equilibrium theory relates an SPD to economic fundamentals. Breeden and Litzenberger (1978) and Cox et al. (1985) show that a state price q_s satisfies

$$\frac{q_s}{p_s} = m_s \tag{2}$$

where p_s is the subjective probability assessed by an investor for state s, and m_s is known as the pricing kernel and is proportional to the marginal utility of a representative investor in that state. In a state where the marginal value of an additional dollar is high, the proportional difference between the state price and the subjective probability is high. Conversely, if one observes a state price far below a subjective probability, then the marginal value of a dollar is low in that state.

Within an exchange economy model such as Rubinstein (1976) and Lucas (1978), the pricing kernel is the ratio of marginal utilities of a representative investor. In this case, the value of an option written on the market portfolio is

$$C = \sum_{s} m_s p_s F_s = \sum_{s} \frac{U'(C_s)}{U'(C_0)} p_s F_s \tag{3}$$

where m is a ratio of marginal utilities of future per capita consumptions (C_s) and present per capita consumption (C_0). This insight – that the pricing kernel is proportional to a ratio of marginal utilities – has led numerous authors to investigate the distributions of equity returns and test a variety of alternative specifications of utilities and endowments for the representative agent. One of the first utility functions tried was power utility. Described in detail by Rubinstein (1976) and investigated empirically by Brown and Gibbons (1985) and others, an implication of power utility is that aggregate consumption is proportional to aggregate wealth.[4] In this case, the pricing kernel m is a nonlinear function of the return on the index measured over the life of the option. Furthermore, because the power utility investor is risk averse, m is a monotonically decreasing function of aggregate wealth at the option expiration.

Jackwerth (2000) estimates q and p using data on the S&P 500 index return and option prices from April 2, 1986 to the end of 1995. Details pertaining to the data are in the appendix. Estimates of m are then obtained from Eq. (2). The maximum smoothness method of Jackwerth and Rubinstein (1996) is applied to the option data and an estimate of q is obtained. This method does not require a representative agent to be specified. Multiple options with various strike prices, but all with 31-day lives, are used. Postcrash option prices exhibit so-called implied volatility smiles and skews.[5] For example, researchers often describe the cross-section

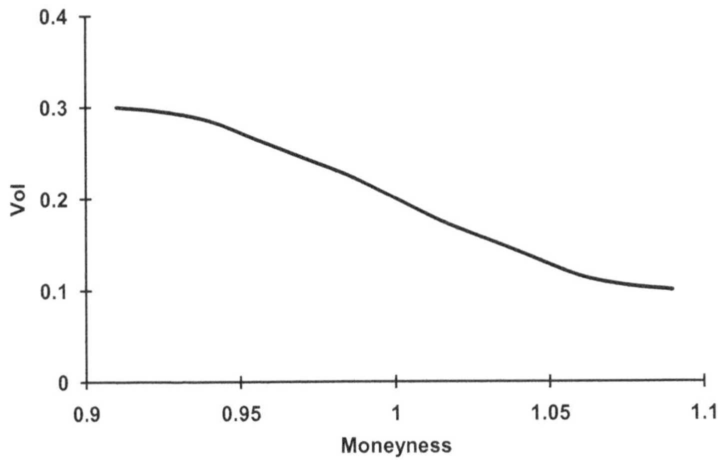

Fig. 1. Empirical Volatility Smile. Typical Post-1987 Stock Market Crash Implied Volatility Smile Across Moneyness (= Ratio of Strike Prices to Index Level).

of options by a plot of implied volatilities against moneyness (= ratio of strike prices to index level) as in Fig. 1.

A consequence of the Black–Scholes option-pricing model is that implied volatilities of all options are equal. If this result held, the plot in Fig. 1 would be flat. Instead, we observe in postcrash index options a "smile," or "skew," or "smirk" depending on your preference in label. The left tail of the plot is substantially above the right.[6] An implication is that the risk-neutral distribution q is left-skewed and leptokurtic, that is, it has a fat left tail and is more peaked in the center than the lognormal distribution.

The subjective probability distribution p is estimated as the historical distribution of four years worth of index returns over 31-day intervals. This is an appropriate method for estimating p provided that investors have rational expectations.[7] Typical estimates of the distributions, say q^* and p^*, are graphed in Fig. 2.

A typical estimate of m, say m^*, appears in Fig. 3 as a function of the return on the S&P 500 index. Rosenberg and Engle (2002) confirm this shape by using a related method, and Jackwerth (2004) provides international evidence for Germany, Japan, and the United Kingdom.[8]

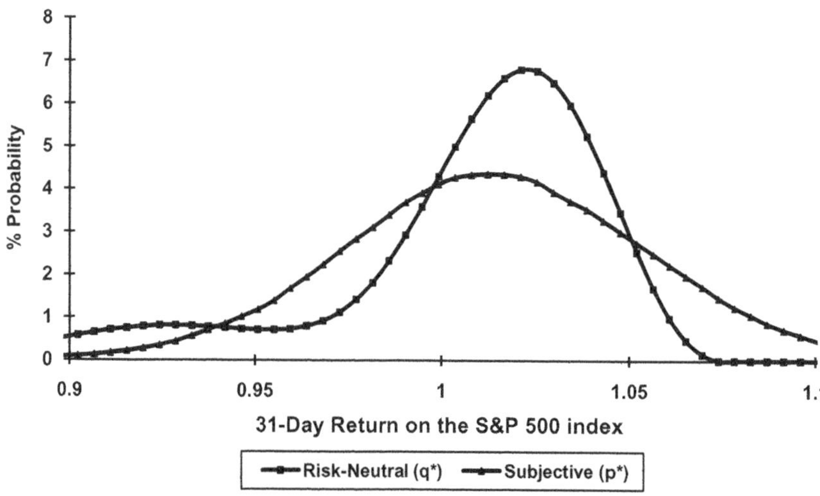

Fig. 2. Risk-Neutral and Subjective Distributions. The Risk-Neutral and the Subjective Return Distributions were Calculated on March 16, 1990. The Subjective Distribution is Approximated by the Smoothed Four-Year Historical Distribution. Returns are Reported as 1 Plus the Rate of Return.

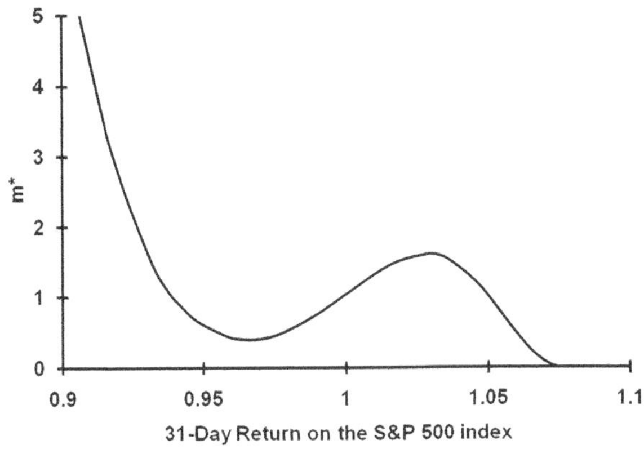

Fig. 3. Empirical Pricing Kernel. Typical Post-1987 Stock Market Crash Implied Pricing Kernel. The Pricing Kernel is Calculated as the Ratio of the Option Implied State-Price Density and the Historical Smoothed Return Distribution. Returns are Reported as 1 Plus the Rate of Return.

For any option-pricing model, the plot of the kernel m (as in Fig. 3) is closely tied to the degree of the smile (like that of Fig. 1).[9] It is important to note that any model used to explain the smile in the S&P 500 index options must provide a kernel m that is consistent with Fig. 3. That is, the kernel implied by a well-constructed model must have a central range that is increasing with the index. The goal of this work is to find models that explain the pricing kernel as shown in Fig. 3. The value of 1 in the center of the horizontal axis represents an ending level of the index (i.e., at the time of option expiration) that is equal to the current level (at the beginning of the 31-day interval). Globally, m^* is a decreasing function of the ending index level. However, for the range from approximately 0.97–1.03, that is, for a range of index levels centered on and within a 3% deviation from the current level, m^* is increasing. This occurs because the proportional difference between the estimates, say q^* and p^*, is increasing over this range, as Eq. (2) implies.

Traditional asset-pricing theory, for example, Rubinstein (1976) and Lucas (1978), assumes that a representative investor exists. It also is common in tests of asset-pricing theories to assume that a market index such as the S&P 500 index represents the aggregate wealth held by this investor. If we make these assumptions, then the empirical m^* of Fig. 3 suggests that the representative investor is locally risk seeking. Over the range of 0.97–1.03, the marginal utility is increasing in wealth, the utility function is convex, and the investor will pay to acquire fair gambles in wealth. Taking this thought experiment to the limit, however, we recognize that our interpretation of m^* in Eqs. (2) and (3) is derived from the optimality conditions of an investor with concave utility. Fig. 3 is inconsistent with these conditions. Hence we arrive at a puzzle. Our estimate m^* is inconsistent with standard approaches in asset pricing.

Our estimation technique does not require the above strong assumptions. To estimate q Jackwerth and Rubinstein (1996) only require that the prices do not offer any arbitrage trading opportunities, while the sample estimator of p requires rational expectations to be valid. Therefore, we interpret m^* somewhat differently. It is a projection of the pricing kernel m onto the space of index returns. This projection is guaranteed to exist, independent of the existence of a representative agent for the economy as a whole. Just the same, m^* may be interpreted as being proportional to the marginal utility of an investor who trades in the S&P 500 index and the options written on the index. In practical terms, m^* represents investors in an index fund that mimics the S&P 500. It is surprising to see that index-fund investors have marginal utilities that are locally increasing in the level of the index.

Before we start modeling this behavior, we first turn to the question if the pricing kernel puzzle might be just spurious. Jackwerth (2000) discusses concerns about the quality of the estimate m^* in detail and has ruled out methodological or data errors. Using simulated data for which we know the true q, a number of different methods generate fairly accurate estimates. Similarly, a variety of standard procedures, both parametric and nonparametric, are used to estimate the historical return distribution p^* and they provide equivalent results. Furthermore, there is no good reason to believe that our index return data is poor. The hump shape of Fig. 3 is also statistically significant since all estimates of m^* in Jackwerth (2000) exhibit it.

A potential further explanation for the existence of the smile is the illiquidity of out-of-the-money options. Options traded in a market with transaction costs or other frictions are priced within an interval determined by these costs. However, the liquidity in the index option market increased 6-fold from an average daily notional volume of \$1.5 billion in 1989 to \$8.5 billion in 1995 (Jackwerth & Rubinstein, 2012), while the steepness of the smile did not change after the 1987 crash. In addition, preliminary research by the authors finds that large trades of out-of-the-money puts have no obvious impact on the steepness of the smile.[10]

Further, while the bid/ask spreads in relation to the option prices are bigger for away-from-the-money options, the hump in the pricing kernel occurs around at-the-money, and is determined by the at-the-money options. Hentschel (2003) suffers from the same criticism when he suggests that option quotes are distributed symmetrically around some true value and are truncated at the intrinsic value. Again, the pricing kernel puzzle arises in the center, whereas the truncation mainly affects the tails of the distribution. Also, it is not clear that market participants do indeed quote options in this particular way.

Market frictions due to margin account requirements might also play a role here. The public, the clearing firms, and the market makers are all subject to margin requirements. However, the requirements have not changed dramatically around the crash of 1987. They were slightly tightened in June of 1988 and more or less remained at that level since then until the end of the sample. To explain the steep smile with transactions costs for trading the out-of-the-money options is probably insufficient, too. For one, transaction costs existed in the precrash period as well as the postcrash period without changes on the day of the crash. However, the smile changed dramatically. Second, transaction costs should affect the out-of-the-money options on both sides of the smile equally. Instead, the index option smile is largely asymmetric.

Although transaction costs are not a likely reason for the index smile, a related concern is the hedging of out-of-the-money puts. Hedging is difficult for sold out-of-the-money puts when one uses only the underlying to hedge. The hedge must offset the positive delta of the position, which is low and grows large as the market crashes. The hedging strategy must have a negative delta that declines to minus one as the market crashes. Thus, the investor must sell into the falling market. However, this problem only applies to investors who desire to stay fully hedged. Investors similar to the representative investor should be able to follow sell and hold strategies even without hedging since we are assuming the existence of a pricing kernel in the economy. A static unhedged position is then still utility-improving.

Note that the historical sample estimate p^* is backward looking. On the other hand, q^* is derived from option prices, and is forward looking in that it represents the beliefs of investors over the life of the index options (31 days in our work). If investors do not have rational expectations, then q^* and p^* may differ greatly. One form of irrationality we call crash-o-phobia or a peso problem. To understand this, suppose that in the period of the 1987 crash investors suddenly became overly fearful of a future market crash. Thus, in the postcrash period, prices of options with strike prices below the current index level are elevated relative to rational levels. As a result, the left tail of q^*, which represents prices for dollars received conditional on a large market decline, is raised upward. Given that q^* always integrates to one, q^*

needs to decline in other ranges. If in addition the statistical distribution p^* is unchanged – so that the change in q^* represents an irrational change in beliefs – then the pricing kernel may take on the shape shown in Fig. 3.

Just the same, it is odd that m^* is locally increasing in all months of our postcrash index sample that currently ends in 1995 when the CBOE stopped distribution of the data. The implication is that crash-o-phobia continued for at least eight years after 1987, and it did so in the absence of another crash. We expect that if investor beliefs changed irrationally in the 1987 crash, then the shape of m^* should revert to its precrash form as memories fade during the postcrash era.[11] Moreover, the S&P 500 index options trade in a large and liquid market, and the crash-o-phobia hypothesis implies that these options are irrationally priced. If so, then over time traders should learn to profitably exploit such mispricing. Over an eight-year period, arbitrage trading should drive option prices and the pricing kernel back to their rational precrash levels. However, we observe no such adjustments. For this reason, we seek rational alternatives to the crash-o-phobia hypothesis as an explanation of the puzzling pricing kernel.

ALTERNATIVE SOLUTIONS TO THE PRICING KERNEL PUZZLE

The extant literature is largely unsatisfactory in explaining the puzzle of Fig. 3. Many authors model the smile that appears in Fig. 1, but this literature generally is one sided and does not tackle the puzzle. Either the index return process in modeled (generating a p distribution) or postcrash option prices are modeled (typically generating a left-skewed q distribution), but a model of $m = q/p$ is not offered.

Consider the leverage effect as an example. As the market value falls, the market debt-equity ratio and therefore index volatility rises. Hence we should expect to see the smile in implied volatilities, as shown in Fig. 1. Note that Black (1976), Christie (1982), and Schwert (1989) discuss the leverage effect on the statistical distribution, and similarly Toft and Prucyk (1997) and Dennis and Mayhew (2000) discuss the effect on the risk-neutral distribution. However, none of these papers calculates the pricing kernel or links the two distributions.

Other examples are the correlation effect (e.g., Campbell, Lettau, Malkiel, & Xu, 2000; Kelly, 1994) and the learning or information aggregation effect (e.g., Gennotte & Leland, 1990; Grossman, 1988; Jacklin,

Kleidon, & Pfleiderer, 1992; Kleidon, 1994; Romer, 1993; Hong & Stein, 2003; Nandi, 1999). The correlation effect says that in down markets correlations across companies increase so that the impact of bad news on the market index is asymmetric. The learning (or information) effect is that an investor learns through trading, and occasionally prices adjust sharply despite the absence of a news event. Each of these effects can imply that volatility increases as the index declines, and thus imply that a smile exists as it appears in Fig. 1. Again, none of the papers listed here model p and q jointly or describe m.

Papers that model the pricing kernel directly include Franke, Stapleton, and Subrahmanyam (1998, 1999), who suggest a pricing kernel with declining elasticity, which follows from undiversifiable background risk faced by investors. Alternatively, Benninga and Mayshar (1997) consider heterogeneous investors, while Campbell and Cochrane (2000) explore utility functions with habit persistence. Grossman and Zhou (1996) describe an economy with demanders and suppliers of portfolio insurance and solve for m. In each of these cases, marginal utility is monotonic in wealth and m is downwards sloping.

The work of Bartunek and Chowdhury (1997) and Bliss and Panigirtzoglou (2004) suffers from a similar problem when they fit the risk-aversion coefficient of a power utility investor in order to explain observed returns best. For that they construct a subjective distribution based on the option implied risk-neutral distribution that they transform through the pricing kernel. But as they assume a power utility, their pricing kernel will by construction be monotonically decreasing. They cannot find a pricing kernel puzzle, even if it is in the data.

A large literature investigates general stochastic processes for the market index together with other variables to explain the smile in implied volatility. Some of these models allow stochastic volatility, for example, the continuous-time model of Heston (1993) and the GARCH model of Duan (1995), or stochastic interest rates. Others consider jumps in the index or in the volatility of the index (e.g., Bakshi, Cao, & Chen, 1997; Bates, 2000; Pan, 2002). These authors assume that jump risk is priced, but also that the compensation for jump risk (in the expected return) is proportional to the intensity of the jump component. Proportional pricing is implied by Cox et al. (1985), who assume time-additive logarithmic utility of a representative agent. To demonstrate that this implies a monotonic m, we simulate Pan's (2002) model according to her estimated parameters. The estimated pricing kernel is monotonically decreasing as shown in Fig. 4.[12]

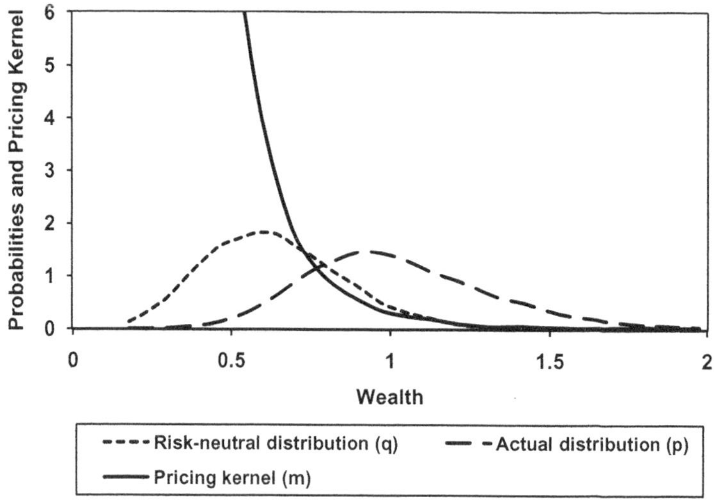

Fig. 4. Simulation of the Pricing Kernel in Pan (2002). The Parameters are Taken from Pan (2002), the Time Horizon is 30 Days with 10 Intradaily Discrete Steps in the Approximation. We Use 10,000 Simulation Runs.

This leaves only two more papers that actually model both the q and the p distribution simultaneously: Branger and Schlag (2003) and Ziegler (2007). Branger and Schlag (2003) model an economy where the index is the average of 30 identical stocks which all are driven by jump-diffusion processes. These processes have a market component and an idiosyncratic component for both the diffusion and the jump parts, respectively. By formally changing to the risk-neutral measure, they change the drift of the diffusion but also the correlation coefficient and the intensity of the jump component. While the correlation coefficient does not have much of an impact, the jump intensity does. Ignoring the idiosyncratic components and focusing on the market component of the index, let the actual jump intensity be very small. Then, the actual return will look almost lognormal. Let the risk-neutral jump intensity be very large and the risk-neutral distribution can exhibit a pronounced left tail and a reduced mode of the distribution. The resulting pricing kernel can in such case exhibit increases in wealth. However, Branger and Schlag (2003) are agnostic about the equilibrium implications of their mechanical change of measure. Thus, while they can generate locally increasing pricing kernels, they do not explain the underlying economics. They do not provide economic restrictions on the price of jump risk that in turn will restrict the pricing kernel in the economy.

In its intent, the work by Ziegler (2007) is closest to this paper. He considers three hypotheses: misestimation of the statistical distribution, misspecification of investor preferences, and heterogeneous investor beliefs. Using a single-factor economy with complete markets, he argues that neither misestimation nor misspecification of preferences are likely to explain the pricing-kernel puzzle. Errors in estimation of the statistical distribution, which we represent as $(q^{*}-q)$, must be very odd and unreasonable in their functional relation to the underlying factor (which in his model is aggregate consumption) if they are to cause the puzzle. With respect to the misspecification of preferences, he investigates commonly used preferences: constant absolute risk aversion, constant relative risk aversion, and decreasing relative risk aversion. For specifications with reasonable parameter values he finds that they all yield very similar transformation from statistical to risk-neutral distributions and vice versa.

Ziegler (2007) argues that his third hypothesis – heterogeneous beliefs – holds more promise as an explanation for the pricing-kernel puzzle. He essentially replaces the actual distribution (which is historically observable to all investors and looks rather lognormal) with a mixture of two lognormal distributions. This mixture is generated by mixing the pessimists' distribution (low mean, low volatility) and the optimists' distribution (high mean, high volatility) in proportions of roughly half and half. Such mix keeps the mean of the actual distribution, but looks rather different, namely left-skewed and leptokurtic. Still, all investors stick to their beliefs and use this mixture as the forward looking subjective distribution. Since it looks much like the risk-neutral distribution in shape, albeit shifted to the right, the resulting pricing kernel is monotonically decreasing. The model hinges on the assumption that no investor checks the statistical fit of the mixture against the historical time-series of index returns. Also, the model needs to have the polar setting of having only pessimists and optimists. A sizeable group of moderates would make the mixture look much more like a lognormal distribution and the pricing kernel puzzle reappears.

A final set of hypotheses we collect under the umbrella of state-dependent utility. By this we mean that the representative investor in the S&P 500 index has state-dependent utility. We do not require a representative agent for the economy as a whole. Instead, we assume the existence of the representative or marginal investor in the S&P 500 index and index options.

State-dependent utility may arise for a number of reasons. One of these is generalized utility, by which we mean that the investor exhibits either habit formation or recursive utility. For example, in the case of habit formation, and unlike with the simple power utility of Hansen and Singleton (1983), the pricing kernel m is a function of an aggregator of historical levels of consumption as well as current consumption. In this setting, an investor becomes accustomed to a level of consumption, which is determined by the aggregator, and strongly dislikes decreases in consumption below that level. Epstein and Zin (1989, 1991) explore the recursive utility model. Here, the uncoupling of the risk-aversion coefficient and the intertemporal substitution rate is not too helpful for our purposes, since it leaves the power utility formulation across wealth in place.[13] However, Fig. 3 is in violation of such power utility.

State-dependent utility may also arise when index volatility, or more generally the distribution of other security returns, is stochastic. In this case, measures of volatility, interest rates, or the prices of other assets enter the index-investor's utility as additional state variables.

We do not detail here every alternative state variable we must consider. It is possible, however, to characterize generally the nature of the relation between the index and the additional state variable that must exist to explain the puzzle. The kernel m is the ratio of expected future marginal utility divided by the current marginal utility. If utility is dependent on a second state variable, and that variable is responsible for the puzzle, then the relation between the additional state variable and the index must be nonmonotonic.

To demonstrate this, consider the optimal consumption (C^*) induced by a level of the S&P 500 index w and a state variable v. We then write

$$m(w) = \frac{E_v\{U'(C^*(w, v))|w\}}{U'(C_0^*(w_0, v_0))} \tag{4}$$

The numerator is the expected marginal utility at the time of the option expiration, where the expectation is conditioned on the index level. For Eq. (4) to behave as in Fig. 3, the distribution of v must change with w so that the numerator rises monotonically in the middle range, that is, where w is close to w_0. However, the relation between w and the v distribution must be decidedly different in the tails. In the tails we expect that the distribution of v changes very little with w. Because marginal utility declines with wealth ceteris paribus, the numerator declines with w either far above or below w_0. We now examine several alternative representations of state-dependent utility with the goal of explaining Fig. 3.

We depict a hypothetical situation of such a state variable v in Fig. 5. Initially, for low wealth levels, the economy is in state 1. As wealth approaches the level of 1, state 2 becomes more likely. However, as wealth increases even further, state 1 is again becoming more likely. Thus, the

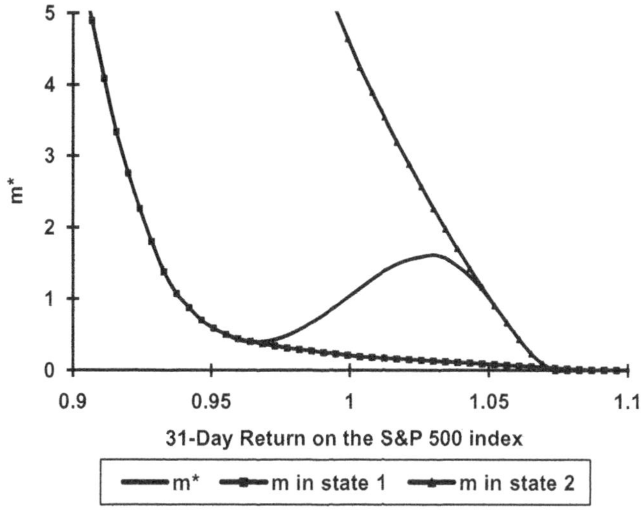

Fig. 5. Hypothetical Pricing Kernels Depending on a Second State Variable v. We Graph the Simplest Setting where the Second State Variable v Can Take Either of Two Values. As Wealth Increases, the Likelihood of Being in State 2 Increases. Taking the Expectation Over v Yields the Desired Empirical Pricing Kernel m^*.

pricing kernel m^* is a weighted average of the two pricing kernels associated with the two states of v. One can think about the following potential explanation: For very low and very high levels of wealth, utility is based on the low marginal utility function (state 1) associated with a high volatility regime. For moderate levels of wealth (close to the initial wealth level of 1), utility is based on the high marginal utility function (state 2) of a low volatility regime. Around the center, the weights shift and the resulting marginal utility function from the above Fig. 3 is obtained.

More recent explanations by Bakshi and Madan (2007) and Bakshi, Madan, and Panayotov (2010) center on investor heterogeneity in beliefs and risk aversion. Hens and Reichlin (2011) argue similarly (and also consider incomplete markets and risk-seeking behavior) but only provide very stylized examples. Bates (2008) focuses on heterogeneity with respect to crash aversion. Ziegler (2002) mentioned investor heterogeneity in beliefs as a potential cause for multimodal risk-neutral distributions already but he argues in Ziegler (2007) that the heterogeneity in beliefs required to explain the pricing kernel puzzle is too large to be realistic.

Chabi-Yo, Garcia, and Renault (2008) provide an alternative argument based on a regime switching model of stock prices driven by a latent variable that can change between two states. Härdle, Krätschmer, and Moro (2009) pick up on the same idea but model it through a micro-economic approach where several investors each switch between different risk attitudes at different wealth levels.

Finally, Benzoni, Collin-Dufresne, and Goldstein (2010) introduce jumps into the stochastic dividend growth process that in turns leads to learning of the investors about the frequency of such jumps. Christoffersen, Heston, and Jacobs (2010) are probably closest to the present paper in that they suggest a pricing kernel that depends not only on returns but also on variance. Once projected onto the space of returns, their model exhibits the pricing kernel puzzle.

A MODEL

For our model, we stay with our above motivation and propose that volatility is a function of a second momentum state variable.

This choice is based on the observation that a candidate state variable would have to exhibit an effect on the pricing kernel that is symmetric in wealth. Namely, the pricing kernel ought to be raised for small changes in wealth and lowered for large changes in wealth in either direction. Volatility naturally has this feature in that it tends to be low if wealth changes little and increases if wealth changes dramatically in either direction. Moreover, we know that in a representative agent economy with power utility and a small risk-aversion coefficient, low volatility will cause the pricing kernel to be high and high volatility will lower the pricing kernel, just as desired. Finally, we are reluctant to model volatility as a function of wealth straightaway since wealth is a nonstationary variable. Thus, we propose to model volatility as a function of a (stationary) momentum variable X_t. X_t follows a simple mean reverting process; it is an exponentially weighted sum of past increments in wealth.

The agent's problem can then be modeled along the lines of Merton (1969) as follows. Let the representative agent choose the rate of consumption $C(W_t, X_t, t)$, and the proportion of wealth in the risky asset $\alpha(W_t, X_t, t)$, and the proportion in the riskless asset $(1-\alpha)$ to maximize expected utility of lifetime consumption:

$$J(W_t, X_t, t) \equiv \underset{\{C_s, \alpha_s\}}{\text{Maximize}}\, E_t\left[\int_t^{\infty} \frac{\exp(-\rho s) C_s^{1-B}}{(1-B)} ds\right] \qquad (5)$$

where

$$dW_t = (W_t\alpha_t(\mu - r_t) + W_t r_t - C_t)dt + \alpha_t W_t \sigma(X_t)dz_t$$
$$dX_t = -\theta X_t dt + \sigma(X_t)dz_t \tag{6}$$

Here, μ and θ are constants, $\sigma(X_t)$ is a function of the second state variable X_t, and a single Brownian motion appears in both diffusion equations. Changes in the state variable are perfectly correlated with changes in wealth. Using Ito's lemma,

$$dJ = J_W dW + J_X dX + J_t dt + \frac{J_{WW}dW^2}{2} + J_{WX}dWdX + \frac{J_{XX}dX^2}{2} \tag{7}$$

Optimal consumption and investment choices satisfy the HJB equation:

$$\begin{aligned} 0 &= \underset{C_t,\alpha_t}{\text{Maximize}} \frac{e^{-\rho t}C_t^{1-B}}{(1-B)} + \frac{E_t[dJ]}{dt} \\ &= \underset{C_t,\alpha_t}{\text{Maximize}} \frac{e^{-\rho t}C_t^{1-B}}{(1-B)} + J_W(W_t\alpha_t(\mu - r_t) + W_t r_t - C_t) + J_X(-\theta X_t) \\ &+ J_t + \frac{J_{WW}\alpha_t^2 W_t^2 \sigma^2(X_t)}{2} + J_{WX}\alpha_t W_t \sigma^2(X_t) + \frac{J_{XX}\sigma^2(X_t)}{2} \end{aligned} \tag{8}$$

From the first-order conditions:

$$C_t = e^{-\rho t/B} J_W^{-1/B}$$
$$\alpha_t = \frac{-J_W}{J_{WW}W_t}\frac{\mu - r_t}{\sigma^2(X_t)} - \frac{J_{WX}}{J_{WW}W_t} \tag{9}$$

In order to find the solution of the model in equilibrium, we posit the following functional form for the utility of wealth of a representative agent,

$$J(W_t, X_t, t) = \frac{e^{-\rho t}h(X_t)W_t^{1-B}}{(1-B)} \tag{10}$$

Substituting partial derivatives (details are in the appendix) into Eq. (9) we obtain

$$\frac{\partial}{\partial C} = 0 = C^{-B} - h(X_t)W^{-B} \Leftrightarrow C_t = h(X_t)^{-1/B}W_t$$
$$\alpha_t = \frac{\mu - r_t}{B\sigma^2(X_t)} + \frac{h'}{Bh} \tag{11}$$

When we assume that the riskless asset is in zero net supply, so that $\alpha_t = 1$, the latter equation identifies the riskless rate:

$$r_t = \mu - B\sigma^2(X_t) + \frac{h'(X_t)}{h(X_t)}\sigma^2(X_t) \tag{12}$$

Now, we use Eq. (11) to identify consumption and investment, Eq. (12) to identify the riskless rate, and Eq. (10) to identify the partial derivatives of J. Eq. (8) is written:

$$\begin{aligned} 0 = (1 - B)\mu h - \rho h + Bh^{1-1/B} - \theta X_t h' \\ + \sigma_t^2(X_t)\left[\frac{1}{2}h'' + (1 - B)h' - \frac{(1 - B)Bh}{2}\right] \end{aligned} \tag{13}$$

This identifies h without knowledge of the riskless rate. The h-function is a second-order ODE with a hyperbolic term that makes it very difficult to solve. However, from the functional form of the pricing kernel we can learn much about the functional form of h. The pricing kernel is given by the ratios of marginal utilities:

$$m_{t,T} = \frac{J_{W_T}}{J_{W_t}} = e^{-\rho(T-t)}\left[\frac{h(X_T)}{h(X_t)}\right]\left(\frac{W_T}{W_t}\right)^{-B} = e^{-\rho(T-t)}\left[\frac{h(X_T)}{h(X_t)}\right] r_{m,t,T}^{-B} \tag{14}$$

The adjustment depends on the ratio of $h(X_T)/h(X_t)$ that will give the desired shape of the pricing kernel if h is shaped like a normal density (Bell-curve) but raised by a constant above the zero line. We thus specify the following parametric form for h:

$$h(X) = d + e^{a+bX+cX^2} \tag{15}$$

We are now in the position to look at results by choosing some reasonable set of parameters. We initialize our economy with unit wealth ($W_0 = 1$) and zero momentum ($X_0 = 0$). The risk-aversion coefficient of the representative agent is set to $B = 0.5$, and the mean reversion of the momentum process is fixed at $\theta = 0.1$. We specify the adjustment function as:

$$h(X) = 8 + e^{-500X^2} \tag{16}$$

and the volatility function as:

$$\sigma(X) = 0.06 + 0.2X^2 \tag{17}$$

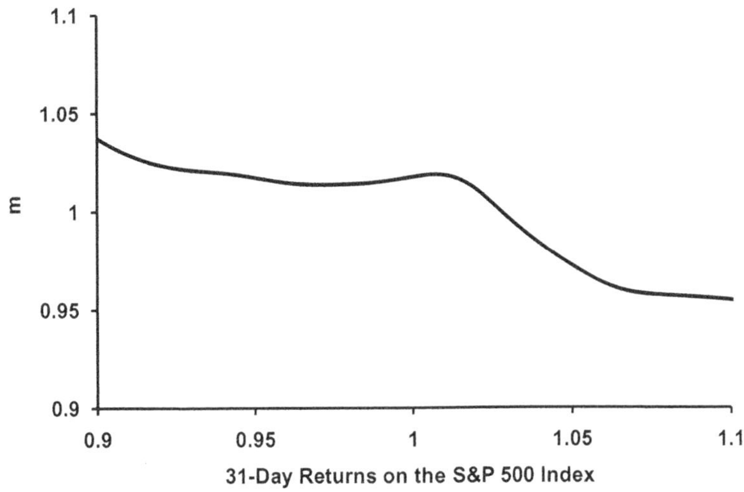

Fig. 6. Simulated Pricing Kernel Based on a Representative Agent Model with a Second State Variable. 10,000 Simulation Runs and Smoothed Through a Kernel Regression.

We are then able to derive the drift μ and the risk-free rate r from Eqs. (12) and (13), respectively. This allows us to simulate the wealth and the momentum processes based on a daily discretization over 31 days. We use 10,000 simulation runs and smooth the resulting graph through a kernel regression. We document in Fig. 6 the simulated pricing kernel that indeed is locally increasing in wealth around a wealth level of 1. It is by design still decreasing in consumption but the second state variable – in our case momentum – introduces a wedge between consumption and wealth. In comparison with Fig. 3 we notice that the model generates a much less pronounced hump in the pricing kernel. This is caused by the economics of the underlying model in which the wedge between consumption and wealth cannot be made arbitrarily large. As a result, the actual and the risk-neutral probability distribution still look more alike than their empirical estimates in Fig. 2. We find that consumption is on the low side at a annualized rate of 1.23–1.56% of wealth.

The realized volatility of the wealth process mimics the u-shaped specification of volatility as a function of momentum (X). We see in Fig. 7 that the realized volatility is also u-shaped when we plot it across 31-day returns and smooth the graph through a kernel regression again. The far edges of the volatility graph ramp up to rather high values.

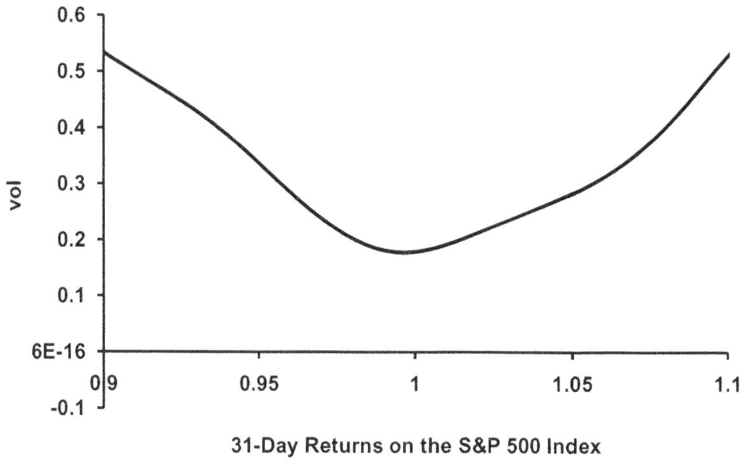

Fig. 7. Annualized Volatility of Simulated Wealth Process Based on a Representative Agent Model with a Second State Variable. 10,000 Simulation runs and Smoothed Through a Kernel Regression.

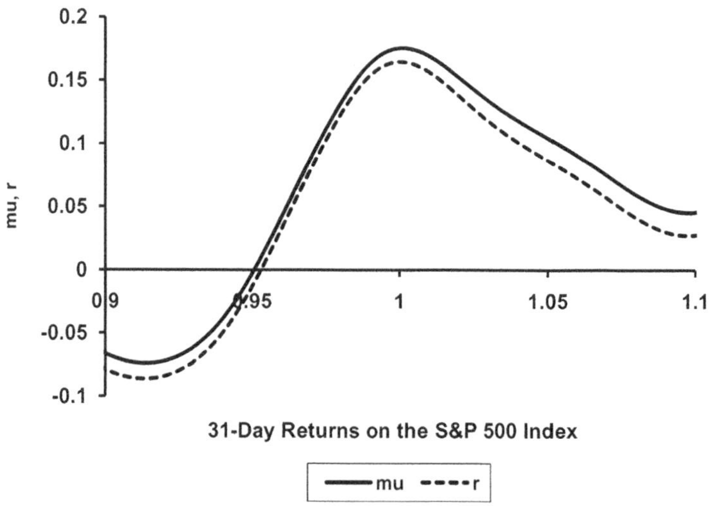

Fig. 8. Annualized Drift and Riskless Rate of Simulated Wealth Process Based on a Representative Agent Model with a Second State Variable. 10,000 Simulation Runs and Smoothed Through a Kernel Regression.

We also find that the model implied function of the drift and the riskless rate change very rapidly as a function of momentum. This is due to the high curvature in the adjustment function around a wealth level of 1. However, when we consider the drift and the riskless rate across wealth, the resulting functions are much better behaved as we show in Fig. 8. The annualized unconditional drift is 8.68% and the annualized unconditional riskless rate is 7.28%. The risk-free rate is thus a little high and the equity risk premium is rather small compared to the historical risk premium. However, that we are faced with the equity premium puzzle is not surprising for this type of model.

SUMMARY

The goal of our work is to explain the pricing kernel puzzle pictured in Fig. 3. This figure demonstrates a surprising pattern of the marginal utility of wealth for investors in the S&P 500 index. It appears that these investors are risk seeking, at least with respect to small risks in the index. This is inconsistent with the basic assumptions of asset-pricing theory, when it is recognized that the S&P 500 index represents a significant proportion of public equity capital in the United States.

Our theoretical model provides for a representative agent model that features volatility as a function of an additional state variable that measures momentum. Through an adjustment function to the pricing kernel, the model is capable of generating the sort of relationship we see in Fig. 3. Future research will examine index returns from markets outside the United States along the lines of Jackwerth (2004). His limited sample seems to suggest that the puzzle is not unique to the S&P 500 index options market but exists internationally. Further empirical work could then use both domestic and foreign market data to test our theoretical explanation of the puzzle.

NOTES

1. For simplicity and without loss of generality, we assume in our discussion that the rate of interest on risk-free assets is zero. As a result, there is no discounting of the expectation needed.In general, the price of a security is the sum of expected future payoffs (using the SPD) discounted at the risk-free rate. The word "density" is usually reserved for a continuous function. For simplicity of discussion, we still refer to the discrete risk-neutral probability distribution under which the expectation is taken as a SPD.
2. See Debreu (1972) for development of a state price.

3. We focus our attention on European options because they are exercised only at expiration. A European call option pays the maximum of zero and the difference between the price of the underlying security, for example, the level of a stock index P_s, and a strike price X defined in the option contract. We write $F_s = \text{Max}[0, P_s - X]$.

4. This result also requires that per capita consumption follows a geometric random walk with drift.

5. That is, the volatility (of returns on the underlying asset) consistent with the Black–Scholes model is obtained, which exactly matches the observed option price. This is the "implied volatility," that is used as a substitute for the option price and makes it an easy task to compare the prices of options.

6. For example, for options on individual equities, the plot is relatively flat compared to Fig. 1. For foreign-exchange options, each tail of the plot tends to be slightly and equally elevated.

7. Investors also need to be solely concerned with the unconditional distribution, or they need to assume that the distribution of returns is stationary. Alas, work by Rosenberg and Engle (2002) uses a nonstationary GARCH model but finds similar subjective distributions.

8. In a further exploratory study, we investigated market frictions in a GMM setting starting with the Euler equation $E[m\ r] = 1$. We use the dataset on options returns from Buraschi and Jackwerth (2001). He and Modest (1995) suggest that the vector of 1's should be replaced with some other value, close to 1 for transaction costs or less than 1 for short sale constraints. However, as the marginal investor (the one with the lowest costs) sets the equilibrium prices, it is hard to imagine that the vector should be vastly different from 1; especially since the market maker and the traders are not short sale constraint. We need to use an expected value of the OTM put returns, which is some 4050 basis points lower than 1, in order to achieve a monotonically decreasing pricing kernel. Such large daily transaction cost is hard to imagine in this liquid market. Such diminished return could also suggest mispricing, a position explored in Jackwerth (2000) and supported by Agarwal and Naik (2004), who find that hedge funds tend to sell out-of-the-money and at-the-money puts. Bondarenko (2003), Coval and Shumway (2001), and Driessen and Maenhout (2003) also find that similar option trading strategies turn out to be very profitable. Given the size and liquidity of this market, our prior is, however, that such profit opportunities should not exist for 10 years without any tendency toward equilibrium.

9. We do not formally demonstrate the link between plots of m and smiles here, but refer to the discussion in Jackwerth (2000) and Rosenberg and Engle (2002).

10. However, Dennis and Mayhew (2000) test for the impact of "market sentiment" variables on the smiles of individual stock options. They find that the ratio of put to call volume is significant and that higher put volume increases the slope of the smile. Still, other measures of "market sentiment", such as the Consumer Confidence Index or the average Price/Earnings ratio for the S&P 500 stock, are not significant in explaining the slope of the smile.

11. See Driessen and Maenhout (2003) for such model with irrational investors.

12. Ziegler (2007) demonstrates this same result.

13. This feature unfortunately only became apparent after we implemented recursive utility into our model below.

ACKNOWLEDGMENTS

The authors thank Jim Hodder, Stewart Hodges, Lars Norden, Mark Rubinstein, and seminar participants at CEPR Summer Symposium at Gerzensee, Tilburg University, European Investment Review Conference – Paris, Insead, London School of Economics, Warwick University, Lancaster University, University of Lausanne, 2nd World Congress of the Bachelier Society – Heraklion for valuable comments. The authors gratefully acknowledge a research grant from INQUIRE UK. This article represents the views of the authors and not of INQUIRE.

REFERENCES

Agarwal, V., & Naik, Y. N. (2004). Risks and portfolio decisions involving hedge funds. *Review of Financial Studies*, *17*(1), 63–98.

Ait-Sahalia, Y., & Lo, A. W. (2000). Nonparametric risk management and implied risk aversion. *Journal of Econometrics*, *94*(1–2), 9–51.

Bakshi, G., Cao, C., & Chen, Z. (1997). Empirical performance of alternative option pricing models. *Journal of Finance*, *52*(5), 2003–2049.

Bakshi, G., & Madan, D.B. (2007). *Investor heterogeneity, aggregation, and the non-monotonicity of the aggregate marginal rate of substitution in the price of market-equity*. Working Paper, University of Maryland.

Bakshi, G., Madan, D. B., & Panayotov, G. (2010). Returns of claims on the upside and the viability of u-shaped pricing kernels. *Journal of Financial Economics*, *97*(1), 130–154.

Bartunek, K., & Chowdhury, M. (1997). Implied risk aversion parameter from option prices. *The Financial Review*, *32*(1), 107–124.

Bates, D. (2000). Post-'87 crash fears in S&P 500 futures options. *Journal of Econometrics*, *94*(1–2), 181–238.

Bates, D. S. (2008). The market for crash risk. *Journal of Economic Dynamics and Control*, *32*(7), 2291–2321.

Benninga, S., & Mayshar, J. (1997). Heterogeneity and option pricing. *Review of Derivatives Research*, *4*(1), 7–27.

Benzoni, L., Collin-Dufresne, P., & Goldstein, R. S. (2010). *Explaining asset pricing puzzles associated with the 1987 market crash*. Working Paper, University of Minnesota.

Black, F. (1976). Studies of stock price volatility changes. *Proceedings of the 1976 Meetings of the American Statistical Association*, Business and Economical Statistics Section (pp. 177–181). Alexandria, VA: American Statistical Association.

Bliss, R., & Panigirtzoglou, N. (2004). Option-implied risk aversion estimates. *Journal of Finance*, *59*(1), 407–446.

Bondarenko, O. (2003). *Why are put options so expensive?* Working Paper. University of Illinois at Chicago.

Branger, N., & Schlag, C. (2003). Why is the index smile so steep? *Review of Finance*, *8*(1), 109–127.

Breeden, D., & Litzenberger, R. (1978). Prices of state-contingent claims implicit in options prices. *Journal of Business*, *51*(4), 621–651.

Brown, D. P., & Gibbons, M. R. (1985). A simple econometric approach for utility-based asset pricing models. *Journal of Finance*, *40*(2), 359–381.

Buraschi, A., & Jackwerth, J. C. (2001). The price of a smile: Hedging and spanning in option markets. *Review of Financial Studies*, *14*(2), 495–527.

Campa, J. M., & Chang, K. P. H. (1998). ERM realignment risk and its economic determinants as reflected in cross-rate options. *Economic Journal*, *108*(449), 1046–1066.

Campbell, J. Y., & Cochrane, J. H. (2000). Explaining the poor performance of consumption-based asset pricing models. *Journal of Finance*, *55*(6), 2863–2878.

Campbell, J. Y., Lettau, M., Malkiel, B. G., & Xu, Y. (2000). Have individual stocks become more volatile? An empirical exploration of idiosyncratic risk. *Journal of Finance*, *56*(1), 1–43.

Chabi-Yo, F., Garcia, R., & Renault, E. (2008). State dependence can explain the risk aversion puzzle. *Review of Financial Studies*, *21*(2), 973–1011.

Christie, A. (1982). The stochastic behavior of common stock variance – Value, leverage and interest rate effects. *Journal of Financial Economics*, *10*(4), 407–432.

Christoffersen, P., Heston, S., & Jacobs, K. (2010). *Option anomalies and the pricing kernel*. Working Paper, University of Maryland.

Coval, J. D., & Shumway, T. (2001). Expected option returns. *Journal of Finance*, *56*(3), 983–1009.

Cox, J. C., Ingersoll, J. E., & Ross, S. A. (1985). An intertemporal general equilibrium model of asset prices. *Econometrica*, *53*(2), 363–384.

Debreu, G. (1972). *Theory of value: An axiomatic analysis of economic equilibrium*. Yale University Press, reprinted, 128pp. Available at http://www.amazon.com/Theory-Value-Equilibrium-Foundation-Monographs/dp/0300015593/ref=sr_1_1?s=books&ie=UTF 8&qid=1335555582&sr=1-1

Dennis, P., & Mayhew, S. (2000). *Implied volatility smiles: Evidence from options on individual equities*. Working Paper. University of Virginia.

Driessen, J., & Maenhout P. (2003). *A portfolio perspective on option pricing anomalies*. Working Paper. University of Amsterdam.

Duan, J.-C. (1995). The GARCH option pricing model. *Mathematical Finance*, *5*(1), 13–32.

Epstein, L. G., & Zin, S. E. (1989). Substitution, risk aversion, and the temporal behavior of consumption and asset returns: A theoretical framework. *Econometrica*, *57*(4), 937–969.

Epstein, L. G., & Zin, S. E. (1991). Substitution, risk aversion, and the temporal behavior of consumption and asset returns: An empirical analysis. *Journal of Political Economy*, *99*(2), 263–286.

Fama, E. F., & French, K. R. (1988). Permanent and temporary components of stock prices. *Journal of Political Economy*, *96*(2), 246–273.

Franke, G., Stapleton, D., & Subrahmanyam, M. (1998). Who buys and who sells options: The role of options in an economy with background risk. *Journal of Economic Theory*, *82*(1), 89–109.

Franke, G., Stapleton, D., & Subrahmanyam, M. (1999). When are options overpriced? The Black–Scholes model and alternative characterisations of the pricing kernel. *European Finance Review*, *3*(1), 79–102.

Gennotte, G., & Leland, H. E. (1990). Market liquidity, hedging, and crashes. *American Economic Review*, *80*(5), 999–1021.

Grossman, S. J. (1988). An analysis of the implications for stock and futures price volatility of program trading and dynamic hedging strategies. *Journal of Business*, *61*(3), 275–298.
Grossman, S. J., & Zhou, Z. (1996). Equilibrium analysis of portfolio insurance. *Journal of Finance*, *51*(4), 1379–1403.
Hansen, L. P., & Singleton, K. J. (1983). Stochastic consumption, risk aversion, and the temporal behavior of asset returns. *Journal of Political Economy*, *91*(2), 249–265.
Härdle, W., Krätschmer, V., & Moro, R. (2009). *A microeconomic explanation of the EPK paradox*. SFB 649 Discussion Paper 2009-010. Humboldt University, Berlin.
He, H., & Modest, D. M. (1995). Market frictions and consumption-based asset pricing. *Journal of Political Economy*, *103*(1), 94–117.
Hens, T., & Reichlin, C. (2011). *Three solutions to the pricing kernel puzzle*. Working Paper. Swiss Banking Institute, University of Zurich.
Hentschel, L. (2003). Errors in implied volatility estimation. *Journal of Financial and Quantitative Analysis*, *38*(4), 779–810.
Heston, S. L. (1993). A closed-form solution for options with stochastic volatility with applications to bond and currency options. *The Review of Financial Studies*, *6*(2), 327–343.
Hong, H., & Stein, J. C. (2003). Differences of opinion, short-sales constraints and market crashes. *Review of Financial Studies*, *16*(2), 487–525.
Jacklin, C. J., Kleidon, A. W., & Pfleiderer, P. (1992). Underestimation of portfolio insurance and the crash of October 1987. *Review of Financial Studies*, *5*(1), 35–63.
Jackwerth, J. C. (1999). Option implied risk-neutral distributions and implied binomial trees: A literature review. *Journal of Derivatives*, *7*(2), 66–82.
Jackwerth, J. C. (2000). Recovering risk aversion from option prices and realized returns. *Review of Financial Studies*, *13*(2), 433–451.
Jackwerth, J. C. (2004). Option implied risk-neutral distributions and risk aversion. Monograph for AIMR, Charlottesville, VA.
Jackwerth, J. C., & Rubinstein, M. (1996). Recovering probability distributions from option prices. *Journal of Finance*, *51*(5), 1611–1631.
Jackwerth, J. C., & Rubinstein, M. (2012). Recovering stochastic processes from option prices. In J. A. Batten & N. Wagner (Eds.), *Contemporary studies in economics and financial analysis: Derivative securities pricing and modelling*. Bingley, UK: Emerald Group.
Kelly, M. (1994). Correlation: Stock answer. *RISK*, *7*(8), 40–43.
Kleidon, A.W. (1994). *Stock market crashes*. Working Paper. Stanford University.
Lucas Jr., R. E. (1978). Asset prices in an exchange economy. *Econometrica*, *46*(6), 1429–1445.
Merton, R. (1969). Lifetime portfolio selection under uncertainty: The continuous-time case. *Review of Economics and Statistics*, *51*(3), 247–257.
Nandi, S. (1999). Asymmetric information about volatility: How does it affect implied volatility, option prices and market liquidity? *Review of Derivatives Research*, *3*(3), 215–236.
Pan, J. (2002). The jump-risk premia implicit in options: Evidence from an integrated time-series study. *Journal of Financial Economics*, *63*(1), 3–50.
Poterba, J. M., & Summers, L. H. (1988). Mean reversion in stock prices. *Journal of Financial Economics*, *22*(1), 27–59.
Romer, D. (1993). Rational asset-price movements without news. *American Economic Review*, *83*(5), 1112–1130.
Rosenberg, J. V., & Engle, R. F. (2002). Empirical pricing kernels. *Journal of Financial Economics*, *64*(3), 341–372.

Rubinstein, M. (1976). The valuation of uncertain income streams and the pricing of options. *Bell Journal of Economics*, *7*(2), 407–425.

Rubinstein, M. (1994). Implied binomial trees. *Journal of Finance*, *49*(3), 771–818.

Schwert, G. W. (1989). Why does the stock market volatility change over time? *Journal of Finance*, *44*(5), 1115–1153.

Toft, K., & Prucyk, B. (1997). Options on leveraged equity: Theory and empirical tests. *Journal of Finance*, *52*(3), 1151–1180.

Ziegler, A. (2002). State-price densities under heterogeneous beliefs, the smile effect, and implied risk aversion. *European Economic Review*, *46*(8), 1539–1557.

Ziegler, A. (2007). Why does implied risk aversion smile? *Review of Financial Studies*, *20*(3), 859–904.

APPENDIX

Formulae

Write the utility of wealth of a representative agent as:

$$J(W_t, X_t, t) = \frac{e^{-\rho t} h(X_t) W_t^{1-B}}{(1-B)} \tag{A.1}$$

so the derivatives of utility of wealth are

$$\begin{aligned} J_W &= e^{-\rho t} h(X_t) W_t^{-B} \\ J_t &= \frac{-\rho e^{-\rho t} h(X_t) W_t^{1-B}}{(1-B)} \\ J_x &= \frac{e^{-\rho t} h'(X_t) W_t^{1-B}}{(1-B)} \\ J_{xx} &= \frac{e^{-\rho t} h''(X_t) W_t^{1-B}}{(1-B)} \\ J_{ww} &= e^{-\rho t}(-B) h(X_t) W_t^{-1-B} \\ J_{wx} &= e^{-\rho t} h'(X_t) W_t^{-B} \end{aligned} \tag{A.2}$$

The derivation of Eq. (13) out of Eq. (8) uses the optimal $\alpha_t = 1$ and proceeds through:

$$\begin{aligned} 0 = {} & \frac{e^{-\rho t}(h(X_t)^{-1/B} W_t)^{1-B}}{(1-B)} \\ & + (e^{-\rho t} h(X_t) W_t^{-B})(W_t(\mu - r) + W_t r_t - (h(X_t)^{-1/B} W_t)) \\ & + \left(\frac{e^{-\rho t} h'(X_t) W_t^{1-B}}{(1-B)}\right)(-\theta X_t) - \frac{\rho e^{-\rho t} h(X_t) W_t^{1-B}}{(1-B)} \\ & + \frac{(e^{-\rho t}(-B) h(X_t) W_t^{-1-B}) W_t^2 \sigma^2(X_t)}{2} \\ & + (e^{-\rho t} h'(X_t) W_t^{-B}) W_t \sigma^2(X_t) + \frac{0.5 e^{-\rho t} \sigma^2(X_t) h''(X_t) W_t^{1-B}}{(1-B)} \end{aligned} \tag{A.3}$$

Data

The empirical tests are based on a database containing all minute-by-minute European option quotes and trades on the S&P 500 index from April 2, 1986 to December 29, 1995. We use only option quotes since we cannot know for actual trades where they occurred relative to the bid/ask spread and our results might be affected. The database also contains all futures trades and quotes on the S&P 500. Our goal is to obtain a panel of daily return observations on the index, the risk-free rate, and on several options with different strike price/index level ratios (moneyness) and constant maturity.

Index Level. Traders typically use the index futures market rather than the cash market to hedge their option positions. The reason is that the cash market prices lag futures prices by a few minutes due to lags in reporting transactions of the constituent stocks in the index. We check this claim by regressing the index on each of the first 20-minute lags of the futures price. The single regression with the highest adjusted R^2 was assumed to indicate the lag for a given day. The median lag of the index over the 1,542 days from 1986 to 1992 was 7 minutes. Because the index is stale, we compute a future-based index for each minute from the future market

$$S_t = \left(\frac{r}{d}\right)^{-\Delta} F_{t+\Delta} \tag{A.4}$$

For each day, we use the median interest rate implied by all futures quotes and trades and the index level at that time. We approximate the dividend yield by assuming that the dividend amount and timing expected by the market were identical to the dividends actually paid on the S&P 500 index. However, some limited tests indicate that the choice of the index does not seem to affect the results of this paper.

Interest Rates. We compute implied interest rates embedded in the European put-call parity relation. Armed with option quotes, we calculate separate lending and borrowing interest returns from put-call parity where we used the above future-based index. We assign, for each expiration date, a single lending and borrowing rate to each day, which is the median of all daily observations across all striking prices. We then use the average of those two interest rates as our daily spot rate for the particular time-to-expiration. Finally, we obtain the interpolated interest rates from the implied forward curve. If there is data missing, we assume that the spot rate curve can be extrapolated horizontally for the shorter and longer time-to-expiration. Again, some limited tests indicate that the results are not affected by the exact choice of the interest rate.

Options with Adjusted Moneyness and Constant Maturity. It is important to use options with adjusted moneyness and constant maturity since our test statistics involve the conditional covariance matrix of option pricing errors. If the maturity of the options were not constant over time, then the conditional covariance matrix of the pricing errors would be time varying, too. This would require additional exogenous assumptions on the structure of the covariance matrix and the estimation of several additional parameters, which could lead to additional estimation error in our test statistics.

In our data set, all puts are translated into calls using European put-call parity. Then, we compute the implied volatilities where we use the Black–Scholes formula as a translation device only. We then adjust throughout each day for the movement of the stock price by assuming that the implied volatilities are independent of the underlying stock price. Then, we pick the stock price closest to 12 pm as our daily stock price and value all options from throughout the day as if they were call options with the implied volatilities measured above and struck at the moneyness level measured above. We do not eliminate any daily observations due to their level of moneyness.

Arbitrage Violations. In the process of setting up the database, we check for a number of errors, which might have been contained in the original minute-by-minute transaction level data. We eliminate a few obvious data-entry errors as well as a few quotes with excessive spreads – more than 200 cents for options and 20 cents for futures. General arbitrage violations are eliminated from the data set. We also check for violations of vertical and butterfly spreads. Within each minute we keep the largest set of option quotes that does not violate:

$$Sd^{-t} \geq C_i \geq \max[0, Sd^{-t} - K_i r^{-t}] \tag{A.5}$$

American early exercise is not an issue as the S&P 500 options are European in nature, and the discreteness of quotes and trades only introduces a stronger upward bias in the midpoint implied volatilities for deep-out-of-the-money puts (moneyness less than 0.6) that we do not use in our empirical work.

RISK-NEUTRAL DENSITIES AND CATASTROPHE EVENTS

Michael Herold and Matthias Muck

ABSTRACT

In this research, we analyze the impact of catastrophe events on risk-neutral densities which can be implied from European option markets. As catastrophe events we consider the destruction of the nuclear power plant at Fukushima and the downgrading of U.S. sovereign debt in 2011. In an event study, we analyze the impact on European blue chip index options traded at EUREX. We find that after a short adaption period, probability mass of especially risk-neutral density functions derived from long-term options is shifted toward the right side. Thus, very good states of the economy become more expensive indicating higher prices for deep out-of-the-money options. This signifies that there has been speculation on a recovery of the German stock market after the shocks.

Keywords: Risk-neutral densities; derivatives

INTRODUCTION

From an abstract point of view, shocks to the capital market are important new information which impact expectations of market participants usually

Derivative Securities Pricing and Modelling
Contemporary Studies in Economic and Financial Analysis, Volume 94, 185–207

ISSN: 1569-3759/doi:10.1108/S1569-3759(2012)0000094010

in a negative way. Examples for events that lead to such shocks are natural disasters, major economic events, terrorist attacks, or other catastrophes. For obvious reasons, it is of primary concern to investors how the market assesses an event and translates it into prices. Option-implied risk-neutral density (RND) functions represent a frequently used tool for analyzing market sentiment since they convey information about the market's expectations regarding the future value of assets. In recent years, a huge body of research has dealt with the estimation of RNDs implied by the market prices of European-style options.

In this study, we apply a simple parametric estimation technique to recover the risk-neutral probability distribution from contemporaneous prices of options on the German blue chip index DAX 30. We consider two different types of shocks that were observed in the year 2011. The first event is the Tōhoku earthquake off the Pacific coast of Japan with the subsequent tsunami and the nuclear disaster at the Fukushima Daiichi power plant. The second one we consider is the downgrading of U.S. government securities in early August 2011. Thus, while the first event is a natural disaster, the second one is a major economic event that might be – especially in the light of the discussion about the power of rating agencies and the sovereign debt crises – of primary concern to economists and policymakers.

We find that especially after a shock RNDs change considerably. Due to volatility increases more probability mass is assigned to the tails of the density. This effect is well known in the literature since major events usually lead to an increase in volatility because market participants become more "nervous." More interesting is the impact on skewness of the distributions. Especially for longer-term options we find that the left tail of the density of returns has a similar shape as before the crises. However, very positive events are assigned higher probabilities under the risk-neutral measure. This observation holds for both events under consideration. An interpretation of this behavior might be that investors speculate on a recovery of the underlying index in the longer-term through investments in out-of-the-money calls. This additional demand makes these options more expensive leading to an increase in the RNDs.

The remainder of the chapter is structured as follows. The second section reviews the concept of RNDs. The third section provides a literature overview over estimation techniques for RNDs and presents the methodology applied in this chapter. The fourth section describes the data. Finally, the fifth section contains the empirical results. The sixth section concludes.

RISK-NEUTRAL DENSITIES AND OPTION PRICES

Standard asset pricing models assume risk-averse investors who require a compensation for risk. For instance the famous Capital Asset Pricing Model (CAPM) states that the time t price of a claim V_t with a time T payoff X_T $(T > t)$ fulfills the equation

$$V_t = \mathbb{E}^P\left[\frac{X_T}{(1 + \text{RADR})^{T-t}}\right] \tag{1}$$

where P is the empirical probability measure, $\mathbb{E}^P[\cdot]$ denotes the P-expectations operator, and RADR stands for the risk adjusted discount rate. According to the CAPM, the RADR compensates investors for time and risk preferences because it is equal to the risk-free rate of interest plus a risk premium. The more risky an investment the higher is the risk premium and thus the risk adjusted discount rate. Obviously, the risk adjusted discount rate is negatively related to time t prices of claims.

Modern option pricing models, however, build on the so-called risk neutral rather than the empirical probability measure. In order to price a contract, they assume that under the risk-neutral probability measure Q all claims meet the requirement

$$V_t = \mathbb{E}^Q\left[\frac{X_T}{(1 + R_f)^{T-t}}\right] \tag{2}$$

The variable R_f stands for the risk-free rate of interest. Thus, investors are treated as if they were risk neutral under Q. Only time preferences are addressed while risk preferences are not considered explicitly. Instead they are reflected in the probability measure. This is highlighted in a discrete one-period model discussed, for example, by Ingersoll (1987) and also by Zimmermann (1998). They consider an economy with a finite number of states $\mathcal{S}$. A representative agent is endowed with initial wealth W_0. Future consumption is financed by the proceeds from the investments on the capital market at $T = 1$. Our agent can trade in $\mathcal{S}$ state securities. For each state $\mathbf{s} \in \mathcal{S}$ there is such a state security that pays off 1 if $\mathbf{s}$ occurs and 0 else. According to Eq. (2) the price of the state security z_s (with payoff in $\mathbf{s}$) is equal to

$$z_s = \frac{\pi_s}{1 + R_f} \tag{3}$$

where π_s is the risk-neutral probability of state **s**. Assume that the representative agent has a concave and additive von Neumann–Morgenstern utility function. Then, she faces the utility maximization problem

$$\max_{C_0, C_1} U(C_0) + \mathbb{E}^P[C_1] = \max U(C_0) + \sum_{s=1}^{\mathcal{S}} p_s C_{1s} \tag{4}$$

The variables C_0 and C_1 denote consumption at time 0 and 1, respectively. Note that since this is a one-period model C_{1s} is equal to the wealth W_{1s}, which in turn depends on the number of state securities purchased. The budget constraint is

$$W_0 = C_0 + \sum_{s=1}^{\mathcal{S}} z_s W_{1s} = C_0 + \sum_{s=1}^{\mathcal{S}} \frac{\pi_s}{1 + R_f} W_{1s} \tag{5}$$

Solving the optimization problem subject to the budget constraint reveals

$$U'(C_0) = \frac{p_s U'(W_s)}{z_s} \Leftrightarrow \pi_s = p_s \frac{U'(W_s)}{U'(C_0)}(1 + R_f) \tag{6}$$

This equation shows that risk-neutral probabilities are equal to empirical probabilities adjusted for preferences (denoted by the differential of marginal utilities) and the risk-free rate of interest. The latter enters the equation because time preferences are taken care of through discounting in Eq. (2) and not in risk-neutral probabilities. The interesting part is the differential of the marginal utilities. The equation highlights that for constant $U'(C_0)$ the differential will be higher for those states which correspond to low levels of wealth (and thus high marginal utility). Thus, risk-neutral probabilities tend to be higher than empirical probabilities in bad states of the economy when investors can consume less. No arbitrage considerations imply that all security-prices must meet Eq. (2). Therefore, securities which provide payoffs in bad states of the economy tend to be priced more expensively than those which pay off in positive states. Certainly, this one-period model is very simple and a stylized picture of reality at best. Nevertheless, the ideas can be generalized to multi-period models and a continuum of future states.

Cox and Ross (1976) apply the theoretical concept of risk-neutral valuation to the pricing of European-style options in continuous time. They show that the theoretical prices of such call and put options $\hat{C}(K, \tau)$ and $\hat{P}(K, \tau)$ with strike prices K and time to expiration $\tau = T - t$ are given by the risk-neutral expectation of future payoffs discounted at the risk-neutral interest rate r (with continuous compounding)

$$\begin{aligned}\hat{C}(K_i,\tau) &= e^{-r\tau}\mathbb{E}^{Q}[S_T - K_i] = e^{-r\tau}\int_{K_i}^{\infty} f(S_T)(S_T - K_i)dS_T \\ \hat{P}(K_i,\tau) &= e^{-r\tau}\mathbb{E}^{Q}[K_i - S_T] = e^{-r\tau}\int_{0}^{K_i} f(S_T)(K_i - S_T)dS_T\end{aligned} \tag{7}$$

Here $f(\cdot)$ denotes the RND function of the terminal price of the underlying asset S_T. Breeden and Litzenberger (1978) show that, given a continuum of European call prices $C(K,\tau)$, the state price density can be computed using the following formula:

$$\frac{\partial^2 C(K_i,\tau)}{\partial K_i^2} = e^{-r\tau} f(S_T = K_i) \tag{8}$$

Intuitively, the second derivative of the European call price function with respect to the strike price leads to state prices which are expressed as the discounted RND associated to the underlying asset taking the value of K_i at expiration of the option. Given the availability of European call prices for a continuum of strike prices, one could infer the whole terminal RND function of the underlying asset using the given formula. In practice, however, there are only a limited number of option prices for discretely spaced strike prices observable. It is therefore necessary to apply an approximation technique to recover option-implied RND functions from real-life options data. The most straightforward method relies on the approximation of the second-order derivative involved in Eq. (8) using finite differences.[1] Given $i = \{1, \ldots, N\}$ pairs of equally spaced strike prices and corresponding prices of European-style call options with the same time to maturity τ, the RND $f(S_T = K_i)$ can be approximated as follows[2]

$$f(S_T = K_i) \cong e^{r\tau}\frac{C(K_{i+1},\tau) - 2C(K_i,\tau) + C(K_{i-1},\tau)}{(\Delta K)^2} \tag{9}$$

The formula applies analogously to European put options $P(K,\tau)$. For illustrative purposes, we apply this approximation to data on German equity index options on March 09, 2011 and August 03, 2011.[3] Fig. 1 shows the computed RNDs plotted against the moneyness of the options involved.

Since equity index options are usually hedged using the corresponding future rather than the index itself, we define moneyness relative to the price of the equity index future with the same time to expiration $F(\tau)$.[4]

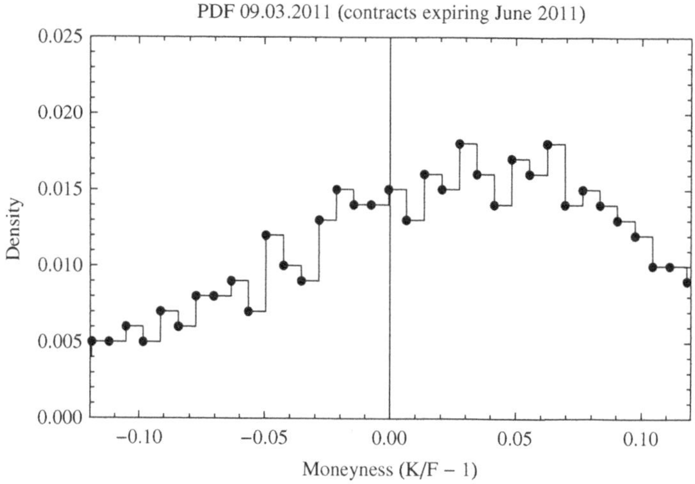

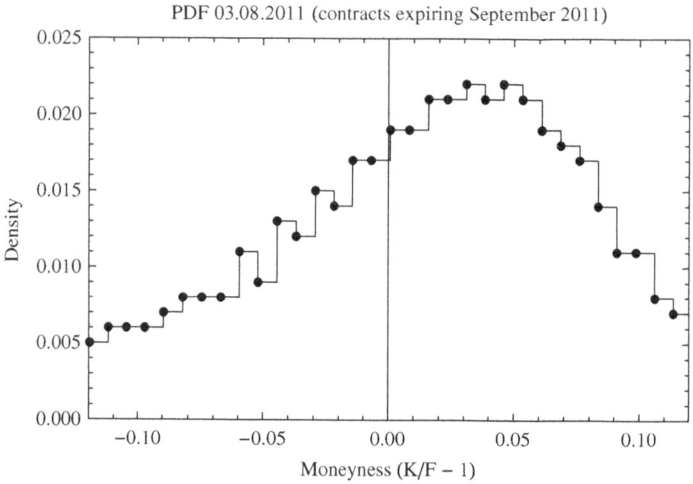

Fig. 1. RNDs Implied by DAX Options on March 09, 2011 and August 03, 2011 Computed Using Finite Differences Approximation.

$$\text{Moneyness} = \frac{K_i}{F(\tau)} - 1 \tag{10}$$

At this point it is important to note that the resulting curves do neither exhibit the smoothness we would expect of a probability density function (pdf) nor do they reveal how the probability mass is allocated to the tails of the distribution. Bliss and Panigirtzoglou (2002) give some reasons for the choppiness of the graph computed from raw options data. These include data errors, non-synchronicity of different data sources and differing levels of liquidity for different strike prices. Hence, we will have to apply a more sophisticated estimation technique to recover the RND from a limited range of discretely spaced option prices.

ESTIMATING THE RND FUNCTION

In recent years, different methods have been explored and applied to estimate RND functions from options data. We follow Jackwerth (1999, 2004) who, in a first step, distinguish parametric and nonparametric approaches. Parametric techniques try to estimate a limited set of parameters so that a specified functional form fits observed option prices. These methods, in turn, can be assigned to three subcategories. First, expansion methods add correction terms to a simple distribution until it fits available options data (Abadir & Rockinger, 2003). Second, generalized distribution methods use more complicated distributions in order to provide increased flexibility. For particular constellations of parameters they simplify to standard distributions (Corrado, 2001). Third, mixture approaches rely on a weighted average of simple distributions. In this research we model the RND as a mixture of two-lognormal densities. Thus, this method will be outlined in greater detail below. Nonparametric methods do not require a specific parametric form but allow more general functions in fitting the RND function to options data. Again, they can be assigned to three major groups. First, maximum-entropy methods try to minimize the amount of information presumed by maximizing the amount of missing information with respect to a prior distribution (Branger, 2004). Second, kernel methods try to fit a nonparametric functional form to observed data. These techniques are related to nonlinear regressions and require a large amount of data. An often cited example is Aït-Sahalia and Lo (1998). Third, curve-fitting methods are primarily used to interpolate between available implied volatility (IV) data points using polynomials or splines. A sufficient number of option prices are then computed from interpolated IVs.[5] Finally, RNDs are recovered using Eq. (9) or a comparable approximation to the second derivative of the option price with the respect to the strike (Figlewski, 2010; Malz, 1997).

A more comprehensive review of research on the estimation of option-implied RNDs is the work of Jackwerth (2004). Other reviews are provided by Bahra (1997), Jackwerth (1999), Bliss and Panigirtzoglou (2002), Mandler (2003), and Figlewski (2010).

We will focus on the class of parametric estimation methods, in particular the lognormal mixture distribution approach (Bahra, 1997; Melick & Thomas, 1997). Rather than assuming a particular stochastic process under the risk-neutral probability measure and estimating its parameters, this approach specifies a parametric form of the terminal RND function itself which is consistent with different underlying stochastic processes. Parameters are then inferred from market data. This method introduces additional degrees of freedom by constructing the terminal RND function as a weighted sum of independent lognormal pdfs and is thus able to capture a wide variety of future outcomes. Since mixture methods exhibit a tendency to overfit the data, we confine ourselves to modeling the RND as a mixture of two lognormal pdfs

$$f(S_T) = \theta\ell(\mu_1, \sigma_1) + (1-\theta)\ell(\mu_2, \sigma_2), \quad 1 > \theta > 0 \tag{11}$$

where θ represents the weighting factor and $\ell(\mu, \sigma)$ the pdf of the lognormal distribution.

$$\ell(\mu, \sigma) = \begin{cases} \dfrac{1}{\sqrt{2\pi}\sigma K} e^{-1/2((\ln K - \mu)/\sigma)^2} & K > 0 \\ 0 & K \leq 0 \end{cases} \quad \mu \in \mathbb{R}, \quad \sigma \in \mathbb{R}^+ \tag{12}$$

The shape of the implied RND is fully determined by five parameters $\{\theta, \mu_1, \sigma_1, \mu_2, \sigma_2\}$. Plugging Eq. (11) into Eq. (7) gives the theoretical pricing formulae for European call and put options

$$\begin{aligned} \hat{C}_t(S, K_i, \tau) &= e^{-r\tau} \int_{K_i}^{\infty} (S_T - K_i)\left[\theta\ell(\mu_1, \sigma_1) + (1-\theta)\ell(\mu_2, \sigma_2)\right] dS_T \\ \hat{P}_t(S, K_i, \tau) &= e^{-r\tau} \int_{0}^{K_i} (K_i - S_T)\left[\theta\ell(\mu_1, \sigma_1) + (1-\theta)\ell(\mu_2, \sigma_2)\right] dS_T \end{aligned} \tag{13}$$

Bahra (1997) derives a closed form solution to Eq. (13) which can be used to avoid numerical errors when evaluating the integrals involved. The prices of European-style options are given by

$$\hat{c}(K,\tau) = e^{-r\tau}\left[\theta(e^{\mu_1+(1/2)\sigma_1^2}\Phi(d_1) - K\Phi(d_2))\right] + (1-\theta)\left[e^{\mu_2+(1/2)\sigma_2^2}\Phi(d_3) - K\Phi(d_4)\right]$$
$$\hat{p}(K,\tau) = e^{-r\tau}\left[\theta(-e^{\mu_1+(1/2)\sigma_1^2}\Phi(-d_1) + K\Phi(-d_2))\right] + (1-\theta)\left[-e^{\mu_2+(1/2)\sigma_2^2}\Phi(-d_3) + K\Phi(-d_4)\right] \quad (14)$$
$$d_1 = \frac{-\ln K + \mu_1 + \sigma_1^2}{\sigma_1}, \quad d_2 = 1 - \sigma_1$$
$$d_3 = \frac{-\ln K + \mu_2 + \sigma_2^2}{\sigma_2}, \quad d_4 = 1 - \sigma_2$$

where $\Phi(\cdot)$ represents the cumulative distribution function (CDF) of the standard normal distribution. As mentioned above, equity index options are hedged using the futures contract on the same underlying with the same time to maturity. They can therefore be priced like options on futures contracts. In view of this fact it comes as no surprise that Eq. (14) can be interpreted as a weighted sum of two Black (1976) models.[6] Similar to Bahra (1997), we will consider equity index options data, that is, options on the German blue chip index DAX 30. Thus, the given closed form solutions are also applicable here.

In order to finally estimate the parameters of the two component lognormal distributions and the weighting factor, we minimize the following objective function using nonlinear methods

$$\underset{\mu_1,\mu_2,\sigma_1,\sigma_2,\theta}{\operatorname{argmin}} \left\{ \sum_{i=1}^{m}[P(K_i,\tau)-\hat{p}(K_i,\tau)]^2 + \sum_{i=m+1}^{n}[C(K_i,\tau)-\hat{c}(K_i,\tau)]^2 + \left[F(\tau)-\hat{F}(\tau)\right]^2 \right\} \quad (15)$$

where $\sigma_1,\sigma_2>0$ and $0\leq\theta\leq 1$. The goal is to find the particular set of parameters $\{\hat{\mu}_1,\hat{\mu}_2,\hat{\sigma}_1,\hat{\sigma}_2,\hat{\theta}\}$ that, for the whole cross section of observed strike prices, minimizes the squared differences between the corresponding call $C(K_i,\tau)$ and put $P(K_i,\tau)$ market prices and their theoretical counterparts computed from Eq. (14). It is common to further add the difference between the observed price of the futures contract on the same underlying with the same time to maturity τ and its theoretical counterpart $\hat{F}(\tau)$ (Bahra, 1997)

$$\hat{F}(\tau) = \mathbb{E}^{Q}[S_T|S_t] = \theta e^{\mu_1+(1/2)\sigma_1} + (1-\theta)e^{\mu_2+(1/2)\sigma_2} \quad (16)$$

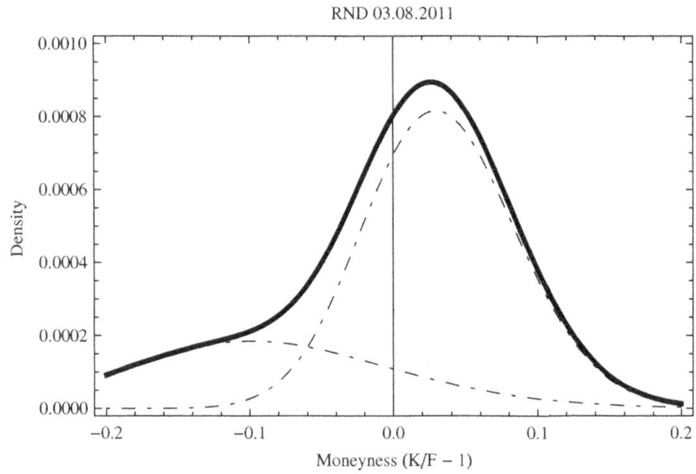

Fig. 2. Mixture RND (Solid Line) and Its Two Weighted Component Lognormal Distributions Estimated from DAX Options Maturing on September 16, 2011 (Parameterization: $\hat{\mu}_1 = 8.858, \hat{\mu}_2 = 8.723, \hat{\sigma}_1 = 0.053, \hat{\sigma}_2 = 0.100, \hat{\theta} = 0.749$).

The theoretical futures price is computed as a weighted sum of the means of the two component lognormal distributions. This is also known as the martingale restriction since it ensures that the parameters are chosen such that the futures price is the best estimator of the future spot price. Fig. 2 shows the estimated mixture RND on August 03, 2011 and its weighted component lognormal pdfs.

THE DATA

We obtain data on European-style call and put options on the German blue chip performance index DAX 30 from Thomson Reuters Datastream. Throughout this study, we use daily exchange settlement prices of contracts with open interest. Bahra (1997) and Söderlind (2000) argue that using these prices should help avoid problems with asynchronous intraday quotes. They further point out that these prices which are fixed after the trading period, are expected to be close to equilibrium prices. We estimate the RND functions using only near-the-money and out-of-the-money call and put options since these are more frequently traded and therefore assumed

Table 1. Prices of DAX Futures and Number of European-Style Option Contracts Used in RND Estimation.

Tōhoku earthquake/Fukushima nuclear accidents, contracts expiring June 17, 2011						
	09.03.2011	10.03.2011	11.03.2011	14.03.2011	15.03.2011	16.03.2011
$F(\tau)$	7154.0	7080.5	7008.0	6899.5	6687.5	6552.5
N	43	42	43	43	41	41
Tōhoku earthquake/Fukushima nuclear accidents, contracts expiring September 16, 2011						
	09.03.2011	10.03.2011	11.03.2011	14.03.2011	15.03.2011	16.03.2011
$F(\tau)$	7179.5	7106.5	7033.5	6924.5	6711.0	6575.0
N	39	40	41	41	42	39
Downgrading of US government securities, contracts expiring September 16, 2011						
	02.08.2011	03.08.2011	04.08.2011	05.08.2011	08.08.2011	09.08.2011
$F(\tau)$	6822.5	6645.0	6417.0	6257.5	5962.5	5941.0
N	42	41	40	39	37	37
	10.08.2011	11.08.2011	12.08.2011	15.08.2011	16.08.2011	17.08.2011
$F(\tau)$	5609.5	5812.5	5994.5	6026.5	5999.0	5956.0
N	35	36	37	38	37	37
Downgrading of US government securities, contracts expiring December 16, 2011						
	02.08.2011	03.08.2011	04.08.2011	05.08.2011	08.08.2011	09.08.2011
$F(\tau)$	6848.5	6670.5	6439.5	6279.0	5982.0	5958.5
N	41	38	34	34	32	34
	10.08.2011	11.08.2011	12.08.2011	15.08.2011	16.08.2011	17.08.2011
$F(\tau)$	5625.5	5829.0	6012.0	6045.0	6017.0	5974.5
N	29	35	37	37	37	38

to have the highest informational content (Clews, Panigirtzoglou, & Proudman, 2000). Furthermore, the estimation is confined to contracts that lie within a moneyness range from −15 to 15%. Again, moneyness is computed based on definition Eq. (10), that is, relative to the price of the corresponding DAX futures contract. Although this range is set rather arbitrarily, this restriction should help bypass liquidity related flaws in deep out-of-the-money options data. Finally, we exclude contracts that violate the following basic no-arbitrage conditions

$$C(K_i, \tau) \geq \max(0; S_t - Ke^{-r\tau}), \quad P(K_i, \tau) \geq \max(0; Ke^{-r\tau} - S_t) \qquad (17)$$

Discount factors for different maturities are computed from EONIA Swap Index interest rates which are also obtained from Thomson Reuters Datastream. It should be noted that the impact of small variations in discount factors on option prices is very limited (Bliss & Panigirtzoglou, 2002). This is particularly true for shorter times to expiration since the discount factor is then close to one.

Our study focuses on two incisive events, that is, the Fukushima nuclear accidents in March 2011 and the downgrading of U.S. government bonds in August 2011. We expect the market sentiment to change considerably in the course of these two events. To reveal the impact of the Fukushima nuclear disaster, option quotes during the period from March 09 to March 16, 2011 are considered. To validate our results, we estimate RNDs based on options that expire on June 17, 2011 and on September 16, 2011. In case of the downgrading of U.S. government securities we consider options data from August 02 to August 17, 2011. Again, the estimation is performed for options with two different expiration dates, that is, September 16, 2011 and December 16, 2011. Table 1 gives an overview of the DAX futures prices on the days under consideration and the number of DAX options employed in the estimation of the corresponding RNDs.

EMPIRICAL RESULTS

When estimating implied RNDs using the objective function in Eq. (15), we choose the transition between put and call options such that the contract which is currently at the money is the first call option, thereby not letting put and call prices overlap. As a consequence, the left side of the estimated pdf is mainly determined by out-of-the-money puts and the right side by out-of-the-money calls. Furthermore, all contracts enter the estimation procedure with equal weight. For a discussion of different error-correcting weighting schemes, see Bliss and Panigirtzoglou (2002). Since we are interested in highlighting changes in the shape of the RND function, we plot the estimated pdfs across a constant moneyness range from −20% to 20%. Further, we numerically compute the mean $\hat{\mu}$ and the absolute standard deviation $\hat{\sigma}$ of the fitted mixture distributions. In order to measure the asymmetry of the estimated pdfs, we rely on two different skewness measures. On the one hand, the median-based skew used by Bliss and Panigirtzoglou (2002)

$$\text{Median skew} = \frac{\hat{\mu} - \hat{X}_{50}}{\hat{\sigma}} \tag{18}$$

where $\hat{X}_{50}$ represents the 50% percentile, that is, the median of the distribution. On the other hand, the coefficient of quartile skewness that is often used as a robust measure of asymmetry

$$\text{Quartile skewness} = \frac{X_{25} - 2X_{50} + X_{75}}{X_{75} - X_{25}} \tag{19}$$

with X_n representing the n% percentile of the mixture distribution. We do not compute any measure of kurtosis. As Campa, Chang, and Reider (1998) point out, using the two-lognormal mixture approach causes the probability mass in the tails of the pdf to decay quickly. This, in turn, might prove too rigid when it comes to interpreting kurtosis measures. Besides, it should be mentioned that the shape of the distribution beyond the moneyness range used for estimation is not grounded on data points. Its informational content is therefore somewhat limited.

We start by computing the parameters of implied RND functions around the Tōhoku earthquake and the subsequent nuclear accidents at the Fukushima I nuclear power plant. The earthquake occurred on Friday, March 11, 2011, at 6.46 h CET, that is, before EUREX opened for trading.[7] Around 16.00 h CET the tsunami hit the Japanese coast which resulted in a power loss at the Fukushima Daiichi nuclear power plant and a subsequent failure of the reactor cooling system in one of the power plant's reactors around 18.30 h CET. On Saturday, March 12, the first hydrogen explosion occurred in the reactor building at unit 1 followed by the failure of the cooling system in unit 3. On Monday, March 14, another hydrogen explosion and the failure of the cooling system in unit 3 were reported. At 22.00 h CET, the Japanese government confirmed that core meltdowns in three reactors could not be ruled out. The situation worsened considerably on March 15, due to a burst of fire in unit 4 and further hydrogen explosions. At 16.15 h CET, the number of experts working on the site was reduced from 800 to 50. With a dramatic rise in the radiation levels, the crisis culminated on March 16, 2011. Fig. 3 shows four panels with RND functions on selected dates during the catastrophe that were recovered from the prices of European put and call options expiring in June 2011 (solid curves). As a reference point, each panel contains the

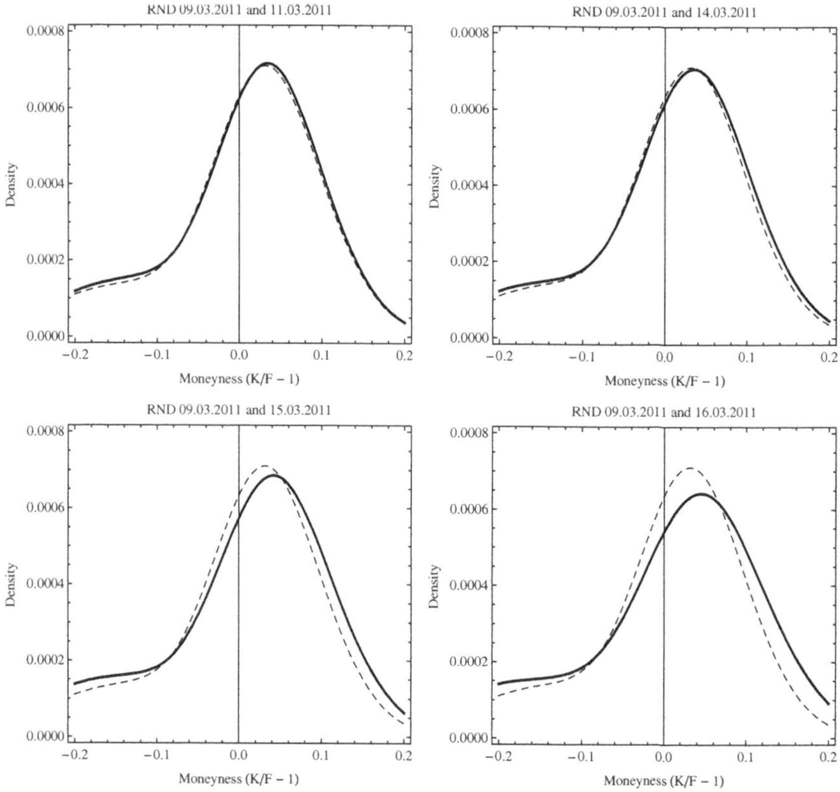

Fig. 3. Implied RNDs Before and in the Course of the Tōhoku Earthquake 2011/ the Fukushima Nuclear Disaster. The pdfs are Estimated Using DAX Options Which Expire on June 17, 2011. The Dashed Line Represents the RND Function on the Reference Date March 09, 2011.

implied RND on March 10, 2011, that is, the day before the catastrophe (dashed curves).

Table 2 gives daily quotes of the DAX future with the same maturity as the options and the summary statistics of the fitted RND functions for the period between March 09 and March 16, 2011.

As one would expect, the mean of the RNDs lies close to the futures price. If and only if there are no changes in the shape of the RND function, changes in the futures price should result in pure sideward movements of the pdf. Furthermore, the RND function is consistently negatively skewed. This

Table 2. DAX Future and Summary Statistics of RND Functions Before and in the Course of the Japan Earthquake with the Subsequent Fukushima Nuclear Disaster.

	09.03.2011	10.03.2011	11.03.2011	14.03.2011	15.03.2011	16.03.2011
$F(\tau)$	7154.0	7080.5	7008.0	6899.5	6687.5	6552.5
$\hat{\mu}$	7157.0	7083.4	7010.2	6903.2	6690.9	6555.2
$\hat{\sigma}$	729.8	729.9	725.0	740.1	768.9	814.1
Median skew	−0.163	−0.169	−0.172	−0.173	−0.187	−0.184
Quartile skew	−0.111	−0.128	−0.129	−0.127	−0.156	−0.156

Note: RNDs are estimated based on DAX options expiring on June 17, 2011.

is confirmed by Figlewski (2010) for RND functions recovered from options on the S&P 500 equity index. Bates (1991) provides an extensive study of negative skewness in implicit distributions recovered from these options around the stock market crash of 1987. Surprisingly, the shape of the RND function on March 11 does not depict any pronounced changes compared to the reference date. This suggests that market participants did not attach too much importance to the earthquake as such, thereby underestimating the potential consequences of the natural disaster. Even after the weekend with the first hydrogen explosion at the Fukushima nuclear power plant, only a slight increase in the left tail can be observed. Nevertheless, increasing volatility is indicative of increasing uncertainty among market participants. With the situation at the Fukushima nuclear power plant becoming worse, we observe a pronounced change in the shape of the RND functions. The left tail becomes much fatter which may be associated to market participants assigning higher probability to extreme downward movements of the DAX. Interestingly, the density function is becoming more negatively skewed. The graphs show that probability mass is shifted toward the right side of the mean of the pdf even though the disaster is still extending and accelerating. One has to be careful when it comes to interpreting this effect. We surmise that speculation on a quick recovery of the underlying index after the catastrophe might be part of the explanation. At this point it is important to note that the RND functions derived from options expiring in June 2011 convey information about the market participants' assessment of the situation in approximately three months' time (as seen from March 2011). If there is indeed speculation on a recovery of the DAX, the second effect should also be observable for a longer time horizon. We therefore repeat our computations based on DAX options that expire in December 2011,

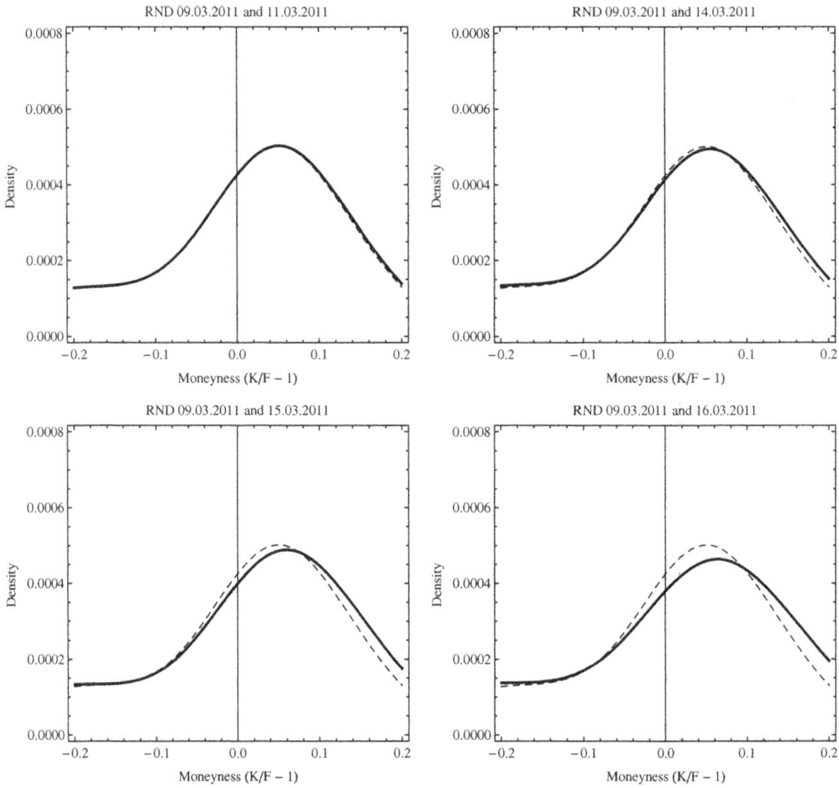

Fig. 4. Implied RNDs Before and in the Course of the Tōhoku Earthquake 2011/the Fukushima Nuclear Disaster. The pdfs are Estimated Using DAX Options Which Expire on September 16, 2011. The Dashed Line Represents the RND Function on the Reference Date March 09, 2011.

implying a time to expiration of approximately six months. Fig. 4 shows the resulting graphs.

Obviously, the peaks of all RND functions derived from options expiring in December 2011 are much less pronounced than those of their counterparts estimated from options that expire in September 2011.[8] Bahra (1997) explains this observation by the higher level of uncertainty implicit in options with longer times to expiration. Furthermore, the graphs confirm our suspicion: Compared to the reference date, probability mass indeed shifts toward the right side of the distribution. The moments reported in

Table 3. DAX Future and Summary Statistics of RND Functions Before and in the Course of the Japan Earthquake with the Subsequent Fukushima Nuclear Disaster.

	09.03.2011	10.03.2011	11.03.2011	14.03.2011	15.03.2011	16.03.2011
$F(\tau)$	7179.5	7106.5	7033.5	6924.5	6711.0	6575.0
$\hat{\mu}$	7181.6	7109.1	7035.5	6928.0	6714.1	6578.2
$\hat{\sigma}$	1020.9	1026.1	1022.1	1031.9	1062.0	1094.7
Median skew	−0.176	−0.179	−0.178	−0.180	−0.189	−0.183
Quartile skew	−0.159	−0.168	−0.160	−0.171	−0.186	−0.191

Note: RNDs are estimated based on DAX options expiring on September 16, 2011.

Table 3 support both observations. In line with the explanation provided by Bahra (1997), the standard deviation is generally higher compared to the RND function recovered from options expiring in June 2011. Further, the distribution is becoming more negatively skewed in the course of the catastrophe. As outlined above, we attribute this in part to speculation on a recovery of the German stock market.

The observation regarding the skewness of the RND functions gives rise to the question if this effect is also observable for other incisive events. We therefore repeat the computations for the downgrading of U.S. government debt securities. After a period of tough negotiations between Democrats and Republicans, congressional leaders of both parties agreed to raise the U.S. debt ceiling and to cut the federal deficit by as much as \$2.5 trillion over a decade. The legislation was passed by both houses of Congress on August 2, 2011. Nevertheless, on August 05, 2011 the rating agency Standard & Poor's (S&P) downgraded the U.S. credit rating from AAA to AA+ for the first time in the country's history. The announcement was made on Friday night, that is, after trading at EUREX had closed for the weekend. On Monday, August 08, 2011 stock markets around the world suffered significant losses. On that day, the DAX closed with a loss of 5%. This marked the beginning of a week of increased financial market volatility fueled by rumors about further downgrading of sovereigns and financial intermediaries. On Wednesday, August 10, 2011 the losses culminated in a stock market crash with the DAX dropping to 5,613 points representing a weekly loss of about 15.5%. In the course of the following days the DAX showed a slight improvement with closing prices remaining around 6,000 points. In contrast to our first example, we consider a longer period of time reaching from August 02 to August 17,

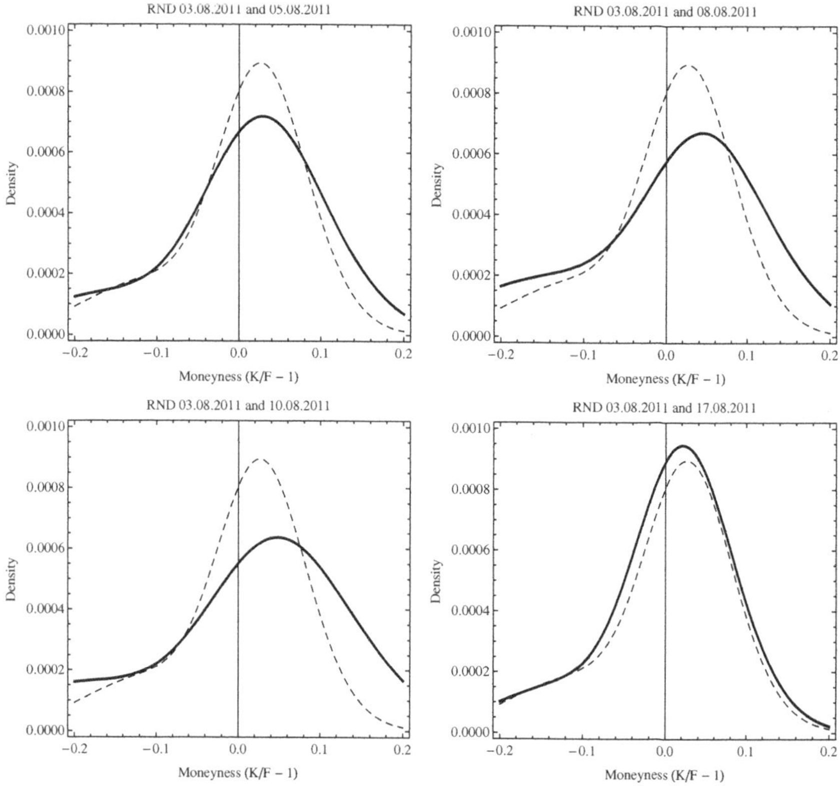

Fig. 5. Implied RNDs Before and After the Downgrading of U.S. Government Securities. The pdfs are Estimated Using DAX Options Which Expire on September 16, 2011. The Dashed Line Represents the RND Function on the Reference Date August 03, 2011.

2011. This enables us to compare the situation on different Wednesdays which should also help avoid potential problems with weekday-effects. Fig. 5 shows fitted RND functions implied by DAX options expiring in September 2011 (solid lines). Further, each panel contains the RND function estimated on Wednesday, August 03, 2011 as a reference point (dashed line).[9]

In order to highlight the differences compared to longer time horizons, we further estimate the implied RNDs using DAX options expiring in December 2011. Fig. 6 shows the corresponding graphs. Table 4 reports the futures prices and pdf summary statistics for both time horizons.

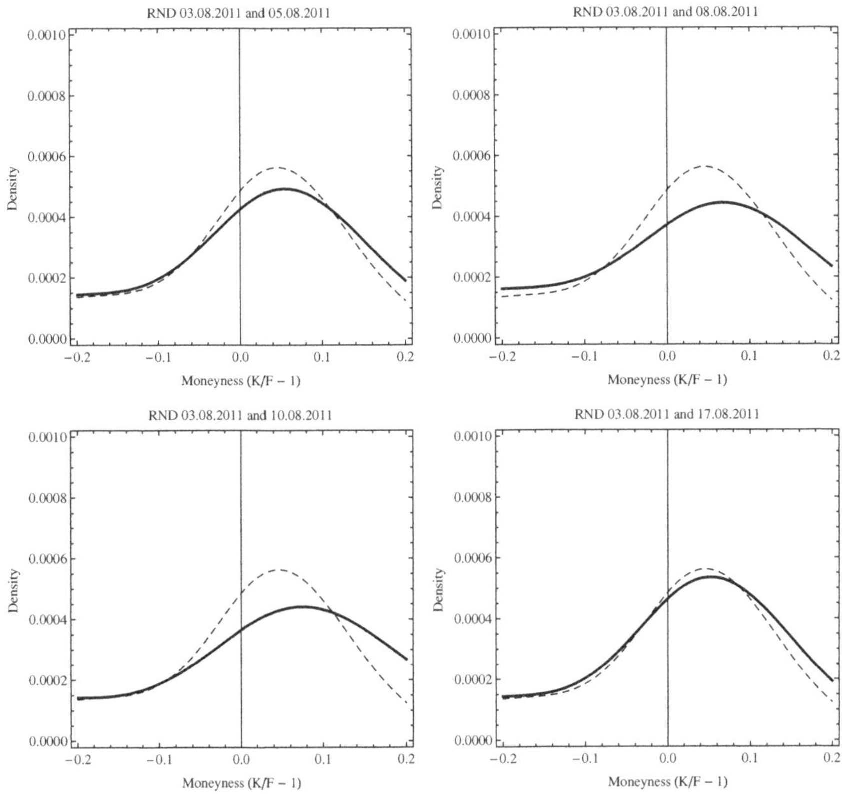

Fig. 6. Implied RNDs Before and After the Downgrading of U.S. Government Securities. The pdfs are Estimated Using DAX Options Which Expire on December 16, 2011. The Dashed Line Represents the RND Function on the Reference Date August 03, 2011.

Despite the fact that S&P announced the downgrading of U.S. sovereign debt on August 05, 2011 after EUREX had closed for the weekend, we find that the RND function changes its shape considerably that day. A possible explanation might be some information leakage prior to the official announcement made by S&P. Further, we observe that probability mass is moved to the left tail of the pdfs, suggesting that market participants assign higher probabilities to bad states of the future. As in case of the Japan earthquake with the subsequent Fukushima nuclear disaster, this effect is much less pronounced for RNDs derived from options with a longer time to

Table 4. DAX Future and Summary Statistics of Implied RND Functions before and after the Announcement of the Downgrading of U.S. Government Debt Securities.

Downgrading of US government securities, contracts expiring September 16, 2011

	02.08.2011	03.08.2011	04.08.2011	05.08.2011	08.08.2011	09.08.2011
$F(\tau)$	6822.5	6645.0	6417.0	6257.5	5962.5	5941.0
$\hat{\mu}$	6824.5	6645.7	6417.8	6258.6	5965.3	5943.2
$\hat{\sigma}$	584.8	567.1	614.3	688.9	730.2	780.4
Median skew	−0.152	−0.156	−0.155	−0.137	−0.161	−0.179
Quartile skew	−0.100	−0.112	−0.133	−0.090	−0.157	−0.146

	10.08.2011	11.08.2011	12.08.2011	15.08.2011	16.08.2011	17.08.2011
$F(\tau)$	5609.5	5812.5	5994.5	6026.5	5999.0	5956.0
$\hat{\mu}$	5611.4	5813.9	5995.5	6027.3	6000.3	5956.4
$\hat{\sigma}$	794.2	755.5	725.4	636.5	587.7	522.8
Median skew	−0.168	−0.164	−0.149	−0.141	−0.138	−0.129
Quartile skew	−0.148	−0.141	−0.107	−0.104	−0.104	−0.076

Downgrading of US government securities, contracts expiring December 16, 2011

	02.08.2011	03.08.2011	04.08.2011	05.08.2011	08.08.2011	09.08.2011
$F(\tau)$	6848.5	6670.5	6439.5	6279.0	5982.0	5958.5
$\hat{\mu}$	6850.6	6672.3	6441.9	6279.6	5984.0	5960.5
$\hat{\sigma}$	925.2	906.3	947.4	1000.5	1070.0	1132.6
Median skew	−0.166	−0.171	−0.165	−0.162	−0.158	−0.177
Quartile skew	−0.136	−0.146	−0.155	−0.158	−0.186	−0.204

	10.08.2011	11.08.2011	12.08.2011	15.08.2011	16.08.2011	17.08.2011
$F(\tau)$	5625.5	5829.0	6012.0	6045.0	6017.0	5974.5
$\hat{\mu}$	5626.0	5831.3	6014.0	6047.4	6020.2	5977.5
$\hat{\sigma}$	1123.6	1093.0	1069.9	1022.0	1013.0	937.3
Median skew	−0.174	−0.171	−0.172	−0.174	−0.169	−0.165
Quartile skew	−0.197	−0.193	−0.168	−0.173	−0.166	−0.148

Note: RNDs are estimated based on DAX options expiring on September 16, 2011 and DAX options expiring on December 16, 2011.

expiration. As one would expect, volatility increases sharply until August 10, 2011 – the day of the stock market crash – and steadily declines afterward back to its level prior to the downgrading announcement. Again, we find that probability mass shifts toward the right side of the density function. This is also reflected in the skewness measures of Table 4 which show that the pdfs at both time horizons become more negatively skewed until August 09, 2011. Afterward, skewness steadily moves back to its pre-crisis level for the shorter time to expiration. For the longer time horizon skewness also moves back, but the shift of probability mass to the right is obviously more persistent. Even though it is difficult to assess what in fact causes this behavior, we believe that speculation on a recovery of the underlying index after the downward movement could be a reasonable explanation.

CONCLUSION

In this research we study the impact of two different types of extreme events on option-implied RNDs. We consider a natural disaster, that is, the Tōhoku earthquake with the subsequent destruction of the nuclear power plant Fukushima Daiichi, and a major economic event, that is, the downgrading of U.S. sovereign debt in 2011. We apply a two-lognormal mixture approach to recover RNDs from European-style call and put options on the German blue chip index DAX 30. Our observations, which hold for both events under consideration, indicate a dichotomous effect on option-implied RND functions: Due to volatility increases in the course of both events more probability mass is moved to the tails of the densities. During the first days after the shocks, considerably more probability mass is assigned to the left tails of the pdfs. A reasonable explanation for this behavior might be that market participants facing bad news become more "nervous" and therefore assign higher probabilities to the bad states of the future. Moreover, we observe an impact on the skewness of the distributions. In particular for longer-term options we find that – besides sideward movements of the pdf – probability mass is shifted toward the right side of the density function. This implies that also positive events are assigned higher probabilities under the risk-neutral measure. An interpretation of this behavior might be speculation on a recovery of the German stock market in the longer term through investments in out-of-the-money calls.

Clearly, there are also some caveats. The mixture of two lognormal distributions may exhibit some undesirable features including too large changes in higher moments of the pdf between consecutive days. Further, there are clear limitations imposed by the data. Bliss and Panigirtzoglou (2002) point out that limiting the range of strike prices used for estimation is equivalent to limiting the information incorporated into the implied RND.

Clews et al. (2000) even argue that end-of-day settlement prices might not reflect true market prices at all.

Nevertheless, in our opinion the observed effects are worth being reconsidered in a more in-depth analysis. RNDs of other extreme events could be analyzed using alternative estimation techniques combined with robustness checks to further support our findings. However, this will be left to future research.

NOTES

1. Breeden and Litzenberger (1978) already propose this approximation. For a discussion and application in greater detail see, for example, Neuhaus (1995).
2. Figlewski (2010) points out that the data points need not necessarily be equally spaced. In this case, he recommends using a weighting procedure to keep the approximation working.
3. More precisely, we use data on out-of-the-money call and put options on the German blue chip index DAX 30 expiring on September 16, 2011. The data employed will be described in greater detail in the subsequent sections.
4. To trade an equity index directly will not be free of problems. One could replicate it using a basket of single stocks. This in turn will most probably lead to significant transaction costs due to rebalancing needs. Alternatively, one could rely on exchange traded funds (ETFs) which are, however, less liquid than the index future.
5. It is important to note that the Black and Scholes (1973) model is used as a tool to convert option prices to implied volatilities and back. Doing this is not equivalent to assuming that this model is true.
6. The Black (1976) model is a modified version of the Black and Scholes (1973) option pricing model which can be used for pricing futures options.
7. Both the DAX options and DAX futures used in this study are traded at EUREX. The general trading hours at EUREX are from 8.00 h to 22.00 h CET.
8. Note that the scale of the ordinate has remained unchanged.
9. The choice of the reference date was based on the observation that the RND function remained relatively stable between August 02 and August 03, 2011.

REFERENCES

Abadir, K. M., & Rockinger, M. (2003). Density functionals, with an option-pricing application. *Econometric Theory*, *19*(5), 778–811. doi:10.1017/S0266466603195047

Aït-Sahalia, Y., & Lo, A. W. (1998). Nonparametric estimation of state-price densities implicit in financial asset prices. *The Journal of Finance*, *53*(2), 499–547. doi:10.1111/0022-1082.215228

Bahra, B. (1997). *Implied risk-neutral probability density functions from option prices: Theory and application*. Working Paper No. 66. Bank of England, London.

Bates, D. S. (1991). The crash of '87: Was it expected? The evidence from options markets. *The Journal of Finance*, *46*(3), 1009–1044Retrieved from http://www.jstor.org/stable/2328552. Accessed on March 6, 2012.

Black, F. (1976). The pricing of commodity contracts. *Journal of Financial Economics*, *3*(1–2), 167–179. doi:10.1016/0304-405X(76)90024-6

Black, F., & Scholes, M. (1973). The pricing of options and corporate liabilities. *The Journal of Political Economy*, *81*(3), 637–654. Retrieved from http://www.jstor.org/stable/1831029. Accessed on March 6, 2012.

Bliss, R. R., & Panigirtzoglou, N. (2002). Testing the stability of implied probability density functions. *Journal of Banking & Finance*, *26*(2–3), 381–422. doi:10.1016/S0378-4266(01)00227-8

Branger, N. (2004). Pricing derivative securities using cross-entropy: An economic analysis. *International Journal of Theoretical and Applied Finance*, *7*(1), 63–82. doi:10.1142/S0219024904002335

Breeden, D. T., & Litzenberger, R. H. (1978). Prices of state-contingent claims implicit in option prices. *The Journal of Business*, *51*(4), 621–651. Retrieved from http://www.jstor.org/stable/2352653. Accessed on March 6, 2012.

Campa, J. M., Chang, P. H. K., & Reider, R. L. (1998). Implied exchange rate distributions: Evidence from OTC option markets. *Journal of International Money and Finance*, *17*(1), 117–160. doi:10.1016/S0261-5606(97)00054-5

Clews, R., Panigirtzoglou, N., & Proudman, J. (2000, February). Recent developments in extracting information from options markets. *Bank of England Quarterly Bulletin*, *40*(1), 50–60.

Corrado, C. (2001). Option pricing based on the generalized lambda distribution. *Journal of Futures Markets*, *21*(3), 213–236. doi:10.2139/ssrn.248696

Cox, J. C., & Ross, S. A. (1976). The valuation of options for alternative stochastic processes. *Journal of Financial Economics*, *3*(1–2), 145–166. doi:10.1016/0304-405X(76)90023-4

Figlewski, S. (2010). Estimating the implied risk neutral density for the US market portfolio. In T. Bollerslev (Ed.), *Volatility and time series econometrics: Essays in honor of Robert F. Engle* (1st ed, pp. 323–353). Oxford: Oxford University Press.

Ingersoll, J. E. (1987). *Theory of financial decision making*. Lanham, MD: Rowman & Littlefield.

Jackwerth, J. (1999). Option-implied risk-neutral distributions and implied binomial trees: A literature review. *Journal of Derivatives*, *7*(2), 66–82. doi:10.3905/jod.1999.319143

Jackwerth, J. C. (2004). *Option-implied risk-neutral distributions and risk aversion*. Charlottesville, VA: Research Foundation of AIMR.

Malz, A. M. (1997). Estimating the probability distribution of the future exchange rate from option prices. *Journal of Derivatives*, *5*(2), 18–36. doi:10.3905/jod.1997.407988

Mandler, M. (2003). *Market expectations and option prices: Contributions to economics*. Heidelberg: Physica-Verl.

Melick, W. R., & Thomas, C. P. (1997). Recovering an asset's implied PDF from option prices: An application to crude oil during the Gulf crisis. *Journal of Financial and Quantitative Analysis*, *32*(1), 91–115. doi:10.2307/2331318

Neuhaus, H. (1995). Der Informationsgehalt von Derivaten für die Geldpolitik: Implizite Volatilitäten und Wahrscheinlichkeiten. *Volkswirtschaftliche Forschungsgruppe der Deutschen Bundesbank: 95,3*. Frankfurt am Main.

Söderlind, P. (2000). Market expectations in the UK before and after the ERM crisis. *Economica*, *67*(265), 1–18. doi:10.1111/1468-0335.00192

Zimmermann, H. (1998). *State-Preference Theorie und Asset Pricing: Eine Einführung*. Studies in Contemporary Economics. Heidelberg: Physica-Verl.

PART III
DERIVATIVES MODELS AND MODEL PERFORMANCE

NON-GAUSSIAN PRICE DYNAMICS AND IMPLICATIONS FOR OPTION PRICING

Miguel Angel Fuentes, Austin Gerig and Javier Vicente

ABSTRACT

It is well known that the probability distribution of stock returns is non-Gaussian. The tails of the distribution are too "fat," meaning that extreme price movements, such as stock market crashes, occur more often than predicted given a Gaussian model. Numerous studies have attempted to characterize and explain the fat-tailed property of returns. This is because understanding the probability of extreme price movements is important for risk management and option pricing. In spite of this work, there is still no accepted theoretical explanation. In this chapter, we use a large collection of data from three different stock markets to show that slow fluctuations in the volatility (i.e., the size of return increments), coupled with a Gaussian random process, produce the non-Gaussian and stable shape of the return distribution. Furthermore, because the statistical features of volatility are similar across stocks, we show that their return distributions collapse onto one universal curve. Volatility fluctuations influence the pricing of derivative

Derivative Securities Pricing and Modelling
Contemporary Studies in Economic and Financial Analysis, Volume 94, 211–225

ISSN: 1569-3759/doi:10.1108/S1569-3759(2012)0000094011

instruments, and we discuss the implications of our findings for the pricing of options.

INTRODUCTION

In his thesis, *Théorie de la Spéculation* (1900), Louis Bachelier modeled price differences as a simple random process (Bachelier, 1900, 1964). It was a seminal publication, not only was it the first mathematical study of stock prices, it also was the first time that the diffusion of a Markovian process was treated analytically, predating by five years the work of Albert Einstein (1905). Bachelier's work laid the foundation for the field of mathematical finance; a field that has blossomed in the last century.

Although pioneering for its time, several modifications to Bachelier's random walk model have been needed. First was the realization that prices move in relative amounts rather than absolute amounts, and that *returns* rather than price differences should be modeled as a random process (Osborne, 1959). Next, several papers showed that returns could not be described by a simple random process because extreme price movements occur much to frequently, causing the return distribution to have *fat* tails (Fama, 1965; Mandelbrot, 1963).

Despite numerous attempts to explain the fat-tailed nature of the return distribution (Bassler, McCauley, & Gunaratne, 2007; Bouchaud & Potters, 2003; Farmer, Gillemot, Lillo, Mike, & Sen, 2004; Gabaix, Gopikrishnan, Plerou, & Stanley, 2003; Mantegna & Stanley, 1995; Viswanathan, Fulco, Lyra, & Serva, 2003), there is still no consensus on the underlying cause.

Characterizing the shape and scaling of the return distribution is important because it determines the probability of observing extreme events, which is needed for proper risk management and for the correct pricing of derivative instruments. If returns are Gaussian, then options are priced according to the standard equation of Black and Scholes (1973). Because returns are ill-described by a Gaussian process, B-S prices exhibit systematic biases across moneyness and time to maturity.

Two explanations for the non-Gaussian shape of the return distribution are often discussed in the literature. The first is known as the *mixture-of-distributions* (MOD) hypothesis (Blattberg & Gonedes, 1974; Praetz, 1972), which states that the return distribution is a mixture of Gaussian distributions with different variances. The second is known as the *stable Paretian* (SP) hypothesis (Lux, 1996; Mandelbrot, 1963; Mantegna & Stanley, 1995), which states that returns are pulled independently and identically from a stable or truncated stable distribution. The MOD hypothesis better describes the shape of the distribution (Blattberg & Gonedes, 1974), but the SP hypothesis better describes the stability of the distribution, that is, that the distribution retains it's non-Gaussian shape when aggregating returns over longer timescales.

In this chapter, we present a model that reproduces both the shape and stability of the return distribution. The model is based on two assumptions about the characteristics of *volatility*, the scale of returns. First, we assume that volatility fluctuates slowly, that is, volatility fluctuations are rather small over short to intermediate intervals (days to weeks), but are quite large over longer timescales (months to years). Second, we assume that the process that generates volatility fluctuations is such that the inverse square of volatility is gamma distributed. As shown below, these assumptions predict that the return distribution will be non-Gaussian (specifically Student's t-distributed), and that the return distribution will keep this shape for short to intermediate timescales. The model, therefore, reproduces empirical results that previously seemed contradictory, and that individually, were used to support one or the other of the two competing hypotheses for non-Gaussian returns (MOD or SP).

We test the predictions of the model using data from six stocks collected from three global exchanges over different time periods. The model performs well for each stock, suggesting it is robust to different time periods, different market sectors, and different countries. These results have implications for the pricing of options, which we discuss after presenting the results.

THEORETICAL APPROACH

We define the return at time t as the difference in logarithmic price from time t to time $t + \tau$,

$$r(t) = \ln[p(t + \tau)] - \ln[p(t)] \quad (1)$$

where the price, $p(t)$, is defined as the midpoint price between the best bid price and offer price in the market (these prices are known as *quotes*).

There are several possibilities to set the unit of the time index, t, and here we study returns over the finest possible timescale, *event-time*. In event-time, t is updated, incremented by a unit, whenever there is a change in the midpoint between the prevailing best quotes.

To begin our analysis we will use the Langevin approach. The proposed stochastic dynamic for the return *during a day* will be the fundamental ordinary differential equation:

$$\frac{dr}{dt} = \sigma\xi(t) \tag{2}$$

Where $\xi(t)$ is a white Gaussian noise of unit variance, that is,

$$\langle \xi(t) \rangle = 0 \tag{3}$$

$$\langle \xi(t)\xi(t') \rangle = \delta(t - t') \tag{4}$$

t is the time, and σ is the *volatility*, or the strength of the noise acting on the return.

Under Ito's calculus, this stochastic dynamic leads immediately to an evolution equation for the probability of the returns, the Fokker–Planck equation, which is

$$\frac{\partial P(x,t)}{\partial t} = \frac{\sigma^2}{2}\frac{\partial^2 P(x,t)}{\partial x^2} \tag{5}$$

This equation has an analytical solution, which is the same that Bachelier found for non *log*-transformed prices in 1900, and five years later Einstein suggested as the distribution for Brownian particles: the normal distribution. "The problem, which corresponds to the diffusion from a single point (ignoring the interactions between diffusing particles) is now mathematically completely defined: its solution is"

$$P(r,t) = \sqrt{\frac{1}{2\pi\sigma^2 t}}\exp\left(-\frac{r^2}{2\sigma^2 t}\right) \tag{6}$$

"Therefore, the distribution of the resulting displacements in a given time t is the same as random error ...," from (Einstein, 1905), author's translations.

In Eqs. (2)–(6), the volatility is fixed, meaning that during any given day, we assume a constant strength for the noise. At this point, the model is nearly identical to Bachelier's original work (using returns instead of price differences). To generate the non-Gaussian, stable shape of the return distribution, we assume that volatility slowly fluctuates. Specifically, we assume that volatility is sufficiently slow varying, such that we can treat σ as a constant over intraday timescales. Over longer periods, we assume that the square of the volatility (the local variance of the price), $v = \sigma^2$, follows a feedback process (Bouchaud & Potters, 2003)

$$v_{k-1} - v_0 = (1 - \varepsilon)(v_k - v_0) - g\varepsilon v_k(\langle\varsigma\rangle - \varsigma) \tag{7}$$

where ς is a centered noise term. This process produces a local variance that is mean-reverting to the value v_0, but which retains memory of past values with coupling parameter g.

The continuous formulation of this discrete Langevin equation leads to the following Fokker–Plank equation for the evolution of the probability:

$$\frac{\partial P(v,t)}{\partial t} = \varepsilon\frac{\partial(v_k - v_0)P(v,t)}{\partial v} + Dg^2\varepsilon^2\frac{\partial^2 P(v,t)}{\partial v^2} \tag{8}$$

where D is the variance of the noise ς. The stationary solution for this equation is an inverse-gamma distribution

$$f(v) = \frac{1}{\Gamma(\mu)v^{1+\mu}}\exp\left(\frac{-v_0}{v}\right) \tag{9}$$

where $\mu = 1 + Dg^2\varepsilon$. Now, if we define

$$v = \frac{1}{\beta} \tag{10}$$

$$\mu = \frac{n}{2} \tag{11}$$

$$\sigma_0 = \frac{n}{2\beta_0} \tag{12}$$

so that the return distribution can be written as

$$P(r,t|\beta) = \sqrt{\frac{\beta}{2\pi\tau}}\exp\frac{\beta r^2}{2\tau} \tag{13}$$

and using the distribution's transformation

$$P(\beta) = P(\sigma^2)\left|\frac{d\sigma^2}{d\beta}\right| \tag{14}$$

we can write

$$f(\beta) = \frac{1}{\Gamma(n/2)}\left(\frac{n}{2\beta_0}\right)^{n/2}\exp\left(-\frac{n\beta}{2\beta_0}\right) \tag{15}$$

which is the equation for a gamma distribution. On any single day, the distribution of returns is Gaussian with variance $v = \sigma^2 = 1/\beta$, as shown in Eq. (6). Because β can vary at longer timescales, the return distribution observed with data pulled from many different days is obtained by marginalizing over β,

$$P(r,\tau) = \int P(r,\tau|\beta)f(\beta)d\beta \tag{16}$$

As seen in this equation, the return distribution is a mixture of Gaussians with different variances.

A straightforward integration of the conditional probability of returns, $P(r,\tau|\beta)$, and the distribution $f(\beta)$ yields the following for the return distribution

$$P(r,\tau) = \frac{\Gamma[(n+1)/2]}{\Gamma[n/2]}\sqrt{\frac{\beta_0}{2\pi\tau}}\left(1+\frac{\beta_0 r^2}{n\tau}\right)^{-(n+1)/2} \tag{17}$$

which is a variant of the Student's t-distribution. The non-Gaussian shape of the distribution results from collecting returns from time periods separated by long intervals where β is different. The stability of this shape for short to intermediate τ results from negligible fluctuations of β over these timescales.

Other papers have reported that returns follow a Student's t-distribution and have fit returns to a generic version of this distribution (see Blattberg & Gonedes, 1974; Bouchaud & Potters, 2003; Praetz, 1972 for examples). Eq. (17) does not represent a fit to the return data, but is determined solely by the two parameters, β_0 and n, from the distribution of the inverse variance, β. In the results we present below, we do not fit a Student's t-distribution, but instead compare the empirical distribution to the predicted distribution as expressed in Eq. (17) and as determined by the independent measurement of β_0 and n. This specifically tests our model rather than the more general result that returns follow a Student's t-distribution.

To facilitate the presentation of the empirical results, we define the following normalized variables

$$r' = r\sqrt{\frac{2\beta_0}{n\tau}}\frac{1}{\beta} \tag{18}$$

$$P'(r') = [\Omega P(r,\tau)]^{2/(n+1)} \tag{19}$$

where $\Omega = \sqrt{2\pi}\Gamma[n/2]/\Gamma[(n+1)/2]$. These normalizations allow results for different timescales and different stocks to collapse on a single curve.

DATA

Our results are produced using a large amount of data (of the order of 10^7 data points) from three stock markets over three time periods: the London Stock Exchange (LSE) from May 2, 2000 to December 31, 2002, the New York Stock Exchange (NYSE) from January 2, 2001 to December 31, 2002, and the Spanish Stock Exchange (SSE) from January 2, 2004 to December 29, 2006. For each market, we choose two highly traded stocks that are from different market sectors. From the NYSE, we study General Motors (GM), an automotive maker, and International Business Machines (IBM), a computer hardware/software maker and consulting firm. From the LSE, we study AstraZeneca (AZN), a pharmaceutical company, and Vodafone (VOD), a mobile telecommunications company. From the SSE we study Santander (SAN), a banking group, and Telefonica (TEF) a broadband and telecommunications company. We consider only the electronic markets for these stocks, and we measure returns whenever the mid-price of a stock fluctuates. This approach allows us to study returns on the finest possible timescale. When aggregating returns over longer timescales, we use nonoverlapping intervals. As mentioned, we measure price fluctuations, or returns, in the standard way (Bouchaud & Potters, 2003) as $r(t) = \ln[p(t+\tau)] - \ln[p(t)]$, where p is the mid-price, t is the time (which is updated by one unit whenever the mid-price changes), and τ is the time increment (also measured in units of mid-price changes).

RESULTS

In this section, we compare empirical results with the assumptions and results of the model. We present supporting evidence for our assumption

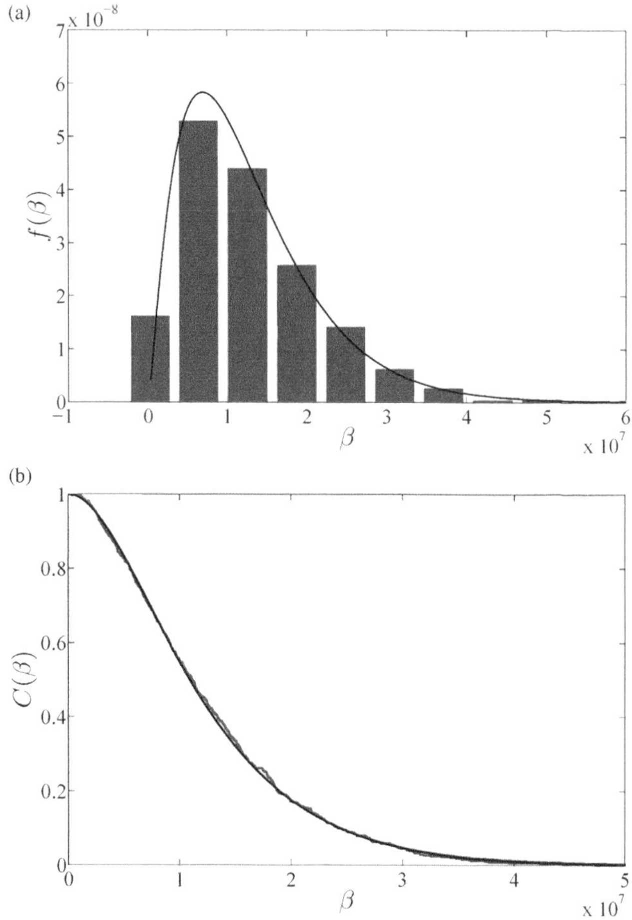

Fig. 1. The Distribution of β for the Stock IBM. (a) The Probability Density of Daily β fit by a Gamma Distribution. The Parameters of the Fit Are $n = 4.4$ and $\beta_0 = 12.8 \times 10^6$. (b) The CCD of β Compared to the Fit.

that the inverse variance of stock returns is gamma distributed. In addition, we show that the return distribution collapses over intraday timescales, supporting our assumption of a slowly fluctuating volatility. Finally, we plot the scaled return distributions for all of the stocks in our study; the collapse of these distributions suggests that the volatility characteristics we've assumed are universally valid.

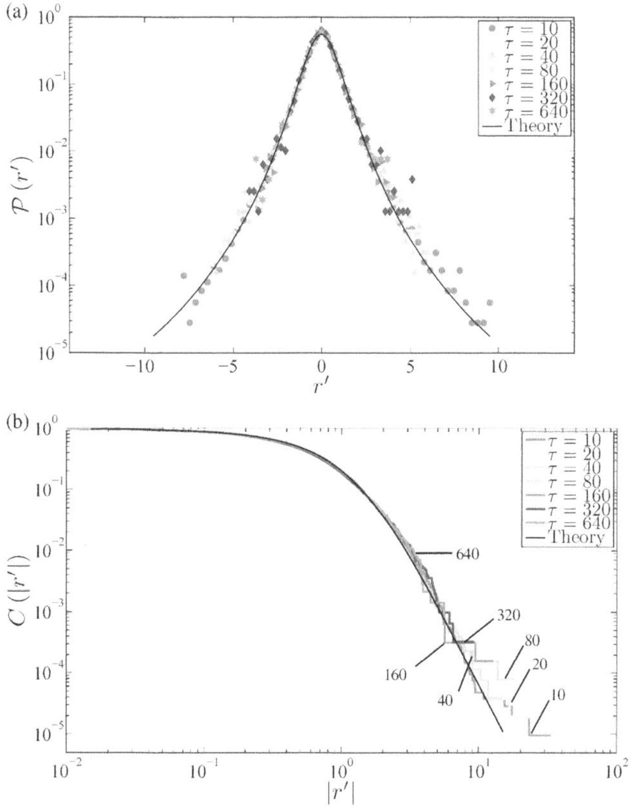

Fig. 2. Collapse of the Distribution of Returns for the Stock IBM Over Various Timescales. (a) The Probability Density Function of Scaled Returns from $\tau = 10$ to $\tau = 640$. (b) The CCD of Scaled Returns for the Same Timescales. In Both Plots, the Solid Black Line is the Calculated from the Theoretical Distribution, Eq. (19) Using $n = 4.4$ and $\beta_0 = 12.8 \times 10^6$.

Figs. 1 and 2 present results only for the stock IBM, although not shown, the results for the other stock in our study are similar in appearance. In Fig. 1(a) we plot the probability density function of β. We overlay the plot with the best fit gamma distribution, that is, the gamma distribution using maximum likelihood estimates (MLEs) for the parameters n and β_0. These MLEs for IBM and the other stocks are reported in Table 1. In Fig. 1(b), we plot the complementary cumulative distribution (CCD) of β and again overlay the plot with the best fit gamma distribution (the CCD is the integral

Table 1. The Total Number of Price Changing Events, Average Number of Events Per Day, and Maximum Likelihood Estimates for n and β_0 for the Six Stocks Studied.

Security	Events	Events/Day	n	β_0 ($\times 10^6$)
GM	505,541	1,025	3.7	6.3
IBM	1,056,636	2,143	4.4	12.8
AZN	1,013,482	1,501	4.8	5.0
VOD	841,492	1,247	8.8	1.8
SAN	243,545	329	15.7	3.0
TEF	315,093	426	30.6	4.8

of the probability function). As seen in both plots, the gamma distribution fits well.

In Fig. 2(a) we plot the probability density function for IBM scaled returns, r', from $\tau = 10$ to $\tau = 640$, which is up to one trading day for the stocks in our study. From the MLEs for parameters n and β_0, we predict the full probability distribution of returns, as derived in Eq. (17) and overlay this prediction on the plot. In Fig. 2(b) we plot the CCD of absolute scaled returns, $C(|r'|)$. We show this plot in logarithmic coordinates to focus on the tails of the distribution, and we overlay the plot with the CCD of the theoretical distribution. As seen in both plots, the model matches the data well in the central region and the tails, and the shape of the distribution is stable over these timescales.

In Fig. 3, we plot the empirical CCD of β versus the fit for all six stocks in the study. This plot is created by first fixing the value of the fit $C(\cdot)$, calculating β at this point, and then plotting the value of the empirical $C(\cdot)$ for this β. The plot is sometimes called a P-P plot, which is used to assess the similarity of the distributions on the x and y axes. If the empirical distribution follows the fitted distribution exactly, the curve will lie on the 45° line. The empirical data shows no systematic deviations from a gamma distribution.

Our model predicts that the functional form of the return distribution is the same for different stocks, and that inconsistencies can be attributed to different parameters of the gamma distribution for β. This is verified in Fig. 4, where we show the collapse of the renormalized probability distribution $P'(r')$, Eq. (19), for all 6 stocks in our study. The return distributions are well fit by the model and collapse over the entire range of returns.

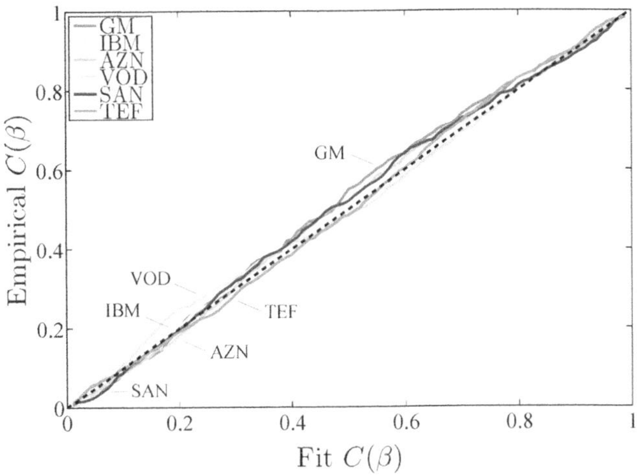

Fig. 3. The Complementary Cumulative Distribution (CCD) of β Compared to the CCD from the Best Fit Gamma Distribution for All the Stocks in Our Study.

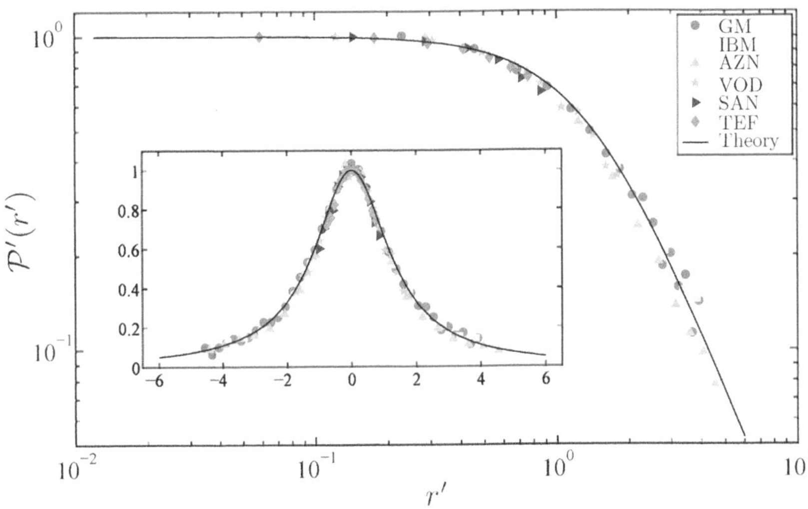

Fig. 4. Collapse of the Return Distribution on the Function $P'(r')$ for the Stocks in Our Study. For Each Stock, the Probability Density Function for $\tau = 80$ is Shown in Logarithmic Coordinates. Inset: The Same Plot in Regular Coordinates.

IMPLICATIONS FOR OPTION PRICING

In the option pricing paper of Black and Scholes (1973), stock prices are assumed to follow geometric Brownian motion with a constant volatility. Because volatility is constant, there exists only one source of randomness that affects both the price of the stock and the price of an option on the stock. The main insight of the B-S model is the following: by holding a certain proportion of stock together with the option (which is dynamically rebalanced) and the randomness of both can be cancelled so that a riskless portfolio results. By setting the return of this portfolio to the risk-free rate, the price of the option can be deduced.

The first study to price options with nonconstant volatility was Merton (1976), who allowed the price process to include random but diversifiable jumps. A number of papers followed that allow for more general changes in volatility. These papers can be separated into two groups, the first group keeps only one source of randomness and assumes that volatility is a deterministic function of price and time (Cox & Ross, 1976; Derman & Kani, 1994; Platen, 2001). The models in these papers are known as *local volatility models*. The second group allows for volatility to be driven by a second source of randomness (Heston, 1993; Hull & White, 1987; Stein & Stein, 1991). These models are known as *stochastic volatility models*. Option pricing within local volatility models can be solved in a similar way as in the B-S model, by forming riskless portfolios. Within stochastic volatility models, pricing options require either the introduction of a hedging instrument for volatility fluctuations or assumptions about the risk preferences of investors.

As seen in the figures above, the returns for the stocks in our study are Student's t-distributed and volatility exhibits slow dynamics. The B-S model no longer applies under these circumstances. Calculating options prices when volatility exhibits both extreme fluctuations and slow dynamics is nontrivial.

Local volatility models that produce Student's t-distributed returns include the models found in Borland (2002) and the minimal market model of Platen (2001). Stochastic volatility models that produce Student's t-distributed returns include the GARCH model (Nelson, 1990) and the 3/2 model (Lewis, 2000). The stochastic volatility model that we adopt in this chapter is a variation in the GARCH model. Option pricing within the GARCH model was treated in Satchell and Timmermann (1992), Amin and Ng (1993), and Duan (1995). Care should be taken when interpreting these results because volatility fluctuations are too fast over longer time periods within the GARCH model. Taylor (2000) studies option pricing when volatility is slowly varying.

To obtain correct option prices, the full dynamics of volatility from short to long timescales must be specified accurately. There is currently no consensus on a volatility model that achieves such a specification, and many of the volatility models above are able to reproduce in a general way the biases observed in B-S option pricing.

CONCLUSIONS

In this chapter, we have presented evidence that the non-Gaussian shape and stable scaling of the return distribution are due to slow, but significant, fluctuations in volatility. Furthermore, our results suggest that return distributions for stocks from different exchanges, time periods, and over different timescales can be described by one functional form.

Our model decomposes individual returns into the product of two terms: a Gaussian noise term and a volatility parameter. On any single day, we assume that volatility is constant so that returns are well described by Gaussian fluctuations. Across many days, however, volatility is driven by a mean-reverting process that produces a gamma distributed β. When combining the local Gaussian behavior of returns with these slow volatility fluctuations, the result is a Student's t-distribution for returns that appears stable over short to intermediate timescales.

The idea that volatility fluctuations produce non-Gaussian returns is not new. It was originally suggested several decades ago (Blattberg & Gonedes, 1974; Clark, 1973; Praetz, 1972). This has competed with an alternative explanation that returns are drawn unconditionally from a fat-tailed, stable distribution (Lux, 1996; Mandelbrot, 1963; Mantegna & Stanley, 1995). Our model can reproduce both the non-Gaussian shape and the apparent stability of the return distribution, two characteristics that previously seemed to be at odds with one another and that individually could be used to support one or the other competing explanations.

Using intraday data for six stocks from three countries, we confirm the predictions of the model. We find that the inverse square of daily volatility is well fit by a gamma distribution. Using the parameters from this fit, we compute the return distribution from the model and find that the empirical distribution matches this prediction extremely well. Furthermore, we find that the return distribution collapses over intraday timescales, a result that supports our assumption of constant intraday volatility. Finally, we show that by appropriately rescaling the returns for each of the stocks in our study, their return distributions collapse onto a single curve, confirming that our model is valid for a variety of different stocks.

ACKNOWLEDGMENTS

Austin Gerig acknowledges support from the European Commission FP7 FET-Open Project FOC-II (no. 255987). Miguel Angel Fuentes acknowledges support from The Omidyar Fellowship and Santa Fe Institute, where this research originated.

REFERENCES

Amin, K., & Ng, V. (1993). *Arch processes and option valuation*. Unpublished manuscript, University of Michigan.

Bachelier, L. (1900). Théorie de la spéculation. Annales scientifiques de l'É.N.S. 3 série, tome 17.

Bachelier, L. (1964). Theory of speculation. In H. P. Cootner (Ed.), *The random character of stock market prices*. Cambridge, MA: MIT Press.

Bassler, K. E., McCauley, J. L., & Gunaratne, G. H. (2007). Nonstationary increments, scaling distributions, and variable diffusion processes in financial markets. *Proceedings of the National Academy of Sciences*, *104*, 17287–17290.

Black, F., & Scholes, M. (1973). The pricing of options and corporate liabilities. *Journal of Political Economy*, *81*(3), 637–654.

Blattberg, R. C., & Gonedes, N. J. A. (1974). Comparison of the stable and Student distributions as statistical models for stock prices. *Journal of Business*, *47*, 244–280.

Borland, L. (2002). Option pricing formulas based on a non-Gaussian stock price model. *Physical Review Letters*, *89*(9), 098701.

Bouchaud, J. P. & Potters, M. (2003). *Theory of financial risks and derivative pricing*. Cambridge: Cambridge University Press.

Clark, P. K. (1973). A subordinated stochastic process model with finite variance for speculative prices. *Econometrica*, *41*, 135–155.

Cox, J. C., & Ross, S. A. (1976). The valuation of options for alternative stochastic processes. *Journal of Financial Economics*, *3*, 145–166.

Derman, E., & Kani, I. (1994). Riding on a smile. *Risk*, *7*(2), 139–145.

Duan, J. (1995). The GARCH option pricing model. *Mathematical Finance*, *5*(1), 13–32.

Einstein, A. (1905). Über die von der molekularkinetischen Theorie der Wärme geforderte Bewegung von in ruhenden Flüssigkeiten suspendierten Teilchen. *Annalen der Physik*, *322*(8), 549–560.

Fama, E. F. (1965). The behavior of stock-market prices. *Journal of Business*, *38*, 34–105.

Farmer, J. D., Gillemot, L., Lillo, F., Mike, S., & Sen, A. (2004). What really causes large price changes? *Quantitative Finance*, *4*, 383.

Gabaix, X., Gopikrishnan, P., Plerou, V., & Stanley, H. E. (2003). A theory of power-law distributions in financial market fluctuations. *Nature*, *423*, 267–270.

Heston, S. L. (1993). A closed-form solution for options with stochastic volatility with applications to bond and currency options. *The Review of Financial Studies*, *6*(2), 327–343.

Hull, J. C., & White, A. D. (1987). The pricing of options on assets with stochastic volatilities. *Journal of Finance*, *42*(2), 281–300.

Lewis, A. (2000). *Option valuation under stochastic volatility*. Newport Beach, CA: Finance Press.

Lux, T. (1996). The stable Paretian hypothesis and the frequency of large returns: An examination of major German stocks. *Applied Financial Economics*, *6*, 463–475.

Mandelbrot, B. B. (1963). The variation of certain speculative prices. *J. Business*, *36*, 394–419.

Mantegna, R. N., & Stanley, H. E. (1995). Scaling behaviour in the dynamics of an economic index. *Nature*, *376*, 46–49.

Merton, R. C. (1976). Option pricing when underlying stock returns are discontinuous. *Journal of Financial Economics*, *3*, 125–144.

Nelson, D. B. (1990). ARCH models as diffusion approximations. *Journal of Econometrics*, *45*, 7–38.

Osborne, M. F. M. (1959). Brownian motion in the stock market. *Operations Research*, *7*, 145–173.

Platen, E. (2001). A minimal financial market model. In M. Colman & S. Tang (Eds.), *Mathematical finance, series: Trends in mathematics* (pp. 293–301). Birkhaeuser: Verlag.

Praetz, P. D. (1972). The distribution of share price changes. *Journal of Business*, *45*, 49–55.

Satchell, S., & Timmermann, A. (1992). *Option pricing with GARCH*. Unpublished manuscript, Birkbeck College, University of London.

Stein, E. M., & Stein, J. C. (1991). Stock price distributions with stochastic volatility: An analytic approach. *Review of Financial Studies*, *4*, 727–752.

Taylor, S. J. (2000). *Consequences for option pricing of a long memory in volatility*. Working Paper. The Department of Accounting and Finance, Lancaster University.

Viswanathan, G. M., Fulco, U. L., Lyra, M. L., & Serva, M. (2003). The origin of fat-tailed distributions in financial time series. *Physica A*, *329*, 273.

ON THE EMPIRICAL BEHAVIOR OF STOCHASTIC VOLATILITY MODELS: DO SKEWNESS AND KURTOSIS MATTER?

Marco M. García-Alonso, Manuel Moreno and Javier F. Navas

ABSTRACT

This chapter analyzes the empirical performance of alternative option pricing models using Black and Scholes (1973) as a benchmark. Specifically, we consider the Heston (1993) and Corrado and Su (1996) models and price call options on the S&P 500 index over the period from November 2010 to April 2011, evaluating each model by computing in- and out-of-sample pricing errors. We find that the two proposed models reduce both types of errors and mitigate the smile effect with respect to the benchmark. Moreover, in most of the cases, the model in Corrado and Su (1996) beats that in Heston (1993). Then, we conclude that skewness and kurtosis matter for option pricing purposes.

Derivative Securities Pricing and Modelling
Contemporary Studies in Economic and Financial Analysis, Volume 94, 227–257

ISSN: 1569-3759/doi:10.1108/S1569-3759(2012)0000094012

INTRODUCTION

Option pricing is one of the most important activities in the field of quantitative finance. Carrying out such task is not easy; before starting, every financial analyst has to choose a pricing model and an estimation procedure. There is a wide range of models available in the literature with Black and Scholes (1973) (BS, from now on) being the seminal paper. This is the most popular and easiest to implement model although not very realistic as it is based on very restrictive assumptions. This model assumes a constant underlying volatility, normal distribution and no jumps for stock returns, and constant interest rates. It has been already illustrated empirically that no stock or market index verifies these conditions. For this reason, many papers after 1973 have relaxed some of the BS assumptions in order to propose more realistic models. For example, Merton (1973) and Amin and Jarrow (1992) developed models introducing stochastic interest rates and Merton (1976), Bates (1991), and Madan, Carr, and Chang (1998) presented new models allowing for jumps in the stock return process.

Researchers have also eliminated a really unrealistic assumption of BS, namely, the constancy of the stock volatility during the option life. There are two ways of doing this, using GARCH models, as in Duan (1995) and Heston and Nandi (2000), or introducing a continuous-time stochastic process for the volatility (or variance) of the stock price, as in Hull and White (1987), Stein and Stein (1991), Heston (1993), and Schöbel and Zhu (1999). Although some of these models manage to incorporate non-normality in the distribution for the stock return, another group of models directly introduced analytical expressions with non-normal skewness and kurtosis in the stock return distribution. This is usually done by adapting expansions of the log-normal distribution as, for instance, Jarrow and Rudd (1982) and Corrado and Su (1996).

This list of alternative models to BS can be easily enlarged by combining stochastic volatility with stochastic interest rates, as in Bakshi and Chen (1997) or by using jump-diffusion processes, as in Bates (1991) and Scott (1997). Both extensions have been compared empirically in Bakshi, Cao, and Chen (1997).

The implementation of the estimation procedure is as important as selecting a model. There are three estimation alternatives. The first one is using a cross-sectional approach by minimizing the sum of the square differences between observed and theoretical prices. This procedure is the most popular and widely used among practitioners, as it is very easy to implement and uses observed option prices to estimate the corresponding parameters. As a disadvantage, the estimates provided by this approach do not take into account the time series properties of stock returns. The second alternative is based on maximum likelihood estimates, using stock or volatility time series. However, this technique does not consider observed option prices in the estimation and can become very complicated if the likelihood function is not easy to obtain, as usually happens when dealing with two-dimensional processes. For these reasons, this procedure is not so extended as the previous one. The third estimation procedure is indirect inference, a two-step approach. See Gouriéroux, Monfort, and Renault (1993) for more details or Fiorentini, León, and Rubio (2002) for an application to a thinly traded option market as the Spanish one.

In this chapter we will develop an empirical study to analyze if option pricing models with stochastic volatility or non-normal distributions provide a better fit than the classical Black and Scholes (1973) model. For our purposes we will use the cross-sectional approach because of its aforementioned advantages. We will test two alternative models, Heston (1993) and Corrado and Su (1996), by considering a sample of prices of call options on the S&P 500 index for a six-month period ranging from November 1, 2010 to April 30, 2011. The comparison between these two models will be based on in- and out-of-sample pricing errors, using Black and Scholes (1973) as benchmark.

As will be seen later, we will find that the two alternative models clearly improve the performance of the Black and Scholes (1973) model, especially in the case of Corrado and Su (1996), which seems slightly superior to Heston (1993). This result is valid for both in- and out-of-sample analyses. However, this improvement is lost when the out-of-sample analysis is extended to higher lags. We also study the shape of the volatility smiles obtained with each model and we find that the alternative models succeed in reducing the skew of the volatility smile obtained in the Black and Scholes framework.

This chapter is organized as follows. We start reviewing briefly some existing literature on empirical option pricing and introducing the three models to be tested. After this, we describe the data and explain the estimation procedure. The next section provides the values obtained for the implied parameters. In- and out-of-sample pricing errors are computed in subsequent sections. Finally, we study the smile effect. The last section summarizes the main findings and conclusions.

LITERATURE REVIEW

Many papers have tested empirically the performance of different option pricing models. A very popular one, Bakshi et al. (1997), compares empirically three stochastic volatility models: a basic one (SV) and two extensions, considering stochastic interest rates (SVSI) and jumps in the stock price process (SVJ), respectively. The authors select a sample of options on the S&P 500 index to estimate the parameters of each model by minimizing the sum of the square errors. For each model, they also evaluate (a) the static performance by computing absolute and relative pricing errors and (b) the dynamic hedging performance using single-instrument and delta-neutral hedges. The static performance is analyzed dividing the sample according to the moneyness and time to maturity of each option. The results show that stochastic volatility leads to a substantial progress in all the categories. Additionally, SVJ provides the minimum pricing errors followed closely by SVSI and SV, although stochastic interest rates seem to provide a marginal effect. Finally, in the dynamic hedging analysis, the SV model provides the minimum hedging errors.

Similar research with BS as benchmark has been developed in subsequent papers. For example, Corrado and Su (1996) developed a skewness- and kurtosis-adjusted BS model that beat the classical BS model when analyzing a sample of (ITM and ATM) European call options on the S&P 500 index. However, Vähämaa (2003) found the opposite results when testing the delta-hedging performance of the Corrado and Su (1996) model. Additionally, Yung and Zhang (2003) illustrated that EGARCH option pricing models improved the out-of-sample performance of the BS model but not its hedging performance. Dealing with Ibex-35 options, Serna (2004) and Prado-Enrico (2005) also illustrated the better performance of Corrado and Su (1996) model.

Moon, Seon, Wee, and Yoon (2009) tested the Heston (1993) and (correlated) Stein and Stein (1991) models on Kospi 200 options and again found a higher performance with these models (relative to BS), being the Heston model slightly better than Stein and Stein (1991). AitSahlia, Goswami, and Guha (2010) extended the empirical test of Heston to the case of American options and also found significant enhancement. Huang, Wang, and Chen (2011) tested GARCH and stochastic volatility models in the Taiwan option market and showed that the GARCH model is superior to that in Hull and White (1987) and that both improve BS performance.

THE MODELS

As previously mentioned, this chapter focuses on testing the empirical performance of two option pricing models by comparing their pricing errors and using the Black and Scholes (1973) model as benchmark. This section reviews briefly this model and the two alternatives to be studied: Heston (1993) and Corrado and Su (1996). From now on, these models will also be called Heston and CS, respectively. For the sake of brevity, closed-form expressions are reported only for call options.

(a) Black and Scholes (1973)

This model assumes that the price of a non-dividend paying stock follows a Geometric Brownian Motion, that is,

$$dS(t) = \mu S(t)dt + \sigma S(t)dW_s(t) \tag{1}$$

where $S(t)$ denotes the underlying asset price at time t, μ is the expected stock return, σ is the stock volatility, and $W_s(t)$ is a standard Brownian motion.

Applying Ito's lemma, a dynamic hedging strategy with stocks and options, and no-arbitrage conditions, Black and Scholes obtain a PDE for the price at time t of a European call option. The solution of this PDE is given by the following closed-form expression

$$C(t,\tau) = S(t)\Phi(d_1) - Ke^{-r\tau}\Phi(d_1 - \sigma\sqrt{\tau}), d_1 = \frac{\ln(S(t)/K) + (r + (1/2)\sigma^2)\tau}{\sigma\sqrt{\tau}} \tag{2}$$

where K is the option strike, r is the (annualized) instantaneous risk-free interest rate, τ is the time to maturity for the option, σ is the volatility of the underlying asset, and $\Phi(\cdot)$ denotes the standard normal cumulative distribution function. All the parameters are known and observed except σ, that needs to be estimated.

(b) Heston (1993)

This model allows the volatility of the underlying asset to be stochastic during the life of the option and, then, this model is much more realistic than BS. Stochastic volatility is introduced by assuming a mean-reverting process for the stock variance[1]

$$dS(t) = \mu S(t)dt + \sqrt{\upsilon(t)}S(t)dW_s(t) \tag{3}$$

$$d\upsilon(t) = \kappa_\upsilon[\theta_\upsilon - \upsilon(t)]dt + \sigma_\upsilon\sqrt{\upsilon(t)}dW_\upsilon(t) \tag{4}$$

As in BS, the stock price follows a Geometric Brownian Motion where $\sqrt{\upsilon(t)}$ is the stock volatility. In expression (4), κ_υ represents the speed of adjustment, θ_υ is the long-run mean of the stock variance, and σ_υ is the variation component of the diffusion variance $\upsilon(t)$. $W_s(t)$ and $W_\upsilon(t)$ are two dependent Brownian motions with $corr_t[dW_s(t)dW_\upsilon(t)] = \rho$. Defining the stock variance with this mean-reverting process is very appropriate since it is consistent with some empirical implications observed in the market. For example, the variance of a stock usually fluctuates around its mean and cannot take negative values as it follows a chi-square distribution (see Cox, Ingersoll, and Ross (1985) for details). In addition, the dependence between the two randomness sources indicates the correlation observed empirically in the market between stock price and its variance. Parameters σ_υ and ρ will have significant implications on the shape of the underlying return distribution as they introduce kurtosis and asymmetry, respectively.

Departing from the two-dimensional process (3)–(4), in a similar way to BS, Heston obtained the corresponding PDE that any derivative price must verify under this model

$$\frac{1}{2}\upsilon S^2\frac{\partial^2 C}{\partial S^2} + rS\frac{\partial C}{\partial S} + \rho\sigma_\upsilon \upsilon S\frac{\partial^2 C}{\partial S \partial \upsilon} + \frac{1}{2}\sigma_\upsilon^2 \upsilon\frac{\partial^2 C}{\partial \upsilon^2} + \kappa_\upsilon[\theta_\upsilon - \upsilon]\frac{\partial C}{\partial \upsilon} + \frac{\partial C}{\partial \tau} - rC = 0 \tag{5}$$

As we assume that the above stochastic structure is set under the risk-neutral measure, the volatility risk premium will be equal to zero and, then, it does not appear in (5). Similarly to BS, Heston (1993) guessed a solution for this PDE substituting the normal cumulative distribution functions by the unknown probabilities P_1 and P_2

$$C(t, \tau) = S(t)P_1 - Ke^{-r\tau}P_2 \tag{6}$$

Substituting the proposed solution (6) into (5), this author obtains two PDEs for the probabilities P_1 and P_2. Analytical expressions for these probabilities are not immediately available but can be obtained by inverting the corresponding characteristic functions. Expressions are written in terms of the logarithm of the spot price $x = \ln(S)$.

The characteristic function solution is given as

$$\mathrm{f_j}(x, \upsilon, t; \phi) = \exp\{C(\tau; \phi) + D(\tau; \phi)\upsilon + i\phi x\}, \quad j = 1, 2 \tag{7}$$

where

$$C(\tau; \phi) = r\phi i\tau + \frac{a}{\sigma^2}\left((b_j - \rho\sigma\phi i + d)\tau - 2\ln\left(\frac{1 - ge^{d\tau}}{1 - g}\right)\right)$$

$$D(\tau; \phi) = \frac{b_j - \rho\sigma\phi i + d}{\sigma^2}\ \frac{1 - e^{d\tau}}{1 - ge^{d\tau}}$$

and

$$g = \frac{b_j - \rho\sigma\phi i + d}{b_j - \rho\sigma\phi i - d}, \quad d = \sqrt{(\rho\sigma\phi i - b_j)^2 - \sigma^2(2u_j\phi i - \phi^2)}, \quad j = 1, 2$$

$$u_1 = \frac{1}{2}, \quad u_2 = -\frac{1}{2}, \quad a = \kappa\theta, \quad b_1 = \kappa - \rho\sigma, \quad b_2 = \kappa$$

Using the characteristic functions (7) we can obtain the desired probabilities

$$P_j(x, \upsilon, T; \ln(K)) = \frac{1}{2} + \frac{1}{\pi}\int_0^\infty \mathrm{Re}\left[\frac{e^{-i\phi\ln(K)} f_j(x, \upsilon, t; \phi)}{i\phi}\right] d\phi, \quad j = 1, 2 \tag{8}$$

Although expression (8) seems a bit complicated, the integral inside can be easily solved using approximations similar to those used to evaluate cumulative normal distributions. Note that the integrand function tends to zero as ϕ increases, then we do not need a high upper limit to solve numerically this integral.[2]

Obtaining the parameter values in the Heston model is not straightforward as we need to estimate five parameters: the volatility $\sqrt{\upsilon(t)}$, the speed of adjustment κ_υ, the long-run mean of the stock variance θ_υ, the variation component of the diffusion variance σ_υ, and the correlation between the spot returns and the spot variance, ρ.

(c) Corrado and Su (1996)

This model starts assuming a certain expression for the distribution of the underlying asset value at maturity. This feature allows us to price European options introducing skewness and excess of kurtosis in the return distribution by adapting a Gram–Charlier expansion of the standard normal density function. This expansion provides the next expression, which is a non-normal density with skewness and excess of kurtosis:

$$g(z) = n(z)\left[1 + \frac{\mu_3}{3!}(z^3 - 3z) + \frac{\mu_4 - 3}{4!}(z^4 - 6z^2 + 3)\right] \tag{9}$$

where $n(z)$ is a normal distribution function, μ_3 and μ_4 are the terms associated to asymmetry and kurtosis, respectively, and $z = \ln(S_t/S_0) - (r - \sigma^2/2)t/(\sigma\sqrt{t})$.[3]

We can use now the density $g(z)$ to derive the theoretical call option price as the discounted value of the expected payoff at maturity, that is,

$$C_{\mathrm{CS}} = e^{-r\tau}\int_K^\infty (S_t - K)g(z(S_t))dz(S_t) \tag{10}$$

Solving this integral, these authors obtained the following option valuation closed-form expression

$$C_{CS} = C_{BS} + \mu_3 Q_3 + (\mu_4 - 3)Q_4 \tag{11}$$

where

$$C_{BS} = S_0\Phi(d) - Ke^{-r\tau}\Phi(d - \sigma\sqrt{\tau}), \quad d = \frac{\ln(S_t/K) + (r + (1/2)\sigma^2)\tau}{\sigma\sqrt{\tau}}$$

is the BS option price formula and

$$Q_3 = \frac{1}{3!}S_t\sigma\sqrt{\tau}((2\sigma\sqrt{\tau} - d)\Phi(d) + \sigma^2\tau\Phi(d))$$
$$Q_4 = \frac{1}{4!}S_t\sigma\sqrt{\tau}((d^2 - 1 - 3\sigma\sqrt{\tau}(d - \sigma\sqrt{\tau}))\Phi(d) + \sigma^3\tau^{3/2}\Phi(d))$$

In this way, the call option price is given by the BS option pricing formula plus some additional terms that reflect corrections for skewness and kurtosis.

Three parameters require estimation in this model: the volatility σ, the skewness μ_3, and the kurtosis μ_4. Note that expression (11) is a little bit different to that in Corrado and Su (1996). This is because we are now using the correction proposed in Brown and Robinson (2002) that identified an error in the original CS formula.

THE DATA

We will analyze the empirical performance of the models introduced previously using data from November 1, 2010 to April 30, 2011. We focus our study on daily closing prices of S&P 500 call options. We have chosen this stock index because of its high liquidity and, then, we think prices are better formed than in other markets.

Our aim is to compute the pricing errors of the alternative pricing models along the sample period. For our analysis we select for each month a wide range of option prices with different strikes and maturing in the following month. Therefore, the models proposed will be tested on options with short-term maturity.

We also need spot stock prices and risk-free interest rate data. Underlying asset prices are obtained from daily closing prices of the S&P 500 index. We have chosen closing prices to reduce timing synchronization problems.

Risk-free rates are obtained from daily yields of US Treasury Bills with the maturity closest to that of the respective option. All data have been downloaded from Bloomberg.

The models under analysis make assumptions about the underlying asset distribution and some parameters determine the main features of such distribution like, for example, volatility (or variance), correlations, skewness, or excess of kurtosis. For this reason we include now some statistical information about the returns of the S&P 500 index in the sample period. Well-specified models should return parameter values similar to those observed in the descriptive statistics, when solving the optimization program.

Fig. 1 shows the evolution of the S&P 500 index (left graph) and its return (right graph) in the selected period. As can be easily noticed from the returns plot, index volatility changes through time. In fact, high volatilities are clustered in November and March, when the underlying asset returns decay significantly. This suggests negative correlation between returns and volatilities, one of the features introduced by the model of Heston.

Fig. 2 plots a histogram of the daily observed spot returns from November 1, 2010 to April 30, 2011. As can be seen, the empirical distribution is far from been normal as both skewness and fat tails are clearly observed in the sample data. This empirical evidence seems consistent with the studies of Heston and CS since both models include parameters that reflect skewness and kurtosis (σ_υ, ρ in Heston and μ_3, μ_4 in CS).

Table 1 reports some descriptive statistics and the result of the Jarque–Bera test of the observed returns. We can corroborate the presence of

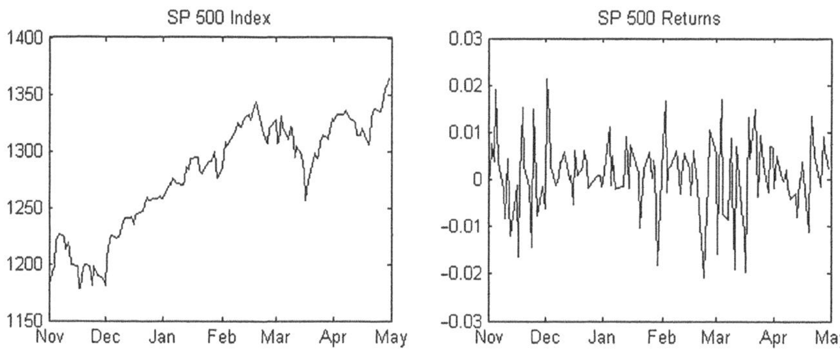

Fig. 1. Daily Evolution of the S&P 500 Index (Left Graph) and its Return (Right Graph) from November 1, 2010 to April 30, 2011.

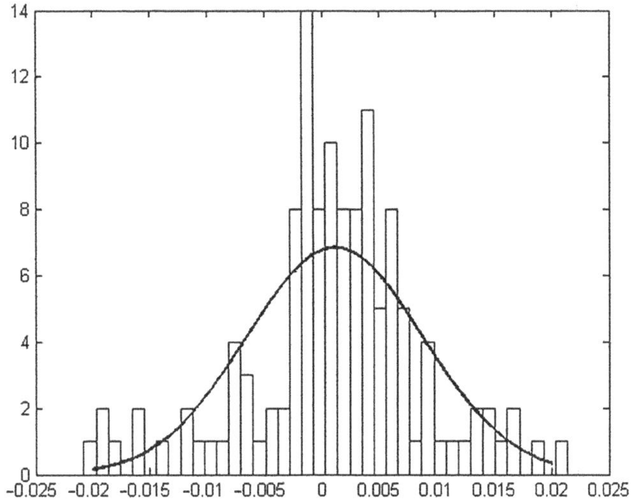

Fig. 2. Histogram of the Daily Observed Spot Returns for the S&P 500 Index from November 1, 2010 to April 30, 2011.

Table 1. Some Descriptive Statistics and the Jarque–Bera (JB) Statistic of the Daily Observed Returns for the S&P 500 Index from November 1, 2010 to April 30, 2011.

Mean	0.0009
Median	0.0010
SD	0.0076
Variance	0.0001
Excess of kurtosis	0.9116
Skewness	−0.3123
JB-statistic (*p*-value)	7.4143 (0.0245)

skewness and kurtosis in the stock returns. We also reject normality in the return distribution, indicating that the BS model cannot be an appropriate model for our underlying asset during our sample period.

ESTIMATION PROCEDURE

To analyze the empirical performance of the proposed models, we will estimate their implied structural parameters following the same estimation technique in all the models. In estimating Heston or CS models we have the difficulty that the spot volatility and structural parameters are not observed. Estimation techniques such as Maximum Likelihood or Generalize Method of Moments would not be convenient because of its stringent requirement on historical data. To circumvent this issue, both practitioners and academics have traditionally used option-implied volatilities based on the model. This practice reduces data requirement and also produces significant improved performance.

Then, our estimation approach will be based on option-implied parameters. To do this, we will follow closely Bakshi et al. (1997). Implied volatility and structural parameters will be estimated jointly by minimizing the sum of the square pricing errors (SSE). We will solve this optimization problem for each day of the sample period in order to obtain daily estimations. Specifically, the estimation procedure is performed in two steps:

1. For each day t, collect N different option closing prices on the same stock.[4] Each of the N options has the same time to maturity (short-term, between 15 and 50 days) and different strikes K_n. For $n=1, \ldots, N$, let $\hat{C}_n(t; K_n)$ and $C_n(t; K_n)$ be the observed and theoretical prices, respectively. The pricing error of the nth option in day t is defined as the difference between both prices, that is,

$$\varepsilon_n[\phi] = \hat{C}_n(t; K_n) - C_n(t; K_n) \tag{12}$$

   and it is a function of the implied parameters vector, ϕ. This vector is $\phi = (\sigma)$ in BS, $\phi = (\upsilon, \kappa_\upsilon, \theta_\upsilon, \sigma_\upsilon, \rho)$ in Heston, and $\phi = (\sigma, \mu_3, \mu_4)$ in CS.

   The value of $C_n(t; K_n)$ will differ along the three models and is obtained from expressions (2), (6)–(7), and (11) for BS, Heston, and CS, respectively.
2. Find the parameter vector ϕ in day t that solves the minimization problem

$$\text{SSE}(t) = \min_{\phi} \sum_{n=1}^{N} w_n(\varepsilon_n[\phi])^2, \quad w_n = 100\frac{Vol(K_n)}{TotVol} \tag{13}$$

   where $Vol(K_n)$ denotes the total amount of options with strike K_n traded in day t and $TotVol$ indicates the amount traded in all options in day t (according to data available in Bloomberg in the sample period).

The number w_n represents each pricing error weight as a function of the volume traded in options with strike K_n in day t. In this way, this practice penalizes very deep in- and out-of-the money (ITM, OTM) options that might bias our estimates. Doing this, the closing prices from the most liquid strikes will have a higher weight in our estimation. Also, pricing errors from very deep ITM options (which are expected to be higher as their price is very high and nonsignificant for our purposes) will be penalized. This step will result in an estimate of the implied parameter vector. After obtaining this vector for day t we go back to step 1 and repeat the same procedure for every day in the sample.[5]

Notice that, in the Heston model, we are estimating the implied volatility as if it were one extra structural parameter, while the return variance is defined as a continuous stochastic process (see expression (4)). Hence, running this estimation procedure in this model would be incorrect if we did not assume that the variance remains unchanged during each period t. Therefore, we will consider that the variance is constant along a day, allowing us to estimate daily parameters for the implied volatility.

There is a wide range of functions that can be applied to obtain the parameters of each model, as the sum of the square percentage errors or the sum of the absolute errors. We will always use function (13) in the estimation procedure in every model. This way all models will be tested under equal circumstances and we obtain consistent conclusions.

IMPLIED PARAMETERS

We apply now the above procedure to call options on the S&P 500 index from November 1, 2010 to April 30, 2011. Therefore, we estimate daily values for the parameters of each model. Table 2 reports descriptive statistics (mean, median, standard deviation, and extreme values (minimum and maximum)) of these parameter estimates.

The first rows of Table 2 includes statistics of the implied volatilities values obtained for each model. The mean volatilities are 14.20%, 12.68%, and 16.52% in BS, Heston, and CS, respectively. These means are representative of the evolution of the parameters through time as the standard deviations do not take very high values, although they are higher in the alternative models than in BS. Then, changes in daily implied volatilities are more significant in CS and Heston models. Medians are similar to means, being slightly higher in CS and a bit lower in Heston than in BS.

Fig. 3 reports the evolution of the daily implied volatilities for the three models during the sample period. We observe similar paths in all the models. Additionally, it can be argued that "Heston implied volatilities are the most

Table 2. Some Descriptive Statistics of the Daily Parameter Estimates for the BS, Heston, and CS Models.

Parameters		BS	Heston	CS
Implied volatility	Minimum	0.0934	0.0100	0.0956
	Mean	0.1420	0.1268	0.1652
	Median	0.1410	0.1348	0.1540
	Maximum	0.2090	0.2183	0.4159
	SD	0.0232	0.0456	0.0501
κ_{υ}	Minimum	–	0.0001	–
	Mean	–	2.0011	–
	Median	–	2.0700	–
	Maximum	–	4.0000	–
	SD	–	1.0674	–
θ_{υ}	Minimum	–	0.0001	–
	Mean		0.1329	
	Median		0.1256	
	Maximum	–	0.3000	–
	SD	–	0.0841	–
σ_{υ}	Minimum	–	0.0001	–
	Mean		0.3740	
	Median		0.3153	
	Maximum	–	1.6968	–
	SD	–	0.2552	–
ρ	Minimum	–	−1.0000	–
	Mean		−0.8323	
	Median		−0.9994	
	Maximum	–	0.9973	–
	SD	–	0.3349	–
μ_3	Minimum	–	–	−2.1772
	Mean			−1.0437
	Median			−0.9647
	Maximum	–	–	0.1972
	SD	–	–	0.4909
μ_4	Minimum	–	–	0.6111
	Mean			4.6666
	Median			4.3916
	Maximum	–	–	11.6737
	SD	–	–	2.2688

Note: The parameters are the following: κ_{υ} is the speed of adjustment of the spot variance, θ_{υ} represents the long run variance, σ_{υ} denotes the diffusion component of the variance process, ρ is the correlation between the underlying asset and the spot stock variance, μ_3 indicates the skewness, and μ_4 is the kurtosis. These parameters have been obtained from closing prices of call options on the S&P 500 index from November 1, 2010 to April 30, 2011.

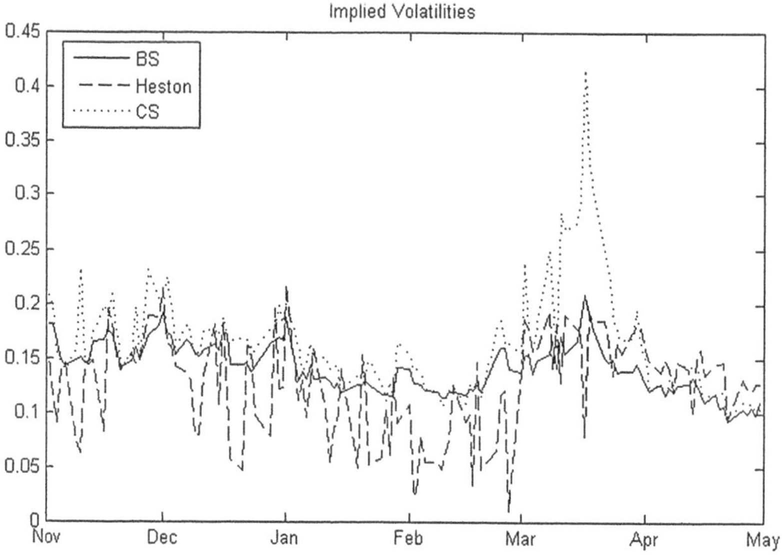

Fig. 3. Evolution of the Daily Implied Volatilities for the BS, Heston, and CS Models from November 1, 2010 to April 30, 2011.

volatile." This assertion makes sense since this model introduces stochastic volatility while the other two assume that volatility is constant. Fig. 3 also shows that CS implied volatilities are significantly similar to BS in the entire sample except in March, where CS reports higher volatilities. This is reasonable as CS just adds two terms for skewness and kurtosis to the BS formula.

Fig. 3 shows that the highest (lowest) implied volatilities are achieved during March (January). These findings are equivalent for all the models and consistent with the evolution of the observed returns. This can be easily seen going back to Fig. 1 and checking in the returns plot that high/low volatilities are clustered in these two months.

According to Fig. 1 and the information reported in the first rows from Table 2 we could say that Heston implied volatilities are lower than in the other two models. One might conclude that Heston model undervalues the risk of the underlying asset. However, this conclusion would be mistaken. Remember that the implied volatility parameter represents the standard deviation of the underlying asset distribution. Standard deviation (or variance) is just one risk measure and represents the mean width of the

Gauss bell. Then, it does not provide information about fat tails or negative skewness. These two factors are also relevant to measure risk and therefore we should not report anticipated conclusions about the underlying asset risk by just looking into implied volatilities.

In Table 2, the next rows include descriptive statistics of the structural parameters in the Heston model. The time evolution of these parameters is included in Fig. 4.

The mean (median) value obtained for the speed of adjustment κ_υ is 2.0011 (2.0700) but the standard deviation is too high to make this value significant. Even though the mean is not representative of the parameter evolution along the period, the upper-left chart in Fig. 4 shows that this parameter always remains positive in the sample period. Then, mean reversion exists in the spot variance process.

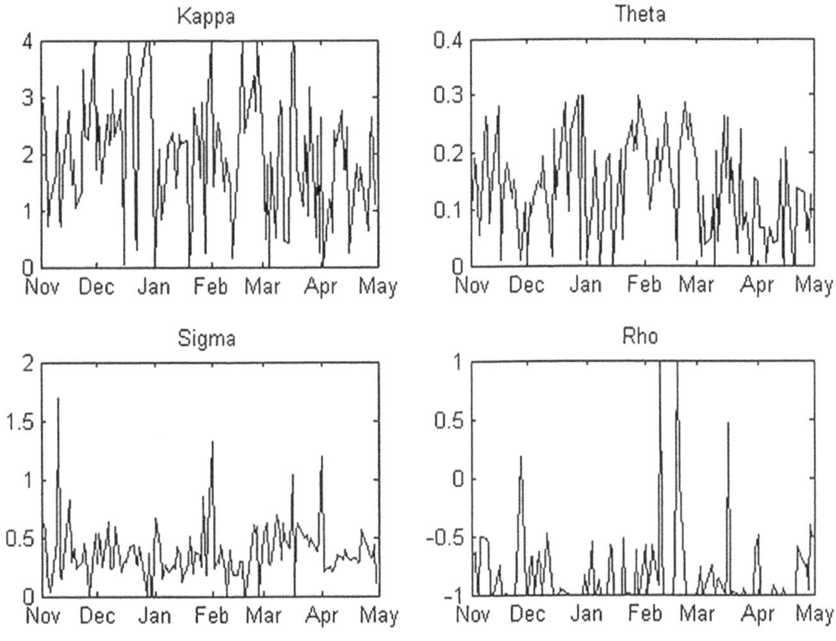

Fig. 4. Time Evolution of the Daily Parameter Estimates for the Heston Model. *Note*: The parameters are the following: κ_υ is the speed of adjustment of the spot variance, θ_υ represents the long run variance, σ_υ denotes the diffusion component of the variance process, and ρ is the correlation between the underlying asset and the spot stock variance. These parameters have been obtained from closing prices of call options on the S&P 500 index from November 1, 2010 to April 30, 2011.

Mean, median, and standard deviation for the long-run variance θ_υ are 0.1329, 0.1256, and 0.0841, respectively. Again, mean is not representative but the upper-right chart in Fig. 4 shows that this parameter remains very low in most of the days although it varies considerably from one day to another.

The parameter σ_υ can be interpreted as the excess of kurtosis. In our case we obtain a mean of 0.3740, median is 0.3153, *and* standard deviation is 0.2552. The lower-left chart in Fig. 4 shows that σ_υ is always positive indicating the presence of kurtosis.

The parameter ρ denotes the correlation between the spot returns and the spot variance in the Heston model. It can also be understood as the skewness of the underlying asset distribution. The lower-right chart in Fig. 4 shows that this parameter is negative in all except four days of the sample period. Mean and median reported in Table 3 are also negative. Then we have obtained parameter values consistent with the skewness observed in the distribution of the observed spot returns (see Fig. 1). However, mean and median values are too negative compared to the skewness coefficient reported in Table 1.

The last rows in Table 2 show the descriptive statistics of the two extra parameters of the CS model. The evolution in time of both parameters is included in Fig. 5.

Similarly to ρ, the parameter μ_3 introduces the skewness component in the underlying distribution and, then, we should observe negative values. This is what we see in almost all of the days looking at the skewness plot in Fig. 5. Mean (median) reported in Table 2 are also negative, −1.0437 (−0.9647); but not representative as the standard deviation is 0.1972. According to the values obtained for μ_3, we can assert that the CS model succeeds in capturing the skewness of the underlying asset distribution. We can note that the most negative values are clustered in March, when the S&P 500 index experiences the strongest correction and its returns are more volatile.

Table 3. Daily Mean and Median SSE (Sum of Square Errors, see expression (13)) for the In-Sample Pricing Errors in the BS, Heston, and CS Models.

		BS	Heston	CS
SSE	Mean	162.1620	41.4268	19.6151
	Median	131.0135	21.1191	11.0602

Note: The SSEs have been calculated from November 1, 2010 to April 30, 2011.

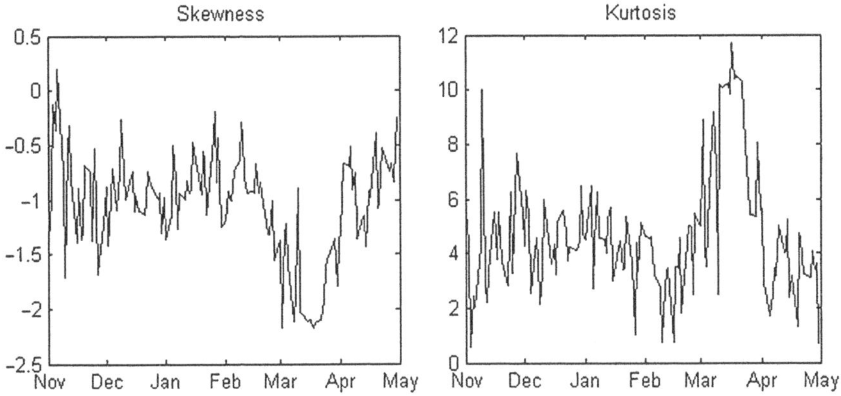

Fig. 5. Time Evolution of the Daily Parameter Estimates for the Skewness and Kurtosis under the CS Model. *Note*: These parameters have been obtained from closing prices of call options on the S&P 500 index from November 1, 2010 to April 30, 2011.

The parameter μ_4 indicates the kurtosis of the stock return distribution in the CS model. We have seen that this distribution is leptokurtic. Hence, parameter values should be greater than three (the kurtosis of the normal distribution). Mean and median values reported in Table 2 are 4.6666 and 4.3916, respectively. Both values show the kurtosis excess that was expected. However, standard deviation is high enough to minor the representativeness of these two values. The reason for this is that sometimes we have obtained extremely high values for the kurtosis (its maximum value is 11.6737). Despite of this, we fairly appreciate that the highest kurtosis values are clustered in March, when the S&P 500 index suffered the strongest correction in our sample period. Therefore, we recognize CS's capability to capture fat tail effects, especially in "bearish" trends.

In this analysis of parameters, we have seen that implied volatilities do not differ significantly in all the models. Parameters obtained for the Heston model seem to be consistent with most of the empirical evidence found in the return distribution and the evolution of spot variance and underlying asset processes. Nonetheless, values change significantly in the sample period, which makes results not very representative. We have also obtained reasonable parameters values for the CS model. Skewness is negative and kurtosis is high enough to capture the leptokurtosis of the observed stock return distribution. In addition, the evolution of these two parameters along the sample period is very satisfactory as they increase significantly in absolute value when the underlying asset reports highest losses.

The outcome of our analysis is consistent with previous empirical research on the Heston model, where similar parameter values were obtained with the same, or alternative, calibration process. For example, applying also a cross-sectional approach, Bakshi et al. (1997) obtained negative (positive) values for the parameter $\rho(\sigma_v)$, supporting the hypothesis of presence of skewness and kurtosis. Alternative assessments were implemented in Aït-Sahalia and Kimmel (2007) for calibration. They applied MLE estimation using proxies of the observed volatility, like the BS implied volatility or an adjusted integrated volatility proxy constructed from the VIX data. In both cases, identical results are obtained, reporting negative values for the correlation between the stock returns and the variance and positive values for kurtosis. This discussion also applies for the CS model when comparing our estimates with other results in the literature, already presented in the section with the literature review.

Therefore, we can say that our estimates for Heston and CS models succeed in capturing the empirical features of the return distribution found in the market. In addition, the dynamic performance of the CS model seems to be better as it captures higher kurtosis and more negative skewness in the "bearish" period. However, this is just a preliminary analysis and we should not arrive at any conclusion until we look more deeply at each model and compare the corresponding in-sample fit and pricing errors. This is the purpose of the next section.

IN-SAMPLE FIT AND PRICING ERRORS

We evaluate now the in-sample fit of each model and calculate pricing errors with the parameters obtained previously using the estimates of day t to calculate the pricing error in this *same* day. We will test each model fitting by evaluating the optimization function given in (13). Table 3 reports the daily mean and median SSE for each model.

We see that the two proposed models clearly improve BS in-sample performance. Specifically, Heston achieves a reduction of 74.45% (83.88%) in mean (median) terms while the SSEs in CS model reduce those in BS by 87.90% and 91.56% in mean and median terms, respectively. Fig. 6 plots the evolution of the SSE during the sample period and evidences the improvement of the alternative models in most of the sample period. This improvement is especially significant in March, when SSE for BS attains the

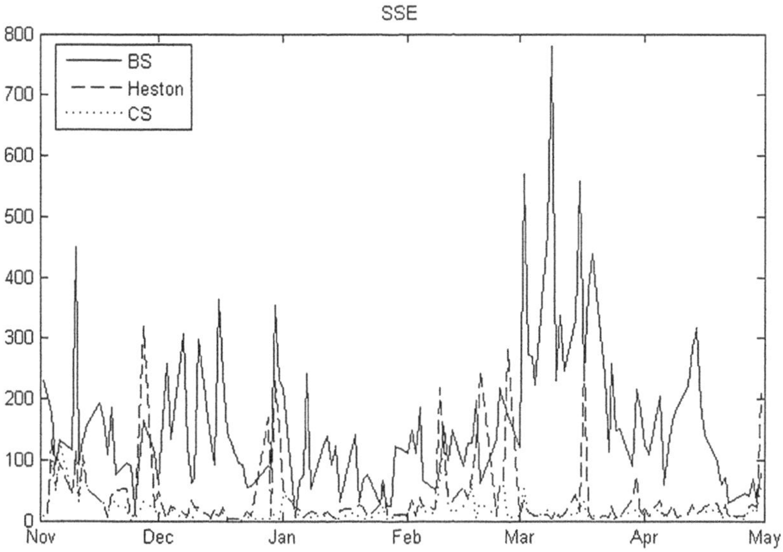

Fig. 6. Evolution of the SSE (Sum of Square Errors, see expression (13)) for the In-Sample Pricing Errors in the BS, Heston, and CS Models. *Note*: The SSEs have been calculated from November 1, 2010 to April 30, 2011.

highest values. According to the analysis in the previous section, this phenomenon can arise from the inability of BS to capture negative skewness and leptokurtosis, which is particularly significant in this month.

We also calculate pricing errors and check which model provides the minimum error. To do this we calculate three different statistics for each day: the median of the absolute errors (MAE), the median of the relative absolute errors (MRAE), and the square root of the median of square errors (RMSE). We report medians instead of means because the robustness of the median to the presence of "outliers" that might appear in very deep ITM and OTM options.

$$\text{MAE}_t = \text{median}(|\varepsilon_n[\phi]|) \tag{14}$$

$$\text{MRAE}_t = \text{median}(|\varepsilon_n[\phi]|/\hat{C}_n(t; K_n)) \tag{15}$$

$$\text{RMSE}_t = \sqrt{\text{median}(|\varepsilon_n[\phi]|^2)} \tag{16}$$

Table 4. Daily Mean and Median for Three Statistics of the In-Sample Pricing Errors (see expression (12)) for the BS, Heston, and CS Models from November 1, 2010 to April 30, 2011.

		BS	Heston	CS
MAE	Mean	1.11	0.48	0.34
	Median	1.04	0.37	0.30
MRAE	Mean	0.1411	0.0469	0.0371
	Median	0.0900	0.0354	0.0311
RMSE	Mean	1.11	0.48	0.34
	Median	1.04	0.37	0.30

Note: The three statistics are the median of the absolute errors (MAE), the median of the relative absolute errors (MRAE), and the square root of the median of square errors (RMSE) (see expressions (14)–(16)).

where the pricing error $\varepsilon_n[\phi]$ is given by (12). Table 4 includes the mean and median of all the daily MAE, MRAE, and RMSE obtained in the sample period for each model.

It is clear that both alternative models provide lower pricing errors in all the categories. The mean for the daily median absolute errors with Heston and CS are, respectively, 63 and 77 cents lower than with BS. Similar results are obtained for the median of MAE. Mean relative absolute errors are 14.11% in BS, 4.69% in Heston and 3.71% in CS. These results do not differ significantly from the median of MRAE. Finally, values for RMSE are identical to those for MAE. Fig. 7 shows the evolution of these statistics for all the models. Again, the highest mispricing reduction is achieved during March.

In summary, we have seen that the two alternative models we have proposed improve the in-sample fit and reduce the pricing errors. This is especially notorious with the CS model as it provides the minimum SSEs and lowest in-sample pricing errors.

OUT-OF-SAMPLE PRICING ERRORS

The previous section shows that lower pricing errors and better in-sample fit are achieved by relaxing BS assumptions and introducing some of the features consistent with the empirical evidences found in the market (such as stochastic volatility, skewness, or kurtosis) in the pricing models. One may

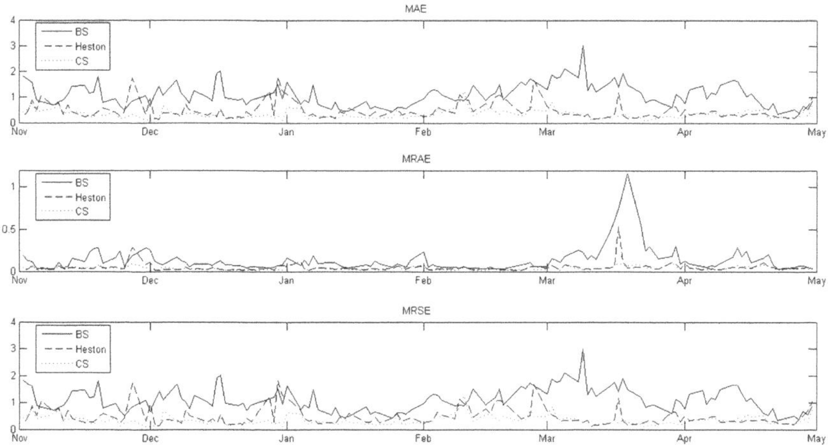

Fig. 7. Time Evolution for Three Statistics of the In-Sample Pricing Errors (see expression (12)) for the BS, Heston, and CS Models from November 1, 2010 to April 30, 2011. *Note*: The three statistics are the median of the absolute errors (MAE), the median of the relative absolute errors (MRAE), and the square root of the median of square errors (RMSE) (see expressions (14)–(16)).

argue that this better fit is a direct consequence of the larger number of structural parameters in the alternative models. However, more parameters may cause over-fitting and penalize the model if the extra parameters do not improve its fitting.

Thus, we perform now an out-of-sample analysis, examining the out-of-sample cross-sectional pricing performance to assess the prediction capacity of each model. If we obtain lower pricing errors in the alternative models than in BS, the conclusions from the previous section would be consolidated. In this analysis, we will use the previous statistics (see expressions (14)–(16)) to measure pricing the errors for each model to find out the best forecasting model.

Out-of-sample pricing errors are calculated as follows. With the parameter values obtained with our estimation procedure, the pricing error for each model in day t is calculated using the structural parameters values from day t-1. That is, today's pricing error is obtained using today's observed data (call option and underlying asset prices, interest rate, etc.) and the previous day's values of the structural parameters. The first day of each month is removed from the analysis since the previous day's structural parameters estimates were obtained from call options with fewer days to

Table 5. Daily Mean and Median for Three Statistics of the One-Day-Ahead Out-Of-Sample Pricing Errors for the BS, Heston, and CS Models from November 1, 2010 to April 20, 2011.

		BS	Heston	CS
MAE	Mean	1.28	1.05	0.92
	Median	1.12	0.83	0.72
MRAE	Mean	0.1728	0.1168	0.1118
	Median	0.1043	0.0718	0.0745
RMSE	Mean	1.28	1.05	0.93
	Median	1.12	0.83	0.72

Note: The three statistics are the median of the absolute errors (MAE), the median of the relative absolute errors (MRAE), and the square root of the median of square errors (RMSE) (see expressions (14)–(16)).

maturity.[6] Table 5 reports the mean and median of the three statistics for each model.

We can see that alternative models also improve BS out-of-sample performance. The mean MAE for Heston (CS) is 23 (36) cents lower than in BS. The mean MRAE is 17.28% in BS while the means in Heston and CS models are 11.68% and 11.18%, respectively. Differences among models found with the median of MAE and MRAE are very similar to those for the means. Results for RMSE are identical to MAE. Hence, a significant improvement is achieved with both Heston and CS models in almost all the days. Errors obtained with CS seem a bit lower. In comparison with the in-sample analysis, we note that differences between BS and both alternatives have been reduced.

To complete this analysis, we calculate now out-of-sample pricing errors using parameters obtained from two to five days before. This means that the error in day t is calculated with parameters from day $t-j$, $j=2,\ldots,5$. In this way, we measure each model's prediction capability and pricing errors deterioration as we increase the forecasting horizon. We obtain MAE and MRAE for the three models in each lag. Table 6 includes the mean and median of both statistics for the three models from lag 0 (in-sample) to lag 5.[7]

Fig. 8 reports the daily evolution of the two statistics calculated using different lags. Fig. 9 returns the mean (left) and median (right) values of MAE (up) and MRAE (down) for the three models in each lag.

Fig. 9 provides very interesting information for our analysis. First, in-sample errors (lag 0) are lower than out-of-sample ones (lags 1–5) in all the

Table 6. Daily Mean and Median for Two Statistics of the In-Sample and (One-Day to Five-Day-Ahead) Out-Of-Sample Pricing Errors for the BS, Heston, and CS Models from November 1, 2010 to April 30, 2011.

		Lag 0			Lag 1		
		BS	Heston	CS	BS	Heston	CS
MAE	Mean	1.11	0.48	0.34	1.28	1.05	0.92
	Median	1.04	0.37	0.30	1.12	0.83	0.72
MRAE	Mean	0.1411	0.0469	0.0371	0.1728	0.1168	0.1118
	Median	0.0900	0.0354	0.0311	0.1043	0.0718	0.0745
		Lag 2			Lag 3		
		BS	Heston	CS	BS	Heston	CS
MAE	Mean	1.40	1.33	1.24	1.47	1.51	1.38
	Median	1.16	0.99	0.85	1.21	1.23	1.06
MRAE	Mean	0.2040	0.1568	0.1422	0.2319	0.1849	0.1672
	Median	0.1101	0.0963	0.0981	0.1359	0.1393	0.0999
		Lag 4			Lag 5		
		BS	Heston	CS	BS	Heston	CS
MAE	Mean	1.54	1.67	1.49	1.62	1.88	1.59
	Median	1.20	1.44	1.03	1.31	1.54	1.14
MRAE	Mean	0.2517	0.2105	0.1844	0.2694	0.2338	0.2071
	Median	0.1473	0.1391	0.1206	0.1547	0.1527	0.1455

Note: The two statistics are the median of the absolute errors (MAE) and the median of the relative absolute errors (MRAE) (see expressions (14)–(15)).

categories. Second, the higher the lag, the worse pricing error obtained in all the models. Third, as lags increase, the worsening is more significant in both Heston and CS models. In fact, Heston pricing errors are higher than BS (or very similar to BS) after the third lag in three charts out of four. Finally, CS always achieves the best performance in mean and median MAE and mean MRAE. Median MRAE in CS is similar to that in Heston in the first two lags but it does not worsen so much as in Heston at the highest lags.

Then, as a final conclusion, we can say that Heston and, especially, CS improve the BS performance. However, most of this improvement is lost as we increase the prediction horizon, that is, higher lags reduce the improvements achieved in relation to BS.

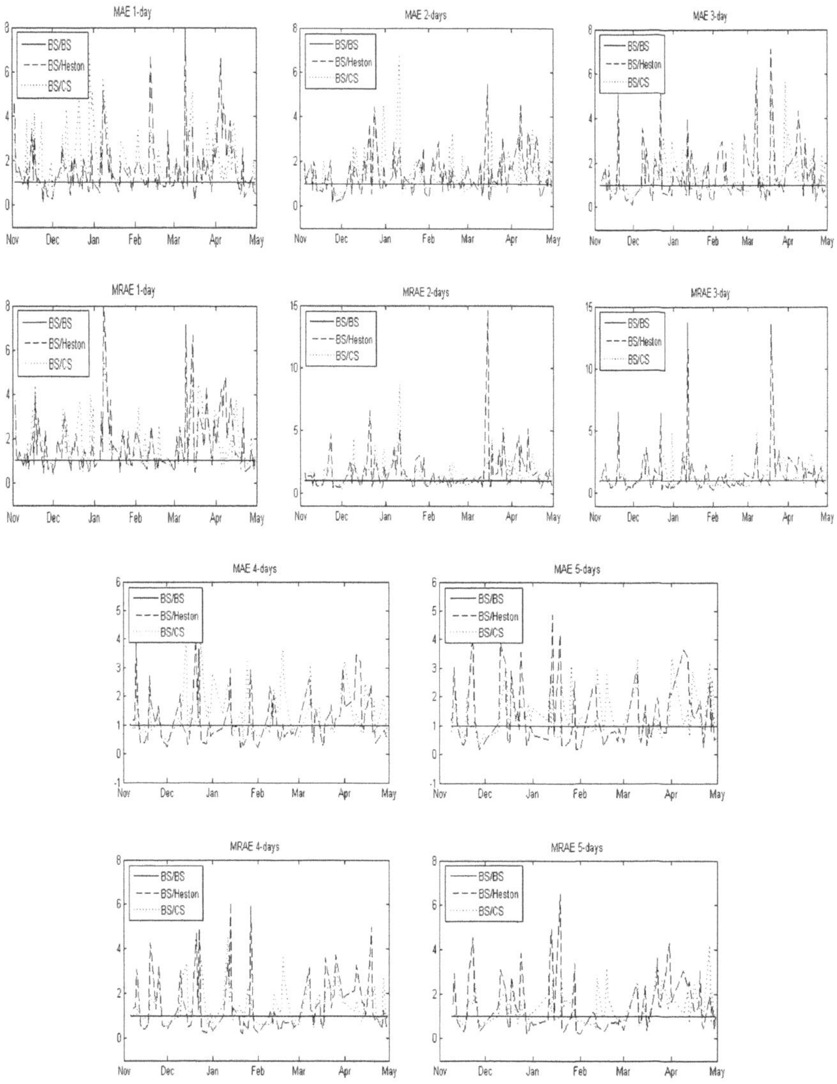

Fig. 8. Time Evolution for Two Statistics of the In-Sample and One-Day to Five-Day-Ahead Out-of-Sample Pricing Errors for the BS, Heston, and CS Models from November 1, 2010 to April 30, 2011. *Note*: The two statistics are the median of the absolute errors (MAE) and the median of the relative absolute errors (MRAE) (see expressions (14)–(15)).

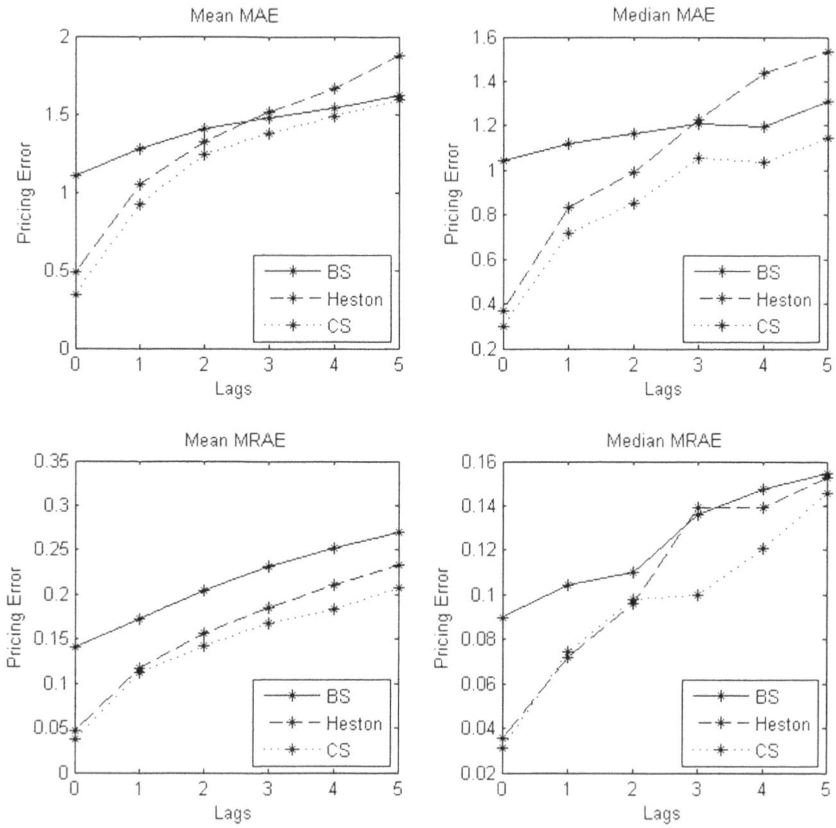

Fig. 9. Mean and Median Values or Two Statistics of the In-Sample and One-Day To Five-Day-Ahead Out-of-Sample Pricing Errors for the BS, Heston, and CS Models from November 1, 2010 to April 30, 2011. *Note*: The two statistics are the median of the absolute errors (MAE) and the median of the relative absolute errors (MRAE) (see expressions (14)–(15)).

After having computed (in- and out-of sample) pricing errors, it can be convenient to analyze each model relative misspecification to complete our study. Introducing stochastic volatility, skewness, and kurtosis has driven us to smaller pricing errors. Therefore, a better specification is expected to be found in both alternative models. The first diagnostic test of the relative model misspecification consists of examining whether each model's implied parameters are consistent with the observed features of the underlying asset distribution and the spot variance process. We have already seen that the estimated parameters succeed in capturing negative skewness, excess of kurtosis, and mean reversion in the spot volatility process. Another way to gauge the model misspecification is to compare the implied-volatility patterns of each model across different levels of moneyness. This is what is performed in the next section.

THE SMILE EFFECT

It is well known that when obtaining the implied volatilities of options traded simultaneously with different strikes, "smile" effects usually appear under the BS model.[8] This fact may be due to the presence of stochastic volatility and non-normal distribution of the spot returns. Hence, we expect to reduce this effect when evaluating each option's implied volatility with the stochastic volatility model (Heston) or other model with non-normal distribution of the spot returns (CS).

Finding the BS implied volatility is easy as it is the only unknown parameter in the option price expression. Using the rest of parameters and data (stock price and interest rate) from day t we can find the volatility value which makes the theoretical option price equal to the observed one. Departing from the parameter values obtained in a previous section, this procedure can be easily extended to obtain the Heston or CS's implied

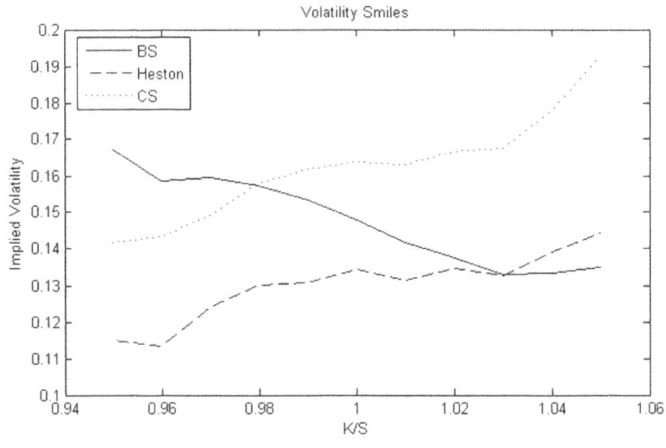

Fig. 10. Average Implied Volatility Value for call options under the BS, Heston, and CS Models from November 1, 2010 to April 30, 2011.

volatility of an option with strike price K_n in day t as follows. Remember that we consider only call options.

At day t, substituting the available data and the structural estimated parameters obtained in that day into the pricing formula of each model, only the spot (implied) volatility remains undetermined. Then, we can find

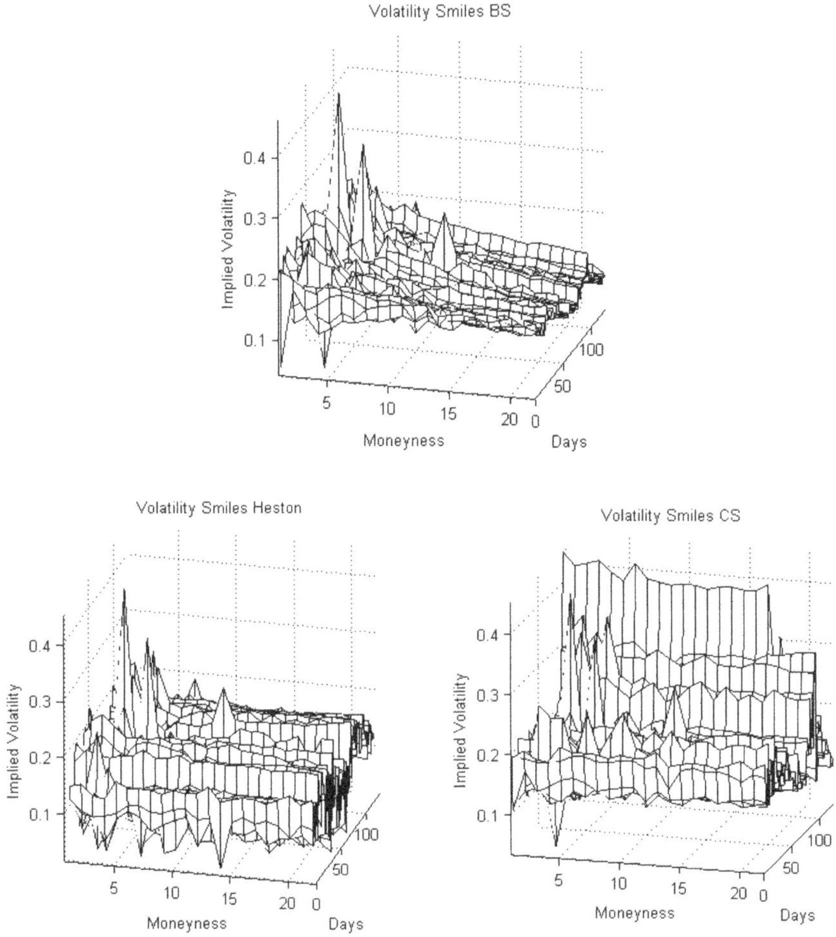

Fig. 11. Daily Smiles for call options under the BS, Heston, and CS Models from November 1, 2010 to April 30, 2011. *Note*: Days in the sample are numbered from 1 (first day) to 124 (last day) and moneyness ranges from 1 to 23, being 1 (23) the deepest ITM (OTM) option in a given day.

numerically the value of the volatility which equates the theoretical option value to the observed one.[9] This procedure has been implemented following the methodology proposed in Bakshi et al. (1997).

We have applied this procedure to the three models for all the data available in our sample. For options traded in the same day, note that the only different input among them will be each option's strike (recall that, in our sample, all options from the same day have the same time to maturity). After this, for each moneyness category, we have calculated the average implied volatility value. Fig. 10 shows the results obtained.

It is clear that "smile" effects with "skew" shape exist. In the case of BS, ITM (OTM) options report higher (lower) implied volatilities. This empirical evidence suggests negative skewness and (left) fat tail in the underlying asset return distribution. In fact, we find high volatilities when the underlying asset price is lower (and vice versa), supporting the idea of negative correlation between asset returns and volatility.

On the contrary, we do not find significant differences between implied volatilities of ITM and OTM options in Heston and CS models, unless we go very deep ITM or OTM. Up to now, it seems we have found enough empirical evidence which suggests that both models succeed in capturing relevant empirical features of the "true" underlying asset distribution. However, this is not the case for deep ITM options ($K/S<0.97$) and deep OTM ones ($K/S>1.03$). This misspecification might arise because these options do not weight too much in the estimation procedure, as they are less traded. Hence, parameters obtained do not fit well these options and the implied volatilities obtained might be more unrealistic. Fig. 11 reports daily smiles for the sample period. In this figure, days in the sample are numbered from 1 (first day) to 124 (last day) and moneyness ranges from 1 to 23, being 1 (23) the deepest ITM (OTM) option in a given day.

CONCLUSIONS

For option pricing purposes, this chapter has analyzed the empirical performance of two alternatives to Black and Scholes (1973): the stochastic volatility model of Heston (1993) and the non-normal distribution one introduced in Corrado and Su (1996). To this aim, we have considered daily closing prices of call options on the S&P 500 index. The sample period goes from November 1, 2010 to April 30, 2011. We have looked into underlying asset returns for this period and we have found that volatility varies with time. In fact, it seems that higher volatility values are clustered in "bearish" periods, suggesting negative correlation between volatility and spot returns. This empirical evidence is consistent with the hypotheses of the Heston (1993) model. The study of the underlying asset dynamics also suggests non-normality in the distribution of the spot returns. The "true" distribution presents negative skewness and "fat tails." For this reason we have also tested the model proposed by Corrado and Su (1996), which introduces skewness and excess of kurtosis in the underlying asset return distribution.

These two models have been evaluated using Black and Scholes (1973) as a benchmark. To accomplish our goal, we have first obtained the daily implied structural parameters of each model by minimizing the sum of the square errors. Values obtained for the parameters of the two alternative models succeed in capturing negative skewness, excess of kurtosis, and mean reversion in the spot volatility process. This is especially notorious in Corrado and Su (1996), where parameter values for skewness and kurtosis are significantly higher when the S&P 500 index experienced important losses.

We have used these implied parameters to evaluate each model's in-sample fit and to compute pricing errors. We obtained that the two alternative models clearly improve the Black and Scholes (1973) performance, especially in the case of Corrado and Su (1996), which performs slightly better than Heston (1993). Then, skewness and kurtosis seem to matter for option pricing purposes. Similar results were obtained from an additional out-of-sample analysis. However, in this case, most of the enhancement achieved with the alternative models is lost when we increase the forecasting horizon, especially after the third lag.

Finally, for the three models, we have investigated the values obtained for the implied volatilities along different moneyness levels. The main finding is that the "skew" of the smile obtained with Black and Scholes (1973) is smaller in the smiles obtained from both Heston (1993) and Corrado and Su (1996) models.

NOTES

1. This process was proposed in Cox et al. (1985) for the term structure of interest rates.
2. We use the function *quadl* in Matlab to solve the integral. This function evaluates integrals using a recursive adaptive Lobatto quadrature.
3. Parameters in z have the same interpretation as in the BS model.
4. N should be greater than or equal to one plus the number of parameters to be estimated.

5. We use the function *fmincon* in Matlab in this estimation procedure.
6. This issue can be verified by going back to section "The Data" and checking the sample.
7. Note that results for lags 0 and 1 are currently included in Tables 4 and 5, respectively. However, we also include these results in Table 6 to provide a complete view to the interested reader.
8. See, for instance, Derman and Kani (1994) for more details.
9. This can be done with the function *fzero* in Matlab.

ACKNOWLEDGMENTS

The authors gratefully acknowledge comments from Unai Ansejo, Ana González-Urteaga, Angel Pardo, Gregorio Serna, Carmen de la Torre, Hipòlit Torró, and attendants at the IX Workshop in Banking and Quantitative Finance. Moreno and Navas acknowledge the financial support from the grants ECO2008-03058 and P08-SEJ-03917. Moreno also ackwoledges the financial support from the grants JCCM PPII11-0290-0305 and UCLM PL20101710. The usual caveat applies.

REFERENCES

Aït-Sahalia, Y., & Kimmel, R. (2007). Maximum likelihood estimation of stochastic volatility models. *Journal of Financial Economics*, *83*(2), 413–452.

AitSahlia, F., Goswami, M., & Guha, S. (2010). American option pricing under stochastic volatility: An empirical evaluation. *Computational Management Science*, *7*(2), 171–187.

Amin, K., & Jarrow, R. (1992). Pricing options on risky assets in a stochastic interest rates economy. *Mathematical Finance*, *2*(4), 217–237.

Bakshi, G. S., Cao, C., & Chen, Z. (1997). Empirical performance of alternative option pricing models. *Journal of Finance*, *52*(5), 2003–2049.

Bakshi, G. S., & Chen, Z. (1997). An alternative valuation model for contingent claims. *Journal of Financial Economics*, *44*(1), 123–165.

Bates, D. (1991). The crash of 87. Was it expected? The evidence from option markets. *Journal of Finance*, *46*(3), 1009–1044.

Black, F., & Scholes, M. (1973). The pricing of options and corporate liabilities. *Journal of Political Economy*, *81*(3), 637–659.

Brown, C. A., & Robinson, D. M. (2002). Skewness and kurtosis implied by option prices: A correction. *Journal of Financial Research*, *25*(2), 279–282.

Corrado, C. J., & Su, T. (1996). Skewness and kurtosis in S&P 500 index returns implied by option prices. *Journal of Financial Research*, *19*(2), 175–192.

Cox, J. C., Ingersoll, J. E., & Ross, S. A. (1985). A theory of the term structure of interest rates. *Econometrica*, *53*(2), 385–408.

Derman, E., & Kani, I. (1994). Riding on a smile. *Risk*, *7*(2), 32–39.

Duan, J. C. (1995). The GARCH option pricing model. *Mathematical Finance*, *5*(1), 13–32.

Fiorentini, G., León, A., & Rubio, G. (2002). Estimation and empirical performance of Heston's stochastic volatility model: The case of a thinly traded market. *Journal of Empirical Finance*, *9*(2), 225–255.

Gouriéroux, C., Monfort, A., & Renault, E. (1993). Indirect inference. *Journal of Applied Econometrics*, *8*(S1), S85–S118.

Heston, S. (1993). A closed form solution for options with stochastic volatility with applications to bond and currency options. *Review of Financial Studies*, *6*(2), 327–343.

Heston, S., & Nandi, S. (2000). A closed form option GARCH valuation model. *Review of Financial Studies*, *13*(3), 585–625.

Huang, H. H., Wang, C. P., & Chen, S. H. (2011). Pricing Taiwan option market with GARCH and stochastic volatility. *Applied Financial Economics*, *21*(10), 747–754.

Hull, J. C., & White, A. (1987). The pricing of options on assets with stochastic volatility. *Journal of Finance*, *42*(2), 281–300.

Jarrow, R., & Rudd, A. (1982). Approximate option valuation for arbitrary stochastic processes. *Journal of Financial Economics*, *10*(3), 347–369.

Madan, D., Carr, P., & Chang, E. (1998). The variance gamma process and option pricing. *European Finance Review*, *2*(1), 79–105.

Merton, R. (1973). Theory of rational option pricing. *Bell Journal of Economics and Management Science*, *4*(1), 141–183.

Merton, R. (1976). Option pricing when underlying stock returns are discontinuous. *Journal of Financial Economics*, *3*(1-2), 125–144.

Moon, K-S., Seon, J.-Y., Wee, I.-S., & Yoon, C. (2009). Comparison of stochastic volatility models: Empirical study on Kospi 200 index options. *Bulletin of the Korean Mathematical Society*, *46*(2), 209–227.

Prado-Enrico, J. M. (2005). *Ibex-35 option pricing under alternative models*, Tesina CEMFI n. 0505.

Schöbel, R., & Zhu, J. (1999). Stochastic volatility with an Ornstein Uhlenbeck process: An extension. *European Finance Review*, *3*(1), 23–46.

Scott, L. O. (1997). Pricing stock options in a jump-diffusion model with stochastic volatility and interest rates: An application of Fourier inversion methods. *Mathematical Finance*, *7*(4), 413–426.

Serna, G. (2004). El modelo de Corrado y Su en el mercado de opciones sobre el futuro del Ibex-35. *Revista de Economía Aplicada*, *34*(12), 101–125.

Stein, E. M., & Stein, J. C. (1991). Stock price distributions with stochastic volatility: An analytic approach. *Review of Financial Studies*, *4*(4), 727–752.

Vähämaa, S. (2003). Skewness and kurtosis adjusted Black–Scholes model: A note on hedging performance. *Finance Letters*, *1*(5), 6–12.

Yung, H. H. M., & Zhang, H. (2003). An empirical investigation of the GARCH option pricing model: Hedging performance. *Journal of Future Markets*, *23*(12), 1191–1207.

RE-EVALUATING HEDGING PERFORMANCE FOR ASYMMETRY: THE CASE OF CRUDE OIL

John Cotter and Jim Hanly

ABSTRACT

We examine whether the hedging effectiveness of crude oil futures is affected by asymmetry *in the return distribution by applying tail-specific metrics to compare the hedging effectiveness of both short and long hedgers. The hedging effectiveness metrics we use are based on lower partial moments (LPM), value at risk (VaR) and conditional value at risk (CVaR). Comparisons are applied to a number of hedging strategies including ordinary least square (OLS), and both symmetric and asymmetric GARCH models. We find that OLS provides consistently better performance across different measures of hedging effectiveness as compared with GARCH models, irrespective of the characteristics of the underlying distribution.*

Keywords: Hedging performance; asymmetry; lower partial moments; value at risk; conditional value at risk

Derivative Securities Pricing and Modelling
Contemporary Studies in Economic and Financial Analysis, Volume 94, 259–280

ISSN: 1569-3759/doi:10.1108/S1569-3759(2012)0000094013

INTRODUCTION

A large literature has examined futures-based hedging strategies. The dominant hedging framework uses the variance as the risk measure despite the fact that it cannot distinguish between positive and negative returns and therefore does not provide an accurate measure of risk for asymmetric distributions. In the literature on optimal hedging, this has been addressed in a number of ways. One option is the use of hedging estimation methods that seek to minimise some measure of risk other than the variance. The second approach is the use of hedging estimation methods that allow for asymmetry in the return distribution.

In this study, we apply tail-specific hedging effectiveness measures together with estimation methods that allow for asymmetry, to a data set consisting of crude oil contracts. This allows us to compare the hedging effectiveness of short and long hedgers under conditions of asymmetry across one of the most important traded assets in commodity markets. Oil commodity markets were chosen as they are particularly suited for an examination into the effects of asymmetry on hedging effectiveness given, their tendency to be non-symmetrically distributed (see Kuper & Van Soest, 2006).

The hedging estimation models used are a naïve hedge, a rolling window ordinary least square (OLS) hedge, and two bivariate GARCH models including an asymmetric GARCH model. Four different hedging effectiveness metrics are applied: variance, lower partial moments (LPM), value at risk (VaR) and conditional value at risk (CVaR). With the exception of the variance, these metrics can account for asymmetries as they can separately measure both left tail and right tail quantiles. This approach allows us to comprehensively examine hedging effectiveness of both short and long hedgers for both symmetric and asymmetric distributions, and to see whether there is a dominant optimal hedge ratio (OHR) estimation method that emerges across a broad range of hedging effectiveness metrics.

Our results show that the rolling OLS model yields the best overall performance irrespective of the distributional characteristics of the contract being hedged, or the hedging effectiveness criteria being applied. We also find that the presence of skewness in the return distribution reduces in-sample and out-of-sample hedging effectiveness. Based on these findings, it would appear that an OLS based hedging strategy is adequate for both non-skewed and skewed distributions.

METHOD

The OHR is defined in the literature as the ratio that minimises the risk of the payoff of the hedged portfolio. The payoff of a hedged portfolio is given as

$$+r_s - \beta r_f \quad \text{(short hedger)} \tag{1a}$$

$$-r_s + \beta_{r_f} \quad \text{(long hedger)} \tag{1b}$$

where r_s and r_f are the returns on the cash and futures, respectively, and β is the estimated OHR. We define a short (long) hedger as being long (short) the cash asset and short (long) the futures asset. In this study, we utilise five different methods for estimating OHRs. The simplest models are a hedge ratio (HR) of zero (no hedge) and a 1:1 or naïve HR where each unit of the cash contract is hedged with equivalent units of the futures contract. The third method applied is an OLS HR, which is the slope coefficient of a regression of the cash on the futures returns. An OHR estimated by OLS was first used by Ederington (1979) and has been applied extensively in the literature. Cecchetti, Cumby, and Figlewski (1988) argue that the OLS method is not optimal because it assumes that the OHR is constant, whereas time-varying volatility is the rule for financial time series, and as the OHR depends on the conditional distribution of cash and futures returns, so too should the HR.

We also use two additional estimation methods that allow the OHR to be time varying. These are a symmetric and an asymmetric GARCH model. The first GARCH model that we use is the Diagonal Vech model proposed by Bollerslev, Engle, and Wooldridge (1988). This model imposes a symmetric response on the variance and is useful for comparison of hedging estimation and performance as it has been extensively applied in the literature to generate OHRs. The second GARCH model that we use is an asymmetric extension of the SDVECH model. We require both a symmetric and an asymmetric GARCH model since we are examining their suitability for symmetric and asymmetric data sets. The key advantage of using an asymmetric model is that it is able to capture the asymmetries both within and between cash and futures markets. It therefore allows the volatility to respond differently to negative and positive returns. This means that dynamic hedging strategies based on an asymmetric GARCH model will differ from those models that impose symmetry, and may provide better hedging performance. The asymmetric GARCH model we use builds on the univariate asymmetric GARCH model of Glosten, Jagannathan, and Runkle (1993). The advantage of GARCH models is that they can jointly estimate the conditional variances and covariances required for optimal HRs, and can also account for asymmetric effects in volatility when extended as appropriate (see, e.g. Kroner & Sultan, 1993). However, the performance of these models has been mixed. Over short time horizons and in-sample they have performed well (see Conrad, Gultekin, & Kaul, 1991), however, over longer hedging horizons and out-of-sample, their performance has been poor (Brooks, Henry, & Persand, 2002). We not turn to hedging effectiveness metrics.

HEDGING EFFECTIVENESS

We address a gap in the literature on commodity hedging, by employing a number of hedging effectiveness metrics in addition to the variance. The hedging effectiveness metrics we use are based on the variance, LPM, VaR and CVaR.

The most popular performance metric applied in the literature on hedging is the percentage reduction in the variance of the cash (unhedged) position as compared to the variance of the hedged portfolio. This was proposed by Ederington (1979) and has been widely adopted. It is given as

$$\mathrm{HE}_1 = 1 - \left[\frac{\mathrm{VARIANCE}_{\text{Hedged Portfolio}}}{\mathrm{VARIANCE}_{\text{Unhedged Portfolio}}}\right] \tag{2}$$

The use of the variance as a measure of risk has been criticised because it fails to distinguish between the tails of the distribution, and therefore, it fails to differentiate in performance terms between short and long hedgers. Where distributions are asymmetric, the variance will over or underestimate risk. For this reason, it is not an adequate measure of risk for hedgers, except where distributions are symmetric. Also, Lien (2005) argues that the findings in the literature, namely, that the OLS hedging strategies tend to perform as well or better than more complex estimation models such as GARCH can be attributed to the use of the Ederington effectiveness measure. This variance performance criterion is only valid for OLS based hedging strategies, and that using it to evaluate non-OLS OHRs will lead to the incorrect conclusion that OLS OHRs offer the best hedging performance. Therefore, while the variance-based measure is appropriate where the hedger seeks to minimise variance, in practice, hedgers may seek to minimise some measure of risk other than the variance. For this reason, we use three additional hedging effectiveness metrics that will allow us to make a robust comparison of different hedging models under both symmetric and asymmetric conditions.

The LPM is the first of a number of hedging effectiveness metrics that we use to address the shortcoming in the variance measure. The LPM distinguishes between the left and right tails of a distribution. Therefore, it can measure risk in the presence of asymmetries, as it is a function of the underlying distribution (Bawa, 1975). The LPM measures the probability of falling below a pre-specified target return. The LPM of order n around τ is defined as

$$\mathrm{LPM}_n(\tau; R) = E\{(\max[0, \tau - R])^n\} \int_{-\infty}^{\tau} (\tau - R)^n \, dF(R) \qquad (3)$$

where $F(R)$ is the cumulative distribution function of the investment return R, and τ is the target return parameter. The value of τ will depend on the level of return or loss that is acceptable to the investor. Some values of τ that may be considered are zero or the risk-free rate of interest. For a hedger, a small negative return may be acceptable to reflect the cost of hedging. The parameter n is the weighting applied to shortfalls from the target return. The more risk averse an investor, the higher the weight (n) that would be attached. Fishburn (1977) shows that $0<n<1$ is suitable for a risk seeking investor, $n=1$ for risk neutral and $n>1$ for a risk adverse investor. We can form a complete set of downside risk measures by changing the τ and n parameters to reflect the position and risk preferences of different types of hedger. The more risk-averse investors may set τ as the disaster level of return and have utilities that would reflect an LPM with $n=2, 3\ldots$ For example, an investor who views the consequences of a disaster level return as being unacceptable may use an order of LPM with $n=5$.

Interest in one-sided risk measures has increased in recent years as investors do not attach the same importance to positive and negative outcomes, but focus on downside or tail-specific risk. The LPM therefore serves as an intuitive measure of risk that is in line with the risk preferences of many investors (Lee & Rao, 1988). A number of studies have compared the hedging effectiveness of short and long hedgers using the LPM methodology (see, e.g. Demirer & Lien, 2003). The results indicate that hedging effectiveness for long hedgers differs from that of short hedgers, with long hedgers deriving more benefit from hedging in terms of risk reduction as measured by reduced LPMs.

Since the majority of hedgers seek to limit losses, it may be appropriate for hedgers to seek to minimise a risk measure that is tail specific. Two additional metrics that are closely related to the LPM and which also have similar advantages as measures of risk for hedging are VaR and CVaR. Both of these measures are also tail specific and may be used to measure downside risk. These are considered in due course.

We calculate the LPM using a target return of zero since the general aim of hedging is to avoid negative outcomes. We also use $n = 3$ as the order of LPM, as this corresponds to a strongly risk-averse investor. The metric we apply to evaluate hedging effectiveness based on the LPM is the percentage reduction in the LPM of each hedging estimation method as compared with a no hedge position.[1]

This is calculated as

$$\text{HE}_2 = 1 - \left[\frac{\text{LPM}_{3\ \text{Hedged Portfolio}}}{\text{LPM}_{3\ \text{Unhedged Portfolio}}}\right] \tag{4}$$

The third hedging effectiveness metric is VaR.[2] This is the loss level of a portfolio over a certain period that will not be exceeded with a specified probability. VaR has two parameters, the time horizon (N) and the confidence level (x). Generally VaR is the (100–x)th percentile of the portfolio over the next N days. We calculate VaR using $x = 99$ and $N = 1$. This corresponds to the first percentile of the return distribution of each portfolio over a one-day period which is consistent with the OHR estimation period used in this study. Similar to the LPM, the performance metric employed is the percentage reduction in the VaR.

$$\text{HE}_3 = 1 - \left[\frac{\text{VaR}_{1\%\ \text{Hedged Portfolio}}}{\text{VaR}_{1\%\ \text{Unhedged Portfolio}}}\right] \tag{5}$$

A shortcoming in VaR is that it is not a coherent measure of risk, as it is not sub-additive.[3] Also in practice two portfolios may have the same VaR but different potential losses. This is because VaR does not account for losses beyond the (100–x)th percentile. We address this by estimating an additional performance metric; CVaR, that addresses the shortcoming in VaR as it is a coherent measure of risk. CVaR is the expected loss conditional that we have exceeded the VaR. It is given as

$$\text{CVaR} = E[L|L > \text{VaR}] \tag{6}$$

This measures the expected value of our losses, L, if we get a loss in excess of the VaR. CVaR is preferable to the VaR because it estimates not only of the probability of a loss, but also the magnitude of a possible loss. In calculating CVaR we use the 1% confidence level which gives us the expected shortfall beyond the 1% VaR. The performance metric we use to evaluate hedging effectiveness is the percentage reduction in CVaR as compared with a no hedge position.

$$\text{HE}_4 = 1 - \left[\frac{\text{CVaR}_{1\%\ \text{Hedged Portfolio}}}{\text{CVaR}_{1\%\ \text{Unhedged Portfolio}}}\right] \tag{7}$$

Few studies in the hedging literature have applied either VaR or CVaR as measures of hedging effectiveness; however, Giot and Laurent (2003) use both the VAR and CVaR measures to examine the risk of short and long trading positions over a one-day time horizon. They estimate volatility using both symmetric and asymmetric GARCH-type approaches. Their findings show that symmetric models underperform models that account for asymmetry; however, their analysis is only applied to unhedged positions. Next we turn to our application of both the hedging models and performance measures outlined to examine hedging effectiveness under conditions of asymmetry.

DATA

Our data consist of daily cash and futures closing prices of crude oil. Crude oil was chosen as it potentially exhibits significant asymmetric effects, because it is the largest traded commodity in the world in terms of monetary value, because of its economic importance and because it is widely hedged. The oil contract is the NYMEX West Texas Light Sweet Crude contract, which was chosen as it is used as an international oil pricing benchmark given its liquidity and price transparency.[4] All data was obtained from commodity systems and daily returns were calculated as the differenced logarithmic prices. Continuous series were formed using the nearby contract with rollover occurring about one week before maturity. Trading volume was used as the criterion in deciding the rollover date meaning that the price of the largest traded contract by volume was used, and that the price switched from one contract to the next when that contract's volume fell below the volume of the next traded contract.

Because we examine the influence of asymmetry and its effects on hedging effectiveness, we require data that exhibits both skewed and non-skewed characteristics in order to facilitate a comparison. These considerations motivated our choice of sample periods. Our initial sample is daily logarithmic returns from 1 January 2000 through 31 December 2010. For each contract our initial search criterion is to have one year each of symmetric and asymmetric returns. Our second search criterion is choosing both in-sample and out-of-sample periods that are consistently symmetrically or non-symmetrically distributed to ensure consistency between in-sample and out-of-sample performance results. From this sample period, we were able to extract two separate data sets, one skewed and one non-skewed. The first data set is asymmetric and runs from January 2001 to December 2001. The second data set is symmetric and runs from January 2002 to December 2002. For each period, the first 160 observations are used for the in-sample estimation of the hedging models. The remaining 100 observations were used to facilitate out-of-sample comparisons for model evaluation. The characteristics of the data are now examined.

Table 1. Summary Statistics.

	2001		2002	
	Crude Oil – Asymmetric		Crude Oil – Symmetric	
	Cash	Futures	Cash	Futures
Mean	−0.0012	−0.0012	0.0018	0.0017
Min	−0.1653	−0.1654	−0.0586	−0.0627
Max	0.1039	0.0807	0.0613	0.0595
SD	0.0277	0.0261	0.0212	0.0208
Skewness	−0.633*	−1.003*	−0.066	−0.041
Kurtosis	6.746*	6.762*	0.421	0.384
B–J	512.36*	541.14*	2.112	1.678
LM	7.17	1.53	9.48	11.41**
Stationarity	−16.25*	−15.43*	−16.83*	−17.51*
Correlation	0.92		0.92	

This table presents summary statistics for the log returns of each cash and futures series for crude oil. The excess skewness statistic measures asymmetry where zero would indicate a symmetric distribution. The excess kurtosis statistic measures the shape of a distribution where a value of zero would indicate a normal distribution. The Bera–Jarque (B–J) statistic combines skewness and kurtosis in comparison to normality. LM with four lags is the Lagrange Multiplier test for ARCH effects proposed by Engle (1982) and is distributed χ^2. Stationarity is tested using the Dickey–Fuller unit root test. The correlation coefficient between each set of cash and futures is also given. *Denotes significance at the 1% level. **Denotes significance at the 5% level.

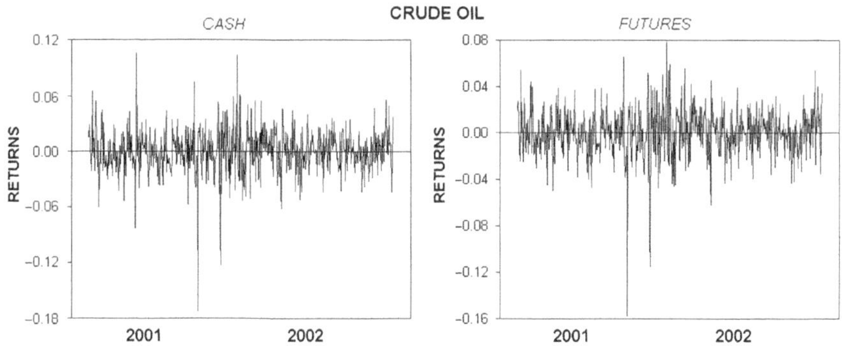

Fig. 1. Returns of Crude Oil. *Note*: This figure displays both the cash and futures return returns series for crude oil. Returns vary over time. For example, the crude oil series displays greater volatility for the year 2001 than for 2002.

Summary statistics for the data are displayed in Table 1. We can see that the characteristics of the return distributions of the two series are markedly different. The first data set for Crude Oil (2001) is non-symmetric and is characterised by significant skewness. In contrast, the second data set of Crude Oil (2002) can be characterised as symmetric given the insignificant skewness figure. We can also see that the volatility differs considerably between the skewed and non-skewed periods. For example, the standard deviation for crude oil cash is 2.7% for the skewed data as compared to 2.1% for the non-skewed data. This is further demonstrated if we examine Fig. 1 which plots the cash and futures return series.

The data were checked for stationarity using Dickey Fuller unit root tests. As expected, the log returns for cash and futures are stationary. The Engle (1982) Lagrange Multiplier (LM) test with four lags was used to check for ARCH effects. The findings indicate significant ARCH effects present for the symmetric period (2002) only. This may limit the advantages of the GARCH models over hedging strategies that assume a constant variance in estimating hedge strategies for the crude oil contract.

EMPIRICAL RESULTS

We compare the short and long hedging effectiveness of five different OHR estimation methods for distributions with symmetric and asymmetric characteristics. We construct hedged portfolios using Eqs. (1a) and (1b) and then evaluate hedging effectiveness using the performance metrics outlined in the second section. The out-of-sample HRs are graphically represented in Fig. 2 together with the associated summary statistics in Table 2.

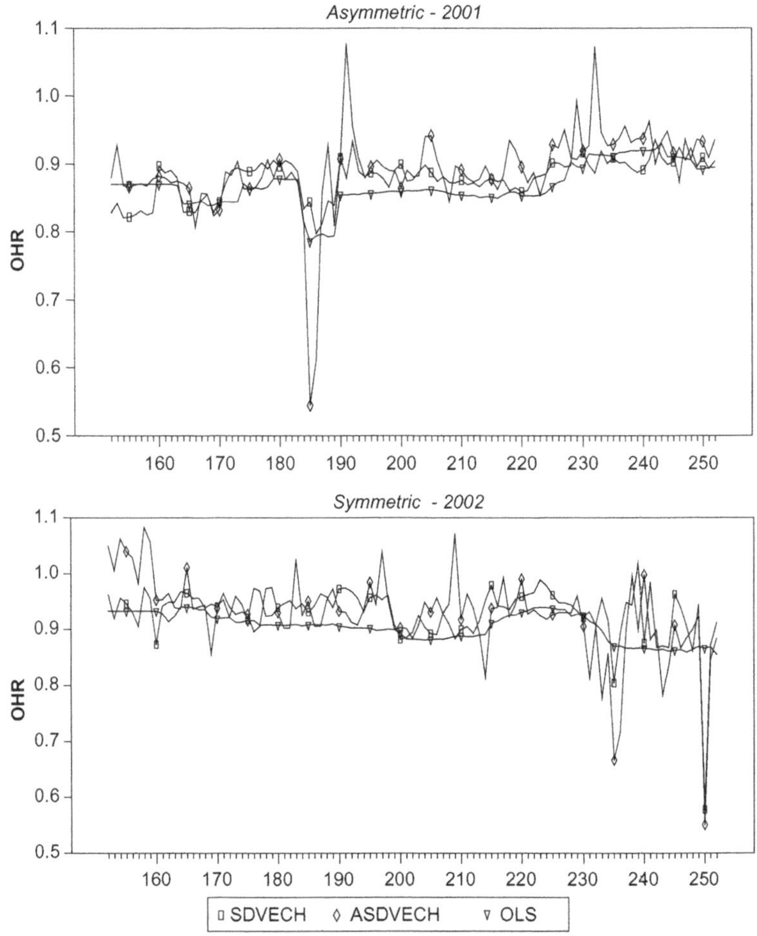

Fig. 2. Out-of-Sample Optimal Hedge Ratios Crude Oil. *Note*: This figure displays the time-varying OHRs for the crude oil series. Three OHRs are presented for both the asymmetric and symmetric distributions which are 2001 and 2002, respectively. The OHRs are the rolling window OLS, symmetric GARCH SDVECH and asymmetric GARCH ASDVECH models.

Table 2. Summary Statistics of Optimal Hedge Ratios.

Hedging Model	2001			2002		
	Crude Oil – Asymmetric			Crude Oil – Symmetric		
	OLS	SDVECH	ASDVECH	OLS	SDVECH	ASDVECH
Mean	0.8722	0.8877	0.8993	0.8994	0.9274	0.9150
Min	0.7857	0.7972	0.5446	0.8554	0.5781	0.5504
Max	0.9409	0.9928	1.0781	0.9407	1.0197	1.0724
SD	0.0336	0.0312	0.0660	0.0248	0.0507	0.0680

This table presents summary statistics for the estimated optimal hedge ratios for each hedging model for crude oil.

A quick glance at Fig. 2 indicates that the different hedging models produce different HRs. In particular we observe from Fig. 2 that the ASDVECH model differs from the SDVECH model. From Table 2, we can see that the range of the HRs is much narrower for the SDVECH model as compared to the ASDVECH model. For example, the OHRs for the asymmetric period range from 0.79 to 0.99 for the SDVECH model as compared with a range of 0.54–1.07 for the ASDVECH model. Again, from Table 2, the OHRs range from about 0.55 to 1.07 for the symmetric crude oil series, using the ASDVECH model. We also observe that the OHRs for both series appear to be stationary. Therefore, while we would expect to see different hedging performance for each of the different hedging models, the performance gap may be narrow in many cases. We now turn to an examination of the hedging performance of the difference models for both short and long hedgers for both the symmetric and asymmetric data.

Tables 3 and 4 present both in-sample and out-of-sample results for hedging effectiveness. Examining first the in-sample results from Table 3, these show that hedging is effective at reducing risk as measured by the variance reduction criterion. For example, if we examine crude oil for the asymmetric period, using a benchmark no-hedge we find a 65.90% reduction in the variance using an OLS hedge. In terms of the overall hedging performance, the average in-sample hedging performance across both asymmetric and symmetric periods and for all hedging models and performance metrics is just 54%.

We also compare the in-sample hedging performance of crude oil based on distributional characteristics. We find better hedging performance across all models and risk measures for the symmetric data. For example, variance

Table 3. In-Sample Hedging Effectiveness – Short versus Long Comparison.

	HE_1 Variance $\times 10^{-2}$	HE_2 LPM $\times 10^{-2}$	HE_3 VaR $\times 10^{-2}$	HE_4 CVaR $\times 10^{-2}$	HE_1 Variance $\times 10^{-2}$	HE_2 LPM $\times 10^{-2}$	HE_3 VaR $\times 10^{-2}$	HE_4 CVaR $\times 10^{-2}$
	Panel A: Short hedgers				Panel B: Long hedgers			
Crude oil – asymmetric								
None	0.00	0.00	0.00	11.61*	0.00	0.00	0.00	0.00
Naïve	64.45	76.18*	13.19	0.00	64.45	36.55	26.38*	29.07*
OLS	65.90	69.97*	20.61	9.91	65.90	55.27	26.55*	22.57*
SDVECH	64.24	72.13*	18.25	3.97	64.24	44.93	30.05*	24.53*
ASDVECH	65.07	74.17*	17.77	3.05	65.07	43.30	29.25*	26.09*
Crude oil – symmetric								
None	0.00	0.00	0.00	0.00	0.00	0.00	0.00	0.00
Naïve	82.95	92.02	42.01	33.18	82.95	87.05	47.17	51.43*
OLS	83.33	90.08	45.59	48.94*	83.33	90.82	47.77	40.47
SDVECH	84.48	93.29	45.45	36.26	84.48	89.26	55.38*	56.17*
ASDVECH	83.52	92.76	43.97	33.86	83.52	88.00	52.74*	54.35*

This table presents the in-sample hedging performance for crude oil for both the asymmetric and symmetric data sets. Figures are in percentages. HE_1 and HE_4 give the percentage reduction in the performance metric from the hedged model as compared with the worst hedged position. Statistical comparisons are made between the performance of short and long hedgers on a metric-by-metric basis using Efron's 1979 bootstrap technique. *Indicates that the percentage reduction in the risk metric is significantly better comparing long to short hedges at the 1% confidence level. For example, using the crude oil asymmetric data set, and the VaR HE_3 as our performance metric, we can see that the in-sample performance of long hedgers is significantly better than that of the short hedgers for each of the four hedging models.

Table 4. Out-of-Sample Hedging Effectiveness – Short versus Long Comparison.

	HE_1 Variance $\times 10^{-2}$	HE_2 LPM $\times 10^{-2}$	HE_3 VaR $\times 10^{-2}$	HE_4 CVaR $\times 10^{-2}$	HE_1 Variance $\times 10^{-2}$	HE_2 LPM $\times 10^{-2}$	HE_3 VaR $\times 10^{-2}$	HE_4 CVaR $\times 10^{-2}$
	Panel A: Short hedgers				Panel B: Long hedgers			
Crude oil – asymmetric								
None	0.00	0.00	0.00	0.00	0.00	0.00	0.00	0.00
Naïve	80.54	79.97	64.02*	59.77*	80.54	93.56*	40.77	36.06
OLS	81.11	85.37	51.69	62.99*	81.11	93.53*	52.08	47.85
SDVECH	80.22	80.87	62.88*	64.23*	80.22	94.12*	37.44	40.00
ASDVECH	80.37	81.62	62.86*	64.90*	80.37	94.14*	37.58	40.55
Crude oil – symmetric								
None	0.00	0.00	0.00	2.90*	0.00	0.00	0.00	0.00
Naïve	70.38	76.82*	15.40	0.00	70.38	62.83	33.43*	26.25*
OLS	71.55	75.63	24.40	16.75	71.55	71.64	29.94	19.71
SDVECH	71.55	78.25*	17.58	3.06	71.55	66.62	35.28*	28.25*
ASDVECH	72.43	81.02*	19.05	2.84	72.43	66.92	35.50*	36.48*

This table presents the out-of-sample hedging performance for both crude oil and S&P500 returns and for both the asymmetric and symmetric data sets. Figures are in percentages. HE_1 and HE_4 give the percentage reduction in the performance metric from the hedged model as compared with the worst hedged position. For example, short hedging the crude oil contract for the asymmetric data set with the naïve model yields an 80.54% reduction in the variance as compared with a no-hedge strategy. Statistical comparisons are made between the performance of short and long hedgers on a metric-by-metric basis using Efron's 1979 technique. *Indicates that the percentage reduction in the risk metric is significantly better comparing long to short hedges at the 1% confidence level. For example, using the crude oil asymmetric data set, and the LPM HE_2 as our performance metric, we can see that the out-of-sample performance of long hedgers is significantly better than that of the short hedgers for each of the four hedging models.

reductions for the symmetric period average 85% as compared with 64% for the asymmetric period when all hedging models are used. This finding persists if we use the tail-specific measures with average differences in hedging performance between the symmetric and asymmetric periods of 27% and 31% for short and long hedgers, respectively.

We derive a number of conclusions from these results. Firstly, the in-sample hedging performance of the crude oil contract is better for symmetric distributions. This suggests that hedging the crude oil commodity using futures is of relatively limited use when returns may be skewed. Secondly, hedging effectiveness is not as good as could be expected when compared with other assets. For example, equity hedges typically show effectiveness in excess of 85% (Cotter & Hanly, 2006).

Examining next the tail-specific performance metrics, hedging is not as effective in reducing VaR and CVaR as it is at reducing the LPM. For example, there are differences in hedging effectiveness typically ranging from 15% to 50%. Also, the different hedging models yield poor performance in terms of reducing the VaR and especially the CVaR. Using the best performing models; for example, the results for the asymmetric data series indicate only an 11% reduction in the CVaR for short hedgers and a 29% reduction for long hedgers. These results may be related to the ability of VaR and CVaR metrics to model extreme tail events whereas the LPM is a more general metric that doesn't pick up the most extreme outliers in the same way.[5] Therefore, hedging crude oil may be quite limited in reducing extreme losses as measured by the VaR or CVaR. Thus, tail-specific hedging effectiveness metrics such as VaR and CVaR may be appropriate for use by strongly risk-averse investors, as a measure of risk for distributions that may be affected by a small number of observations. A key point is that hedges may not be as effective in volatile markets that are skewed. In hedging terms, this means that investors may face the risk that their hedges will not fulfil their function of risk reduction during stressful markets conditions when they are most needed.

We also make a statistical comparison of the hedging effectiveness of short and long hedgers using Efron's (1979) bootstrap methodology, by employing t-tests of the differences between short and long hedgers based on the point estimates of our results.[6] This approach is also adopted in tests of model hedging effectiveness and allows us to make statistical as well as economic inferences from our results.[7] Taking the crude oil asymmetric sample first, the hedging effectiveness differences between short and long hedgers are significant at the 1% level in every single case whereas for the symmetric sample they are significant in only 50% of cases in-sample.

The differences between short and long hedgers even for the symmetric period demonstrates the importance of using tail-specific hedging effectiveness metrics irrespective of the characteristics of the return distribution. This finding is supported across each of the different tail-specific metrics of hedging performance.

We now turn to the out-of-sample results which are of importance in determining the hedging performance under real world conditions. From Table 4, the first thing to note is that hedging is still effective in terms of reducing risk across each of the risk measures. For example, variance reductions are of the order of 80% for the asymmetric sample and 72% for the symmetric sample. Also, we can again see the limited use of hedging in reducing risk as measured by VaR and CVaR metrics. For example, using the symmetric period, we can see that effectiveness as measured by CVaR is as low as 2.84% using the ASDVECH model.

Using the tail-specific performance metrics, we also examine the out-of-sample hedging performance of short and long hedgers for asymmetric as compared to symmetric periods. For the asymmetric data, the differences in hedging effectiveness between short and long hedgers are significant at the 1% level in 92% of cases out-of-sample whereas for the asymmetric data they are significant in only 69% of cases out-of-sample. These results indicate the importance of using tail-specific performance measures even for data with symmetric distributional characteristics.

We now turn our attention towards model performance. Tables 5 and 6 present absolute figures for the performance effectiveness measures of each of the hedging models, for in-sample and out-of-sample hedges, respectively. The lower values represent better hedging performance. For example, the variance figure of 0.481 in Table 5 for the asymmetric crude oil hedge represents the risk associated with an unhedged position, whereas the OLS model is the best hedging model as it yields the lowest risk with a variance of 0.164. Looking first at the in-sample results, we can see that the best hedging model depends on the hedging performance metric. For example, we can see from Table 5, using the asymmetric data for short hedgers, that the OLS model yields the best performance in terms of both the variance (0.164) and the VaR (4.19), whereas using the LPM as the performance criterion, the naïve hedge (0.328) is the best performer.

In terms of the best overall model, Table 7 presents a summary of the best performing model for both short and long hedgers; in-sample and out-of sample. The best overall in-sample hedging model for the asymmetric data is the OLS model which performs best in 50% of cases across both short and

Table 5. Statistical Comparison of Hedging Model Performance – In-Sample.

	Variance $\times 10^{-3}$	LPM $\times 10^{-5}$	VaR $\times 10^{-2}$	CVaR $\times 10^{-2}$	Variance $\times 10^{-3}$	LPM $\times 10^{-5}$	VaR $\times 10^{-2}$	CVaR $\times 10^{-2}$
	Panel A: Short hedgers				Panel B: Long hedgers			
Crude oil – asymmetric								
None	0.481*	1.375*	5.278*	5.700[a]	0.481*	0.722*	5.917*	8.107*
Naive	0.171	0.328[a]	4.582*	6.449*	0.171	0.458*	4.356	5.750[a]
OLS	0.164[a]	0.413*	4.190[a]	5.810	0.164[a]	0.323[a]	4.346	6.277*
SDVECH	0.172	0.383	4.315	6.193	0.172	0.398*	4.139[a]	6.118*
ASDVECH	0.168	0.355	4.340	6.252	0.168	0.410*	4.186	5.992*
Crude oil – symmetric								
None	0.522*	1.075*	5.115*	5.587*	0.522*	0.895*	5.518*	6.131*
Naïve	0.089*	0.086*	2.966*	3.733*	0.089*	0.116*	2.915*	2.978*
OLS	0.087*	0.107*	2.783[a]	2.853[a]	0.087*	0.082[a]	2.882*	3.650*
SDVECH	0.081[a]	0.072[a]	2.790	3.561*	0.081[a]	0.096*	2.462[a]	2.687[a]
ASDVECH	0.086	0.078	2.866	3.695*	0.086	0.107*	2.608*	2.799*

This table presents the in-sample hedged portfolio statistics upon which we base our performance measures. The best performing model is the model that yields the lowest value for each risk measure and is denoted by superscript alphabet a. For example, the OLS model yields the lowest variance of 0.164 when hedging the crude oil asymmetric data. Statistical comparisons are made for each hedging model against the best performing model using Efron's 1979 technique. For example, taking the asymmetric data set for a short hedger, we can see that there is a significant difference between the in-sample variance of the no hedge 0.481 as compared with the best performing OLS model 0.164. *Denotes a better performance being recorded for the best performing benchmark relative to that measure at the 1% significance level.

Table 6. Statistical Comparison of Hedging Model Performance – Out-of-Sample.

	Variance $\times 10^{-3}$	LPM $\times 10^{-5}$	VaR $\times 10^{-2}$	CVaR $\times 10^{-2}$	Variance $\times 10^{-3}$	LPM $\times 10^{-5}$	VaR $\times 10^{-2}$	CVaR $\times 10^{-2}$
	Panel A: Short hedgers				Panel B: Long hedgers			
Crude oil – asymmetric								
None	1.240*	2.862*	12.183*	16.531*	1.240*	8.110*	9.399*	10.395*
Naïve	0.241	0.573*	4.383[a]	6.650*	0.241	0.522	5.567*	6.647*
OLS	0.234[a]	0.419[a]	5.885*	6.118	0.234[a]	0.524	4.504[a]	5.421[a]
SDVECH	0.245	0.548*	4.522	5.913	0.245	0.476	5.880*	6.237*
ASDVECH	0.243	0.526*	4.525	5.803[a]	0.243	0.475[a]	5.867*	6.180*
Crude oil – symmetric								
None	0.341*	0.634*	4.278*	4.312*	0.341*	0.469*	4.974*	5.353*
Naïve	0.101*	0.147*	3.619*	4.441*	0.101*	0.174*	3.311	3.948*
OLS	0.097	0.154*	3.234[a]	3.697[a]	0.097	0.133[a]	3.485*	4.298*
SDVECH	0.097	0.138*	3.526*	4.305*	0.097	0.157*	3.219	3.841*
ASDVECH	0.094[a]	0.120[a]	3.463*	4.315*	0.094[a]	0.155*	3.208[a]	3.400[a]

This table presents the out-of-sample hedged portfolio statistics upon which we base our performance measures. The best performing model is the model that yields the lowest value for each risk measure and is denoted by superscript alphabet a. Statistical comparisons are made for each hedging model against the best performing model using Efron's 1979 technique. For example, taking the crude oil asymmetric data set for a short hedger, we can see that there is a significant difference between the in-sample variance of both the no hedge model 1.240 as compared with the best performing OLS model 0.234. *Denotes a better performance being recorded for the best performing benchmark relative to that measure at the 1% significance level.

Table 7. Summary of Best Performing Hedging Model.

	Variance	LPM	VaR	CVaR	Variance	LPM	VaR	CVaR
	Panel A: Short hedgers				Panel B: Long hedgers			
					In-sample Crude oil			
Asymmetric	OLS	Naïve	OLS	None	OLS	OLS	SDVECH	Naïve
Symmetric	SDVECH	SDVECH	OLS	OLS	SDVECH	OLS	SDVECH	SDVECH
					Out-of-sample Crude oil			
Asymmetric	OLS	OLS	Naïve	ASDVECH	OLS	ASDVECH	OLS	OLS
Symmetric	ASDVECH	ASDVECH	OLS	OLS	ASDVECH	OLS	ASDVECH	ASDVECH

This table summarises the best hedging model for both short and long hedgers for each measure of hedging effectiveness. For example, the best in-sample hedging model in terms of risk reduction for the asymmetric crude oil data set is the OLS model in four out of eight cases across both sets of hedgers.

long hedgers. For the symmetric data the best overall model is the SDVECH model which performs best for five out of eight performance metrics spread across both short and long hedgers. The out-of sample results show that the OLS and ASDVECH models are the best overall performers for the asymmetric and symmetric data, respectively

While these findings highlight the best hedging models for a given scenario, a key issue is whether there are significant differences in the performance of the different hedging models. To test this we compared the performance of the different hedging models, again employing Efron's (1979) bootstrap methodology. The results of these tests are presented in Tables 5 and 6. We find significant differences between model hedging performances in 54% of cases in-sample and 56% of cases out-of-sample. Indeed if we look at the actual performance metrics for the different hedging models, while there may be statistical differences between them, the absolute differences between models are small and not economically significant. What this demonstrates is that the OLS and GARCH models tend to provide better hedging performance than a naïve hedge. These findings show that when hedging commodities such as crude oil, the choice of hedging model is important but it also indicates that the OLS model provides consistently good performance across different assets.

The failure of the asymmetric GARCH model to provide better performance for asymmetric distributions contrasts with that of Giot and Laurent (2003). This may relate to the earlier point relating to the ability of the ASDVECH model to model positive and negative return innovations separately; however, this is not the same as being able to model skewness in the distribution. Based on these findings, we would have to conclude that there is little to be gained from the more complex GARCH models in performance terms over the simpler OLS model irrespective of the characteristics of the return distribution. This finding supports the broad literature on optimal hedging that the OLS model provides an efficient outcome across a selection of risk measures.

CONCLUSIONS

This chapter compares the hedging effectiveness of crude oil for both symmetric and asymmetric distributions. We also compare the hedging effectiveness of short and long hedgers using a variety of hedging estimation methods that are tail-specific. We find that both in-sample and out-of-sample hedging effectiveness is significantly reduced by the presence of skewness in the return distribution. This is an important finding as it means that hedging may not be as effective during asymmetric return periods, and therefore investors may not be effectively hedging during the periods when they most require it.

We also find larger differences in hedging performance between the short and long hedgers for the asymmetric distribution when compared with a symmetric distribution. Therefore, the use of one-sided hedging performance measures that are consistent with modern risk management techniques such as VaR and CVaR is to be recommended, as the traditional variance reduction criterion is not adequate and will provide inaccurate measures of risk for different types of hedgers both for symmetric and especially asymmetric distributions.

Also, the best hedging estimation model to emerge is the OLS model. This provides the best overall hedging performance across all measures of hedging effectiveness for both short and long hedgers. This finding suggests that there is little economic benefit to be gained by the use of more complex hedging estimation models over the simpler OLS model irrespective of the characteristics of the return distribution.

ACKNOWLEDGMENTS

Cotter's contribution to the study has been supported by Science Foundation Ireland under Grant Number 08/SRC/FM1389.

NOTES

1. Cotter's contribution to the study has been supported by Science Foundation Ireland under Grant Number 08/SRC/FM1389.
2. As stated we choose a weight of $n = 3$ to describe a strongly risk averse investor. However, our measures of VaR and CVaR can also encompass attitudes to risk. VaR can be viewed as a special case of the LPM in Eq. (3) setting $n = 0$ and CVaR sets $n = 1$. By fixing the probability LPM_0, the corresponding VaR/CVaR can be calculated.
3. Coherent measures of risk are sub-additive. What this means is that the risk of two positions when added together is never greater than the sum of the risks of the two individual positions (see, e.g. Artzner, Delbaen, Eber, & Heath, 1999).
4. The contract trades in units of 1,000 barrels on the NYMEX through open outcry. Further details of the contract and its trading characteristics are available at http://www.nymex.com/lsco_fut_descri.aspx. Accessed on 7 March 2012.
5. While each of these measures is one sided, the LPM with a target rate set $t = 0$ will include all observations less than 0, whereas both the VaR and CVaR

calculated at the 1% interval will include only extreme observations located in the left or right tails of the distribution. Also, modelling the tail of the distribution is more statistically reliable as compared with the exceeding method that relates to the LPM.

6. The returns of the hedged portfolios as compiled using Eqs (1a) and (1b) were bootstrapped by re-sampling with replacement from the returns. One hundred simulations were used allowing for the construction of confidence intervals around each point estimate.

7. For each hedging model, we compare the performance metric for short hedgers with the performance metric for long hedgers again employing bootstrap confidence intervals. To illustrate, examining Crude Oil hedges and taking the asymmetric data for example, the difference between the Naïve model VaR figures of 13.19 and 26.38, respectively, is statistically significant at the 1% level.

REFERENCES

Artzner, P., Delbaen, F., Eber, J., & Heath, D. (1999). Coherent measures of risk. *Mathematical Finance*, *9*, 203–228.

Bawa, S. (1975). Optimal rules for ordering uncertain prospects. *Journal of Financial Economics*, *2*, 95–121.

Bollerslev, T., Engle, R., & Wooldridge, J. (1988). A capital asset pricing model with time-varying covariances. *Journal of Political Economy*, *96*, 116–131.

Brooks, C., Henry, O., & Persand, G. (2002). The effects of asymmetries on optimal hedge ratios. *Journal of Business*, *75*, 333–352.

Cecchetti, S., Cumby, R., & Figlewski, S. (1988). Estimation of the optimal futures hedge. *Review of Economics and Statistics*, *70*, 623–630.

Conrad, J., Gultekin, M., & Kaul, G. (1991). Asymmetric predictability of conditional variances. *Review of Financial Studies*, *4*, 597–622.

Cotter, J., & Hanly, J. (2006). Re-examining hedging performance. *Journal of Futures Markets*, *26*, 657–676.

Demirer, R., & Lien, D. (2003). Downside risk for short and long hedgers. *International Review of Economics and Finance*, *12*, 25–44.

Ederington, L. (1979). The hedging performance of the new futures markets. *Journal of Finance*, *34*, 157–170.

Efron, B. (1979). Bootstrap methods: Another look at the jack-knife. *The Annals of Statistics*, *7*, 1–26.

Engle, R. (1982). Autoregressive conditional heteroskedasticity with estimates of the variance of United Kingdom inflation. *Econometrica*, *50*, 987–1008.

Fishburn, P. (1977). Mean-risk analysis with risk associated with below-target returns. *The American Economic Review*, *67*, 116–126.

Giot, P., & Laurent, S. (2003). Value-at-risk for long and short trading positions. *Journal of Applied Econometrics*, *18*, 641–663.

Glosten, L., Jagannathan, R., & Runkle, D. (1993). On the relationship between the expected value and the volatility of the normal excess return on stocks. *Journal of Finance*, *48*, 1779–1801.

Kroner, K., & Sultan, J. (1993). Time varying distribution and dynamic hedging with foreign currency futures. *Journal of Financial and Quantitative Analysis*, *28*, 535–551.

Kuper, G., & Van Soest, D. (2006). Does oil price uncertainty affect energy use? *Energy Journal*, *27*, 55–78.

Lee, W., & Rao, R. (1988). Mean lower partial moment valuation and lognormally distributed returns. *Management Science*, *34*, 446–453.

Lien, D. (2005). The use and abuse of the hedging effectiveness measure. *International Review of Financial Analysis*, *14*, 277–282.

ON THE BINOMIAL-TREE APPROACH TO CONVERTIBLE BONDS PRICING AND RISK ASSESSMENT

Krasimir Milanov and Ognyan Kounchev

ABSTRACT

In this chapter we concentrate at the most popular model for convertible bond (CB) valuation in a one-factor, stochastic underlying stock price setting. Through the last decade, the Tsiveriotis–Fernandes model (1998) has become a widely commented model that involves the state of default of the issuer of the CB. A routine approach to the solution of this model is the usage of methods of finite difference schemes (FDS). However, for many people trained in finance these methods are not very intuitive and they tend to ignore them and prefer to use binomial-tree approach as more intuitive technique. For that reason, our primary focus is to highlight the answer of the so far unanswered question: Does the binomial-tree approach to CBs provide accurate pricing, hedging, and risk assessment? We show on a set of representative examples that by using binomial-tree methodology one is unable to provide a consistent analysis of the pricing, hedging, and risk assessment. We start the chapter with the basics of CBs and CB market. We then explain the implementation of TF model within binary-tree approach. We conclude the chapter with performance

Derivative Securities Pricing and Modelling
Contemporary Studies in Economic and Financial Analysis, Volume 94, 281–302

ISSN: 1569-3759/doi:10.1108/S1569-3759(2012)0000094014

valuation of binomial-tree approach showing unexpected behavior in practice areas such as pricing (profile of CB's price versus underlying stock price), hedging (performance of CB's delta, gamma, and convertible arbitrage strategy versus underlying stock), and risk assessment (Monte Carlo VaR with respect to the underlying).

Keywords: Convertible bonds; binomial-tree; Tsiveriotis–Fernandes model; convertible arbitrage; delta-hedging of convertible bonds; risk assessment of convertible bonds

CONVERTIBLE BONDS

Convertible bonds (CBs or simply "convertibles") are a widely used type of contract, playing a major role in the financing of the companies (De Spiegeleer & Schoutens, 2011; Gushchin & Curien, 2008; Hull, 2002; Wilmott, 2000). From a pricing and hedging perspective, they are highly complex instruments. They have the early exercise feature of American options but in three forms: the option to be converted, the option to be called and the option to be put. Hence, sometimes they behave like a bond and sometimes like a stock. To be more precise, CBs are the bonds issued by a company where the holder has the option to exchange (to convert) the bonds for the company's stock at certain times in the future. The "conversion ratio" is the number of shares of stock obtained for one bond (this can be a function of time). If the conversion option is executed, then the rights to future coupons are lost. The bonds are almost always callable (i.e., the issuer has the right to buy them back at certain times at predetermined prices). Sometimes the holder's "call option" is conditional on the price of the company's stock being above a certain level. Some CBs incorporate a put feature. This right permits the holder of the bond to return it to the issuing company for a predetermined amount.

About the volume of the CB market, let us mention that in year 2000, the global convertible securities market has reached an approximate value of \$470 billion and in 2011 it is \$226 billion in United States. A significant feature of the recent trends in the CB market during the last 7 years, has been the relative shift in the investor base, away from the investors behind convertible arbitrage hedge funds and toward institutional investors such as pension funds and insurance companies which make up the so-called "outright" (or long-only) segment of the investor structure.

PRICING OF CBs

In the present research, we address a very important and so far unanswered question regarding the binomial-tree approach to the Tsiveriotis–Fernandes (TF) model for pricing CBs. Namely, does the binomial-tree framework provide accurate pricing, hedging and risk assessment? We show on a set of representative examples that by applying the binomial-tree methodology one is unable to provide a consistent analysis of the pricing, hedging, and risk assessment.

An important feature of the pricing of CBs is that similar to the American options there is no closed form solution, and the numerical computation of the solution is a challenge due to the free boundaries arising. Respectively, in our study we will employ the natural properties of CBs which are usually exploited in practice. Depending on the underlying stock we examine the profile of CB's price, of CB's sensitivities, convertible arbitrage strategy, and the Monte Carlo VaR estimation.

Throughout the years different CB pricing methodologies were developed. The main development was in the area of modeling the CB's price dynamics, as well as toward design of numerical methods for evaluating the CB pricing function. One of the most advanced and popular ideas for modeling CB's price dynamics was introduced in the seminal paper by Tsiveriotis and Fernandes (1998). They have proposed to split the CB value into two components: a cash-only part which is subject to credit risk, and an equity part, which is independent of the credit risk. This leads to a pair of coupled partial differential equations under certain constraints (in fact boundary and free boundary conditions) that can be solved to value the price of the convertibles. From numerical point of view Tsiveriotis and Fernandes have proposed explicit finite difference method for solving their system of equations. On the other hand, as in Hull (2002) one may use binomial-tree approach for solving the same system. More precisely, the approach in Hull (2002) is based on Cox, Ross, and Rubinstein (CRR) tree.

Currently, there are two basic numerical approaches for CB pricing, hedging, and risk assessment. The first one that is based on trees (binomial and trinomial) (Citigroup, 2003; De Spiegeleer & Schoutens, 2011; Gushchin & Curien, 2008; Hull, 2002), and the second one which is based on finite difference techniques (Andersen & Buffum, 2002; Ayache, Forsyth, & Vetzal, 2003; Tsiveriotis & Fernandes, 1998).

There is a gap in the above studies as they do not provide a complete report on the methodology performance. In the present chapter, we want to indicate essential drawbacks of the binomial-tree methodology and mistakes that are made when this methodology is used in major practice areas as hedging and risk assessment.

In general, we have to mention that the TF model provides an adequate pricing methodology for a still financial market, without involving credit default. However, if one needs to emphasize the credit default, which is very important for the present situation of the financial markets, then the approach of Ayache et al. (2003) exposes a negative convexity with respect to the stock price (for smaller values) is a more appropriate model. In a separate chapter, we will develop a CB pricing based on binomial-tree that is convergent to the Ayache et al. (2003) model.

The chapter is organized as follows. In the third section we explain the binomial-tree scheme for approximation of the TF model. Our main results are in the fourth section where we provide the performance valuation. Finally, in the appendix we provide a short but closed and informative outline of the model of Tsiveriotis and Fernandes.

THE TF MODEL AND ITS BINOMIAL-TREE APPROXIMATION

We follow the binomial-tree approximation to the TF model that is widely used in practice (cf. Hull, 2002). It involves modeling the issuer's stock price. It is assumed that the stock price process follows geometric Brownian motion and its dynamics is represented by the usual binomial-tree of Cox, Ross, and Rubinstein.

First of all, let us recall shortly the TF model; however, more details are presented in the last section. The pricing of CB has two main periods: before 1998, and after 1998 when the TF model has appeared, cf. Tsiveriotis and Fernandes (1998). It represents a major breakthrough in the area which revolutionized the price computation. The system of TF represents a prettily complicated system of equations which has solutions with free boundary. This makes it much more complicated for analysis and numerical solution than the American options. For that reason a binomial-tree model represents a very intuitive approximation to the model of TF, and this is completely analogous to the situation in options theory where binomial-tree models are very popular.

The idea of the TF model is that the CB price V is represented as a sum of two components

$$V = B + E$$

where B is the cash component and E is the equity component. B is related to the future payments in cash, given at moment t. They satisfy the following system of partial differential equations:

$$V_t + \frac{1}{2}\sigma^2 S^2 V_{SS} + rSV_S - rV - Br_c = 0$$
$$B_t + \frac{1}{2}\sigma^2 S^2 B_{SS} + rSB_S - (r + r_c)B = 0$$

and a set of boundary and "free interior boundary" conditions in the domain $0 \leq t \leq T$, and $0 \leq S < \infty$. The derivation is outlined in the appendix.

The life of the tree denoted by T is set equal to the life of the CB denoted also by T. The value of the CB at the final nodes (at time T) of the tree is calculated based on the conversion option that the holder has at that time T. We then roll back through the tree.

At nodes where the terms of the instrument allow calling back the bond, we test whether the position of the issuer can be improved by calling the bond. We also test whether the terms of the instrument allow improvement of the holder's position by selling back the bond to the issuer. Finally, we test whether conversion is optimal. This is equivalent to setting the CB value denoted as usually by V at a node equal to

$$max[min(Q_1, Q_2), Q_3, Q_4]$$

where Q_1 is the value given by the rollback (assuming that the bond is neither converted nor called, nor putted at the node), Q_2 refers to the dirty call price, Q_3 refers to the dirty put price, and Q_4 is the value if conversion takes place.

Following the idea of Tsiveriotis and Fernandes, the value of the bond at each node is represented as a sum of two components, $V = E + B$, namely, a component E that arises from situations where the bond ends up as equity, and a component B that arises from the situations where the bond ends up as a debt. In addition, the computation of the equity component E of Q_1 is based on risk-free discount rate, and the debt component B of the Q_1 is based on risky discount rate.

In order to complete the credit risk concept of TF model, we assume a non-zero value for the debt component B only when either cash redemption at maturity or put back of the bond takes place (Ayache et al., 2003, Eq. 47; Tsiveriotis & Fernandes, 1998, Eqs. 6 and 12).

PERFORMANCE VALUATION OF THE BINOMIAL-TREE APPROXIMATION

In our practice we have met a lot of examples for which the above-mentioned binomial-tree approach of TF model has unsatisfactory performance. To demonstrate this, we will choose the widely known and typical example presented in the chapter of Tsiveriotis and Fernandes (1998, Exhibit 5). Namely, our current performance evaluations are based on terms and conditions that are given in Table 1.

In the next subsections, we exhibit the following inconsistencies to market expectations about:

- profile of the price, delta, and gamma sensitivities;
- performance of delta-hedge strategy;
- movement of probability mass of simulations for, for example, one day holding period.

Taking into account these inconsistencies we believe a methodology that is based on binomial-tree approach would lead very often to impossibility to make any consistent analysis.

CB Price Performance Valuation

Regarding the underlying stock, the CB price has such important properties as strong monotonicity and convexity. In this section we show that the CB

Table 1. Example Terms and Conditions.

Parameter	Value
Issue date	January 6, 2009
Maturity date	January 6, 2014
Conversion	January 6, 2009 to January 6, 2014 into 1 share
Call	January 6, 2011 to January 6, 2014 at 110
Nominal	100
Coupon rate	4% paid semi-annually
Day count convention	*act*/365
Business day convention	*Actual*
Risk-free interest rate	5% (continuously compounded)
Credit spread	2% (continuously compounded)
Stock volatility	30%

price V obtained by means of the binary-tree method, misses the strong monotonicity and convexity, and exposes spurious oscillations. This misbehavior is persistent no matter how many steps of the binomial-tree method we use.

To demonstrate the above statements, in Figs. 1 and 2 we present the evolution of the CB price V with respect to the underlying stock during the time till maturity using a binary-tree with 500 and 750 time steps, respectively. The time value 0, corresponds to the issue date, and the time value 5, corresponds to the maturity date. For reader's convenience in Fig. 3 we provide the section $V(2, S)$ of the CB price V of Fig. 1, that is, we look at 2 years after the issue date. It is clearly seen that it is not convex and not strictly monotone in the range of S between 108 and 110. Also, in Fig. 4 we provide $V(2, S)$ of the CB price of Fig. 2 and have the same observations as above. Let us emphasize that for 750 tree steps we have a tree levels at every 1 ½ days or so, and for 500 tree steps – every 2 days or so. We make the final conclusion that even such a detailed binary-tree approximation does not

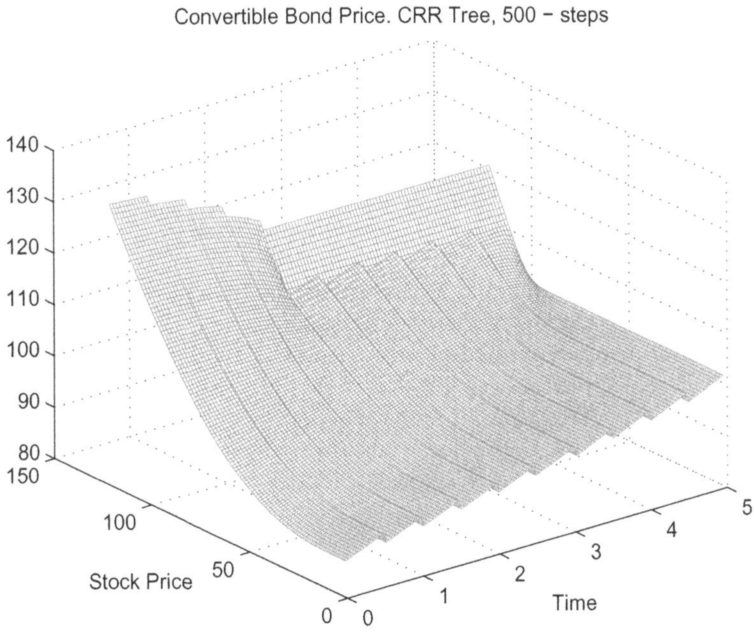

Fig. 1. CB Price, 500 Steps.

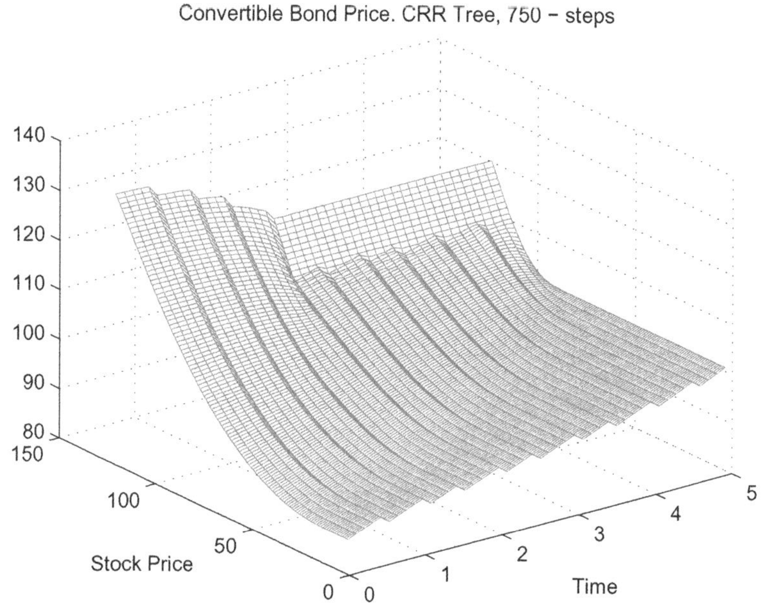

Fig. 2. CB Price, 750 Steps.

guarantee a satisfactory result. *Both figures in identical way highlight the wrong pricing performance of the approach.*

CB Delta and Gamma Sensitivities

CB delta and gamma quantify the sensitivity of the convertible price with respect to a small change in the underlying stock.

CB delta, sometimes referred to as hedge ratio, is the number of units of the stock we should short for each CB that we hold in order to create a risk-less portfolio. On the other hand, it is the slope of the curve that relates the CB price to the underlying stock price. Thus, the natural definition of CB delta is

$$\Delta = \frac{\partial V}{\partial S}$$

Traders and market makers prefer to use the following form of delta to illustrate the equity sensitivity of the CB (De Spiegeleer & Schoutens, 2011, p. 23)

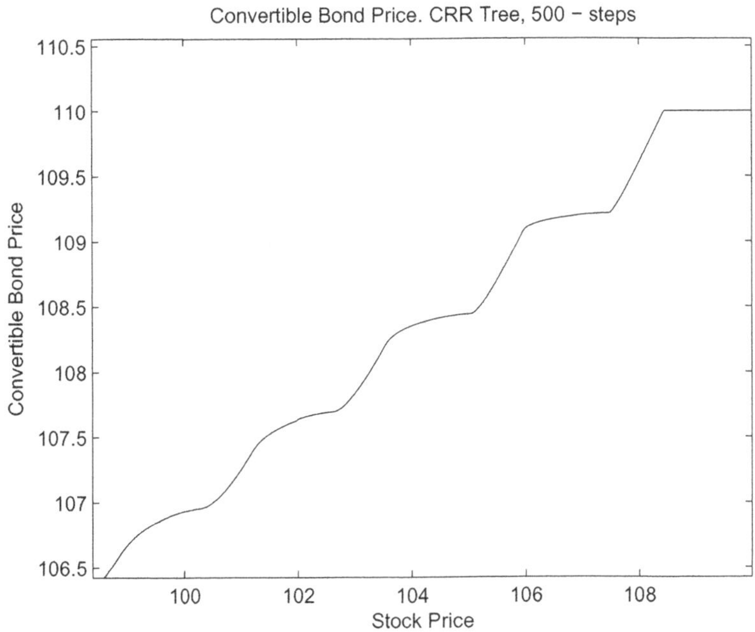

Fig. 3. CB Price Profile at $t = 2$.

$$\Delta_{\%} = \frac{\Delta}{C_r}$$

where C_r refers to the conversion ratio (the number of shares per 100 nominal that bond holder gets when converting the bond). This number ranges between 0% and 100% whereas the previous delta definition would have values in the interval $[0, C_r]$.

CB gamma is a representative measure for convexity or non-linearity of the instrument. It measures the change in Δ for a change in the price of the underlying common stock,

$$\Gamma = \frac{\partial^2 V}{\partial^2 S} = \frac{\partial \Delta}{\partial S}$$

From a hedging point of view, CB gamma illustrates how often the position must be re-hedged in order to maintain a delta-neutral position. That is, if gamma is small, delta changes slowly, and adjustments to keep a position

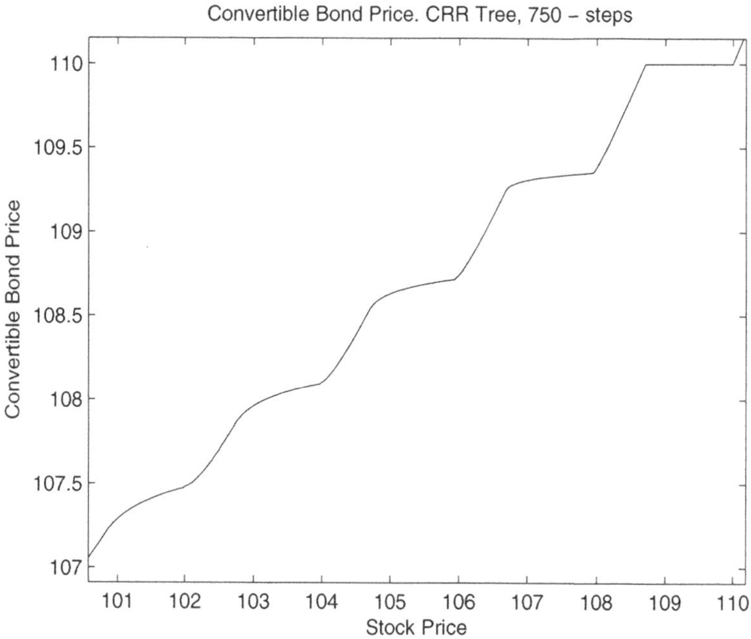

Fig. 4. CB Price Profile at $t = 2$.

delta-neutral need to be made only relatively infrequently. However, if the absolute value of gamma is large, delta is highly sensitive to the price of the underlying asset. It is then quite risky to leave a delta-neutral position unchanged for any length of time.

As we have seen, the path dependency and the possibilities of terminating the bond before the maturity date prohibit the derivation of a closed form pricing formula. Thus, the absence of closed form formula imposes the use of numerical methods to calculate the Greeks.

Finally, let us remark that it is a notorious fact that finite differences provide a bad approximation to delta and gamma, and are also computationally expensive. A satisfactory approach has been given for the computation of delta in (Hull, 2002; Wilmott, 2000) and for the computation of gamma, in Wilmott, 2000), and we will follow these references.

Within the binomial-tree framework CB delta is defined by (cf. Hull, 2002, p. 398 formula (1.8), p. 170):

$$\Delta = \Delta(t, S) = \frac{V^+ - V^-}{(u - d)S}$$

where t is the time and S is the stock price at this time; u and d are the parameters of the CRR tree, and V^+ and V^- are estimated CB values at one step forward when the stock price is Su and Sd, respectively.

In a similar way, the CB gamma is defined by

$$\Gamma = \Gamma(t, S) = \frac{\Delta^+ - \Delta^-}{(u - d)S}$$

where Δ^+ is the value of delta at one step forward for the stock price Su, that is, $\Delta^+ = \Delta(t + \delta t, Su)$ and Δ^- is the value of delta at one step forward for the stock price Sd, that is $\Delta^- = \Delta(t + \delta t, Sd)$.[1]

Now, let us come back to market activities as pricing (Dollar Nuking or Delta Neutral pricing, cf. De Spiegeleer & Schoutens, 2011), analyzing, and hedging where the existence of delta is of crucial importance.

Using the example from Table 1, in this section we demonstrate that throughout half of the CB life-span there exist stock prices for which the CB delta is not well defined and atypically oscillates although the computation that we have made where based on large number of time steps. Similarly to the results of delta, the results for the CB gamma are quite inconsistent.

In support of the above statements, in Figs. 5 and 6 we present the evolution of the CB delta and gamma with respect to the underlying stock during the time till maturity using a binary-tree with 500 time steps. As before, the time value 0 corresponds to the issue date, and the time value 5, corresponds to the maturity date. Also, in order to ease the reader, we look at 2 years after the issue date, and in Figs. 7 and 8 we exhibit the profile of CB delta and gamma on the basis of 500 tree steps, namely the one-dimensional sections $\Delta(2, S)$ and $\Gamma(2, S)$. Both figures in identical way highlight the wrong performance of the approach corresponding to CB delta and gamma.

Delta-Hedging (Convertible Arbitrage) of CB

The delta-hedging in the case of CBs is called convertible arbitrage.

Convertible arbitrage is a market-neutral investment strategy often employed by hedge funds (arbitrageurs). It involves the simultaneous purchase of convertible securities and the short sale of the same issuer's common stock.

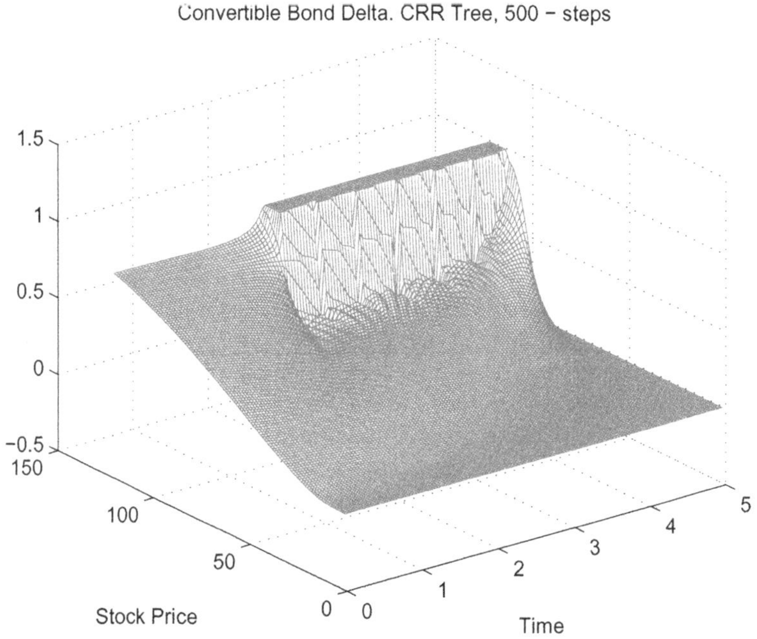

Fig. 5. CB Delta, 500 Steps.

The number of shares sold short usually reflects a delta-neutral or market-neutral ratio. As a result, under normal market conditions, the arbitrageur expects the combined position to be insensitive to fluctuations in the price of the underlying stock.

A main reason for the popularity of binary-tree methods is that in the financial math community the following myths are widely spread: first, the delta-hedging is only possible in binary-tree framework and Black–Scholes framework, and second, the binomial delta becomes, in the limit of time, the Black–Scholes (BS) delta.

In real-life situations the arbitrageurs expect that the Hedged position is insensitive with respect to the fluctuations in the price of the underlying stock.

In the following example we provide the graph of the relative change of the convertible arbitrage strategy (hedged position) calculated by means of the binomial-tree, where the shock of the stock price is equal to 0.5. The contract size of the position of CB given by Table 1 is 1 million, which is a

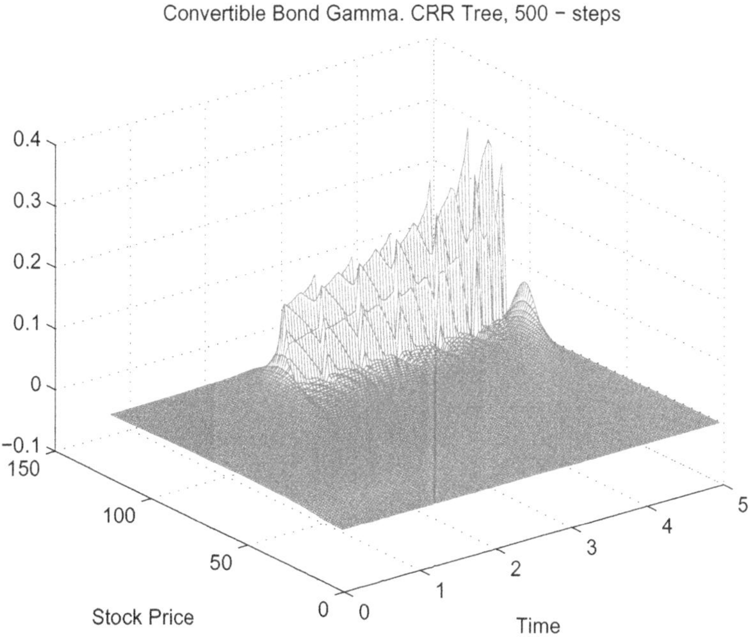

Fig. 6. CB Gamma, 500 Steps.

realistic example. We assume that the settlement date is the issue date t. The delta-hedged position (representing the convertible arbitrage strategy) is given by

$$\Pi(S) = V(S,t) - \frac{\partial V(S,t)}{\partial S} \times S$$

while its variation (resulting by the 0.5 shock) is given by

$$\Pi(S+0.5) = V(S+0.5,t) - \frac{\partial V(S,t)}{\partial S} \times (S+0.5)$$

The increment (the change) $\Pi(S)$ of the portfolio is given by the difference

$$\Pi(S+0.5) - \Pi(S) = V(S+0.5,t) - V(S,t) - 0.5 \times \frac{\partial V(S,t)}{\partial S}$$

In Fig. 9 we see that the binomial-tree with 500 steps does not meet the expectations of the arbitrageur since it oscillates considerably.

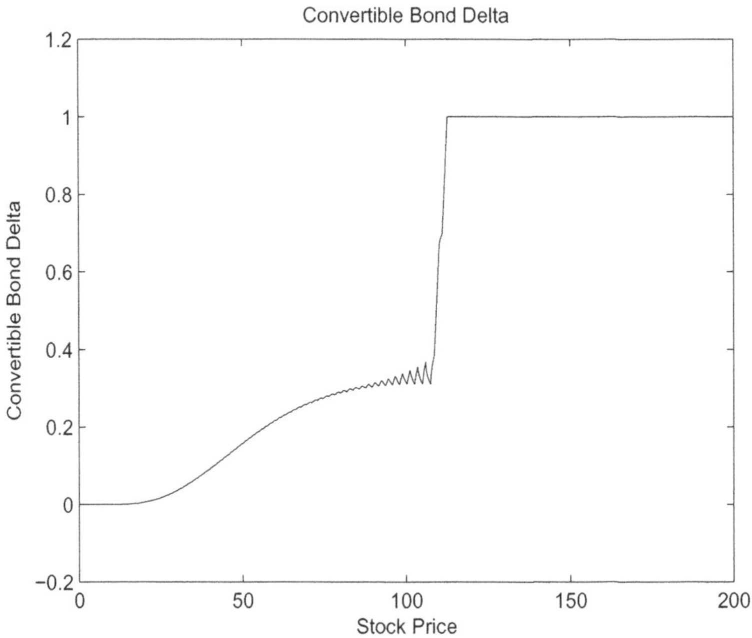

Fig. 7. CB Delta Profile at $t = 2$.

Risk Assessment

As an example of the bad performance of the binomial-tree approximation to risk assessment we will present a simple case of market risk assessment.

Market risk assessment explores the impact of market observable variables over the value of an investment (single position or a portfolio). Such variables are stock prices, interest rates, exchange rates, etc. which are sometimes referred to as market risk drivers or simply risk drivers.

A commonly used methodology for estimation of market risk is Value-at-Risk (VaR) (see, e.g., Fabozzi & Rachev, 2005). The importance of VaR arises from the fact that regulators and the financial industry advisory committees recommend VaR as way of measuring risk. The real boost in the use of VaR came when the Basel Committee on Banking Supervision adopted banks to use VaR as an internal model to set their capital requirements.

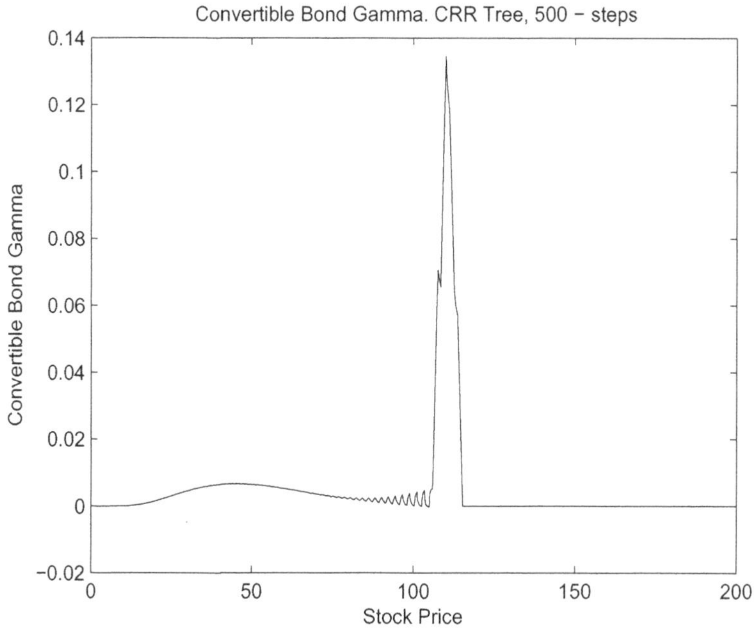

Fig. 8. CB Gamma Profile at $t = 2$.

The VaR measure is the highest possible loss over a certain period of time h at a given confidence level (De Spiegeleer & Schoutens, 2011; Fabozzi & Rachev, 2005). The VaR with confidence level $1 - \alpha$ is defined as

$$\mathrm{VaR}_{1-\alpha} = -min\{x : P(X \leq x) > \alpha\}$$

Here $1 - \alpha$ is the confidence level, α usually takes values like 1% or 5% and X is the change in the portfolio value, that is $X = V_h - V_0$. As usually portfolio values V_0 and V_h correspond to the initial time and the end of the holding period. The mostly used holding period, over which the expected CB loss is calculated, is one day or one month (22 business days).

It is clear that to calculate VaR values we need the probability density function of the portfolio value. The VaR methodologies mainly differ in ways of constructing the probability density function. The widely used in

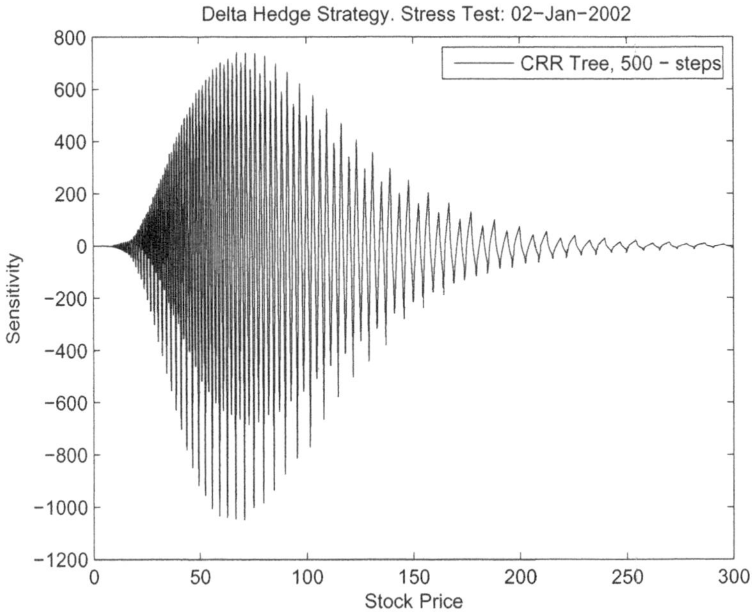

Fig. 9. Delta Hedge Strategy Stress Test.

practice are the following methodologies (De Spiegeleer & Schoutens, 2011; Fabozzi & Rachev, 2005):

- parametric method;
- historical simulation;
- Monte Carlo simulation.

We will apply the mostly used third method, namely, the MC simulation. The reason is that the parametric method is based on delta and gamma valuation and we have seen in the previous section that their computation by means of the binomial-tree is inefficient. Also, the application of the historical method would require to tie down the evidence with a partial historical environment.

Let us point out, that the use of binomial-tree approach in building a VaR methodology is too inadequate due to the fact that the probability density function in many examples of CBs is inadequate. In support of this statement we consider the typical CB example considered in Table 1 and provide its simplified VaR analysis as described in Table 2.

Table 2. VaR Analysis Conditions.

Parameter	Value
Pricing model	CRR tree with 500 time steps
Evaluation date	January 6, 2011
Holding period	1 day
Confidence level	99%
Source of risk	Underlying stock, only
Stock price scenario type	Log-normal: mean = 0.05, variance = 30%
Number of scenarios	10,000
Stock spot price	100

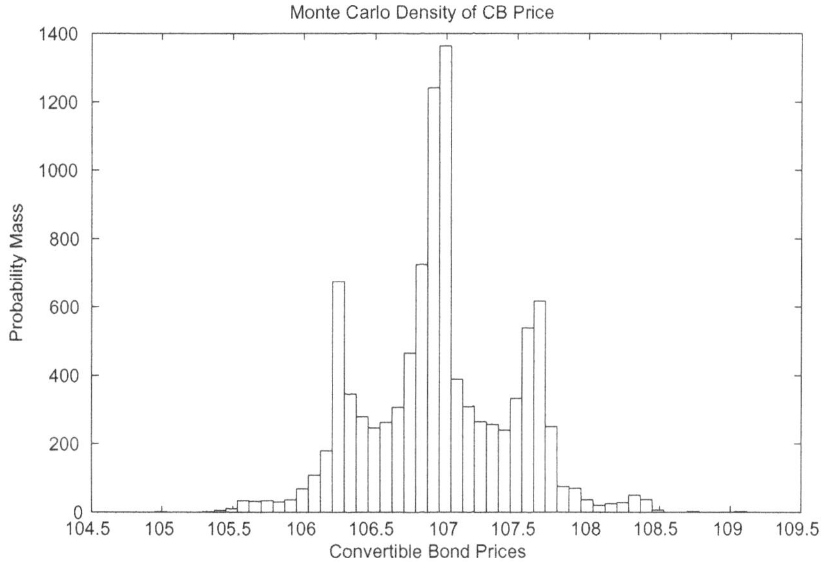

Fig. 10. MC Density of CB Price.

Although the VaR value at 99% given by $\text{VaR}_{99} = 1.1285\%$ looks good as a level of risk, in fact it and all other VaR values are very questionable since they are obtained from the wrongly constructed probability density ρ. Indeed, we compute the density ρ by means of MC simulation for the underlying stock that are valid for the end of the holding period. In Fig. 10 we see that ρ exhibits the atypical movements of probability mass caused by the atypical price profile of CB price at the end of the holding period.

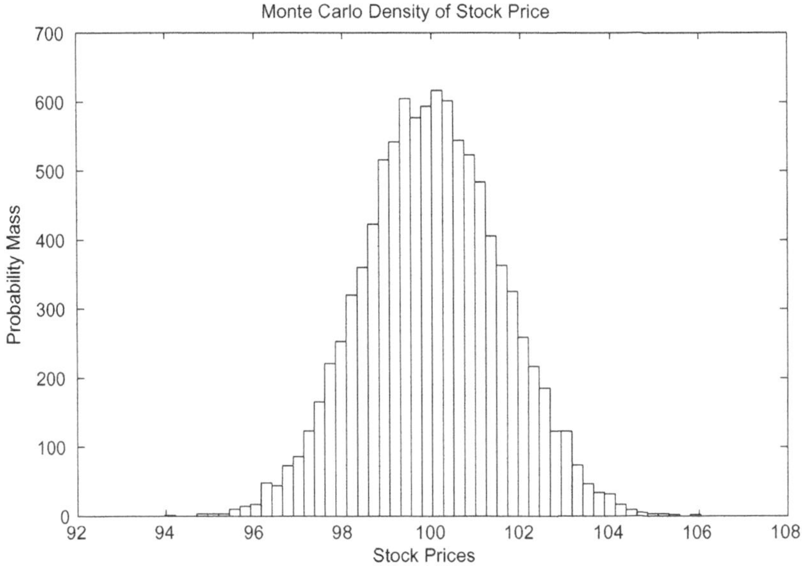

Fig. 11. MC Density of Stock Price.

Finally, for completeness sake, in Fig. 11 we show Monte Carlo scenarios for the underlying stock which are valid for the end of the holding date.

CONCLUSION

In this chapter we have made performance evaluation of the widely used and popular techniques of binomial-tree for approximation of the TF model for price dynamics of CBs. Our results show that in many typical examples the binomial-tree techniques do not meet practitioners' criteria. Let us mention that even the simplest finite difference schemes (FDS) technique (the explicit method) has a much better performance and this will be the subject of our next chapter.

NOTE

1. We have to note that although the expressions for Γ are different in Hull (2002) and Wilmott (2000), they provide the same approximation.

ACKNOWLEDGMENTS

The second author would like to acknowledge the partial support of the Alexander von Humboldt Foundation.

REFERENCES

Andersen, L., & Buffum, D. (2002). *Calibration and implementation of convertible bond models*. Working Paper. Bank of America Securities. Available at http://ssrn.com/abstract=355308

Ayache, E., Forsyth, P. A., & Vetzal, K. (2003). Valuation of convertible bonds with credit risk. *The Journal of Derivatives*, *11*(Fall), 9–29.

Citigroup. (2003, December). *Convertible bonds: A guide*. December 2003. Availalbe at http://www.scribd.com/doc/19605748/Citibank-Convertible-Bonds-A-Guide

De Spiegeleer, J., & Schoutens, W. (2011). *The handbook of convertible bonds: Pricing, strategies and risk management*. The Wiley Finance Series. Chichester, England: Wiley.

Fabozzi, F., & Rachev, Z. (2005). *Fat-tailed and skewed asset return distributions. implications for risk management, portfolio selection, and option pricing*. Chichester, England: Wiley.

Gushchin, V., & Curien, E. (2008). The pricing of convertible bonds within Tsiveriotis and Fernandes framework with exogenous credit spread: Empirical analysis. *Journal of Derivatives & Hedge Funds*, *14*, 50–64.

Hull, J. (2002). *Options, futures and other derivatives* (5th ed.). Upper Saddle River, NJ: Prentice-Hall.

Tsiveriotis, K., & Fernandes, C. (1998). Valuing convertible bonds with credit risk. *Journal of Fixed Income*, *8*(2), 95–102.

Wilmott, P. (2000). *Derivatives: The theory and practice of financial engineering*. Chichester, England: Wiley.

APPENDIX: THE TF MODEL

For readers' convenience in the present section we provide in detail the TF model for computation of CBs. We continue this presentation which we started in the third section.

We construct a risk neutral portfolio

$$\Pi = B - \Delta S$$

In case of no default in the time interval $[t, t + \delta t]$, for

$$d\Pi = \Pi_{t+\delta t} - \Pi_t$$

we have

$$d\Pi = (B_t + \frac{1}{2}\sigma^2 S^2 B_S S)dt$$

On the other hand, on default in the same time interval the model assumption is that the bond holder will lose all future cash flows, that is

$$d\Pi = -B$$

Because of this, the expected value of $d\Pi$ is equal to

$$E(d\Pi) = (B_t + \frac{1}{2}\sigma^2 S^2 B_S S - r_c B)dt$$

Finally, from non-arbitrage arguments

$$B_t + \frac{1}{2}\sigma^2 S^2 B_{SS} + rSB_S - (r + r_c)B = 0$$

On the other hand, the value $E = V - B$ represents the value of the CB related to payments in equity, and it should therefore satisfy the Black–Scholes equation

$$(V - B)_t + \frac{1}{2}\sigma^2 S^2 (V - B)_{SS} + rS(V - B)_S - r(V - B) = 0$$

Now, replacing the equation for B we obtain equation

$$V_t + \frac{1}{2}\sigma^2 S^2 V_{SS} + rSV_S - rV - r_c B = 0$$

Thus we have the system of two equations:

$$\begin{aligned} &V_t + \tfrac{1}{2}\sigma^2 S^2 V_{SS} + rSV_S - rV - Br_c = 0 \\ &B_t + \tfrac{1}{2}\sigma^2 S^2 B_{SS} + rSB_S - (r + r_c)B = 0 \end{aligned} \quad \text{(A.1)}$$

where V is the price of CB; B is the price of cash-only part of the CB; S is the stock price $S \in 0, \infty)$; k is the conversion ratio; N is the nominal (par value) of the CB; r is the risk-free rate; r_c is the yield spread or credit spread; t is the evaluation date $t \in [0, T]$; and T is the maturity date.

We have the "conversion function":

$$cnv(S,t) := \begin{cases} k \cdot S \text{ if } t \in \text{Conversion periods of the contract} \\ 0 \quad \text{otherwise} \end{cases}$$

The "Put Back function" is defined by

$$B^{Put}(t) = \begin{cases} b(t) \text{ for } t \in \text{Put periods of the contract} \\ 0 \quad \text{otherwise} \end{cases}$$

for a contracted function $b(t)$;

The "Call Back function" is defined by

$$B^{Call}(t) = \begin{cases} c(t) \text{ for } t \in \text{Call periods of the contract} \\ +\infty \quad \text{otherwise} \end{cases}$$

We have the following boundary conditions and constraints:

Expiry conditions (for $t = T$):

$$V(S,T) = max(cnv(S,T), N)$$

$$B(S,T) = \begin{cases} N, & cnv(S,T) \leq N \\ 0, & \text{otherwise} \end{cases}$$

and the boundary conditions (for $S = 0$ and $S = \infty$)

$$\text{when} \quad S = 0, \quad 0 \leq t \leq T$$

$$V(0,t) = max(B^{\text{Put}}(t), V(t))$$

$$B(0,t) = max(B^{\text{Put}}(t), B(t))$$

$$\text{where} \quad V = V(t) \text{ and } B = B(t) \text{ are}$$

$$V(t) = B(t) = N \cdot e^{-(r+r_c)(T-t)}$$

$$\text{when} \quad S \to \infty: \quad \text{for } 0 \leq t \leq T$$

$$V(S,t) = cnv(S,T), \quad B(S,t) = 0$$

The Payoff constraints:

$$V(S,t) = max(B^{Put}(t), cnv(S,t), min(B^{Call}(t), V_{held}(S,t)))$$
$$0 \leq S < +\infty, 0 \leq t < T$$

We have to note that all conditions and constraints above are for zero coupon CB which is enough for our present considerations.

An essential extension of the TF model has been considered in Ayache et al. (2003) who have incorporated a recovery rate R in the case of default. They obtain an equation which is similar to Eq. (A.1) without decomposition of the price into two components:

$$V_t + (r + p\eta)SV_S + \frac{\sigma^2 S^2}{2} V_{SS} - (r+p)V + p\ max(\kappa S(1-\eta), RN) = 0 \quad \text{(A.2)}$$

where R is the recovery rate, p is intensity of default, η is the percentage of the stock price drop upon default, and κ is the conversion ratio. This model describes better the process of default.

PART IV
DERIVATIVES MODELS, RISK MANAGEMENT, CREDIT AND CORPORATE CONTROL

A NEW PARADIGM FOR INFLATION DERIVATIVES MODELING

Lixin Wu

ABSTRACT

In this chapter, we define the "inflation forward rates" based on arbitrage arguments and develop a dynamic model for the term structure of inflation forward rates. This new model can serve as a framework for specific no-arbitrage models, including the popular practitioners' market model and all models based on "foreign currency analogy." With our rebuilt market model, we can price inflation caplets, floorlets, and swaptions with the Black formula for displaced-diffusion processes, and thus can quote these derivatives using "implied Black's volatilities." The rebuilt market model also serves as a proper platform for developing models to manage volatility smile risks.

Through this chapter, we hope to correct two major flaws in existing models or with the current practices. First, a consumer price index has no volatility, so models based on the diffusion of the index are essentially wrong. Second, the differentiation of models based on zero-coupon inflation-indexed swaps and models based on year-on-year inflation-indexed swaps is unnecessary, and the use of "convexity adjustment," a common practice to bridge models that are based on the two kinds of swaps, is redundant.

Derivative Securities Pricing and Modelling
Contemporary Studies in Economic and Financial Analysis, Volume 94, 305–330

ISSN: 1569-3759/doi:10.1108/S1569-3759(2012)0000094015

INTRODUCTION

Government inflation-indexed bond first appeared in Finland in 1945, but it began to be treated as an asset class only after the first issuance of inflation-indexed bond, called Gilt, in 1981 by UK government. Since then, more European governments had started to issue inflation-protected sovereignty debts. The U.S. Treasury joined the rank in 1997 with the issuance of Treasury Inflation-Protected Securities (TIPS), which spurred the growth of the inflation derivatives markets.

Research on pricing models for inflation-rate derivatives has also become active since 1997 (Barone & Castagna, 1997; van Bezooyen, Exley, & Smith, 1997). A theoretical framework, the so-called "foreign currency analogy", first suggested by Hughston (1998) and completely established by Jarrow and Yildirim (2003), had become very influential. Under this framework, the real interest rate, defined as the difference between nominal interest rate and the inflation rate, is treated as the interest rate of a foreign currency, while the consumer price index (CPI) is treated as the exchange rate between the domestic and the foreign currencies. To price inflation derivatives, one needs to model the domestic (nominal) interest rate, the foreign (real) interest rate, and the exchange rate (CPI). A handy solution for modeling inflation derivatives is to adopt Heath, Jarrow, and Morton (1992) framework for both interest rates, and bridge them using a lognormal process for the exchange rate. Manning and Jones (2003) push to the limit of the analytical tractability of this approach and obtain price formulae for inflation caplets and floorlets. For general inflation derivatives, one resorts to Monte Carlo simulations.

Although elegant in theory, a Heath–Jarrow–Morton (HJM)-type model is inconvenient to use. The model takes unobservable instantaneous (nominal and/or real) forward rates as state variables, while the payoffs of most inflation derivatives are written on CPI or simple compounding inflation rates, making the models hard to calibrate.

Aimed at more convenient pricing and hedging of inflation derivatives, a number of alternative models have been developed since 2003. Some researchers adopted normal or lognormal dynamics for certain observable inflation-related variables, for example, the CPI index (Belgrade & Benhamou, 2004a; Korn & Kruse, 2004), the forward price of real zero-coupon bonds (Kazziha, 1999; Mercurio, 2005), or inflation forward rates (Kenyon, 2008). Extensions to these models have also been developed so that risk factors other than diffusion, like stochastic volatility (Kenyon, 2008; Kruse, 2007; Mercurio & Moreni, 2006, 2009) and jumps (Hinnerich, 2008), are incorporated. Other researchers adopted the square-root process of Cox, Ross, and Ingersoll (1985) to model the spot inflation rate, in conjunction with a short-rate model for the nominal spot rate (see, e.g., Chen, Liu, & Cheng, 2006; Falbo, Paris, & Pelizzari, 2009). Over the years, nonetheless, practitioners have been using a model of their own, the so-called market model that is based on the displaced-diffusion dynamics for simple inflation forward rates and has not been documented in the publicly available literature. There are also researches that study various issues in inflation-rate modeling. Among others, Cairns (2000) considers inflation models where nominal interest rates are ensured positive; Chen et al. (2006) estimate inflation risk premium; and Belgrade and Benhamou (2004b) examine seasonality in inflation rates and manage to take it into account in their CPI-based model.

While important advancements were made over the years, a certain degree of disorder in the literature has also been created. Now there are at least three "market models" (Beldgrade, Benhamou, & Koehler, 2004; Mercurio-Moreni, 2006, and the practitioners' model), and at least two versions of "inflation forward" respectively adopted by models based on zero-coupon inflation-indexed swaps (ZCIIS) and models based on year-on-year inflation indexed swaps (YYIIS). When using a ZCIIS-based model to price derivatives on YYIIS, the technique of convexity adjustment is used to calculate the YYIIS swap rates.

With this article we hope to sort out this field. We will redefine the notion of inflation forward rate as the fair rate for a forward contract on inflation rate, which will be shown to be replicable statically and thus is unique. We will then justify the lognormal martingale dynamics for displaced inflation forward rates, and thus rigorously rebuild the practitioners' model. With these works the notion of market model should be clarified. Moreover, we will establish a HJM-type equation for instantaneous inflation forward rates and, by also making use of the classic HJM equation for nominal forward rates, rederive the HJM-type equation for real forward rates established by Jarrow and Yildirim (2003), along with a correction that the notion of the "volatility of the consumer price index" is flawed and should not be used for modeling.

This article has other important implications. First, we show that the ZCIIS- and YYIIS-based market models are identical and the use of "convexity adjustment" is redundant. Second, we unify the closed-form pricing of inflation caplets, floorlets, and swaptions with the Black formula for displaced-diffusion processes that allows us to quote these derivatives using "Black's implied volatilities." Finally, we provide a proper platform for developing smile models.

The rest of the chapter is organized as follows. In the second section, we introduce major inflation derivatives and highlight real zero-coupon bonds, part of our primitive state variables. In the third section, we define the notion of inflation forward rates, rebuild the market model, and develop a HJM-type model in terms of continuous compounding nominal and inflation forward rates. The fourth section is devoted to pricing major inflation-indexed derivatives under the market model, where we produce closed-form formulae for caps, floors, and swaptions. In the fifth section, we briefly discuss the calibration of the market model and demonstrate some calibration results with market data. In the sixth section, we demonstrate the construction of smile models using, in particular, the SABR methodology. Finally in the seventh section, we conclude the chapter. The proofs of some propositions are put in the appendix.

CPI INDEX AND INFLATION DERIVATIVES MARKET

Inflation-rate security markets have evolved steadily over the past fifteen years. Among developed countries, the outstanding notional values of inflation-linked government bonds have grown from about 50 billion dollars in 1997 to over 1.4 trillion dollars in 2009.[1] There are inflation-linked securities in most major currencies, including pound sterling, Canadian dollar, yen, and, of course, Euro and U.S. dollar. The global daily turnover on average was about $10 billions a day in 2009, which is largely dominated by Euro and dollar-denominated securities. For more information on global inflation-indexed security markets, we refer readers to the 2010 Annual Report by Barclays Capital. By comparing to the sizes of LIBOR or credit markets, one has to conclude that the interest on inflation securities has been tepid in the past. Nonetheless, since the 2007–2008 financial crisis, there has been concern for potential high inflation, caused by the expansionary monetary policy adopted across the globe (Jung, 2008).

The payoff functions of inflation-linked securities often depend on inflation rates, which are defined as the percentage change rates of the CPI. The CPI represents an average price of a basket of services and goods, and the average price is compiled by official statistical agencies of central governments. The evolution of CPI indexes in both Europe and United States is displayed in Fig. 1, which shows a trend of steady increase.[2]

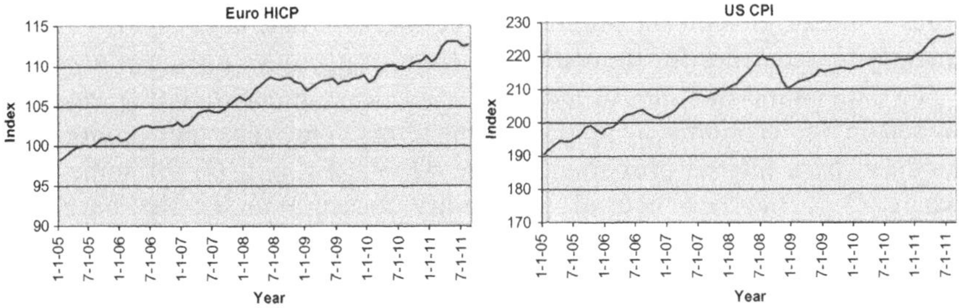

Fig. 1. Consumer Price Indexes of United States and Euro Zone.

The inflation rate of a country is defined in terms of its CPI. Denoted by $I(t)$ the CPI of time t, then the inflation rate over the time period $[t, T]$ is defined as the percentage change of the index:

$$\hat{i}(t, T) = \frac{I(T)}{I(t)} - 1$$

For comparison purpose, we will more often use annualized inflation rate:

$$i(t, T) = \frac{1}{T - t}\left(\frac{I(T)}{I(t)} - 1\right)$$

Suppose the limit of the annualized inflation rate exists for $T \rightarrow t$ from above, we obtain the so-called instantaneous inflation rate, $i(t)$, which will be used largely for mathematical and financial arguments instead of modeling. An important feature that distinguishes inflation rates from interest rates is that the former can be either positive or negative, while the latter have to be positive or otherwise we were in a situation of arbitrage.

Inflation-indexed bonds are mainly issued by central governments, while inflation-rate derivatives are offered and traded in the OTC markets by various financial institutions. The dollar-denominated inflation-linked securities have been predominately represented by TIPS, followed by ZCIIS and YYIIS. In recent years, caps, floors, and swaptions on inflation rates have been gaining popularity. In the following subsections, we will spend some length to describe these inflation-linked securities. In our modeling approach, ZCIIS will be taken as the underlying securities of the inflation derivatives markets and used for the construction of "inflation forward rates", unlike the current practice of the markets that takes YYIIS as the underlying securities for derivatives pricing.

To understand the roles of the basic securities in model building, we need to set up the economy in mathematical terms. The uncertain economy is modeled by a filtered probability space $(\Omega, \mathscr{F}, \{\mathscr{F}_t\}_{t\in[0,\tau]}, Q)$ for some $\tau > 0$ where Q is the risk neutral probability measure under the uncertain economical environment, which can be defined in a usual way in an arbitrage-free market (Harrison & Krep, 1979; Harrison & Pliska, 1981), and the filtration $\{\mathscr{F}_t\}_{t\in[0,\tau]}$ is generated by a d-dimensional Q-Brownian motion $\mathbf{Z} = \{\mathbf{Z}_t : t \geq 0\}$.

TIPS

TIPS are coupon bonds with fixed coupon rates but floating principals, and the latter is adjusted according to the inflation rate over the accrual period of a coupon payment. Note that typically there is a floor on the principal value of a TIPS, which is often the initial principal value. The existence of floors, as a matter of fact, turns TIPS into coupon bonds with embedded options. So strictly speaking the pricing of TIPS needs a model.

Note that the CPI index is measured with a two-month lag. Yet this lagged index plays the role of the current index for the principal adjustments of TIPS and the payoff calculations of inflations derivatives. From modeling point of view, lagging or not makes no difference. With this understanding in mind, we will treat the lagged index as the current index throughout the chapter.

ZCIIS

The ZCIIS is a swap contract between two parties with a single exchange of payments. Suppose that the contract was initiated at time t and will be expired at $T > t$, then the payment of one party equals to a notional value times to the inflation rate realized over the contract period, that is,

$$Not. \times \hat{i}(t, T)$$

while the counterparty makes a fixed payment in the amount

$$Not. \times ((1 + K(t, T))^{T-t} - 1)$$

where *Not.* stands for the notional value of the contract and $K(t, T)$ is the quote for the contract. Because the value of the ZCIIS is zero at initiation,

ZCIIS directly renders the price of the so-called real zero-coupon bond that pays inflation adjusted principal:

$$P_R(t,T) = E^Q\left[e^{-\int_t^T r_s ds}\frac{I(T)}{I(t)}\middle|\mathcal{F}_t\right] = P(t,T)(1+K(t,T))^{T-t} \tag{1}$$

Here, r_s is the short rate and $P(t, T)$ is the nominal discount factor from T back to t. For real zero-coupon bonds with the same maturity date T but an earlier issuance date, say, $T_0 < t$, the price is

$$P_R(t,T_0,T) = E^Q\left[e^{-\int_t^T r_s ds}\frac{I(T)}{I(T_0)}\middle|\mathcal{F}_t\right] = \frac{I(t)}{I(T_0)}P_R(t,T) \tag{2}$$

We emphasize here that $P_R(t, T_0, T)$, instead of $P_R(t, T)$, is treated as the time t price of a traded security. The latter is merely the initial price of a new security.

For modeling inflation-rate derivatives, we will take the term structure of real and nominal zero-coupon bonds, $P_R(t, T_0, T)$ and $P(t, T)$ for a fixed T_0 and all $T \geq t \geq T_0$, as model primitives. Note that $\{P_R(t, T), \forall T > t\}$ alone carries information on the term structure of real interest rates only. To see that, we make use of the relationship between the instantaneous inflation rate and CPI:

$$\frac{I(T)}{I(T_0)} = e^{\int_{T_0}^T i(s)ds} \tag{3}$$

Plugging Eq. (3) into Eq. (1) and then making use of Fisher's equation (Fisher, 1930, also see Cox et al., 1985),

$$r_t = R(t) + i(t) \tag{4}$$

where $R(t)$ is the real interest rate, we obtain

$$\begin{aligned} P_R(t,T) &= E^Q\left[e^{-\int_t^T (r_s - i(s))ds}|\mathcal{F}_t\right] \\ &= E^Q\left[e^{-\int_t^T R(s)ds}|\mathcal{F}_t\right] \end{aligned} \tag{5}$$

According to Eq. (5), the real zero-coupon bond implies the discount factor associated to real interest rates. This is the reason why we use the subindex "R" for the price.

Note that the real interest rates are not good candidates for state variable, because most inflation derivatives are written on inflation rates.

YYIIS

YYIIS are contracts to swap an annuity against a sequence of floating payments indexed to inflation rates over future periods. The fixed-leg payments of a YYIIS are $Not.\Delta\phi_i K$, $i = 1, 2, \ldots, N_x$, where $\Delta\phi_i$ is the year fractions between two consecutive payments, while the floating-leg payments are of the form

$$Not.\left(\frac{I(T_j)}{I(T_{j-1})} - 1\right)$$

and are made at time T_j,$j = 1, 2, \ldots, N_f$. Note that the payment gaps $\Delta\phi_i = \phi_i - \phi_{i-1}$ and $\Delta T_j = T_j - T_{j-1}$ can be different, yet the terms for payment swapping are the same, that is, $\Sigma_{i=1}^{N_x}\Delta\phi_i = \Sigma_{j=1}^{N_f}\Delta T_j$. The price of the YYIIS equals to the difference in values of the fixed and floating legs. The former can be calculated simply by discounting, yet the later involves the evaluation of an expectation:

$$V_{float}^{(j)}(t) = Not.E^Q\left[e^{-\int_t^{T_j} r_s ds}\left(\frac{I(T_j)}{I(T_{j-1})} - 1\right)\middle|\mathscr{F}_t\right]$$

We will show that, contrary to the current practices, the theoretical pricing of the floating leg should be model independent.

Inflation Caps and Floors

An inflation cap is like a YYIIS with embedded optionality: with the same payment frequency, payments are made only when a netted cash flow to the payer (of the fixed leg) is positive, corresponding to cash flows of the following form to the cap holder

$$Not.\Delta T_i\left[\frac{1}{\Delta T_i}\left(\frac{I(T_i)}{I(T_{i-1})} - 1\right) - K\right]^+, \; i = 1, \ldots, N$$

Accordingly, the cash flow of an inflation floor is

$$Not.\Delta T_i\left[K - \frac{1}{\Delta T_i}\left(\frac{I(T_i)}{I(T_{i-1})} - 1\right)\right]^+, i = 1, \ldots, N$$

Apparently, the prices of caplets and floorlets depend on the variance of the future inflation rates, thus making their pricing model dependent.

Inflation Swaptions

An inflation swaption is an option to enter into a YYIIS swap in the future. At the maturity of the option, the holder of the option should enter into the underlying YYIIS if the option ends in the money. The underlying security of the swaption is YYIIS. With the establishment of the theory of this chapter, the pricing of the underlying YYIIS will become model independent, which consequently will make the pricing of inflation swaptions easier.

REBUILT MARKET MODEL AND THE NEW PARADIGM

Inflation Discount Bonds and Inflation Forward Rates

The cash flows of several major inflation-indexed instruments, including YYIIS, inflation caplets, and floorlets, are expressed in term rates of simple inflation rates. For pricing and hedging, we need to define inflation forward rates as the fair rates for forward-rate agreements on inflation rates, parallel to the definition nominal forward rates. We know that the prices of nominal zero-coupon bonds imply nominal forward rates. Not surprisingly, the prices of nominal zero-coupon bonds and real zero-coupon bonds jointly imply the inflation forward rates. To be precise, we introduce

Definition 1. The discount bond associated to inflation rate is defined by

$$P_I(t,T) \triangleq \frac{P(t,T)}{P_R(t,T)} \tag{6}$$

Here, "$\triangleq$" means "being defined by."

Alternatively, with $P_I(t, T)$ and $P_R(t, T)$, we effectively factorize the nominal discount factor into real and inflation discount factors:

$$P(t,T) = P_R(t,T)P_I(t,T) \tag{7}$$

Note that neither $P_I(t, T)$ nor $P_R(t, T)$ is a price of a tradable security,[3] yet both quantities are observable.

We define inflation forward rates as the returns implied by the inflation discount bonds.

Definition 2. The *inflation forward rate* for a future period $[T_1, T_2]$ seen at time $t \leq T_2$ is defined by

$$f^{(I)}(t, T_1, T_2) \triangleq \frac{1}{(T_2 - T_1)} \left(\frac{P_I(t, T_1)}{P_I(t, T_2)} - 1 \right) \tag{8}$$

There is a slight problem with the above definition: the inflation forward rate is fixed at $t = T_2$, beyond the life of the T_1-maturity inflation bond, so we need to define $P_I(t, T_1)$ for $t > T_1$. In view of Eq. (2), we have

$$P_I(t, T_1) = \frac{I(t)}{I(T_0)} \frac{P(t, T_1)}{P_R(t, T_0, T_1)} \tag{9}$$

The second ratio on the right-hand side of Eq. (9) is the relative price between two traded bonds with an identical maturity date, and thus its value beyond T_1 can be defined by constant extrapolation, yielding

$$P_I(t, T_1) = \frac{I(t)}{I(T_0)} \frac{I(T_0)}{I(T_1)} = \frac{I(t)}{I(T_1)}, \quad \forall t \geq T_1 \tag{10}$$

Given Eq. (10), we have the value of the forward rate at its fixing date to be

$$f^{(I)}(T_2, T_1, T_2) = \frac{1}{T_2 - T_1} \left(\frac{I(T_2)}{I(T_1)} - 1 \right) \tag{11}$$

so the inflation forward rate converges to inflation spot rate at maturity.

Next, we will argue that $f^{(I)}(t, T_1, T_2)$ so defined is the fair rate seen at time t for a forward contract on the inflation rate over $[T_1, T_2]$. We can rewrite Eq. (8) into

$$f^{(I)}(t, T_1, T_2) = \frac{1}{(T_2 - T_1)} \left(\frac{F_R(t, T_1, T_2) P(t, T_1)}{P(t, T_2)} - 1 \right) \tag{12}$$

where

$$F_R(t, T_1, T_2) \triangleq \frac{P_R(t, T_2)}{P_R(t, T_1)} = \frac{P_R(t, T_0, T_2)}{P_R(t, T_0, T_1)} \tag{13}$$

is the relative price between two tradable securities. The following result is the corner stone of our theory, with its proof given in the appendix.

Proposition 1. At time $t \leq T_1 \leq T_2$, the price of the real zero-coupon bond with reference date T_1 and maturity T_2 is $P(t, T_1) F_R(t, T_1, T_2)$.

In view of Eq. (12), we can treat $f^{(I)}(t, T_1, T_2)$ as the T_2-forward price for the payoff of $f^{(I)}(T_2, T_1, T_2)$ at T_2, and thus have proven.

Proposition 2. The inflation forward rate $f^{(I)}(t, T_1, T_2)$ is the unique arbitrage-free rate seen at the time t for a T_1-expiry forward contract on the inflation rate over the future period $[T_1, T_2]$.

Proposition 2 should help to end the situation of the coexistence of multiple definitions of inflation forward rates. Note that our definition Eq. (8) coincides with one of the definitions of inflation forward rates, $Y_i(t)$ given in Mercurio and Moreni (2009).

The Consistency Condition

We now proceed to the construction of dynamic models for inflation forward rates of both simple and instantaneous compounding. Under the risk neutral measure Q, $P(t, T)$ and $P_R(t, T_0, T)$ are assumed to follow the lognormal dynamics:

$$\begin{aligned} dP(t, T) &= P(t, T)(r_t dt + \Sigma(t, T) \cdot dZ_t) \\ dP_R(t, T_0, T) &= P_R(t, T_0, T)(r_t dt + \Sigma_R(t, T) \cdot dZ_t) \end{aligned} \tag{14}$$

where the short rate r_t can be stochastic, $\Sigma(t, T)$ and $\Sigma_R(t, T)$ are d-dimensional $\mathscr{F}_t$ – adaptive volatility functions of $P(t, T)$ and $P_R(t, T_0, T)$, respectively,[4] and "·" means scalar product. The volatility function are assumed sufficiently regular in t and T so that the SDE (14) admits a unique strong solution, and their partial derivatives with respect to T exist and have finite L_2 norms w.r.t. t. Moreover, the volatility functions must satisfy[5]

$$\Sigma(t, t) = \Sigma_R(t, t) = 0$$

By making use of the dynamics of $P_R(t, T_0, T)$ and the dynamics of the CPI,

$$dI(t) = i(t)I(t)dt$$

we can derive the dynamics of $P_R(t, T)$:

$$dP_R(t, T) = P_R(t, T)((r_t - i(t))dt + \Sigma_R(t, T) \cdot dZ_t) \tag{15}$$

Being a T_1-forward price of a tradable security, $F(t, T_1, T_2)$ should be a lognormal martingale under the T_1-forward measure whose volatility is the difference between those of $P_R(t, T_0, T_2)$ and $P_R(t, T_0, T_1)$, that is,

$$\frac{dF_R(t,T_1,T_2)}{F_R(t,T_1,T_2)} = (\Sigma_R(t,T_2) - \Sigma_R(t,T_1))^T (d\mathbf{Z}_t - \Sigma(t,T_1)dt) \tag{16}$$

Note that $d\mathbf{Z}_t - \Sigma(t,T_1)dt$ is (the differential of) a Brownian motion under the T_1-forward measure, Q_{T_1}, defined by the Radon–Nikodym derivative:

$$\left.\frac{dQ_{T_1}}{dQ}\right|_{\mathscr{F}_t} = \frac{P(t,T_1)}{B(t)P(0,T_1)}$$

where $B(t) = \exp\left(\int_0^t r_s ds\right)$ is the unit price of money market account.

There is an important implication by Eq. (16). By Ito's lemma, we also have

$$\frac{dF_R(t,T_1,T_2)}{F_R(t,T_1,T_2)} = (\Sigma_R(t,T_2) - \Sigma_R(t,T_1))^T (d\mathbf{Z}_t - \Sigma_R(t,T_1)dt) \tag{17}$$

The coexistence of Eqs. (16) and (17) poses a constraint on the volatility functions of the real zero-coupon bonds.

Proposition 3. (Consistency condition) For arbitrage pricing, the volatility functions of the real bonds must satisfy the following condition:

$$(\Sigma_R(t,T_2) - \Sigma_R(t,T_1)) \cdot (\Sigma(t,T_1) - \Sigma_R(t,T_1)) = 0 \tag{18}$$

Its differential version is, by letting $T_2 \to T_1 = T$,

$$\dot{\Sigma}_R(t,T) \cdot \Sigma_I(t,T) = 0 \tag{19}$$

where the overhead dot means partial derivative with respect to T, the maturity.

Let us try to comprehend the consistency condition. We know obviously that $\Sigma_I(t,T_1) \triangleq \Sigma(t,T_1) - \Sigma_R(t,T_1)$ is the percentage volatility of $P_I(t,T)$, while $\Sigma_R(t,T_2) - \Sigma_R(t,T_1)$ is the volatility of the real forward rate, defined by

$$f_R(t,T_1,T_2) \triangleq \frac{1}{T_2 - T_1}\left(\frac{P_R(t,T_1)}{P_R(t,T_2)} - 1\right)$$

Literally, Eq. (18) means that the price of inflation discount bond with maturity T_1 must be uncorrelated with real forward rates of any future period beyond T_1. This sounds reasonable and is nonrestrictive at all.

The differential version of the consistency condition, Eq. (19), will be used later to derive an HJM-type model for inflation rates.

Rebuilding the Market Model

For generality, we let $T = T_2$ and $\Delta T = T_2 - T_1$, we can then cast Eq. (12) into

$$f^{(I)}(t, T - \Delta T, T) + \frac{1}{\Delta T} = \frac{1}{\Delta T}\frac{F_R(t, T - \Delta T, T)P(t, T - \Delta T)}{P(t, T)}$$

The dynamics of $f^{(I)}(t, T - \Delta T, T)$ follows readily from those of F_R and P's.

Proposition 4. Under the risk neutral measure, the governing equation for the simple inflation forward rate is

$$d\left(f^{(I)}(t, T - \Delta T, T) + \frac{1}{\Delta T}\right)$$
$$= \left(f^{(I)}(t, T - \Delta T, T) + \frac{1}{\Delta T}\right)\{\gamma^{(I)}(t, T) \cdot (d\mathbf{Z}_t - \Sigma(t, T)dt)\} \qquad (20)$$

where

$$\gamma^{(I)}(t, T) = \Sigma_I(t, T - \Delta T) - \Sigma_I(t, T)$$

is the percentage volatility of the displaced inflation forward rate.

In formalism, Eq. (20) is just the practitioners' model. Yet in applications, practitioners bootstrap the inflation forward rates from YYIIS and calibrate the model to inflation caps/floors for $\gamma^{(I)}(t,T)$.

Let us present the market model for inflation rates in comprehensive terms. The state variables consist of two streams of spanning nominal forward rates (Brace, Gatarek, & Musiela, 1997; Miltersen, Sandmann & Sondermann, 1997; Jamshidian, 1997) and inflation forward rates, $f_j(t) \triangleq f(t, T_j, T_{j+1})$ and $f_j^{(I)}(t) \triangleq f^{(I)}(t, T_{j-1}, T_j)$, $j = 1, 2, \ldots, N$, that follow the following dynamics:

$$\begin{cases} df_j(t) = f_j(t)\gamma_j(t) \cdot (d\mathbf{Z}_t - \Sigma(t, T_{j+1})dt) \\ d\left(f_j^{(I)}(t) + \dfrac{1}{\Delta T_j}\right) = \left(f_j^{(I)}(t) + \dfrac{1}{\Delta T_j}\right)\gamma_j^{(I)}(t) \cdot (d\mathbf{Z}_t - \Sigma(t, T_j)dt) \end{cases} \qquad (21)$$

where

$$\Sigma(t, T_{j+1}) = -\sum_{k=\eta_t}^{j} \frac{\Delta T_{k+1} f_k(t)}{1 + \Delta T_{k+1} f_k(t)}\gamma_k(t)$$

and $\eta_t = min\{i|T_i > t\}$. The initial nominal and inflation forward rates are derived from prices of nominal and real discount bonds. We want to highlight here that $f_j^{(I)}(t)$ is also a martingale under its own "cash flow measure," that is, the T_j-forward measure.

The New Paradigm

Analogously to the definition of nominal forward rates, we define the instantaneous inflation forward rates by

$$f^{(I)}(t,T) \triangleq -\frac{\partial \ln P_I(t,T)}{\partial T}, \quad \forall T \geq t \tag{22}$$

or through

$$P_I(t,T) = e^{-\int_t^T f^{(I)}(t,s)ds}$$

By the Ito's lemma, we have

$$\begin{aligned} - d \ln P_I(t,T) &= d \ln\left(\frac{P_R(t,T)}{P(t,T)}\right) \\ &= -\left(i(t) + \frac{1}{2}\left\|\Sigma_I(t,T)\right\|^2\right)dt - \Sigma_I(t,T)\cdot(d\mathbf{Z}_t - \Sigma(t,T)dt) \end{aligned} \tag{23}$$

Differentiating the above equation with respect to T and making use of Eq. (19), the consistency condition, we then obtain

$$df^{(I)}(t,T) = -\dot{\Sigma}_I \cdot (d\mathbf{Z}_t - \Sigma(t,T)dt) \tag{24}$$

Eq. (24) shows that $f^{(I)}(t,T)$ is a Q_T-martingale.

In an HJM context, the volatilities of nominal and inflation forward rates, $\sigma(t,T) = -\dot{\Sigma}(t,T)$ and $\sigma^{(I)}(t,T) = -\dot{\Sigma}_I(t,T)$, are first prescribed, and the volatilities of the zero-coupon bonds follow from

$$\Sigma(t,T) = -\int_t^T \sigma(t,s)ds \quad \text{and} \quad \Sigma_I(t,T) = -\int_t^T \sigma^{(I)}(t,s)ds$$

Then, the extended HJM model with nominal and inflation forward rates is

$$\begin{cases} df(t,T) = \sigma(t,T)\cdot d\mathbf{Z}_t + \sigma(t,T)\cdot\left(\int_t^T \sigma(t,s)ds\right)dt \\ df^{(I)}(t,T) = \sigma^{(I)}(t,T)\cdot d\mathbf{Z}_t + \sigma^{(I)}(t,T)\cdot\left(\int_t^T \sigma(t,s)ds\right)dt \end{cases} \tag{25}$$

which takes the initial term structures of nominal and inflation forward rates as initial inputs. Yet again the dynamics of the forward rates is fully specified by their volatilities.

If we treat Eq. (25) as a framework of no-arbitrage models, then the market model Eq. (21) fits into the framework with the volatility function:

$$\sigma^{(I)}(t,T) = -\dot{\Sigma}_I(t,T) = \frac{\partial}{\partial T}\left(\sum_{k=0}^{\left[\frac{T-t}{\Delta T}\right]} \gamma^{(I)}(t, T-k\Delta T)\right)$$

where $[x]$ is the integer part of x.

Unifying the Jarrow–Yildirim Model

According to their definitions, nominal, inflation, and real forward rates for continuous compounding satisfy the relationship:

$$f_R(t,T) = f(t,T) - f^{(I)}(t,T)$$

Subtracting the two equations of Eq. (25) and applying the consistency condition, Eq. (19), we arrive at

$$df_R(t,T) = \sigma_R(t,T)\cdot d\mathbf{Z}_t + \sigma_R(t,T)\cdot\left(\int_t^T \sigma_R(t,s)ds\right)dt \tag{26}$$

where

$$\sigma_R(t,T) = \sigma(t,T) - \sigma^{(I)}(t,T) = -\dot{\Sigma}_R(t,T)$$

In contrast, under our notations the equation established by Jarrow and Yildirim (2003) for the real forward rates is

$$df_R(t,T) = \sigma_R(t,T)\cdot d\mathbf{Z}_t + \sigma_R(t,T)\cdot\left(\int_t^T \sigma_R(t,s)ds - \sigma_I(t)\right)dt \tag{27}$$

where $\sigma_I(t)$ is the volatility of the CPI index. As we now understand that $\sigma_I(t) \equiv 0$, thus the two equations are actually identical.

Even if the CPI volatility were not zero, we can still rederive the Jarrow and Yildirim model by recognizing that the volatility of $P_R(t, T_0, T)$ satisfies $\Sigma_R(t, t) = \sigma_I(t)$ and redoing the arguments. Based on the above analysis, we claim that market model is consistent with the framework of "foreign currency analogy."

In a two-currency economy, the exchange rate is usually stochastic with volatility. Having no volatility, the CPI behaves like a money market account instead of an exchange rate. Hence we comment that the inflation derivatives modeling is not completely analogous to cross-currency derivatives modeling.

PRICING INFLATION DERIVATIVES

We have established for the first time that simple inflation forward rates are lognormal martingales under respective forward measures. As a result, the current practices on pricing some inflation derivatives must undergo some changes.

YYIIS

The price of a YYIIS is the difference in value of the fixed leg and floating leg. While the fixed leg is priced as an annuity, the floating leg is priced by discounting the expectation of each piece of payments under its cash-flow measure:

$$\begin{aligned} V_{float}^{(j)}(t) &= Not.P(t, T_j)E_t^{Q_{T_j}}\left[\frac{I(T_j)}{I(T_{j-1})} - 1\right] \\ &= Not.\Delta T_j P(t, T_j)E_t^{Q_{T_j}}\left[f_j^{(I)}(T_j)\right] \\ &= Not.\Delta T_j P(t, T_j) f_j^{(I)}(t) \end{aligned} \tag{28}$$

where we have made use of the martingale property of the inflation forward rates. The value of the floating leg is the aggregation of the values of the pieces, and the value of the YYIIS is the difference between the values of the fixed and floating legs.

In the market place, YYIIS are treated as another set of securities parallel to ZCIIS, and the "inflation forward rates" implied by YYIIS and ZCIIS can be different. In existing literatures, pricing YYIIS using a ZCIIS-based model goes through the procedure of "convexity adjustment," which is, as was just shown, unnecessary. Our theory, for the first time, suggests that such differences should create arbitrage opportunities.

Caps

In view of the displaced-diffusion processes for simple inflation forward rates, we can price a caplet with \$1 notional value straightforwardly as follows:

$$\begin{aligned}
&\Delta T_j E_t^Q\left[e^{-\int_t^{T_j} r_s ds}(f_j^{(I)}(T_j) - K)^+\right] \\
&= \Delta T_j P(t, T_j) E_t^{Q_{T_j}}\left[\left(\left(f_j^{(I)}(T_j) + \frac{1}{\Delta T_j}\right) - \left(K + \frac{1}{\Delta T_j}\right)\right)^+\right] \\
&= \Delta T_j P(t, T_j)\{\mu_j(t)\Phi(d_1^{(j)}(t)) - \tilde{K}_j \Phi(d_2^{(j)}(t))\} \qquad (29)
\end{aligned}$$

where $\Phi(\cdot)$ is the standard normal accumulative distribution function, and

$$\mu_j(t) = f_j^{(I)}(t) + 1/\Delta T_j, \quad \tilde{K}_j = K + 1/\Delta T_j$$

$$d_1^{(j)}(t) = \frac{\ln \mu_j/\tilde{K}_j + \frac{1}{2}\sigma_j^2(t)(T_j - t)}{\sigma_j(t)\sqrt{T_j - t}}, \quad d_2^{(j)}(t) = d_1^{(j)}(t) - \sigma_j(t)\sqrt{T_j - t}$$

with $\sigma_j(t)$ to be the mean volatility of $\ln\left(f_j^{(I)}(t) + \frac{1}{\Delta T_j}\right)$:

$$\sigma_j^2(t) = \frac{1}{T_j - t}\int_t^{T_j} \|\gamma_j^{(I)}(s)\|^2 ds \qquad (30)$$

The inflation-indexed cap with maturity T_N and strike K is the addition of a series of inflation-indexed caplets with the cash flows at T_j for $j = 1, \ldots, N$. Denote by IICap(t;N,K) the price of the inflation-indexed cap at time $t < T_1$. Then, based on Eq. (29), we have

$$\text{IICap}(t; N, K) = \sum_{j=1}^{N} \Delta T_j P(t, T_j)\{\mu_j \Phi(d_1^{(j)}(t)) - \tilde{K}_j \Phi(d_2^{(j)}(t))\} \qquad (31)$$

Eq. (29) is like an old bottle filled with new wine: the input inflation forward rates should be implied by ZCIIS instead of YYIIS. Given inflation caps of various maturities, we can consecutively bootstrap $\sigma_j(t)$, the "implied caplet volatilities," in either a parametric or a nonparametric way. With additional information on correlations between inflation rates of various maturities, we can determine $\gamma_j^{(I)}$, the volatility vector of inflation rates and thus fully specify the displace-diffusion dynamics for inflation forward rates. We may also include inflation swaption prices to the input set for the determination of $\gamma_j^{(I)}$'s.

Swaptions

Discussions on the pricing of inflation swaptions have been rare (Hinnerich, 2008). An inflation swaption is an option to enter into a YYIIS at the option's maturity. Without loss of generality, we consider here an underlying swap that has the same payment frequency for both fixed and floating legs. Similar to the situation of swaps on nominal interest rates, it is straightforward to show that the market prevailing inflation swap rate (that nullifies the value of a swap) is

$$S_{m,n}(t) = \frac{\sum_{i=m+1}^{n} \Delta T_i P(t, T_i) f_i^{(I)}(t)}{\sum_{i=m+1}^{n} \Delta T_i P(t, T_i)} \tag{32}$$

The above expression can be recast into

$$S_{m,n}(t) + \frac{1}{\Delta T_{m,n}} = \sum_{i=m+1}^{n} w_i(t) \mu_i(t) \tag{33}$$

where

$$w_i(t) = \frac{\Delta T_i P(t, T_i)}{A_{m,n}(t)}, \quad A_{m,n}(t) = \sum_{i=m+1}^{n} \Delta T_i P(t, T_i)$$

and

$$\frac{1}{\Delta T_{m,n}} = \sum_{i=m+1}^{n} w_i(t) \frac{1}{\Delta T_i}$$

We have the following results on the dynamics of the swap rate.

Proposition 5. The displaced forward swap rate $S_{m,n}(t)+\frac{1}{\Delta T_{m,n}}$ is a martingale under the measure $Q_{m,n}$ corresponding to the numeraire $A_{m,n}(t)$. Moreover,

$$d\left(S_{m,n}(t)+\frac{1}{\Delta T_{m,n}}\right)=\left(S_{m,n}(t)+\frac{1}{\Delta T_{m,n}}\right)\times\left[\sum_{i=m+1}^{n}\alpha_i(t)\gamma_j(t)+(\alpha_i(t)-w_i(t))\Sigma(t,T_i)\right]\cdot d\mathbf{Z}_t^{(m,n)} \quad (34)$$

where $d\mathbf{Z}_t^{(m,n)}$ is a $Q_{m,n}$-Brownian motion and

$$\alpha_i(t)=\frac{w_i(t)\mu_i(t)}{\sum_{j=m+1}^{n}w_j(t)\mu_j(t)}.$$

The martingale property is easy to see because it is the relative value between its floating leg and an annuity, both are tradable securities. The proof of Eq. (34) is supplemented in the appendix.

By appropriately freezing coefficients of Eq. (34), the displaced inflation forward swap rate $S_{m,n}(t)+\frac{1}{\Delta T_{m,n}}$ becomes a lognormal variable, and closed-form pricing of inflation swaptions will then follow. Consider a T_m-maturity swaption on the YYIIS over the period $[T_m,T_n]$ and with strike K, we can derive its value as

$$V_t=A_{m,n}(t)\left[\left(S_{m,n}(t)+\frac{1}{\Delta T_{m,n}}\right)\Phi(d_1^{(m,n)})-\tilde{K}_{m,n}\Phi(d_2^{(m,n)})\right] \quad (35)$$

where

$$\tilde{K}_{m,n}=K+\frac{1}{\Delta T_{m,n}}$$

$$d_1^{(m,n)}=\frac{\ln(S_{m,n}(t)+1/\Delta T_{m,n})/\tilde{K}_{m,n}+\frac{1}{2}\sigma_{m,n}^2(t)(T_m-t)}{\sigma_{m,n}(t)\sqrt{T_m-t}}$$

$$d_2^{(m,n)}=d_1^{(m,n)}-\sigma_{m,n}(t)\sqrt{T_m-t}$$

$$\sigma_{m,n}(t)=\frac{1}{T_m-t}\int_t^{T_m}\left\|\sum_{i=m+1}^{n}[\alpha_i(t)\gamma_i^{(I)}(s)+(\alpha_i(t)-w_i(t))\Sigma(s,T_i)]\right\|^2 ds$$

Treatments of freezing coefficients similar to what we have done to Eq. (34) are popular in the industry, and they are often very accurate in applications. A thorough analysis on the error estimation of such approximations, however, is still pending. For interesting insights about the magnitude of errors, we refer to Brigo, Liinev, Mercurio, and Rapisarda (2004).

The swaption formula, Eq. (35), implies a hedging strategy for the swaption. At any time t, the hedger should long $\Phi(d_1^{(m,n)})$ units of the underlying inflation swap for hedging. Proceeds from buying or selling the swap may go in or go out of a money market account. Besides, the swpation formula also contains the caplet formula, Eq. (29), as a special case when $n = m + 1$.

Finally we emphasize that, with the Black's formula (for displaced-diffusion processes), inflation caps, floors and swaptions can be quoted using implied volatilities, regardless the sign (i.e., either positive or negative) of input inflation forward rates or swap rates.

MODEL CALIBRATION

A comprehensive calibration of the inflation-rate model Eq. (21) means simultaneous determination of volatility vectors of nominal and inflation

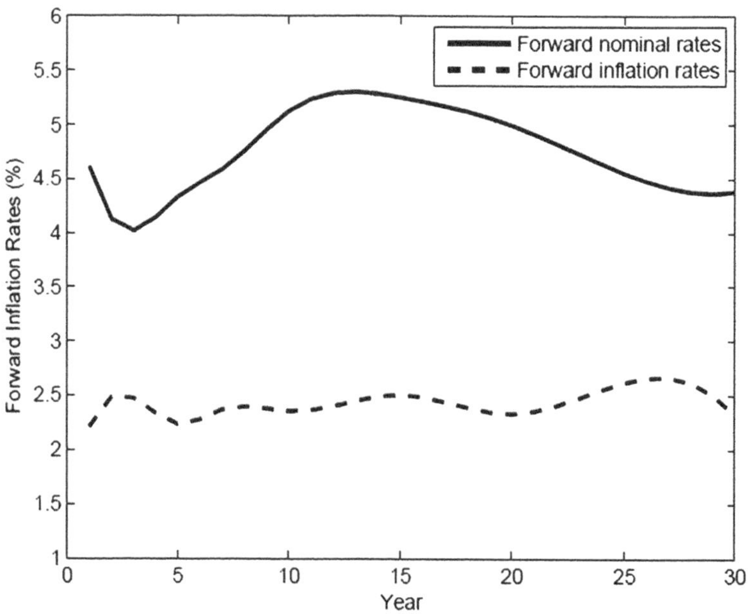

Fig. 2. Term Structure of the Nominal Forward Rates and Inflation Forward Rates.

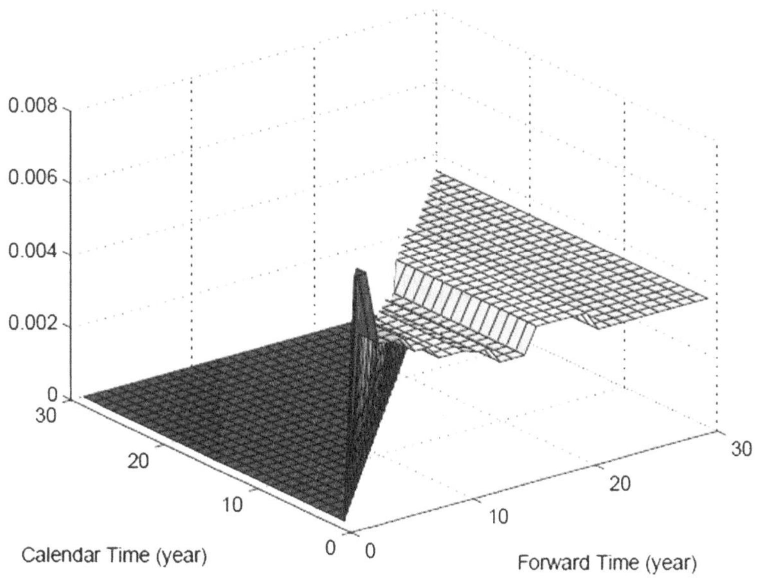

Fig. 3. Calibrated Local Volatility Surface, $\gamma_i^{(I)}(t)$.

forward rates, based on market data of caps, floors, and swaptions of both nominal interest rates and inflation rates. It is not hard to see that the calibration of nominal forward-rate and inflation forward-rate dynamics can be decoupled. For nonparametric calibration, one can apply the methodology of Wu (2003) to the separate calibration of the two dynamics.

For demonstration, we have calibrated the two-factor market model to price data of Euro ZCIIS and (part of the) inflation caps as of April 7, 2008,[6] and observed very nice performance. Fig. 2 shows the term structures of inflation forward rates as well as nominal forward rates. Fig. 3 shows the local volatility function obtained by calibrating the model to implied cap volatilities of various maturities but a fixed strike $K=2\%$.

SMILE MODELING

With the dynamics of displaced diffusions only, the market model cannot price volatility smiles in cap/floor markets. For that purpose, we should extend or modify the current model in ways parallel to the extensions to the LIBOR market model, on which there are rich literatures (see, e.g., Brigo & Mercurio, 2006 for an introductions of smile models).

One quick solution for smiles modeling is to adopt the SABR (Hagan Kumar, Lesnieski, & Woodward, 2002) dynamics for the displaced inflation forward rates, $\mu_j(t)$, and consider the following model:

$$\begin{cases} d\mu_j(t) = \mu_j(t)\gamma_j^{(I)} dZ_j(t) \\ d\gamma_j^{(I)} = \varepsilon_j \gamma_j^{(I)} dW_j(t) \end{cases} \tag{36}$$

where β_j and ε_j are constants, and both $Z_j(t)$ and $W_j(t)$ are one-dimensional (correlated) Brownian motions under the T_j-forward measure. Mecurio and Moreni (2009) proposed and studied the above model for $\beta_j = 1$, and demonstrate a quality fitting of implied volatility smiles.

CONCLUSION

Taking prices of real zero-coupon bonds as model primitives that are tradable through ZCIIS, we define the term structure of inflation rates, rebuild the market model, and create an HJM-type model for the term structure of inflation rates. The HJM-type model with inflation forward rates is shown to be consistent with the HJM model with real forward rates developed through "foreign currency analogy." With the market model we can price inflation caplets/floorlets and swaptions in closed form, and quote these derivatives by "implied Black's volatilities." The market model also serves as a proper platform for developing models to manage volatility smile risk in those inflation-rate derivatives.

NOTES

1. See James (2010).
2. *Source*: U.S. Bureau of Labor Statistics and European Central Bank. Available at ftp://ftp.bls.gov/pub/special.requests/cpi/cpiai.txt and http://appsso.eurostat.ec.europa.eu/nui/show.do?dataset=prc_hicp_midx&lang=en
3. $P_R(t, T)$ is treated as the price of a zero-coupon bond of a virtue "foreign currency" by Jarrow and Yildirim (2003).
4. It is not hard to see that the volatility of $P_R(t, T_0, T)$ does not depend on T_0.
5. Note that both $P_R(t, t)$ and $I(t)$ have no volatility.
6. For brevity the data are not presented here, which are however available upon request.

ACKNOWLEDGMENTS

Parts of the results of this chapter have been presented in the financial mathematics seminar of Peking University, December 2007, BFS 2008 London Congress, International Conference on Applied Statistics and Financial Mathematics, Hong Kong 2010, and Problems and Challenges in Financial Engineering, Shanghai 2011. The author is thankful for comments from participants of these seminars/conferences. All errors are mine.

REFERENCES

Barone, E., & Castagna, A. (1997). *The information content of TIPS*. Internal Report, SanPaolo IMI, Turin and Banca IMI, Milan.

Belgrade, N., & Benhamou, E. (2004a). Reconciling year on year and zero coupon inflation swap: A market model approach. Preprint, CDC Ixis Capital Markets. Available at http://papers.ssrn.com/sol3/papers.cfm?abstract-id = 583641. Accessed on March 7, 2012.

Belgrade, N., & Benhamou, E. (2004b). *Smart modeling of the inflation market:taking into account the seasonality*. Preprint, CDC Ixis Capital Markets.

Belgrade, N., Benhamou, E., & Koehler, E. (2004). A market model for inflation. Preprint, CDC Ixis Capital Markets. Available at http://papers.ssrn.com/sol3/papers.cfm?abstract-id=576081. Accessed on March 7, 2011.

Brace, A., Gatarek, D., & Musiela, M. (1997). The market model of interest rate dynamics. *Mathematical Finance*, *7*(2), 127–155.

Brigo, D., Liinev, J., Mercurio, F., & Rapisarda, F. (2004). *On the distributional distance between the lognormal LIBOR and Swap market models*. Working Paper. Banca IMI, Italy.

Brigo, D., & Mercurio, F. (2006). *Interest rate models: Theory and practice: With smile, inflation and credit* (2nd ed). Berlin: Springer Finance.

Cairns, A. J. G. (2000). *A multifactor model for the term structure and inflation for long-term risk management with an extension to the equities market*. Preprint, Heriot-Watt University, Edinburgh.

Chen, R.-R., Liu, B., & Cheng, X. (2006). *Pricing the term structure of inflation risk premia: Theory and evidence from TIPS*. *Journal of Empirical Finance*, *17*(4), 702–721.

Cox, J., Ingersoll, J., & Ross, S. A. (1985). A theory of the term structure of interest rates. *Econometrica*, *53*(2), 385–408.

Falbo, P., Paris, F., & Pelizzari, C. (2009). Pricing inflation-link bonds. *Quantitative Finance*, 1–15.

Fisher, I. (1930). *The theory of interest* (ISBN: 978-0879918644.). New York: The Macmillan Company.

Hagan, P., Kumar, D., Lesnieski, A., & Woodward, D. (2002). Managing smile risk. *Wilmott Magazine*, July 26, pp. 84–108.

Harrison, J. M., & Krep, S. (1979). Martingales and arbitrage in multiperiod securities markets. *Journal of Economic Theory*, *20*, 381–408.

Harrison, J. M., & Pliska, S. (1981). Martingales and stochastic integrals in the theory of continuous trading. *Stochastic Processes and Their Application*, *11*, 215–260.
Heath, D., Jarrow, R., & Morton, A. (1992). Bond pricing and the term structure of Interest rates: A new methodology for contingent claims valuation. *Econometrica*, *60*, 77–105.
Hinnerich, M. (2008). Inflation indexed swaps and swaptions. *Journal of Banking and Finance*, *32*(11), 2293–2306.
Hughston, L. P. (1998). *Inflation derivatives*. Merrill Lynch, Working Paper, London.
James, A. (2010). *Global inflation-linked products: A user's guide*. Barclay Capital, London.
Jamshidian, F. (1997). LIBOR and swap market models and measures. *Finance and Stochastic*, *1*, 293–330.
Jarrow, R., & Yildirim, Y. (2003). Pricing treasury inflation protected securities and related derivatives using an HJM model. *Journal of Financial and Quantitative Analysis*, *38*(2), 409–430.
Jung, J. (2008). Real growth. *RISK*, February.
Kazziha, S. (1999). *Interest Rate Models, Inflation-based Derivatives, Trigger Notes And Cross-Currency Swaptions*. Ph.D. thesis, Imperial College of Science, Technology and Medicine, London.
Kenyon, C. (2008). Inflation is normal. *RISK*, 76–82.
Korn, R., & Kruse, S. (2004). A simple model to value inflation-linked financial products (in German). *Blätter der DGVFM*, *XXVI*(3), 351–367.
Kruse, S. (2007). *Pricing of inflation-indexed options under the assumption of a lognormal inflation index as well as under stochastic volatility*. Bonn, Germany: University of Applied Sciences.
Manning, S., & Jones, M. (2003). Modeling inflation derivatives-a review. The Royal Bank of Scotland Guide to Inflation-Linked Products. Incisive RWG Ltd, London.
Mercurio, F. (2005). Pricing inflation-indexed derivatives. *Quantitative Finance*, *5*(3), 289–302.
Mercurio, F., & Moreni, N. (2006). Inflation with a smile. *RISK*, *19*(3), 70–75.
Mercurio, F., & Moreni, N. (2009). Inflation modelling with SABR dynamics. *RISK*, 106–111.
Miltersen, K., Sandmann, K., & Sondermann, D. (1997). Closed-form solutions for term structure derivatives with lognormal interest rates. *Journal of Finance*, 409–430.
van Bezooyen, J. T. S., Exley, C. J., & Smith, A. D. (1997). *A market-based approach to valuing LPI liabilities*. London: Group for Economic and Market Value-Based Studies.
Wu, L. (2003). Fast at-the-money calibration of LIBOR market model through Lagrange multipliers. *Journal of Computational Finance*, *6*(2), 39–77.

APPENDIX

Proofs of Propositions

Proof of Proposition 1

Do the following zero-net transactions.

1. At time, $t \geq T_0$
   (a) long the forward contract to buy $\frac{I(T_1)}{I(T_0)}$ dollars of T_2-maturity real zero-coupon bond (for the payoff of $\frac{I(T_2)}{I(T_1)}$) at time T_1 with the unit price $F_R(t, T_1, T_2)$;
   (b) long one unit of T_1-maturity real bond at the price of $P_R(t, T_0, T_1)$;
   (c) short $\frac{P_R(t,T_0,T_1)}{P_R(t,T_0,T_2)}$ unit(s) of T_2-maturity real bond at the unit price of $P_R(t, T_0, T_2)$.
2. At time T_1, exercise the forward contract to buy the T_2-maturity real zero-coupon bond at the unit price $F_R(t, T_1, T_2)$, applying all proceeds from the T_1-maturity real bond.
3. At Time T_2, close out all positions.

The net profit or loss from the transactions is

$$P\&L = \left(\frac{1}{F_R(t, T_1, T_2)} - \frac{P_R(t, T_0, T_1)}{P_R(t, T_0, T_2)}\right)\frac{I(T_2)}{I(T_1)} \tag{A.1}$$

For the absense of arbitrage, the forward price must be set equal to Eq. (13), and the spot price is obtained by discounting.

Proof of Proposition 5

According to Eq. (33),

$$S_{m,n}(t) + \frac{1}{\Delta T_{m,n}} = \sum_{i=m+1}^{n} w_i(t)\mu_i(t) \tag{A.2}$$

so the dynamics of the displaced swap rate will arise from, by Ito's lemma,

$$d\left(S_{m,n}(t) + \frac{1}{\Delta T_{m,n}}\right) = \sum_{i=m+1}^{n} \mu_i(t)dw_i(t) + w_i(t)d\mu_i(t) + dw_i(t)d\mu_i(t) \tag{A.3}$$

One can easily show that

$$dw_i(t) = w_i(t)(\Sigma(t, T_i) - \Sigma_A(t)) \cdot (d\mathbf{Z}_t - \Sigma_A(t)dt) \tag{A.4}$$

where $\Sigma_A(t) = \sum_{i=m+1}^{n} w_i \Sigma(t, T_i)$. Making use of Eqs. (17) and (A.4), we have

$$\begin{aligned}
d\left(\sum_{i=m+1}^{n} w_i(t)\mu_i(t)\right) &= \sum_{i=m+1}^{n} w_i(t)\mu_i(t)[(\Sigma(t,T_i)-\Sigma_A(t))\cdot(d\mathbf{Z}_t-\Sigma_A(t)dt) \\
&\quad +\gamma_j^{(I)}(t)\cdot(d\mathbf{Z}_t-\Sigma(t,T_i)dt)+\gamma_i^{(I)}(t)\cdot(\Sigma(t,T_i)-\Sigma_A(t))dt] \\
&= \sum_{i=m+1}^{n} w_i(t)\mu_i(t)[(\Sigma(t,T_i)-\Sigma_A(t)+\gamma_i(t))\cdot(d\mathbf{Z}_t-\Sigma_A(t)dt)] \\
&= \left(\sum_{i=m+1}^{n} w_i(t)\mu_i(t)\right)\left[\sum_{i=m+1}^{n} \alpha_i(t)\big(\gamma_j(t)+\Sigma(t,T_i)\big)-\Sigma_A(t)\right] \\
&\quad \cdot(d\mathbf{Z}_t-\Sigma_A(t)dt)
\end{aligned}$$

which is Eq. (34).

Finally, we point out that $d\mathbf{Z}_t - \Sigma_A(t)dt$ is a Brownian motion under the martingale measure corresponding to the numeraire $A_{m,n}(t)$. Let $Q_{m,n}$ denote this measure, then it is defined by the Radon–Nikodym derivative with the risk neutral measure by Q

$$\left.\frac{dQ_{m,n}}{dQ}\right|_{\mathscr{F}_t} = \frac{A_{m,n}(t)}{A_{m,n}(0)B(t)} = m_s(t) \quad for \quad t \leq T_n$$

where $B(t)$ be the money market account under discrete compounding:

$$B(t) = \left(\prod_{j=0}^{\eta_t-2}(1+f_j(T_j)\Delta T_j)\right)(1+f_{\eta_t-1}(T_{\eta_t-1})(t-T_{\eta_t-1}))$$

By Ito's lemma,

$$dm_s(t) = m_s(t)\Sigma_A(t)\cdot d\mathbf{Z}_t \tag{A.5}$$

The $Q_{m,n}$ Brownian motion corresponding to $\mathbf{Z}_t$ is defined by

$$\begin{aligned}
d\mathbf{Z}_t^{(m,n)} &= d\mathbf{Z}_t - \left\langle d\mathbf{Z}_t, \frac{dm_s(t)}{m_s(t)}\right\rangle \\
&= d\mathbf{Z}_t - \Sigma_A(t)dt
\end{aligned} \tag{A.6}$$

AN OPTION-PRICING FRAMEWORK FOR THE VALUATION OF FUND MANAGEMENT COMPENSATION

Axel Buchner, Abdulkadir Mohamed and Niklas Wagner

ABSTRACT

Compensation of funds managers increasingly involves elements of profit sharing that entitle managers to option-like payoffs. An important example is the compensation of private equity fund managers. Compensation of private equity fund managers typically consists of a fixed management fee and a performance-related carried interest. The fixed management fee resembles common compensation terms of mutual funds and hedge funds, while the performance-related carried interest is uncommon among most mutual funds. Moreover, the performance-related carried interest typically differs from variable hedge fund fees. In this chapter, we derive the value of the variable components of private equity fund managers' compensation based on a risk-neutral option-pricing approach.

Derivative Securities Pricing and Modelling
Contemporary Studies in Economic and Financial Analysis, Volume 94, 331–350

ISSN: 1569-3759/doi:10.1108/S1569-3759(2012)0000094016

INTRODUCTION

Compensation of funds managers increasingly involves elements of profit sharing that entitle managers to option-like payoffs that are contingent on the performance of the managed fund. An important example is the compensation of private equity fund managers, to which only limited research has been devoted so far. In this chapter, we show how to value the variable components of private equity fund managers' compensation based on a risk-neutral option-pricing approach.

Private equity funds are typically organized as limited partnerships, with private equity firms serving as General Partners (GPs) of the funds, and large institutional investors and wealthy individuals providing bulk of the capital known as Limited Partners (LPs). These limited partnerships typically last for 10 years, and partnership agreements signed at a fund initiation define the expected payments to GPs. These payments consist of two components. A fixed component (called "management fee") and a performance-related component (called "carried interest" or simply "carry"). The fixed management fee resembles well pricing terms of mutual funds and hedge funds, while the performance-related carried interest is uncommon among most mutual funds and is different from the variable incentive fees of hedge funds.

For the GPs, carried interest is an option-like position on the total proceeds of all investments of the fund. In practice, multiple, staggered investments and stepwise liquidation of the investments make carried interest considerably more complex than a simple call option on a traded asset. In particular, the option payoffs are typically contingent upon the performance of the fund, where performance is typically measured by the internal rate of return of the fund cash flows. To derive solutions to the problem of valuing these option-like positions, we first develop a continuous-time model of the cash flow dynamics of private equity funds. This model consists of three main components. (1) The modeling of the capital drawdowns, (2) the modeling of the investment value, and (3) the modeling of the return repayments. To keep the model simple, a geometric Brownian motion is utilized for the dynamics of the investment value and two mean-reverting square root processes are applied for the dynamics of the drawdown and the distribution dynamics. Second, we use risk-neutral valuation to estimate the value of the carried-interest option at the fund inception date. This is conducted using a numerical Monte-Carlo simulation of the fund cash flows.

This chapter is related to the literature that investigates the fee terms of private equity partnerships. The first paper to address this issue is Gompers and Lerner (1999a), who explore cross-sectional and time-series variation in the terms of venture capital funds. Similar issues are addressed by Litvak (2004), who extends the analysis of Gompers and Lerner (1999a) from a more legal perspective. Neither of these papers uses an option-pricing framework to value the carried interest. An exception to this is Metrick and Yasuda (2010), who also use a risk-neutral valuation framework to estimate the value of various pricing terms. However, they do not develop a comprehensive model for the cash flow and value dynamics of private equity funds, as done in this chapter. As shown, this framework allows us to analyze how the value of the pricing terms is related to the cash flow dynamics and the risk/return characteristics of a fund. This gives rise to several important determinants of fund fee value that have not previously been studied.

The remainder of this chapter is organized as follows. In the next section, we set forth the notation, assumptions, and structure of the model underlying our fee valuation. The third section presents the risk-neutral valuation framework for lifetime private equity fund fees. The fourth section present the results of a model calibration and analyzes determinants of private equity fund fee value. The conclusions are presented in the fifth section.

THE FRAMEWORK

The aim of this section is to develop the framework in which we derive the value of private equity fund fees. We start with a brief description that lays out the typical construction of private equity funds and explain the two components of private equity fund fees. This gives the motivation for the subsequent model of the dynamics of private equity funds.

Institutional Setting

Investments in private equity are typically intermediated through private equity funds. Thereby, a private equity fund denotes a pooled investment vehicle whose purpose is to negotiate purchases of common and preferred stocks, subordinated debt, convertible securities, warrants, futures, and other securities of companies that are usually unlisted. As the vast majority of private equity funds, the fund to be modeled here is organized as a limited partnership in which the private equity firm serves as the GP. The bulk of the capital invested in private equity funds is typically provided by institutional investors, such as endowments, pension funds, insurance companies, and banks. These investors, called LPs, commit to provide a certain amount of capital to the private equity fund (the so-called committed capital). The GP then has an agreed time period in which to invest this committed capital – usually on the order of five years. This time period is commonly referred to as the fund commitment period. In general, when a GP identifies an investment opportunity, he "calls" money from the LPs up to the amount committed, and A GP can do so at any time during the pre-specified commitment period. The capital calls usually occur unscheduled over the commitment period, where the exact timing only depends on the investment decisions of the GPs. However, total capital calls over the commitment period do not exceed the total committed capital. The capital calls are also called drawdowns or takedowns. As those drawdowns occur, the available cash is immediately invested in managed assets and the size of the portfolio begins to increase. When an investment is liquidated, the GP distributes the proceeds to its LPs either in marketable securities or in cash. The GP also has an agreed time period in which to return capital to the LPs – usually on the order of ten to fourteen years. This time period is also called the total legal lifetime of the fund.[1]

Following the typical structure of private equity funds, the GPs receive two types of compensations for managing the investments: a fixed component (called "management fee") and a performance-related component (called "carried interest" or simply "carry").[2] The management fee is generally expressed as a percentage of the committed capital and is paid annually. Typically, the fees are around 2 percent yearly and vary based on fund sizes (see Metrick and Yasuda (2010)). Often the fees decrease after the commitment period to reflect the fact that less time is required in managing activities, especially when investments are mature or partly realized. Tapering the management fee is effected by either reducing the accounting basis on which the rate is applied – or through reduction of the percentage rate paid for compensation. Tapered fee corresponds to the real purpose of the management fee to cover the costs of running and administering the fund. For example, if a fund charges a fixed 2 percent annual management fees on committed capital for the entire fund lifetime of ten years, then the lifetime management fees of the fund amount to 20 percent of the committed capital. Thus only the remaining 80 percent of the committed capital will be available for investments into portfolio companies. We will denote this fraction as fund investment capital in the following. Using these definitions, total fund committed capital can be split into two components according to:

$$\text{Committed Capital} = \text{Investment Capital} + \text{Lifetime Management Fees}$$

The second source of compensation is the carried interest or carry, which entitles venture capital firms a certain share of the capital gains from the fund. Typically, the carried interest is only paid if LPs received initial investment plus some other form of pre-specified interests. Most LPs require interests on their capital known as a hurdle rate. This hurdle rate is not a guaranteed interest payment to the fund providers, but rather represents target returns above which venture capital firms are entitled to receive the carried interest. The hurdle rate is typically 8 percent and the carried interest level as prevailed in the industry is 20 percent (see Metrick and Yasuda, 2010).

Table 1 illustrates the computation of the carried interest using a simple numerical example. Assume a private equity fund with a committed capital of $100M, a carried interest level of 20 percent, a hurdle rate of 8 percent, and a fixed lifetime of ten years. For simplicity, we assume that there are no management fees and that the committed capital of the fund is fully drawn by the fund and hence, the absolute value of the negative cash flows during the first four years represents committed capital (i.e., $100M). The fund has exited some of their portfolio companies beginning of year five and continued to the end of year ten. The table shows that the fund generates profits of $150M net of investments or equivalently a multiple of 2.5 (250/100) at the end of fund life.

The calculated cash flow based internal rates of return (IRR) show that the distribution schedule of the fund satisfies the 8 percent hurdle rate requirement in year seven. One year later, the GPs are entitled to receive carried interest. The exact amount of the carried interest is thereby affected by the existence of a catch-up clause, as shown in Table 1. With no catch-up clause, the GPs receive 20 percent of the capital distributions beginning of year eight and continued to the end of year ten. This results in total carried

Table 1. Carried Interest Calculation.

Year	1	2	3	4	5	6	7	8	9	10	Total
Cash flows	−50	−30	−10	−10	30	50	60	50	40	20	150
IRR (in % p.a.)	−100	−100	−100	−100	−33	−6	8	14	17	18	18
Carried interest (no catch-up)	0	0	0	0	0	0	0	10	8	4	22
Carried interest (with catch-up)	0	0	0	0	0	0	0	18	8	4	30

Note: This table illustrates carried interest calculation for a $100M fund with a carried interest level of 20 percent, a hurdle rate of 8 percent, and a lifetime of ten years. The calculation is shown for a fund with no catch-up clause and fund with a catch-up clause of 100 percent.

interest payments of \$22M, which is lower than the carried interest level of 20 percent times the net profits of \$150M of the fund. Thus the GPs receive a lower fraction of the net profits of the fund than the defined carried interest level when no catch-up clause exists. The key idea of a catch-up clause is that the GPs of a fund with a catch-up and hurdle rate receive a fraction of the profits of the fund equal to the carried interest level as long as the fund is sufficiently profitable (i.e., the fund has an IRR that exceeds the hurdle rate). Table 1 shows that the catch-up provision in this example implies that the GPs receive \$18M carried interest in year eight, which is equal to the carried interest level of 20 percent times the net profits of the fund of \$90M (\$190M of distributions on \$100M of committed capital) up to year eight. After year eight, the GPs also receive a fraction of 20 percent of the capital distributions. This results in total carried interest payments of \$30M, which is exactly the carried interest level of 20 percent times the net profits of \$150M of the fund. In this example, we have chosen a catch-up provision of 100 percent. A fund with a catch-up percentage below 100 percent will still receive a proportion equal to the carried interest level of the fund profits, but at a somewhat slower pace than in the example shown here.

The above description has made clear that carried interest is an option-like position on the total proceeds of the fund investments. Valuing such a contingent claim requires modeling the cash flow dynamics of private equity funds.

Private Equity Fund Dynamics

Following the typical construction of private equity funds outlined above, modeling the cash flow dynamics of private equity funds requires three main ingredients: the modeling of the capital drawdowns, the modeling of the investment value, and the modeling of the return repayments.

Capital Drawdowns

We consider a private equity fund with a total legal lifetime of T_l. We begin by assuming that the fund to be modeled has total commitments given by CO, total lifetime management fees given by MF_{T_l}, and an investment capital given by IC. As defined above, it must hold that

$$CO = IC + MF_{T_l} \tag{1}$$

Cumulated capital drawdowns from the LPs up to some time t during the commitment period T_c are denoted by D_t, undrawn capital up to time t

by U_t. When the fund is set up at $t=0$, $D_0=0$, and $U_0=IC$ are given by definition. Furthermore, at any time $t \in [0,T_c]$, the simple identity

$$D_t = IC - U_t \tag{2}$$

must hold. In the following, assume capital to be drawn over time at some non-negative rate from the remaining undrawn investment capital $U_t = IC - D_t$.

Assumption 1. The dynamics of the cumulated capital drawdowns D_t can be described by the ordinary differential equation

$$dD_t = \delta_t U_t 1_{\{0 \leq t \leq Tc\}} dt \tag{3}$$

where $\delta_t \geq 0$ denotes the rate of contribution, or simply the fund's drawdown rate.

In most cases, capital drawdowns of private equity funds are heavily concentrated in the first few years or even quarters of a fund's life. After high initial investment activity, drawdowns of private equity funds are carried out at a declining rate, as fewer new investments are made, and follow-on investments are spread out over a number of years. This typical time-pattern of the capital drawdowns is well reflected in the structure of Eq. (3). Under the specification (3), cumulated capital drawdowns D_t are given by

$$D_t = IC - IC \exp\left(-\int_0^{\leq Tc} \delta_u du\right) \tag{4}$$

Eq. (4) shows that the initially high capital drawdowns at the start of the fund decrease over the commitment period T_c of the fund. This follows as undrawn amounts of the investment capital, $U_t = IC \exp\left(-\int_0^{\leq Tc} \delta_u du\right)$, decay exponentially over time. A condition that leads to the realistic feature that capital drawdowns are highly concentrated in the early times of a fund's life. Furthermore, Eq. (4) shows that the cumulated drawdowns D_t can never exceed the total investment capital IC under this model setup, that is, $D_t \leq IC$ holds for all $t \in [0,T_c]$. At the same time the model also allows for a certain fraction of the investment capital IC not to be drawn, as the commitment period T_c represents a cutoff point for capital drawdowns.

As investment opportunities typically do not arise constantly over the commitment period T_c, we introduce a stochastic process for the drawdown rate δ_t.

Assumption 2. The drawdown rate δ_t is given by a stochastic process $\{\delta_t, 0 \leq t \leq T_c\}$. Its specification under the objective probability measure $\mathbb{P}$ is

$$d\delta_t = \kappa_1(\theta_1 - \delta_t)dt + \sqrt{\sigma_1}\delta_t dB_{1,t} \tag{5}$$

where $\theta_1 > 0$ is the long-run mean of the drawdown rate, $\kappa_1 > 0$ *governs the rate of reversion to this mean,* $\sigma_1 > 0$ reflects the volatility of the drawdown rate, and $B_{1,t}$ is a standard Brownian motion.

The drawdown rate behavior implied by the above square-root diffusion ensures that negative values of the drawdown rate are precluded[3] and that the drawdown rate randomly fluctuates around some mean level θ_1. We are now equipped with the first component of our model. The following turns to the modeling of the capital distributions.

Capital Distributions

As capital drawdowns occur, the available capital is immediately invested in managed assets and the portfolio of the fund begins to accumulate. As the underlying investments of the fund are gradually exited, cash or marketable securities are received and finally returns and proceeds are distributed to the LPs. Let cumulated capital distributions up to some time $t \in [0, T_l]$ during the legal lifetime T_l of the fund be denoted by R_t. Recognizing that the size and timing of repayments are based on the performance of the fund, it is assumed that capital distributions occur at a non-negative rate ρ_t from the total investment portfolio value V_t of the fund at time t.

Assumption 3. The dynamics of the cumulated capital distributions R_t can be described by

$$dR_t = \rho_t V_t dt, \quad \text{if} \quad t < T_l \quad \text{and} \quad R_t = \int_0^t \rho_u V_u du + V_t 1_{\{t=T_l\}} \tag{6}$$

where $\rho_t \geq 0$ denotes the rate of repayment, or simply the fund's distribution rate.

The ordinary differential equation in specification (6) illustrates that capital repayments occur at a non-negative rate ρ_t. This, however, holds only in case $t < T_l$. As funds are fully liquidated at the end of their legal lifetime, cumulated capital distributions over the entire life of the fund must also include the final reimbursement of the assets of the fund at maturity T_l, that is, $R_{T_l} = \int_0^t \rho_u V_u \, du + V_t 1_{\{t=T_l\}}$. Note also that the model developed here allows cumulated distributions to be greater (or smaller) than the cumulated drawdowns, implying a possibly positive (or negative) performance of the fund over its lifetime.

To capture the erratic feature of real world private equity fund capital distribution, we also introduce a stochastic process for the distributions rate ρ_t.

Assumption 4. The distribution rate ρ_t is given by a stochastic process $\{\rho_t, 0 \leq t \leq T_l\}$. Its specification under the objective probability measure $\mathbb{P}$ is

$$d\rho_t = \kappa_2(\theta_2 - \rho_t)dt + \sigma_2\sqrt{\rho_t}dB_{2,t} \quad (7)$$

where $\theta_2 > 0$ is the long-run mean of the distribution rate, $\kappa_2 > 0$ governs the rate of reversion to this mean, $\sigma_2 > 0$ reflects the volatility of the distribution rate, and $B_{2,t}$ is a second standard Brownian motion.

We model distributions and drawdowns separately and, therefore, must similarly restrict capital distributions to be strictly non-negative at any time t during the legal lifetime T_l of the fund. This is again achieved by assuming a square-root diffusion for the dynamics of the distributions rate.[4] Additionally, the specification (7) has the attractive feature that the distributions rate will randomly fluctuates around the mean level θ_2.

Besides the stochastic distributions rate, ρ_t, capital distributions of a fund are also driven by the evolution of the fund value V_t over time, which is specified in the following.

Investment Value

The last step in the modeling of private equity funds is characterizing the dynamics of the value of the fund V_t over the legal lifetime T_l. Fund values are affected by three variables: capital drawdowns, capital distributions, and investment performance. It is assumed that the return on any cash flow invested in the fund can be described by a normal distribution with constant mean μ and constant (non-negative) volatility σ.

Assumption 5. The dynamics of the fund values V_t under the objective probability measure $\mathbb{P}$ can be described by the stochastic differential equation

$$dV_t = \mu V_t dt + \sigma V_t dB_{3,t} + dD_t - dR_t \quad (8)$$

where μ is the constant mean rate of return, $\sigma > 0$ is the constant return volatility, and $B_{3,t}$ is a third standard Brownian motion.

From specification (8), one can infer that the change in value of the fund is made of the performance of the existing investment V_t. Randomness in returns is introduced into the model by the standard Brownian motion $B_{3,t}$. Besides, the value of the fund is augmented by the capital drawdowns and decreased by the capital distributions.

Substituting the definition of dR_t, Eq. (8) can be simplified to

$$dV_t = (\mu - \rho_t)V_t dt + \sigma V_t dB_{3,t} + dD_t, \quad \text{if } t < T_l \tag{9}$$

which is the stochastic differential equation of a so-called inverse gamma process that turns into a standard geometric Brownian motion in case of $t > T_c$.[5] Note here that final value is $V_{T_l} = 0$ because of the final cash flow repayment inherent in specification (6). In addition, note that also $V_0 = 0$ holds in the model by definition.

RISK-NEUTRAL FEE VALUATION

In this section, we derive the value of lifetime private equity fund fees using risk-neutral pricing techniques. We start with a formal definition of the two fee components. Then, the risk-neutral valuation framework is presented.

Definition of Fee Components

As outlined in the section "Institutional Setting" GPs typically receive two forms of compensations for managing the partnership interests. The first, is fixed revenue and paid as management fees, while the second is performance-based revenue and payable as carried interest.

The formal definition of the management fees in a continuous-time framework is straightforward. Let MF_t denote cumulated management fees up to some time $t \in [0, T_l]$. If management fees are defined as a percentage c_{mf} of the committed capital CO and paid continuously, the dynamics of the management fees can be represented by the ordinary differential equation

$$dMF_t = c_{mf} CO dt \tag{10}$$

The definition of the carried interest is slightly more complex as this performance-based compensation depends on the fund cash flows. Let CI_t denote the cumulated carried interest up to some time $t \in [0, T_l]$. The carried interest entitles the GPs a certain share of the capital gains from the fund. If the carried interest level is given by c_{ci}, the GPs receive the fraction c_{ci} of the net cash flows of the fund after management fees. Mathematically, the dynamics of the carried interest can be described by

$$dCI_t = c_{ci} \max\{dR_t - dD_t - dMF_t, 0\} 1_{\{IRR_t > h\}} \quad (11)$$

where taking the maximum of the net cash flows after management fees and zero, $\max\{dR_t - dD_t - dMF_t, 0\}$, ensures that instantaneous carried interest payments are non-negative. In addition, multiplying by the indicator function $1_{\{IRR_t > h\}}$ guarantees that the performance-related carried interest is only payable at time t if the internal rate of return of the fund at that time, IRR_t, exceeds the specified hurdle rate h, that is, $IRR_t > h$ holds. The internal rate of return is the performance measure commonly employed in the private equity industry to evaluate the return of a fund. In continuous-time, the internal rate of return IRR_t of the net fund cash flows after management fees at time t is a solution to[6]

$$\int_0^t e^{-IRR_t u}(dR_u - dD_u - dMF_u) = 0 \quad (12)$$

Eq. (11) implicitly assumes that the carried interest is paid without the existence of a catch-up clause. If the carried interest is paid with a 100 percent catch-up provision, the dynamics of the carried interest become more complex. Again, carried interest is only payable at time t if $IRR_t > h$ holds. In addition, if the fraction of the cumulated carried interest of the net profits of the fund is equal to the carried interest level, that is $CI_t/(R_t - CO) = c_{ci}$ holds, the GPs receive an instantaneous carried interest of $c_{ci} \max\{dR_t - dD_t - dMF_t, 0\}$. This is similar to the definition of the carried interest without a catch-up in Eq. (11). In contrast, if $CI_t/(R_t - CO) < c_{ci}$ holds, instantaneous carried interest payments are equal to $\min\{c_{ci}(R_t - CO) - CI_t, dR_t - dD_t - dMF_t\}$. Thereby, taking the minimum here means that the catch-up payments, $c_{ci}(R_t - CO) - CI_t$, cannot exceed instantaneous net fund cash flows after management fees, $dR_t - dD_t - dMF_t$.

Risk-neutral valuation

Based on our stochastic cash flow models and the definitions made above, we can now derive the value of lifetime fund fees of the GPs. The value of the outstanding fund fees V_t^{GP} at time $t \in [0, T_l]$ is defined by the discounted value of all expected outstanding lifetime fund fees, including management fees and the carried interest. Applying a risk-neutral valuation approach, the arbitrage-free value of the fund fees is given by

$$V_t^{GP} = V_t^{MF} + V_t^{CI} = E_t^{\mathbb{Q}}\left[\int_t^{T_l} e^{-r_f(u-t)} dMF_u\right] + E_t^{\mathbb{Q}}\left[\int_t^{T_l} e^{-r_f(u-t)} dCI_u\right] \quad (13)$$

where $E_t^{\mathbb{Q}}[\cdot]$ denotes the expectations operator conditional on the information set available at time t. This conditional expectations operator is defined under the risk-neutral probability measure $\mathbb{Q}$. Therefore, discounting at the riskless rate r_f is appropriate in Eq. (13). From specification (13), the value of lifetime fund fees consists of two components. The first term, V_t^{MF}, is the value of the outstanding management fees. The second term, V_t^{CI}, corresponds to the value of the outstanding carried interest.

The evaluation of the first integral for the value of the management fees is trivial. This is since the fixed management fee is a contractual arrangement that is paid riskless and by a constant amount per time period. Therefore, we can eliminate the first expectation in Eq. (13), as the expectation of a constant is simply the constant itself.[7] Substituting Eq. (10), the value of the outstanding management fees turns out to be

$$V_t^{MF} = c_{mf} CO\left[\int_t^{T_l} e^{-r_f(u-t)} du\right] = c_{mf} CO \frac{1 - exp(-r_f(T_l - t)}{r_f} \quad (14)$$

Substituting Eq. (11), the value of the outstanding carried interest (with no catch-up) can be evaluated by solving

$$V_t^{CI} = E_t^{\mathbb{Q}}\left[\int_t^{T_l} e^{-r_f(u-t)} c_{ci} \max\{dR_u - dD_u - dMF_u, 0\} 1_{\{IRR_u > h\}}\right] \quad (15)$$

From Eq. (15), one can directly infer that the value of the carried interest is a contingent claim on the capital drawdowns and distributions of a private equity fund. The complication here arises from the fact that the state variables underlying the valuation, that is, the assumed cash flow processes, do not represent traded assets. In such an incomplete market setting, risk-neutral pricing based on arbitrage considerations alone is not feasible. Hence, the risk sources underlying our model have to be transformed.

Applying Girsanov's Theorem, as for example outlined in Duffie (2001), it follows that the underlying stochastic processes for the drawdown rate, distribution rate, and the investment value under the risk-neutral probability measure $\mathbb{Q}$ are given by

$$d\delta_t = [\kappa_1(\theta_1 - \delta_1) - \lambda_1\sigma_1\sqrt{\delta_t}] + \sigma_1\sqrt{\delta_t}dB^{\mathbb{Q}}_{1,t} \quad (16)$$

$$d\rho_t = [\kappa_2(\theta_2 - \rho_t) - \lambda_2\sigma_2\sqrt{\rho_t}] + \sigma_2\sqrt{\rho_t}dB^{\mathbb{Q}}_{2,t} \quad (17)$$

$$dV_t = (\mu - \lambda_3\sigma)V_t dt + \sigma V_t dB^{\mathbb{Q}}_{3,t} - dR_{t+}dD_t \quad (18)$$

where $B^{\mathbb{Q}}_{1,t}$, $B^{\mathbb{Q}}_{2,t}$, and $B^{\mathbb{Q}}_{3,t}$ are $\mathbb{Q}$ Brownian motions and λ_1, λ_2, and λ_3 are the corresponding market prices of risk. To simplify the valuation, we assume that the drawdown and distribution rate carry zero systematic risk. Under this condition, the market prices of risk λ_1 and λ_2 are equal to zero and the drift coefficients of the stochastic processes δ_t and ρ_t are not affected by the change of the probability measure.

The third market price of risk λ_3 can be derived using a version of the intertemporal capital asset pricing model (ICAPM) of Merton (1973).[8] It follows that the market price of risk is given by:

$$\lambda_3 = Corr(dV_t, dM_t)Std(dM_t) \quad (19)$$

That is, the market price of risk is simply computed by the correlation $Corr(dV_t, dM_t)$ between the fund returns and the market portfolio returns multiplied by the volatility $Std(dM_t)$ of the market portfolio returns.

Unfortunately, valuation Eq. (15) cannot be solved analytically because of the path-dependent structure of the carried interest that is contingent on the internal rate of return of the fund. Therefore, we have to resort to a numerical technique. This is done here by using Monte Carlo simulations based on discrete-time approximations of the stochastic cash flow and fee model. The details of the numerical procedure to solve Eq. (15) are outlined in the appendix.

NUMERICAL EXAMPLE

In this section, the fee valuation is applied using a set of reasonable input parameters. We assume a fund with a committed capital equal to \$100 and a legal lifetime of 10 years. The fee terms are a 2 percent management fee, a carried interest level of 20 percent, and a hurdle rate of 8 percent. For the dynamics of the capital drawdowns and capital distribution, we rely on the parameters estimated by Malherbe (2004) for the buyout segment: $\kappa_1 = 8.74$, $\theta_1 = 0.32$, $\sigma_1 = 1.46$, $\kappa_2 = 17.47$, $\theta_2 = 0.20$, and $\sigma_2 = 1.93$.

For the value dynamics, we assume an expected return of $\mu = 0.15$ and a volatility of $\sigma = 0.30$. To compute the market price of risk λ_3, we assume a

Table 2. Estimated Fee Values.

	Management Fee Value	Carried Interest Value	Total Fee Value
No catch-up	15.86	3.80	19.66
With catch-up	15.86	4.16	20.02

Note: This table summarizes the outputs of the fee valuation. Fee values are expressed in dollars per $100 of committed capital. The fee terms employed for the calculations are a 2 percent management fee, a carried interest level of 20 percent, and a hurdle rate of 8 percent. Calculations are shown for a fund with no catch-up clause and fund with a catch-up clause of 100 percent.

correlation coefficient of 0.5 between the fund and market returns and a volatility of the market returns equal to 0.2. For this set of model parameters, the market price of risk turns out to be to be $\lambda_3 = 0.1$. Finally, the riskless rate of interest is set to 5 percent.

Table 2 summarizes the fee values that can be computed using this set of model parameters. All fee values are expressed in dollars per $100 of committed capital. The table shows that the total value of lifetime fees is $19.66 for a fund with no catch-up and $20.02 for a fund with a 100 percent catch-up provision. That is, total value of lifetime fee revenues amounts to around 20 percent of the committed capital of the fund. Management fees account for the largest portion of the value of the lifetime fees and are not affected by the existence of a catch-up clause. In both categories, close to four-fifth of the value of the total revenues derive from the fixed management fee and only one-fifth from the variable revenue generated by the carried interest payments. As expected, the existence of a catch-up clause increases the value of the carried interest. However, the figures provided in Table 2 imply that the magnitude of this effect is relatively low.

Besides calculating fee values it is also interesting to explore how they are affected by the various model parameters. The factors influencing the value of the outstanding management fees, V_t^{MF}, can directly be inferred from Eq. (15). Table 3 summarizes these factors and indicates their directional influence on the value of the outstanding management fees. As shown in the table, the value increases as the remaining fund lifetime $T_l - t$, the committed capital CO, or the management fee level c_{mf} are increased. In contrast, the value of outstanding management fees decreases with higher levels of the riskless rate r_f , as this leads to higher discounting of the outstanding management fees.

Table 4 summarizes the parameters influencing the value of the carried interest, V_t^{CI}.[9] First, the value of the carried interest depends on the fund

Table 3. Factors Determining Management Fee Value.

Parameter	Symbol	Direction
Remaining fund lifetime	T_l-t	Increases
Committed capital	CO	Increases
Management fee level	c_{mf}	Increases
Riskless rate	r_f	Decreases

Note: This table summarizes the factors determining the value of the outstanding management fees. The column labeled direction indicates how the value of the management fees changes if the corresponding parameter is increased.

Table 4. Factors Determining Carried Interest Value.

Parameter	Symbol	Direction
Remaining fund lifetime	T_l-t	Increases
Committed capital	CO	Increases
Carried interest level	c_{ci}	Increases
Hurdle rate	h	Decreases
Speed of adjustment for the drawdown rate	κ_1	(Decreases)
Long-term drawdown rate	θ_1	Increases
Volatility drawdown rate	σ_1	(Increases)
Speed of adjustment for the distribution rate	κ_2	(Increases)
Long-term distribution rate	θ_2	Decreases
Volatility distribution rate	σ_2	(Decreases)
Expected return	μ	Increases
Asset volatility	σ	Increases
Riskless rate	r_f	Decreases

Note: This table summarizes the main factors determining the value of the outstanding carried interest. The column labeled direction indicates how the value of the carried interest changes if the corresponding parameter is increased. For parameters with only a small impact on the carried interest value, the direction is shown in brackets. Note that the relationships shown in this table hold for carried interest payments with and without a catch-up clause.

terms. Similar to the value of the management fees, the value of the carried interest increases as the remaining fund lifetime $T_l - t$ or the committed capital CO increases. The carried interest entitles the GPs a percentage of the capital gains of the fund equal to the carried interest level c_{ci} if the fund's return exceeds the hurdle rate h. Therefore, the value increases (decreases) with an increasing carried interest level c_{ci} (hurdle rate h).

Second, the value of the carried interest is also influenced by the parameters governing the stochastic dynamics of the drawdown and distribution rate. The main model parameters affecting the carried interest value here are the long-term drawdown rate θ_1 and the long-term distribution rate θ_2. A higher long-term drawdown rate θ_1 increases the value of the carried interest. This holds as a higher parameter θ_1 on average leads to a faster drawdown schedule. A faster drawdown schedule in turn results in earlier carried interest payments on average. Through the effect of a lower discounting of earlier carried interest payments this results in higher carried interest values. Conversely, increasing the long-term distribution rate θ_2 decreases the value of the carried interest. This holds because a higher level of θ_2 decreases the average period over which the capital is tied up in portfolio companies which also decreases the probability of fund returns that exceed the hurdle rate. Increasing the volatility parameters σ_1 and σ_2 has a similar effect on the value of the carried interest. However, note that the impact of a variation of σ_1 or σ_2 is much smaller than the impact of a variation of θ_1 or θ_2. The impact is about the same relative magnitude than that of a variation of the speed of adjustment parameters κ_1 and κ_2. The speed of adjustment parameters has an opposite effect on the carried interest value, which can be explained by the fact that a high speed of adjustment can absorb some of the volatility of the drawdown and distribution rate.

Third, the value of the carried interest is influenced by the asset value dynamics and the riskless rate of interest. The higher the expected return of the assets μ, the more likely the fund's return will exceed the defined hurdle rate, h. Therefore, a higher expected rate of return μ increases the value of the carried interest. Likewise, a higher asset volatility σ increases the probability of high carried interest payments and thus increases the value of the carried interest. Finally, the value of the carried interest decreases with higher levels of the riskless rate r_f, as this parameter leads to higher discounting of future carried interest payments.

CONCLUSION

This chapter demonstrates the application of a risk-neutral option-pricing approach to value private-equity fund fees. Our numerical analysis shows that the performance-related compensation accounts only for a relatively small portion of the total compensation of private equity fund managers. The framework also enables a detailed analysis of the determinants of private equity fund fee value. The results of this imply that a GP has various ways to influence the value of his future fee payments. For example, he can make riskier investments to increase the carried interest value. Thus, the fee structure of private equity funds gives rise to classical risk-shifting problems. However, the framework developed here does not take into account that such a risk-shifting behavior might also affect the ability of the GP to raise future funds. Undoubtedly, the ability for a GP to raise future funds will also be a very important consideration in his investment decisions. An extension of the model in this direction is a fruitful topic for future research.

NOTES

1. For a more thorough introduction on the subject of private equity funds, for example, refer to Gompers and Lerner (1999b) or to the recent survey article of Phalippou (2007).
2. Besides management fee and the carried interest, private equity funds also often receive transaction and monitoring fees. Both types of additional fees are more common for buyout than for venture capital funds. A transaction fee is typically charged by buyout funds to their LPs when buying or selling a portfolio company. Additionally, many buyout funds charge monitoring fees to their portfolio companies. This is to compensate the fund for the time and effort spent by the GPs in advising and monitoring the portfolio companies. In most cases, these fees are shared with the LPs that receive 80 percent of the monitoring fees and GPs that receive 20 percent. Transaction and monitoring fees are not covered in the analysis of this paper and the interested reader is referred to Metrick and Yasuda (2010) for a more detailed overview.
3. As we model capital distributions and capital drawdowns separately, we have to restrict capital drawdowns to be strictly non-negative at any time t during the period $[0,T_c]$. The square-root diffusion was initially proposed by Cox, Ingersoll, and Ross (1985) as a model of the short rate and is frequently denoted as CIR model. If κ_1, $\theta_1 < 0$, then δ_t will never be negative. If $2\kappa_1\theta_1 \geq \sigma_1^2$, then δ_t remains strictly positive for all t, almost surely. See Cox et al. (1985, p. 391).
4. Note here that under the specification (7), it will again hold that ρ_t will never be negative if κ_1, $\theta_1 < 0$ holds. If $2\kappa_2\theta_2 \geq \sigma_2^2$, then ρ_t remains strictly positive for all t, almost surely.
5. This follows as dD_t for $t > T_c$ hold by definition.
6. Note that the internal rate of return is defined here by the continuously compounded rate of return that makes the net present value of the fund cash flows equal to zero.
7. Note that this relationship holds regardless of whether the expectation is defined under the objective measure $\mathbb{P}$ or under the risk-neutral measure $\mathbb{Q}$.
8. In this version of the ICAPM the expected return μ_i of an asset i satisfies the relation $\mu_i - r_f = \sigma_{iM}$, where σ_{iM} is the covariance of the return on asset i with the return of the market portfolio M. This specification arises from the assumption of logarithmic utility. It permits to omit terms that are related to stochastic shifts in the investment opportunity set, which otherwise arise. See Merton (1973) and Brennan and Schwartz (1982) for a detailed discussion.

Note that this relationship holds regardless of whether the expectation is defined under the objective measure $\mathbb{P}$ or under the risk-neutral measure $\mathbb{Q}$.

9. For simplicity, we assume here that no management fees are paid to analyze the impact of the various model parameters on the value of the carried interest. Note that the management fees decrease the investment capital by the mechanism shown in Eq. (1) and therefore will also affect the carried interest payments.

10. For simplicity, we assume here that the commitment period T_c is equal to the legal lifetime of the fund T_l, that is, $T_c = T_l$ holds.

11. With its second-order Taylor approximation, the *Milstein scheme* here provides a better approximation of the SDEs compared to the standard *Euler scheme* which is only based on a first-order Taylor approximation. For an arbitrary SDE, $dX_t = \mu(X_t)dt + \sigma(X_t)dB_t$, the Milstein approximation takes the form

$$\Delta X_{k+1} = \mu(X_k)\Delta t + \sigma(X_k)\sqrt{\Delta t}\ \varepsilon_{k+1} + \tfrac{1}{2}\,\sigma(X_k)\sigma'(X_k)\Delta t[(\varepsilon_{k+1})^2 - 1]$$

where ε_{k+1} is a standard normal variable and $\sigma'(X_k) = d\sigma(X_k)/dX_k$ holds. For more details on how to approximate SDEs in discrete-time, see, for example, Glasserman (2003) or Kloeden and Platen (1999).

REFERENCES

Brennan, M., & Schwartz, E. (1982). Consistent regulatory policy under uncertainty. *The Bell Journal of Economics*, *13*(2), 506–521.

Cox, J. C., Ingersoll, J. E., & Ross, S. A. (1985). A theory of the term structure of interest rates. *Econometrica*, *53*(2), 385–408.

Duffie, D. (2001). *Dynamic asset pricing theory* (3rd ed.). Princeton University Press.

Glasserman, P. (2003). *Monte Carlo methods in financial engineering*. Springer.

Gompers, P., & Lerner, J. (1999a). An analysis of compensation in the U.S. venture capital partnership. *Journal of Financial Economics*, *51*(1), 3–44.

Gompers, P., & Lerner, J. (1999b). *The venture capital cycle*. Cambridge: MIT Press.

Kloeden, P. E., & Platen, E. (1999). *Numerical solution of stochastic differential equations*. Springer.

Litvak, K. (2004). Venture capital limited partnership agreements: Understanding compensation arrangements. Working Paper No. 29. University of Texas at Austin, Austin, TX.

Malherbe, E. (2004). Modeling private equity funds and private equity collateralised fund obligations. *International Journal of Theoretical and Applied Finance*, *7*(3), 193–230.

Merton, R. C. (1973). An intertemporal capital asset pricing model. *Econometrica*, *41*(4), 867–888.

Metrick, A., & Yasuda, A. (2010). The economics of private equity funds. *Review of Financial Studies*, *23*(6), 2303–2341.

Phalippou, L. (2007). Investing in private equity funds: A survey. Working Paper. University of Amsterdam, Amsterdam.

APPENDIX

In this appendix we present a numerical solution of valuation Eq. (15) using Monte Carlo simulation of a discrete-time approximation of the stochastic cash flow model presented in the section "Private Equity Fund Dynamics."

In order to implement the Monte Carlo simulation, we divide the time interval $[0,T_l]$ into K discrete intervals each of length Δt. Then, we simulate all relevant quantities at equidistant time points $t_k = k\Delta t$, where $k = 1, \ldots, K$ and $K = T_l/\Delta t$ holds.

Using these definitions, the dynamics of the capital drawdowns, Eq. (3), can be represented in discrete-time by[10]

$$\Delta D_{k+1} = \delta_{k+1} U_k \Delta t \tag{A.1}$$

Similarly, it holds that an appropriate discrete-time specification of the dynamics of the capital distributions, Eq. (6), is given by

$$\Delta R_{k+1} = \rho_{k+1} V_k \Delta t, \quad \text{if} \quad k+1 < K \quad \text{and} \quad \Delta R_k = V_k \tag{A.2}$$

An appropriate scheme for approximating the risk-neutral dynamics of the drawdown and distribution rate, Eqs. (16) and (17), is the *Milstein scheme.*[11] Applying this scheme, it turns out

$$\delta_{k+1} = \delta_k + k_1(\theta_1 - \delta_k)\Delta t + \sigma_1\sqrt{\delta_k \Delta t}\varepsilon_{1,k+1} + \tfrac{1}{4}\sigma_1^2\,\Delta t[(\varepsilon_{1,k+1})^2 - 1] \tag{A.3}$$

$$\rho_{k+1} = \rho_k + k_2(\theta_2 - \rho_k)\Delta t + \sigma_2\sqrt{\rho_k \Delta t}\varepsilon_{2,k+1} + \tfrac{1}{4}\sigma_2^2\,\Delta t[(\varepsilon_{2,k+1})^2 - 1] \tag{A.4}$$

where $\varepsilon_{1,1}, \varepsilon_{2,2}, \ldots, \varepsilon_{1,k}$ and $\varepsilon_{2,1}, \varepsilon_{2,2}, \ldots, \varepsilon_{2,k}$ are *i.i.d.* sequences of standard normal variables that are assumed to be uncorrelated.

Finally, approximating the risk-neutral dynamics of the investment value, Eq. (18), using the *Milstein scheme* gives

$$\begin{aligned} V_{k+1} = {} & V_k[1 + (\mu + \lambda_3\sigma)\Delta t] + \sigma V_k \varepsilon_{3,k+1}\sqrt{\Delta t} + \tfrac{1}{2}\sigma^2 V_k \Delta t[(\varepsilon_{3,k+1})^2 - 1] \\ & - \Delta R_{k+1} + \Delta D_{k+1} \end{aligned} \tag{A.5}$$

where $\varepsilon_{3,1}, \varepsilon_{3,2}, \ldots, \varepsilon_{3,k}$ is a third *i.i.d.* sequence of standard normal variables that is assumed to be uncorrelated with the sequences $\varepsilon_{1,1}, \varepsilon_{2,2}, \ldots, \varepsilon_{1,k}$ and $\varepsilon_{2,1}, \varepsilon_{2,2}, \ldots, \varepsilon_{2,k}$.

Using these discrete-time specifications, the risk-neutral carried interest dynamics (assuming no catch-up) can be approximated by

$$\Delta CI_k = c_{ci} \max\{\Delta R_k - \Delta D_k - \Delta MF_k, 0\} 1_{\{IRR_k > h\}} \tag{A.6}$$

where IRR_k is a solution to

$$\sum_{s=1}^{k} \frac{\Delta R_s - \Delta D_s - \Delta MF_s}{(1 + IRR_k)^s} = 0 \tag{A.7}$$

To numerically solve Eq. (15), consider a Monte Carlo sampling experiment composed of M independent replications of the discrete-time approximations (A.1) to (A.8). Let $\Delta R_{k,i}$ ($\Delta D_{k,i}$) denote the kth observation of the capital distributions (capital drawdowns) in the mth replication. Similarly, $IRR_{k,i}$ denotes the kth observation of the internal rate of return in the mth replication. If the number of simulation iterations M is considerably large, the value of the outstanding carried interest with no catch-up in Eq. (15) can be approximated by computing

$$V_k^{CI} = \frac{1}{M} \sum_{i=1}^{M} \sum_{s=k}^{K} \left[\frac{c_{ci} \max\{\Delta R_{s,i} - \Delta D_{s,i} - \Delta MF_s, 0\} 1_{\{IRR_{s,i} > h\}}}{(1 + r_f \Delta t)^{s-k}} \right] \tag{A.8}$$

Note that the same approach can also be used to determine the value of the outstanding carried interest with a 100 percent catch-up provision. Throughout this chapter, we choose $M = 100{,}000$ simulation iterations to evaluate Eq. (A.8).

AN EQUITY-BASED CREDIT RISK MODEL

Gaia Barone

ABSTRACT

This chapter presents a structural model à la Leland (1994) that is, at the same time, novel, simple, and able to explain the quotes of credit default swaps (CDS), equity, and equity options. The model gives a closed-form formula for the term structure of default probabilities and can be calibrated to fit the CDS spreads. It also offers closed-form formulas for equity, equity volatility, and equity options. Differently from other structural models, debt has been modeled as a perpetual fixed-rate bond, instead of a zero-coupon bond with finite maturity. Therefore, default can happen at any time, and not only at the bond's maturity. The model (which belongs to the class of first-passage models) specifies default as the first time the firm's asset value hits a lower barrier. The barrier is endogenously determined as a solution of an optimal stopping problem (stockholders' equity maximization). Equity is seen as a portfolio that contains a perpetual American option to default and can be valuated by using the results of Rubinstein-Reiner (1991) for barrier options. Equity options are valued by a closed-form formula that requires only an extra parameter (leverage) with respect to the standard input list of Black–Scholes–Merton equation. The formula is consistent with the volatility skew that is generally observed in the equity options markets and can be

Derivative Securities Pricing and Modelling
Contemporary Studies in Economic and Financial Analysis, Volume 94, 351–378

ISSN: 1569-3759/doi:10.1108/S1569-3759(2012)0000094017

used to estimate the firms' implied leverage, as it is perceived by traders. The chapter concludes with an application of the model to the case of Goldman Sachs.

INTRODUCTION

The aim of this chapter is to define a model that allows traders to assess the value of equity and equity/credit derivatives in a unified framework. We propose closed-form formulas that traders could use to evaluate equity, equity options, and credit default swaps (CDS) in a consistent manner. The model can also be used to solve the *inverse problem* that is to extract credit–risk-sensitive information from market quotes. In particular, the model allows to estimate the firm's leverage, as it is perceived by traders.

In *equity option markets*, traders often quote the implied volatilities of European options – calculated according to the Black–Scholes–Merton model – rather than prices. The quotes reflect the shape of the probability distribution of future returns of the underlying asset. The implied volatilities generally decrease as the strike price increases, showing a typical downward-sloping *volatility skew*. This is consistent with the hypothesis that the actual distribution of future returns used by option traders has extra weight on the left tail with respect to the normal distribution of Black–Scholes–Merton model.

One possible explanation for the volatility skew in equity options concerns leverage:

> As a company's equity declines in value, the company's leverage increases. This means that the equity becomes more risky and its volatility increases. As a company's equity increases in value, leverage decreases. The equity then becomes less risky and its volatility decreases. This argument suggest that we can expect the volatility of a stock to be a decreasing function of the stock price ... Hull (2011, p. 415)

To define leverage, we need first to define debt. A useful approach is to assume that the mixture of bonds with different coupons, bank loans, and leases of a firm can be approximated by a single issue of a *perpetual* fixed-rate bond with the same "stochastic duration" of the actual debt.[1] The assumption of a infinitely lived security is not only mathematically convenient but also a good proxy for a short-term debt rolled over again and again as with perpetual floaters. This assumption has been extensively used by Leland (1994, 1995, 2006, 2009).[2] In his model, stockholders have a perpetual American option to default. Our changes with respect to the original Leland model (1994) are in the spirit of Goldstein, Ju, and Leland (2001), where equity depends on the tax rate.

In the markets for *credit default swaps*, the term structure of CDS spreads reflects the expectations of market participants about the firm's default risk for various time horizons (typically 1, 3, 5, 7, 10 years) and the requested (credit/liquidity) premia. The main advantage of our structural model is that the default barrier is *endogenously* given as solution of a stockholders' maximization problem. This allows to derive closed-form formula for default probabilities and credit spreads that make use of the first-passage time distribution function. We do not need to separately estimate ad hoc values of recovery rates.

The structure of the chapter is as follows. First, we characterize the different claims hold by the firm's main *stakeholders*, then we argue that the actual debt can be approximated by a single perpetual-bond equivalent issue and highlight the model's differences with respect to Leland original article. After defining leverage, we show the stochastic nature of equity volatility and derive the term structures of default probabilities and CDS spreads. Then, we derive new formulas for equity options and show how the model's parameters can be estimated by using quotes of equity and equity options. In particular, we show how to use market data to extract the traders' perceptions of a firm's leverage, measured in terms of a single perpetual-bond equivalent issue.

CAPITAL STRUCTURE

The contractual relationships among the various firm's "stakeholders," considered in the Leland model, can be synthesized as in Table 1. The firm's ownership is shared between stockholders, bondholders, third parties (lawyers, accountants, courts, etc.), and the tax authority, which have the right to receive the share θ of the firm's earnings (θ is the tax rate). The assets' value, V, is divided in two parts: θV to the tax authority and $(1-\theta)V$ to the other stakeholders.

Stockholders issue a perpetual bond with nominal value Z, coupon $C=rZ$, and market value B. Because of firm's limited liability, they have an option to default that is the (perpetual) right to sell the assets at price Z to the bondholders. In other terms, they have a perpetual American put option, with strike Z and market value P, written on V.

When $V=V_b$, stockholders exercise their option to default. This prevents equity's value to become negative. When the (put) option is exercised,

Table 1. Contracts Between Stakeholders.

Contracts	Stakeholders			
	Stockholders	Bondholders	Third parties	Tax authority
Firm's assets	V_0	–	–	–
Risk-free bond	$-Z$	Z	–	–
Option to default	$P \equiv (Z-V_b)\, p_b$	$-P \equiv -(Z-V_b)\, p_b$	–	–
Bankruptcy security	–	$-A \equiv -\alpha\, V_b\, p_b$	$A \equiv \alpha\, V_b\, p_b$	–
Tax claims	$-G_S \equiv -\theta\,(V_0-Z+P)$	$-G_B = -\theta\,(Z-P-A)$	$-G_U \equiv -\theta\, A$	$G_0 \equiv G_S+G_B+G_U$
Total	$S_0 \equiv (1-\theta)\,(V_0-Z+P)$	$B_0 \equiv (1-\theta)\,(Z-P-A)$	$U_0 \equiv (1-\theta)\, A$	$G_0 \equiv \theta\, V_0$

Note: p_b is the value of a *perpetual* first-touch digital option that pays $1 when $V=V_b$ at default time τ.

stockholders sell the firm's assets, whose value is V_b, and receive Z from bondholders. Such a bankruptcy triggers the execution of another contract. When the firm defaults, third parties claim a share α of the firm.

Therefore, the contracts "negotiated" among the various parties are as follows:

1. *Stockholders* use their own capital to buy the firm's assets. Assets, whose current value is V_0, can be tangible and intangible (including human capital);
2. *Tax Authority* claims a share θ of the firm's assets as soon as the firm is created (the *Tax Authority* is a "special partner" of *stockholders*);
3. *Bondholders* buy a perpetual fixed-rate bond from stockholders. The face value of the *corporate bond*, with coupon C, is Z. The bond contains two embedded options: a short perpetual option to default in favor of *stockholders*, and a short perpetual digital option (or *bankruptcy security*) in favor of *third parties*. The option to default, with strike Z, is optimally exercised at the default time τ, when $V=V_b$. The perpetual digital option, with barrier V_b, offers a rebate αV_b $(0<\alpha<1)$ at τ. As soon as the bond is issued, the tax burden θV_0 is redistributed among the three firm's claimants, to include the newcomers (bondholders and third parties).

The current values of the four securities (stock, corporate bond, bankruptcy security, tax claim) are, respectively, S_0, B_0, U_0, G_0.

Here we assume that individuals (stockholders, bondholders, third parties) are taxed at the same effective rate, θ. Besides, we assume that stockholders, bondholders, third parties are taxed, respectively, only when dividends, interests, and fees are paid. This means, in particular, that – in order to avoid double taxation – retained earnings are not taxed.[3]

Stakeholders

The *Tax Authority* is long on a simple linear contract, with current value

$$G_0 = \theta V_0 \tag{1}$$

This is the result of three claims:

1. A claim toward stockholders, with current value $G_S = \theta(V_0 - Z + P)$;
2. A claim toward bondholders, with current value $G_B = \theta(Z - P - A)$;
3. A claim toward third parties, with current value $G_U = \theta A$.

Third parties (lawyers, etc.) have a portfolio with current value

$$U_0 = (1 - \theta)A \tag{2}$$

They are

1. Long on a perpetual *bankruptcy security*, with current value A.
2. Short on the tax claim $G_U \equiv \theta A$.

Bondholders have a portfolio with current value

$$B_0 = (1 - \theta)(Z - P - A) \tag{3}$$

They are

1. Long on a perpetual *risk-free bond*, with constant value Z.
2. Short on a perpetual *option to default*, with current value P.
3. Short on a perpetual *bankruptcy security*, with current value A.
4. Short on the tax claim $G_B = \theta(Z - P - A)$.

Finally, *stockholders* have a portfolio with current value

$$S_0 = (1 - \theta)(V_0 - Z + P) \tag{4}$$

They are

1. Long on the firm's assets, with current value V_0.
2. Short on a perpetual *risk-free bond*, with constant value Z.
3. Long on a perpetual *option to default*, with current value P.
4. Short on the tax claim $G_S = \theta(V_0 - Z + P)$.

Note that the total value of liabilities, $S_0 + B_0 + U_0 + G_0$, should be equal to the value of the firm's assets, V_0:

$$S_0 + B_0 + U_0 + G_0 = (1-\theta)(V_0 - Z + P) + (1-\theta)(Z - P - A) + (1-\theta)A + \theta V_0 = V_0 \quad (5)$$

Dynamics of Assets' Value

The dynamics for the value, V, of the firm's assets is described by a diffusion-type stochastic process with stochastic differential equation

$$dV = (\mu_V - q_V)V dt + \sigma_V V\, dz$$

where

μ_V is the instantaneous expected rate of return on the firm per unit time;
q_V is the payout rate (to shareholders, bondholders and Tax Authority);
σ_V is the asset volatility (i.e., the standard deviation of the assets' rate of return per unit of time);
dz is a standard Wiener process.

Because of Merton's hedging argument, the price, f, of any time-insensitive derivative with no intermediate payments (as the *perpetual option to default* or the *bankruptcy security*) should satisfy the following differential equation

$$\frac{1}{2}\frac{d^2 f}{dV^2}\sigma_V^2 V^2 + (r - q_V)V\frac{df}{dV} - rf = 0$$

where r is the risk-free interest rate.

In this context, it is appropriate to note that Merton's hedging argument *does* hold even if all of the firm's assets are not tradable nor observable. Although V may not be the value of a traded asset, trading of equity (or other contingent claims) allows use of V as the state variable:

> To understand the intuition of the replication argument, consider an analogy with an ordinary stock option model. Fundamentally, the option can be priced precisely because we can replicate its payoff using the stock and risk free bonds. However, we can just as well value the stock by replicating its payoff using the (traded) option. In the same fashion, we can value the firm's assets using stocks and risk free bonds. Ericsson and Reneby (2002, p. 5)

Under the assumption of a geometric Brownian motion for V, we can price the contracts negotiated by the various stakeholders.

Contracts

The current value, A, of the *bankruptcy security* is equal to

$$A = \alpha V_b p_b \tag{6}$$

where

α is the ratio between (direct and indirect) bankruptcy costs and the market value of assets prior to bankruptcy;[4]
V_b is the optimal default trigger, chosen by stockholders to maximize the value of equity:[5]

$$V_b = Z \frac{\gamma_2}{\gamma_2 - 1} \tag{7}$$

p_b is the value of a *perpetual* first-touch digital option that pays \$1 when $V = V_b$:[6]

$$p_b = \left(\frac{V_0}{V_b}\right)^{\gamma_2} \tag{8}$$

γ_2 is the elasticity of the perpetual first-touch digital option with respect to V:

$$\gamma_2 = \frac{-(r - q_V - \sigma_V^2/2) - \sqrt{(r - q_V - \sigma_V^2/2)^2 + 2\sigma_V^2 r}}{\sigma_V^2}$$

Z is the constant value of a *perpetual risk-free bond*:

$$Z = \frac{C}{r} \tag{9}$$

C is the instantaneous coupon per year of a *perpetual risk-free bond.*

The current value, P, of the *option to default* is equal to[7]

$$P = (Z - V_b) p_b \tag{10}$$

Therefore, substituting Eq. (10) into Eq. (4) gives the current value, S_0, of equity as

$$S_0 \equiv (1 - \theta)\left[V_0 - Z + (Z - V_b)\left(\frac{V_0}{V_b}\right)^{\gamma_2}\right] \tag{11}$$

Payouts

The model does not allow the firm to change its business risk, measured by σ_V, which is a constant, but allows for the liquidation of assets to make interest, dividend, and tax payments. The firm's payout policy is defined by q_V

$$\begin{aligned} q_V V &= \text{net interests} + \text{net dividends} + \text{taxes} \\ &= \text{gross interests} + \text{gross dividends} \\ &= q_B \frac{B}{1-\theta} + q_S \frac{S}{1-\theta} \end{aligned} \tag{12}$$

where

q_B is the before-tax bond yield

$$q_B = r\frac{(1-\theta)Z}{B} \tag{13}$$

q_S is the before-tax dividend yield.

The payout rate, q_V, determines the cash flow $q_V V$ that is taken out of the assets of the firm. What is left out of this cash flow (after paying interest on debt) is paid out to shareholders as dividends. If $q_V V$ is insufficient to cover coupons on the bonds, shareholders receive a negative dividend (i.e., contribute additional cash to the firm). A negative dividend (a cash-flow crisis) does not mean that that it is optimal to default: Expected future cash flows could be sufficiently high to induce stockholders to keep the firm alive.

Default Point and Renegotiation

Stockholders have to determine the optimal default point, V_b. We will suppose that V_b is not affected by renegotiation. Renegotiation is suboptimal, for both stockholders and bondholders.

> A natural question at this point is, if the firm is bankrupt at time *T*, why should the bondholders not renegotiate the contract in hopes that subsequent good fortune would allow the firm to pay them in full? The answer should be clear. Under the current contract they have the right to receive all the assets of the firm. Why should they settle for less? If the firm is fortunate, they can have all of the profits rather than sharing them. Of course, they would renegotiate if the shareholders made the right concession – add

> more money to the firm. However, they would have to add enough to make up the bankruptcy shortfall plus an amount equal to whatever claim on the refinanced firm they would like to own. But again, why should they do that? It would cost more than the value they would receive in return. Ingersoll (1987, p. 419)

Therefore, we will assume that, if bankruptcy occurs, bondholders receive all assets (*after costs*) and stockholders none.

The optimal default point, V_b, is chosen by stockholders as the level of V that maximizes the value of equity. By Eq. (11), maximizing S_0 with respect to V_b gives

$$V_b = Z\frac{\gamma_2}{\gamma_2 - 1} \tag{14}$$

Greeks

By Eq. (4), the value of equity is

$$S_0 \equiv (1-\theta)(V_0 - Z + P) \tag{15}$$

and, by Eqs. (10) and (8), the value of the perpetual option to default is

$$P = (Z - V_b)\left(\frac{V_0}{V_b}\right)^{\gamma_2}$$

Therefore, the delta, Δ_P, and gamma, Γ_P, of the perpetual option to default are

$$\Delta_P \equiv \frac{\partial P}{\partial V} = \gamma_2 \frac{P}{V}$$
$$\Gamma_P = \frac{d^2P}{dV^2} = \frac{\gamma_2(\gamma_2 - 1)P}{V^2} \tag{16}$$

and the delta, Δ_S, and gamma, Γ_S, of equity are

$$\Delta_S \equiv \frac{dS}{dV} = (1-\theta)(1+\Delta_P)$$
$$\Gamma_S \equiv \frac{d^2S}{dV^2} = (1-\theta)\Gamma_P \tag{17}$$

By taking the limits of Δ_S for $V \to V_b$ and $V \to \infty$, we can see that $0 \leq \Delta_S <$ $(1-\theta)$. Besides, $\Gamma_S > 0$. Therefore, S is a convex function of V, consistently with the "option-like" nature of equity. Fig. 1 reports equity, S, as a function of asset's value, V, for different levels of debt's notional value, Z.

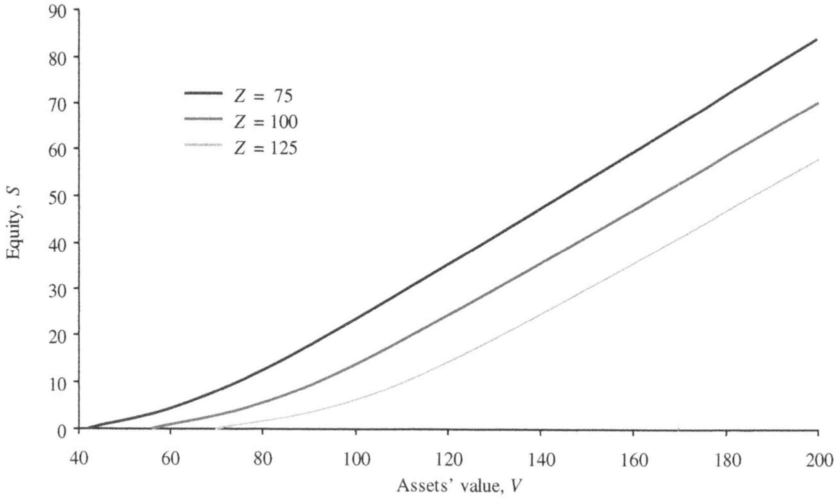

Fig. 1. Equity, S, as a Function of Asset's Value, V, for Different Levels of Debt's Face Value, Z ($r=4\%$, $q_V=6\%$, $\sigma_V=10\%$, $\theta=35\%$, $\alpha=5\%$).

Leverage

We define leverage, L, as the ratio between the nongovernment value, $(1-\theta)V$, of firm's assets and the value, S, of equity:

$$L = \frac{(1-\theta)V}{S} \tag{18}$$

Substituting Eq. (15) into Eq. (18) and taking the limits of L for $V \to \infty$ and $V \to V_b$ shows that $1 < L < +\infty$.

Equity Volatility

By Itô's lemma, the equity volatility, σ_S, is

$$\sigma_S = \frac{\Delta_S V \sigma_V}{S} \tag{19}$$

Substituting Eqs. (16)–(18) into Eq. (19) gives

$$\sigma_S = \left(1 + \gamma_2 \frac{P}{V}\right) L \sigma_V \tag{20}$$

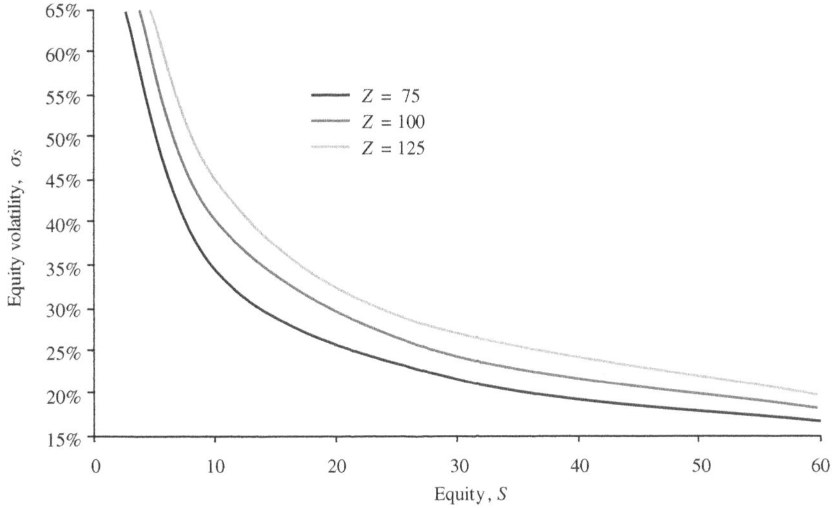

Fig. 2. Equity Volatility, σ_S, as a Function of Equity's Value, S, for Different Levels of Debt's Face Value, Z ($r=4\%$, $q_V=6\%$, $\sigma_V=10\%$, $\theta=35\%$, $\alpha=5\%$).

Eq. (20) reveals the stochastic nature of equity volatility, which is a complex function of V.[8] Taking the limits of σ_S for $V\rightarrow\infty$ and $V\rightarrow V_b$ shows that $\sigma_V<\sigma_S<+\infty$.

Fig. 2 reports equity volatility, σ_S, as a function of equity's value, S, for different levels of debt's nominal value, Z.

The Case for Debt with Infinite-Maturity

A fundamental property of the Leland model is that debt is approximated by a single perpetual bond. While equity is simply a perpetual, residual claim on firm's assets, debt is much more difficult to define in general terms. It can be devised in various ways.

Often debt has a finite maturity, but this is not always the case. Leland (1994) assumes that it has an infinite maturity:

> Very long time horizons for fixed obligations are not new, either in theory or in practice. The original Modigliani and Miller (1958) argument assumes debt with infinite maturity. Merton (1974) and Black and Cox (1976) look at infinite maturity debt in an explicitly dynamic model. Since 1752 the Bank of England has, on occasion, issued Consols, bonds promising a fixed coupon with no final maturity date. And preferred stock typically pays a fixed dividend without time limit. Leland (1994, p. 1215)

Debt can be coupon-bearing or have no coupon, can be repaid by amortization or by a balloon payment at maturity, can pay a fixed, variable or step (mixed) interest, can be assisted by option-like covenants (in favor of the issuer or the holder), can include not-paid salaries and delayed payments to suppliers, can have different priority and subordination in the event of dissolution of the firm. Last, but not least, debt is always embedded in derivatives contracts that the firm could have entered into. The debt embedded in derivatives contracts can be extremely relevant:

> Long-Term Capital Management used its \$2.2 billion in capital from investors as collateral to buy \$125 billion in securities, and then used those securities as collateral to enter into exotic financial transactions valued at \$1.25 trillion. Kahn and Truell (1998)

In the well-known Moody's KMV approach, the reference debt – used to define the "default point" – is simply equal to the short-term liabilities plus half of long-term liabilities, both measured in nominal, accounting, book units.[9]

Over time, the firm's financial structure (leverage, maturity, etc.) changes. Debt can be rolled-over into other longer-maturity loans. In particular, firms can use revolving credit lines or loan commitments – made by a bank or other financial institution – to increase the flexibility of their financial structure.

Theoretically, firms can roll-over their debt an infinite number of times. This makes reasonable to approximate the actual debt structure with a unique perpetual *fixed-rate* bond, as in Merton (1974), Black-Cox (1976), Leland (1994), Goldstein et al. (2001), and many other papers.[10]

From a theoretical standpoint, the time independency of perpetual securities assures that the firm's capital structure does not change abruptly over time, thus simplifying the analysis.[11]

From an empirical standpoint, the assumption of a single perpetual issue is an important advantage with respect to models that assume a finite-maturity debt, because there is no need to estimate the debt's maturity parameter, T.[12]

Differences with Respect to Leland's Original Model

The firm's capital structure we defined is different from that used by Leland (1994) in his original article. As in Leland, the value of equity, S, does not depend on the parameter α, which measures bankruptcy costs. However, differently from Leland, equity *does* depend on the effective tax rate, θ.

The definitions of debt, D, and equity, E, used by Leland (1994, Eqs. (7) and (13)) can be obtained, respectively, by merging the claims of bondholders with the claims of the Tax Authority towards bondholders and by merging the claims of stockholders with the claim of the Tax Authority towards stockholders plus "the value of the tax deduction of coupon payments," $TB(V) = \theta Z(1{-}p_b)$.

By Table 1 and Eqs. (8) and (10):

$$\begin{aligned} D &\equiv B_0 + G_B \\ &= (1-\theta)(Z-P-A) + \theta(Z-P-A) \\ &= Z-P-A \\ &= Z-(Z-V_b)p_b - \alpha V_b p_b \\ &= Z+[(1-\alpha)V_b - Z]p_b \\ &= Z+[(1-\alpha)V_b - Z]\left(\frac{V_0}{V_b}\right)^{\gamma_2} \end{aligned}$$

and

$$\begin{aligned} E &\equiv S_0 + G_S + \theta Z(1-p_b) \\ &= (1-\theta)(V_0 - Z + P) + \theta(V_0 - Z + P) + \theta Z(1-p_b) \\ &= V_0 - Z + P + \theta Z(1-p_b) \\ &= V_0 - Z + (Z - V_b)p_b + \theta Z(1-p_b) \\ &= V_0 - (1-\theta)Z + [(1-\theta)Z - V_b]p_b \\ &= V_0 - (1-\theta)Z + [(1-\theta)Z - V_b]\left(\frac{V_0}{V_b}\right)^{\gamma_2} \end{aligned}$$

Our stricter definition of equity, S_0, is equal to the definition of equity, E_{solv}, used by Goldstein et al. (2001), Eq. (19).[13] Some of the consequences of our different approach, with respect to Leland (1994), are

1. The value of equity *does* depend on the tax rate θ.[14]
2. The default trigger, V_b, is different from (higher than) the default trigger obtained by Leland.
3. It is not possible to derive an optimal capital structure by balancing tax advantages with potential default costs.

Another consequence is that – for evaluating equity options – we cannot use the formulas derived *within* the original Leland model.

DEFAULT PROBABILITIES AND CDS SPREADS

Default Probabilities

Let $Q(T)$ denote the probability of default between time 0 and time T (included). This is equal to the probability that V reaches V_b before T (or in T). Therefore, $Q(T)$ is equal to the first-passage time distribution function:[15]

$$Q(T) = N(-z_1) + \left(\frac{V_0}{V_b}\right)^{2(1-\lambda)} N(-z_2) \tag{21}$$

where

$$z_1 = \frac{\ln(V_0/V_b) + (r - q_V - \sigma_V^2/2)T}{\sigma\sqrt{T}}$$

$$z_2 = \frac{\ln(V_0/V_b) - (r - q_V - \sigma_V^2/2)T}{\sigma\sqrt{T}}$$

$$\lambda = 1 + \frac{r - q_V - \sigma_V^2/2}{\sigma_V^2}$$

Eq. (21) gives the term structure of unconditional (cumulative) default probabilities and allows an easy calculation of the term structure of conditional default probabilities (or *hazard rates/default intensities*).

Table 2 shows that, by using the *actual* drift rate μ_V instead of r, the model can be calibrated to fit the term structures of *actual* default probabilities.[16] In the table, historical default frequencies calculated by Moody's for different rating classes have been reported together with theoretical default probabilities obtained for different values of the model's parameters Z and σ_V.

CDS Spreads

Standard single-name CDS, where the protection buyer makes periodic payments and has the right to sell at par the bonds issued by the reference entity, can be priced in the framework given by the model.[17]

To explain the calculations, let us consider a n-year CDS whose payment dates are at times t_i $(1 \leq i \leq m \times n)$, where m is the number of payments per year. The value, A_1, of an annuity that pays $1/m$ at each payment date until default, τ, or maturity, $T = t_{m\times n}$, whichever comes first, is

Table 2. Default Probabilities.

Rating	Maturity (years)								
	1	2	3	4	5	7	10	15	20
Actual Default Probabilities (%)									
Aaa	0.000	0.012	0.012	0.037	0.105	0.245	0.497	0.927	1.102
Aa	0.022	0.059	0.091	0.159	0.234	0.384	0.542	1.150	2.465
A	0.051	0.165	0.341	0.520	0.717	1.179	2.046	3.572	5.934
Baa	0.176	0.494	0.912	1.404	1.926	2.996	4.851	8.751	12.327
Ba	1.166	3.186	5.583	8.123	10.397	14.318	19.964	29.703	37.173
B	4.546	10.426	16.188	21.256	25.895	34.473	44.377	56.098	62.478
Caa	17.723	29.384	38.682	46.094	52.286	59.771	71.376	77.545	80.211

Rating	Maturity (years)										
	1	2	3	4	5	7	10	15	20	Z	σ_V (%)
Theoretical Default Probabilities (%)											
Aaa	0.000	0.001	0.015	0.057	0.127	0.316	0.614	0.992	1.220	60	11.5
Aa	0.000	0.005	0.051	0.159	0.314	0.683	1.208	1.829	2.196	65	12.0
A	0.001	0.106	0.461	0.973	1.530	2.567	3.766	4.991	5.658	70	12.5
Baa	0.210	2.036	4.528	6.858	8.860	11.970	15.092	18.097	19.768	80	15.0
Ba	1.933	8.363	14.220	18.859	22.533	27.943	33.240	38.468	41.594	90	20.0
B	4.708	16.491	26.138	33.488	39.216	47.592	55.841	64.196	69.418	110	35.0
Caa	13.644	30.656	41.560	49.063	54.588	62.289	69.526	76.567	80.829	140	40.0

Source: Moody's (1970–2009).
Note: The theoretical default probabilities are based on Eq. (21), where the risk-free interest rate r has been replaced with the *actual* drift rate μ_V. The model's parameters are $V=100$, $\mu_V=5\%$, $q_V=0\%$, $\theta=35\%$, $\alpha=5\%$ (the values of Z and σ_V are a function of the rating class).

$$A_1 = \frac{1}{m}\sum_{i=1}^{m\times n} e^{-y_i t_i}[1 - Q(t_i)] \tag{22}$$

where y_i is the risk-free interest rate for maturity t_i and $Q(t_i)$ is the default probability given by Eq. (21).

We assume "instant recovery." In other terms, we assume that – at default time, τ – the protection buyer receives an instant payment equal to 1–R, where the recovery rate R is *endogenously* given by the following formula:

$$R = \frac{(1-\alpha)V_b}{Z} \tag{23}$$

Substituting Eq. (14) into Eq. (23), the instant payoff 1–R to the protection buyer is equal to

$$1 - R = \frac{1 - \alpha\gamma_2}{1 - \gamma_2}$$

The present value of the payoff is

$$(1 - R)p_b(T) \tag{24}$$

where $p_b(T)$ is the value of a *T-maturity* first-touch digital option, which pays a unit *at time* τ ($\tau \leq T$) if the firm defaults at τ.

Generally, CDS specify that the protection buyer must, at default, pay the CDS spread that has accrued since the last coupon date. In order to take this accrual payment into account, we subtract one-half of the regular payment from the instant payoff 1–R:

> For reasonably small default probabilities and intercoupon periods, the expected difference in time between the credit event and the previous coupon date is just slightly less than one-half, in expectation, of the length of an intercoupon period, assuming that the default risk is not concentrated at a coupon date. Thus, for purposes of pricing in all but extreme cases, one can think of the credit swap as equivalent to payment at default of face value less recovery value less one-half of the regular default-swap premium payment. Duffie-Singleton (2003, pp. 183–184)

Therefore, the present value, A_2, of the *net* CDS payoff is

$$A_2 = \left[(1 - R) - \frac{1}{2}\frac{s}{m}\right]p_b(T) \tag{25}$$

where s is the CDS spread per year.

The CDS contract is fair when the present value, sA_1, of the payments equals the present value, A_2, of the net payoff, or

$$sA_1 = A_2 \tag{26}$$

By substituting Eqs. (22) and (25) into Eq. (26),

$$s = \frac{(1 - R)p_b(T)}{(1/m)\{(1/2)p_b(T) + \sum_{i=1}^{m\times n} e^{-y_i t_i}[1 - Q(t_i)]\}} \tag{27}$$

where the value, $p_b(T)$, of a finite-maturity first-touch digital option, with barrier $V_b < V_0$, has been derived by Rubinstein and Reiner (1991) as:

$$p_b(T) = \left(\frac{V_b}{V_0}\right)^{a+b} N(-z) + \left(\frac{V_b}{V_0}\right)^{a-b} N(-z + 2b\sigma_V\sqrt{T}) \tag{28}$$

with

$$z \equiv \frac{\ln(V_b/V_0)}{\sigma_V\sqrt{T}} + b\sigma_V\sqrt{T} \quad a \equiv \frac{r - q_V - \sigma_V^2/2}{\sigma_V^2} \quad b \equiv \frac{\sqrt{(r - q_V - \sigma_V^2/2)^2 + 2\sigma_V^2 r}}{\sigma_V^2}$$

It can be shown that Eq. (28) converges to Eq. (8) when $T \to \infty$.

EQUITY OPTIONS

Similarly to Toft (1994), Toft and Prucyk (1997), and Barone (2011), we can derive the value, c, of a European call, with strike K and maturity T, written on S as:

$$\begin{aligned} c &= e^{-rT}E(S_T - K | V_T > V_T^* \cap V_t > V_b) \times \text{Prob}(V_T > V_T^* \cap V_t > V_b) \\ &= (1 - \theta)(V_{\text{doc}} + P_{\text{uop}} - ZR_{\text{doc}}) - KR_{\text{doc}} \end{aligned} \tag{29}$$

where

V_{doc} is the value of a down-and-out asset-or-nothing call, with strike V_T^* and barrier V_b, which pays V_T at time T if $V_T > V_T^*$ and $V_t > V_b$ $(0 < t \leq T)$:

$$V_{\text{doc}} = V_0 e^{-q_V T}\left[N(x) - \left(\frac{V_b}{V_0}\right)^{2\lambda} N(y)\right]$$

P_{uop} is the value of an up-and-out asset-or-nothing put, with strike P_T^* and barrier P_b, which pays P_T at time T if $P_T < P_T^*$ and $P_t < P_b$:

$$P_{\text{uop}} = P_0\left[N(-x_P) - \left(\frac{P_b}{P_0}\right)^{2\lambda_P} N(-y_P)\right]$$

R_{doc} is the value of a down-and-out cash-or-nothing call, with strike V_T^*, barrier V_b and unit rebate R, which pays $R = \$1$ in T if $V_T > V_T^*$ and $V_t > V_b$:

$$R_{\text{doc}} = e^{-rT}\left[N(x - \sigma_V\sqrt{T})\left(\frac{V_b}{V_0}\right)^{2\lambda - 2} N(y - \sigma_V\sqrt{T})\right]$$

V_T^* is the critical asset value that makes the call finish at the money;

$$V_T^* = V_0 e^{(r - q_V - \sigma_V^2/2)T + \varepsilon^* \sigma_V \sqrt{T}}$$

P_T^* is the value of the perpetual first-touch digital when $V = V_T^*$;

$$P_T^* = P_0 e^{(r - \sigma_P^2/2)T - \varepsilon^* \sigma_P \sqrt{T}}$$

ε^* is the standardized normal shock that makes the equity call finish at the money;
$N(\cdot)$ is the standard normal distribution function;

and

$$x \equiv \frac{\ln(V_0/V_T^*)}{\sigma_V\sqrt{T}} + \lambda\sigma_V\sqrt{T} \quad x_P \equiv \frac{\ln(P_0/P_T^*)}{\sigma_P\sqrt{T}} + \lambda_P\sigma_P\sqrt{T}$$

$$y \equiv \frac{\ln[V_b^2/(V_0V_T^*)]}{\sigma_V\sqrt{T}} + \lambda\sigma_V\sqrt{T} \quad y_P \equiv \frac{\ln[P_b^2/(P_0P_T^*)]}{\sigma_P\sqrt{T}} + \lambda_P\sigma_P\sqrt{T}$$

$$\lambda \equiv 1 + \frac{r + q_V - \sigma_V^2/2}{\sigma_V^2} \quad \lambda_P \equiv 1 + \frac{r - \sigma_P^2/2}{\sigma_P^2} \quad \sigma_P = -\gamma_2\sigma_V$$

Under the hypothesis that – if the firm defaults at τ – the buyer receives K at T (and not at τ), the value, p, of a European put, with strike K and maturity T, written on S is

$$\begin{aligned} p &= e^{-rT}E[K - S_T | V_T < V_T^* \cap V_t > V_b] \times \text{Prob}(V_T < V_T^* \cap V_t > V_b) \\ &\quad + E[e^{-rT}K | V_t \leq V_b] \times \text{Prob}(V_t \leq V_b) \\ &= K(R_{\text{dop}} + R_{\text{di}}) + (1-\theta)(ZR_{\text{dop}} - V_{\text{dop}} - P_{\text{uoc}}) \end{aligned} \tag{30}$$

where

R_{dop} is the value of a down-and-out cash-or-nothing put, with strike V_T^*, barrier V_b and unit rebate R, written on V, which pays $R = \$1$ at time T if $V_T < V_T^*$ and $V_t > V_b$ $(0 < t \leq T)$:

$$\begin{aligned} R_{\text{dop}} &= e^{-rT}[N(-x + \sigma_V\sqrt{T}) - N(-x_1 + \sigma_V\sqrt{T})] \\ &\quad + e^{-rT}\left(\frac{V_b}{V_0}\right)^{2\lambda-2}[N(y - \sigma_V\sqrt{T}) - N(y_1 - \sigma_V\sqrt{T})] \end{aligned}$$

V_{dop} is the value of a down-and-out asset-or-nothing put, with strike V_T^* and barrier V_b, written on V, which pays V_T at time T if $V_T < V_T^*$ and $V_t > V_b$:

$$V_{\text{dop}} = V_0e^{-q_VT}\left\{N(-x) - N(-x_1) + \left(\frac{V_b}{V_0}\right)^{2\lambda}[N(y) - N(y_1)]\right\}$$

P_{uoc} is the value of an up-and-out asset-or-nothing call, with strike P_T^* and barrier P_b, written on P, which pays P_T at time T if $P_T > P_T^*$ and $P_t < P_b$:

$$P_{\mathrm{uoc}} = P_0\left\{N(x_P) - N(x_{1P}) + \left(\frac{P_b}{P_0}\right)^{2\lambda_P}[N(-y_P) - N(-y_{1P})]\right\}$$

R_{di} is the value of a down-and-in (*at expiry*) cash-or-nothing, with barrier V_b and unit rebate R, written on V, which pays $R = \$1$ at time T if $V_t \leq V_b$ $(0 < t \leq T)$:

$$R_{\mathrm{di}} = e^{-rT}\left[N(-x_1 + \sigma_V\sqrt{T}) + \left(\frac{V_b}{V_0}\right)^{2\lambda-2} N(y_1 - \sigma_V\sqrt{T})\right]$$

and

$$x_1 \equiv \frac{\ln(V_0/V_b)}{\sigma_V\sqrt{T}} + \lambda\sigma_V\sqrt{T} \quad x_{1P} \equiv \frac{\ln(P_0/P_b)}{\sigma_P\sqrt{T}} + \lambda_P\sigma_P\sqrt{T}$$

$$y_1 \equiv \frac{\ln(V_b/V_0)}{\sigma_V\sqrt{T}} + \lambda\sigma_V\sqrt{T} \quad y_{1P} \equiv \frac{\ln(P_b/P_0)}{\sigma_P\sqrt{T}} + \lambda_P\sigma_P\sqrt{T}$$

Put-Call Parity

Formulas (29) and (30) satisfy the following put-call parity

$$c - p = (1 - \theta)S_{\mathrm{do}} - Ke^{-rT}$$

where

S_{do} is the value of a down-and-out asset-or-nothing, with barrier 0, written on S, which pays S_T at time T if $S_t > 0$ $(0 < t \leq T)$:

$$S_{\mathrm{do}} = V_{\mathrm{do}} + P_{\mathrm{uo}} - ZR_{\mathrm{do}}$$

and

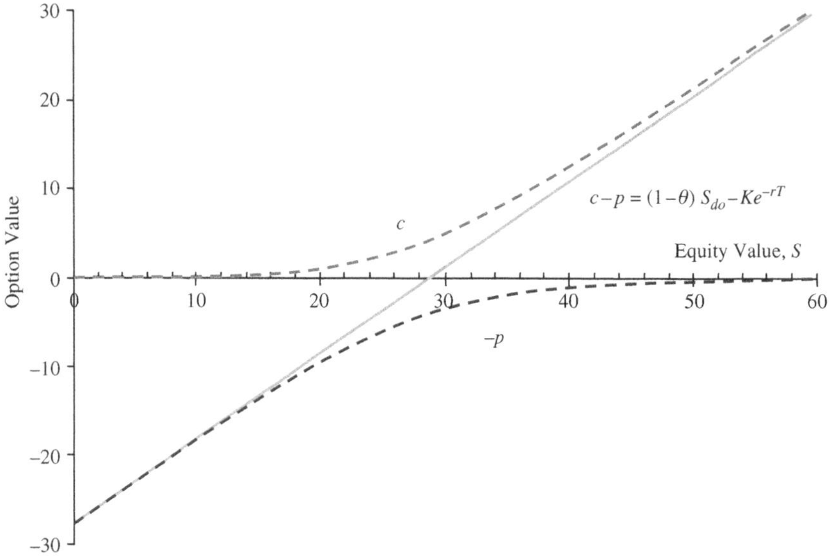

Fig. 3. Equity Put-Call Parity ($r = 5.5\%$, $q_V = 3.5\%$, $\sigma_V = 20\%$, $Z = 50$, $\theta = 35\%$, $V_b = 31.19$, $K = 30$, $T = 1$).

$$V_{\text{do}} = V_0 e^{-q_V T}\left[N(x_1) - \left(\frac{V_b}{V_0}\right)^{2\lambda} N(y_1)\right]$$

$$P_{\text{uo}} = P_0\left[N(-x_{1P}) - \left(\frac{P_b}{P_0}\right)^{2\lambda_P} N(-y_{1P})\right]$$

$$R_{\text{do}} = e^{-rT}\left[N(x_1 - \sigma_V\sqrt{T}) - \left(\frac{V_b}{V_0}\right)^{2\lambda-2} N(y_1 - \sigma_V\sqrt{T})\right]$$

and the other variables have already been defined.

Fig. 3 shows the values of call and put options, as a function of the equity value, for some model's parameters. The chart also shows the put-call parity relationship, measured by the difference *c–p*.

AN APPLICATION: GOLDMAN SACHS

In the third section, Table 2 showed the solution of an *inverse problem*: the calculation of *implied* default probabilities based on *actual* default probabilities reported by Moody's for some rating classes.

Here we show how to solve another inverse problem: the model's calibration based on the spreads of CDS and the quotes of equity and equity options. We considered market daily data on Goldman Sachs (GS). On July 29, 2011, the latest available date, we observed CDS spreads, options quotes, equity, and equity volatility. The implied volatilities of CBOE options quotes of GS exhibit the usual downward-sloping relationship with respect to strike prices (Fig. 4), which confirms the negative correlation between historical volatility and stock prices (Fig. 5).

After fixing θ, α, and r, we estimated the other model's parameters (V, Z, q_V, σ_V), by minimizing a loss function defined as the sum of weighted squared *log* differences between actual and theoretical values of CDS spreads, call options' quotes, equity, and equity volatility.[18]

Log differences have been used because CDS spreads, options' quotes, equity, and equity volatility are measured in different units (and have different levels). Weights allow for the *perfect fit* of single contracts. The calibration's results are shown in Table 3.

The model fit is good enough. However, the valuations made in the market for 3–10 year CDS seem to be relatively optimistic about the future of GS and the out-of-the-money longer-term equity options seem to be

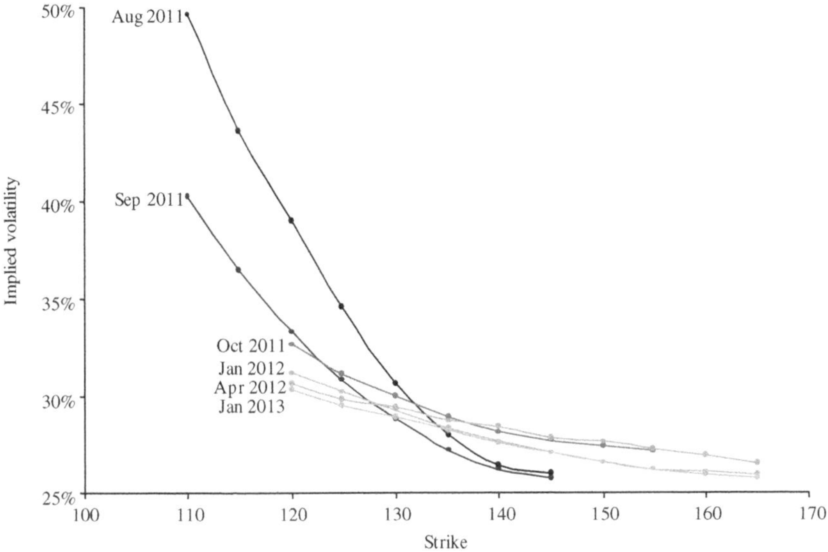

Fig. 4. CBOE Options Quotes of Goldman Sachs: Implied Volatilities (July 29, 2011).

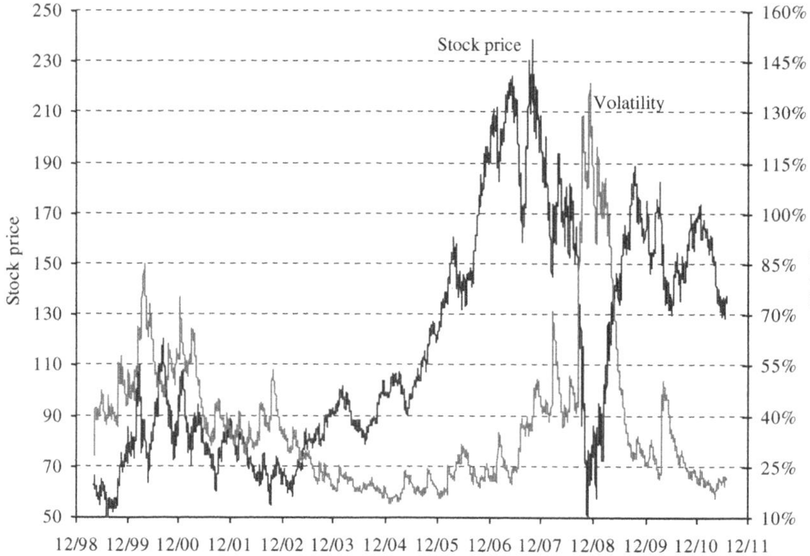

Fig. 5. Goldman Sachs: Stock Price and Historical Volatility (EWMA: $\lambda = 0.96$).

relatively cheap.[19] If one trusts the model, there should have been room for convergence trading.

CONCLUSIONS

This chapter proposes an integrated continuous-time structural model for the consistent pricing of a firm's liabilities (debt as equity) as well as of some key derivative securities (equity, equity options and CDS). The underlying model is essentially that of Leland (1994). In this model, the firm obtains a stochastic stream of cash flows from its operations (modeled as a geometric Brownian motion) and has liabilities consisting of perpetual coupon bonds and equity. Residual cash flows after interest and taxes are distributed as dividends to the shareholders. If the cash flows are insufficient to cover interest and taxes, the shareholders have the option of either defaulting or contributing additional equity. The decision of whether to default or not is made optimally by the shareholders taking into account expected future cash flows should the firm continue its operations, that is by solving an optimal stopping problem. Since interest payments are made continuously

Table 3. Goldman Sachs: Model's Calibration.

Current Date	Maturity	Zero Rate	Default Prob.	Survival Prob.	Default Intensity	Actual Spread	Theoret. Spread	Squared Error
t	$T-t$	r	Q	$1-Q$	λ	s_{mkt}	s	$\ln(s_{mkt}/s)^2$
CDS								
7/29/11	1	0.445%	1.02%	98.98%	1.03%	57	27	53.73%
	3	0.854%	18.14%	81.86%	6.67%	116	167	13.38%
	5	1.648%	34.49%	65.51%	8.46%	150	207	10.49%
	7	2.361%	46.32%	53.68%	8.89%	165	218	7.83%
	10	3.061%	58.52%	41.48%	8.80%	173	221	6.10%
								91.52%

Maturity	Strike	Market Value	Theoret. Value	Squared Error	Maturity	Strike	Market Value	Theoret. Value	Squared Error
T	K	c_{mkt}	c	$\ln(c_{mkt}/c)^2$	T	K	c_{mkt}	c	$\ln(c_{mkt}/c)^2$
Equity options									
8/20/11	125	11.675	5.507	56.46%	9/17/11	125	12.625	9.485	8.18%
	130	7.575	3.897	44.18%		130	8.850	7.662	2.08%
	135	4.150	2.677	19.21%		135	5.700	6.120	0.51%
	140	1.870	1.786	0.21%		140	3.400	4.833	12.37%
	145	0.715	1.156	23.08%		145	1.890	3.774	47.81%
				143.14%					70.94%
10/22/11	125	14.100	13.044	0.61%	1/21/12	125	16.700	19.519	2.43%
	130	10.675	11.144	0.18%		130	13.525	17.582	6.88%
	135	7.750	9.463	3.99%		135	10.700	15.798	15.18%
	140	5.400	7.987	15.32%		140	8.300	14.161	28.54%
	145	3.650	6.702	36.92%		145	6.300	12.664	48.75%
				57.02%					101.79%

Table 3. (*Continued*)

Maturity	Strike	Market Value	Theoret. Value	Squared Error	Maturity	Strike	Market Value	Theoret. Value	Squared Error
T	K	c_{mkt}	c	$\ln(c_{mkt}/c)^2$	T	K	c_{mkt}	c	$\ln(c_{mkt}/c)^2$
4/22/12	125	18.650	24.202	6.79%	1/19/13	125	23.750	33.450	11.73%
	130	15.700	22.281	12.26%		130	21.075	31.625	16.47%
	135	12.975	20.485	20.85%		135	18.400	29.884	23.52%
	140	10.575	18.807	33.15%		140	16.200	28.225	30.83%
	145	8.525	17.243	49.62%		145	14.000	26.646	41.42%
				122.67%					123.96%

Current Date	Market Value	Theoret. Value	Squared Error	Market Value	Theoret Value	Squared Error	SSE
t	S_{mkt}	S	$\ln(S_{mkt}/S)^2$	σ_{mkt}	σ_S	$\ln(\sigma_{mkt}/\sigma_S)^2$	
Equity				*Equity volatility*			*Sum of squared errors*
7/29/11	135.67	118.74	8.88%	49.63%	70.74%	62.82%	782.75%

Asset Value	Bond's Par Value	Payout Rate	Asset Volatility	Leverage	Default Trigger	Option to Default	Option to Def. Vol.	Bond	Bond Yield	Recovery Rate
V	Z	q_V	σ_V	L	V_b	P	σ_P	B_0	y	R
Model's parameters				*Model's output*						
9,113.6	10,709.2	3.68%	3.90%	49.9	8,195.1	1,778.3	12.70%	5,617	3.79%	72.70%

Note: The model's exogenous parameters are $\theta = 35\%$, $\alpha = 5\%$, $r = 3.06\%$. All the weights have been set to 1.

and debt is perpetual, default can happen at any time, rather than just at the debt's maturity as in the model of Merton (1974).

In his original paper, Leland focused on the pricing of a firm's debt and equity. Toft and Prucyk (1997) were the first to derive a closed formula for the pricing of equity options within Leland's model. Relative to simple option-pricing models (such as Black–Scholes–Merton), these formulas are complicated both by the possibility of default and by the fact that, due to the effect of leverage, the value of the firm's equity has stochastic volatility.

This chapter, built on the results I developed in a previous paper concerning the pricing of European compound options on American options within the Black–Scholes–Merton model, makes a more significant contribution by deriving new closed formulas for the pricing of CDS within the Leland model. Therefore, the Leland model can be calibrated jointly to equity option and CDS quotes in order to identify trading opportunities across the two markets and/or to measure and manage equity and credit risk within a unified framework.

The model's usefulness in linking credit and equity markets is shown by an example at the end of the chapter (using market quotes for GS) that points to some of the empirical work that could be done to implement model-based strategies.

NOTES

1. The stochastic duration of a bond is defined as the time to maturity of a zero-coupon bond with the same sensitivity to changes of interest rates, that is, with the same basis risk. "If we wish stochastic duration, D_3, to be a proxy for basis risk of coupon bonds with the units of time, then it is natural to define it as the maturity of a discount bond with the same risk" (p. 56). See Cox, Ingersoll, and Ross (1979).
2. See Leland (1994, 1995, 2006, 2009).
3. In the notation used by Goldstein et al. (2001), interest payments to investors are taxed at a personal rate τ_i, "effective" dividends are taxed at τ_d, and corporate profits are taxed at τ_c. We assume that $\tau_d = \tau_i$ and $\tau_c = 0$. Therefore, the effective tax rate, τ_{eff}, defined by $(1-\tau_{\text{eff}}) = (1-\tau_c)(1-\tau_d)$ is simply equal to $\tau_d = \tau_i$ (and to θ, in our notation).
4. Goldstein et al. (2001, footnote 20, p. 497) report that direct bankruptcy costs, estimated by Warner (1977), are about 1% of assets' value: "As measured here, the cost of bankruptcy is on average about one percent of the market value of the firm prior to bankruptcy" (Warner, 1977, p. 377). However, taking account for indirect costs, Goldstein–Ju–Leland choose $\acute{a} = 5\%$ in their base case.
5. As we will see later, this is different from the default trigger originally derived by Leland (1994, Eq. (14), p. 1222).
6. For a proof of p_b see, for instance, Barone (2010).

7. Note that our $Z–P$ is equal to $F(V)$ in Black and Cox (1976, Eq. (16), p. 364), where $c = rZ$, $\bar{V} = V_b$, $V = V_0$ and $\alpha = -\gamma_2$:

$$F(V) = \frac{c}{r} + \left(\bar{V}^{\alpha+1} - \frac{c}{r}\bar{V}^{\alpha}\right)V^{-\alpha}$$

8. Eq. (20) shows that σ_S is a function of the random asset value, V. Strictly speaking, our model is a *local-volatility* model, which belongs to the more general class of *stochastic-volatility* models. The term *fully stochastic-volatility* has been often used to describe models where the asset volatility has a randomness of its own and is driven by a different Wiener process.

9. Moody's KMV "Credit Monitor Quick Reference (2004)" defines the default point as "The point to which a firm's asset value must fall before the firm is unable to raise capital to meet either a principal or interest payment. It is approximately equal to the total amount of short-term liabilities, plus half of the long-term liabilities (precise definition varies by industry)." See Moody's KMV "Credit Monitor Quick Reference," 2004.

10. See Black and Cox (1976) and Goldstein et al. (2001).

Leland (1995) has also proposed an "exponential model" where the firm retires the perpetual debt at a proportional rate m through time. This roll-over debt structure, with regular repayments and renewals of principal and coupon, should guarantee a stationary debt structure. However, Décamps and Villeneuve (2008) show that this extension of Leland's original model does not allow close-form formulas because the default point is not constant anymore, but depends on time.

11. Note that, because the debt is fixed in nominal terms, the actual leverage tends to decrease in real terms over time. An alternative assumption would be to model debt as a perpetual *floating-rate* bond. However, if coupons were continuously paid at the rate r, the basis risk, that is, the bond's sensitivity to interest rates would be null (and this would contradict the empirical evidence). See Cox, Ingersoll, and Ross (1980).

12. See Merton (1974). There is some evidence that the longer is T the better is the Merton model fit: "Experimenting with different choices, we find that choosing a longer maturity, and hence giving a larger weight to volatility, generates predictions more correlated with market observations. We present our results based on $T = 10$" (Bai & Wu, 2010, p. 9).

13. According to Eq. (19) of Goldstein et al.(2001), $E_{solv} = (1-\tau_{eff})\ (V_{solv} - V_{int})$ where $V_{int} = (C/r)\ (1-p_B)$. In our notation, $S_0 = E_{solv}$, $\theta = \tau_{eff}$, $V_0 - V_b\ p_b = V_{solv}$, $Z(1-p_b) = V_{int}$, $p_b = p_B$. Therefore, $S_0 = (1-\theta)[V_0 - V_b \quad p_b - Z(1-p_b)] = (1-\theta)$ $[V_0 + (Z - V_b)\ p_b - Z] = (1-\theta)(V_0 + P - Z)$. In the notation used by Goldstein et al. (2001), $BC_{def} = \alpha V_{def} = \alpha V_b p_b$ is the value of the bankruptcy claim. We assume that also third parties have to pay taxes. Therefore, our expression for the value, U_0, of the bankruptcy claim is equal to $\alpha V_b p_b$ pre-multiplied by $(1-\theta)$.

14. "In contrast to Leland (1994), equity is a decreasing function of τ_{eff}" (Goldstein et al., 2001, p. 497).

15. See Eq. (34b), p. 353, in Ingersoll (1987). Transformed into our notation, $x_0 = \ln(V_0/V_b)$, $\mu = r - q_V - \sigma_V^2/2$, $2\mu/\sigma^2 = 2(\lambda - 1)$, $t_0 = 0$.

16. It should be noted that *actual* default probabilities shown in the table *do not* include the (high) risk premiums asked by bond traders as a compensation for the (high) systematic risk of bond portfolios.

17. See Duffie and Singleton (2003), Section 8.4.

18. The Solver routine in Excel has been used to search for the values of the parameters that minimize the loss function. The routine works well provided that the spreadsheet is structured so that the parameters being searched for have roughly equal values. Since occasionally Solver gives a local minimum, a number of different starting values for the model's parameters have been tested.

19. Some new empirical evidence documents a "slow information diffusion between the CDS market and the stock market." See Han and Zhou (2011).

ACKNOWLEDGMENTS

I owe an irreducible debt to Domenico Cuoco for introducing me to continuous-time finance and for acting as an always positive and encouraging mentor. A couple of sentences from him are always sufficient to straighten out my brain wiring. Jeffrey Williams deserves a special acknowledgment for the supportive and precious suggestions. He thoroughly analyzed a preliminary draft of this work and provided many detailed comments. Useful suggestions have also been provided by Stefano Herzel and Roberto Renò. I am also grateful to Michele Bagella, Fabrizio Cacciafesta, Gennaro Olivieri, and Gustavo Piga for their precious advices. Last but not the least, I wish to thank Darrell Duffie, Steve Ross, and Mark Rubinstein, whose paths I had the good fortune to cross. Without them, finance would not be as fascinating as it is.

REFERENCES

Bai, J., & Wu, L. (2010). *Anchoring corporate credit spreads to firm fundamentals*. Working Paper.

Barone, G. (2010). *European compound options written on perpetual American options*. Working Paper. University of Rome, Tor Vergata.

Barone, G. (2011). *Equity options and bond options in the Leland model*. Working Paper. University of Rome, Tor Vergata.

Black, F. S., & Cox, J. C. (1976). Valuing corporate securities: Some effects of bond indenture provisions. *Journal of Finance*, *31*(2), 351–367.

Cox, J. C., Ingersoll, J. E., & Ross, S. A. (1979). Duration and the measurement of basis risk. *Journal of Business*, *52*(1), 51–61.

Cox, J. C., Ingersoll, J. E., & Ross, S. A. (1980). An analysis of variable rate loan contracts. *Journal of Finance*, *35*(2), 389–403.

Décamps, J.-P., & Villeneuve, S. (2008). *On the modeling of debt maturity and endogenous default – A caveat*. Working Paper.

Duffie, D. & Singleton, K. J. (2003). *Credit risk*. Princeton, NJ: Princeton University Press.

Ericsson, J., & Reneby, J. (2002). *A note on contingent claims pricing with non-traded assets.* SSE/EFI Working Paper Series in Economics and Finance No. 314.

Goldstein, R., Ju, N., & Leland, H. (2001). An EBIT-based model of dynamic capital structure. *Journal of Business*, *74*(4), 483–512.

Han, B. & Zhou, Y. (2011). *Term structure of credit default swap spreads and cross-section of stock returns.* Working Paper.

Hull, J. C. (2011). *Options, futures, and other derivatives* (8th ed.). Boston, MA: Pearson.

Ingersoll, J. E. (1987). *Theory of financial decision making.* Totowa, NJ: Rowman & Littlefield.

Kahn, J., & Truell, P. (1998). Troubled investment fund's Bets now estimated at $1.25 trillion. *Wall Street Journal*, September 26.

Leland, H. (1994). Corporate debt value, bond covenants, and optimal capital structure. *Journal of Finance*, *49*(4), 1213–1252.

Leland, H. (1995). *Bond prices, yield spreads, and optimal capital structure with default risk.* Finance Working Paper No. 240, Haas School of Business, University of California at Berkeley.

Leland, H. (2006). "Princeton Lectures" [*Lecture 1* – Pros and Cons of Structural Models – An Introduction, Lecture 2 – A New Structural Model, *Lecture 3* – Financial Synergies and the Optimal Scope of the Firm-Implications for Mergers and Structured Finance].

Leland, H. (2009). *Structural models and the credit crisis.* Guangzhou: China International Conference in Finance.

Merton, R. C. (1974). On the pricing of corporate debt: The risk structure of interest rates. *Journal of Finance*, *29*(2), 449–470. reprinted in Merton, R. C. (1990). *Continuous-time finance* (Chapter 12, pp. 388–412). Malden, MA: Blackwell.

Modigliani, F., & Miller, M. H. (1958). The cost of capital, corporation finance and the theory of investment. *American Economic Review*, *48*(3), 267–297.

Moody's KMV. (2004). Credit monitor quick reference. Retrieved from http://www.moodys.com/sites/products/ProductAttachments/CM4_QuickRefCard.pdf

Rubinstein, M., & Reiner, E. (1991). Unscrambling the binary code. *Risk*, *4*(9), 75–83.

Toft, K. B. (1994). *Options on leveraged equity with default risk.* Working Paper No. 238. Walter A. Haas School of Business, University of California at Berkeley.

Toft, K. B., & Prucyk, B. (1997). Options on leveraged equity: Theory and empirical tests. *Journal of Finance*, *52*(3), 1151–1180.

Warner, J. B. (1977). Bankruptcy costs: Some evidence. *Journal of Finance*, *32*(2), 337–347.

BUSINESS CYCLES AND THE IMPACT OF MACROECONOMIC SURPRISES ON INTEREST RATE SWAP SPREADS: AUSTRALIAN EVIDENCE

Victor Fang, A. S. M. Sohel Azad,
Jonathan A. Batten and Chien-Ting Lin

ABSTRACT

This study examines the response of Australian interest rate swap spreads to the arrival of macroeconomic news information during the economic expansion and contraction periods. We find that the impact of news announcements on swap spread change differs and largely depends on the state of the economy. The unexpected inflation rate is the only news released that has significant impact on swap spreads across all maturities during contractions and remains the important news announcement throughout the business cycles, while the unanticipated unemployment rate tends to be more relevant to 10-year swap and the unanticipated change in money supply tends to be more relevant to 4- and 7-year swaps during expansions. We also find shocks from these news surprises appear to have significant impact on the conditional volatility of the swap spread

Derivative Securities Pricing and Modelling
Contemporary Studies in Economic and Financial Analysis, Volume 94, 379–398

ISSN: 1569-3759/doi:10.1108/S1569-3759(2012)0000094018

change during both economic phases. The macroeconomic shocks in general are negatively related to the conditional volatility of the swap spread change, suggesting that the newsworthy announcements tend to reduce uncertainty on the news announcement days in the swap market during expansion and contraction periods.

Keywords: Interest rate swap spreads; macroeconomic news; business cycles; probability of default

INTRODUCTION

Macroeconomic news plays an essential role in financial markets by revealing new information about the fundamentals of the economy. Periodic news announcements such as unemployment rate and consumer price index (CPI) are, therefore, closely watched by market participants who respond quickly and accordingly to unexpected element of the news. These news surprises, therefore, form an important part of the price discovery process in financial assets. More importantly, the concept of market efficiency is closely related to the reaction of asset returns to news announcements. Analyzing the effects of news shocks on asset returns might shed some light on market efficiency.

An extensive literature examining the impact of macroeconomic news surprises on financial assets has well been documented, mostly on bonds, stocks, and foreign exchange. For example, Chen, Roll, and Ross (1986), Fleming and Remolona (1997), Almeida, Goodhart, and Payne (1998), Bollerslev, Cai, and Song (2000), Furfine (2001), Balduzzi, Elton, and Green (2001), Flannery and Protopapadakis (2002), Anderson, Bollerslev, Diebold, and Vega (2003), Green (2004), Simpson, Ramchander, and Chaudhry (2005), Tang & Yan (2006), and Brenner, Pasquariello, and Subrahmanyam (2009) find that news surprises from GDP, interest rate, inflation rate, unemployment rate, or consumer confidence are significantly related to changes in Treasury yields, stock prices, and foreign exchange rates.

In addition, a number of empirical studies find that macroeconomic fundamentals play an important role in determining credit spread dynamics. For examples, Jaffee (1975) and Fama and French (1989) show that credit spreads (the difference between corporate bond yield and Treasury bond yield with an equivalent maturity) are significantly related to macroeconomic conditions and widen during recession periods. Ewing (2003) shows that the default risk premium is relatively higher during recessionary conditions. Wilson (1997a, 1997b), Ramchander, Simpson, and Webb (2003), Ramchander, Simpson, and Chaudhry (2005), and Duffie, Saita, and Wang (2007) show that macroeconomic fundamentals have an impact on default rates or yield spread changes. A recent study by Azad, Fang, and Wickramanayake (2011) shows that macroeconomic surprises and volatility of yen interest rate swap are closely related, albeit volatility of swap leads the relationship on Granger causal sense. However, Azad et al. (2011) have not examined whether yen swap spread is influenced by macroeconomic news surprises. In terms of methodology and empirical approach, this study is similar to that of Fang, Lin, and Parbhoo (2008), who examine the influence of macroeconomic news announcements on Australian financial markets (excluding interest rate swaps) under different economic conditions.

Thus, little empirical work has been done to examine the impact of macroeconomic variables on swap spreads outside the United States. In this study, we examine the effects of macroeconomic fundamentals on swap spreads under different state of economy. Specifically, our study addresses the following sets of questions. First, how do unanticipated macroeconomic news announcements impact on the Australian dollar interest rate swap spreads? Second, do these unanticipated macroeconomic announcements affect swap spreads differently across different state of the economy? Third, are these influences consistent with existing theories on interest rate determination?

The swap spread is the difference between the fixed rate of a plain-vanilla swap and the yield of a government bond of similar maturity. Since an interest rate swap is an OTC derivative and is not exchange traded, it does not enjoy a payment guarantee by a clearing organization or exchange. Consequently, the pricing of swaps and the corresponding swap spreads reflect credit risk across different maturities. Changes in the swap spreads due to news surprises, the unexpected component of the news announcements, should therefore contain new information about default risk and the overall credit worthiness of the Australian corporate sector in addition to interest rate risk.

A broad consensus has been reached that only a small number of macroeconomic factors have a significant impact on pricing and return. For interest rate swaps in particular, Fornari (2004) finds that only six macroeconomic variables are influential on US implied volatilities that are extracted from swaption prices – namely US non-farm payrolls, the US Institute for Supply Management (ISM) index, jobless claims, the Chicago Purchasing Managers (CPM) index, durable goods orders and retail sales announcements. Because some of the news announcements are not available in Australia and they tend to provide similar information on the economy, hence, we restrict our analysis to the most closely watched economic indicators. Specifically, we focus on the news of money supply growth, unemployment rate, and CPI. We choose these macroeconomic announcements because they are well known to offer insight into the intrinsic health of the economy, the future direction of interest rates, and the performance of financial markets.

Besides being the first study outside United States, to our knowledge this is the first study in which we introduce a state contingent framework to examine whether these news announcements carry the same influence in both periods of economic expansion and contraction. A rise in inflation rate during expansion, for example, may carry more weight than an increase in money supply growth because Central Bank may need to respond to the rising inflation by raising interest rate whereas the same rise of inflation rate may have less effect on interest rate during contractions. One of the aims in this study is therefore to extend the existing literature by examining which news announcements play a dominant role in providing information during each phase of the business cycles.

The state contingent framework also allows us to investigate the interaction of the risk factors where they may vary across different phase of the business cycles. As evidenced by Boyd, Hu, and Jagannathan (2005) that information provided by the news arrivals may be interpreted differently depending on the state of the economy.[1] They find that stock market is more responsive to rising unemployment news during expansions but not during contractions. For example, a negative macroeconomic surprise related to an unexpected rise in unemployment rate during an expansion may lower market expectations on future economic activities that lead to a rise in the probability of default on private sector debt. At the same time, the expected decline in the economic activities may push interest rate lower, thereby producing a counter effect. Determining which macroeconomic variable is the dominant effect could depend on the state of the economy.

In addition, using an exponential generalized autoregressive conditional heteroskedasticity (EGARCH) specification in our analysis, we address whether the macroeconomic surprises (positive and negative shocks) have an asymmetric effect on the conditional volatility of the swap spreads within each state of the economy and the macroeconomic shocks remain persistent during both economic growth and slowdowns. Finally, unlike earlier studies that only identify surprise arrivals, our study takes into account both the direction and size of the unexpected component of a news announcement, an improvement that we believe will better capture the impact of news surprises.

We find that over the full sample period, news surprise from CPI is the only significant news announcement affecting the interest rate swap spread change across all maturities. That is, a lower (higher) than expected inflation is related to an increase (decrease) in the swap spreads. However, when we decompose the full sample period into periods of expansion and contraction, unanticipated news on money supply (on 4- and 7-year swap spreads) and unemployment rate (on 10-year swap spread) are more important during expansions while unexpected inflation rate news is the only factor that has an impact on swap spreads across all maturities during contractions.

Within each phase of the business cycles, we further find that the EGARCH modeling has clearly captured the characteristics of swap spreads volatility. The conditional volatility of swap spreads exhibits volatility clustering behavior (measured by $\beta_{i,1}$) across all maturities. The asymmetric effect (measured by $\beta_{i,2}$) is not statistically significant for all sample periods. Looking at the effects of macroeconomic announcements on the conditional volatility of swap spreads, it appears that shocks from CPI are the only shocks that are persistent during both expansions and contractions. However, these shocks are found to reduce conditional volatility.

The rest of the paper is structured as follows. Section 2 describes and provides summary statistics of the swap spread, macroeconomic news announcements, and business cycles. Section 3 discusses the methodologies used to examine the impact of the macroeconomic news announcements. Section 4 reports the results of our empirical tests. Section 5 concludes the paper.

DATA AND SUMMARY STATISTICS

For the 2, 3, 4, 5, 7, and 10-year interest swap rates, we use the daily closing mid-rates from DataStream over the period from January 3, 1995 to January 31, 2007. The Treasury bond yields of corresponding maturities are obtained from the Reserve bank of Australia (RBA). Swap spreads for the 6 maturities are then calculated by subtracting the swap rates from the Treasury bond yields of the same maturity.

Table 1 provides some descriptive statistics for the swap spreads. It shows that the average swap spread rises as the maturity of the swap increases, capturing the risk premium embedded in the swap rates. The volatility of the swap spread however appears to be fairly constant across all maturities.

Table 1. Descriptive Statistics of the Interest Rate Swap Spreads.

	2-Year Swap Spreads	3-Year Swap Spreads	4-Year Swap Spreads	5-Year Swap Spreads	7-Year Swap Spreads	10-Year Swap Spreads
Mean	0.2495	0.2827	0.3454	0.3502	0.3535	0.3797
Median	0.2350	0.2950	0.3550	0.3700	0.3670	0.4070
Standard deviation	0.1375	0.1501	0.1423	0.1563	0.1521	0.1520
Minimum	−0.1350	−0.4550	−0.0300	−0.4250	−0.0700	−0.0800
Maximum	0.6100	0.7250	0.9370	1.1100	0.8870	0.9470
Skewness	0.1280	−0.3676	0.0066	0.3293	0.0302	−0.0053
Kurtosis	2.2820	2.8081	2.8535	4.1391	2.3828	2.3314
Observations	2533	2533	2533	2533	2533	2533
ADF t-ratio	−3.4044	−2.8550	3.3722	−3.4030	−2.5578	−2.5060

Notes: This table reports the summary statistics of the daily interest rate swap spreads from January 1995 to January 2007. The critical value for t-ratio at 1% and 5% significant level significant are −3.43 and −2.87 m, respectively.

Across all maturities, the skewness and the kurtosis of the swap spread show non-normality with some skewness and thin tails. Each of the swap spreads also exhibits non-stationarity based on the Augmented Dickey-Fuller (ADF) test.

We also collect 3 different scheduled macroeconomic announcements over the same 12-year period as the swap spreads. Monthly unemployment rate is compiled by the Australian Bureau of Statistics and released at 11:30 am on the second Thursday of the month. Information on money supply growth is announced at 11:30 am on the first Friday of the month by the Reserve Bank of Australia. Finally, quarterly CPI is made public at 11:30 am on the last Wednesday of the month following every quarter (e.g., March quarter CPI is released on the last Wednesday of April). In order to examine the extent to which these economic fundamentals affect the swap market, it is important to understand and properly model the news information arrivals. Releases of macroeconomic announcements are partly anticipated by the market. At the point of announcement release, the market only reacts to the unexpected component of the news, that is, to the news information that deviates from market expectations. While the announcement of expected component of news information has little influence since it has largely been absorbed in the current price by the market prior to the release.[2]

To measure the news surprises in terms of both direction and magnitude, we subtract the expected values of the macroeconomic news from the actual data of the news releases. Since consensus estimates on the news announcements is not available in Australia where they are collected by Money Market Services (MMS) in the United States, we follow Connolloy and Wang (2003) and build an ARIMA model for each actual news announcement series and use residuals from the model to estimate the unexpected value of each of the macroeconomic information.[3]

Table 2 reports some summary statistic of the macroeconomic announcements and their news surprises. The change in unemployment rate over the sample period averaged −0.031% and ranged from −0.41% to 0.38%. This period is often characterized by high growth especially in the last several years where the unemployment rate stays at a low of 5–6%. Money supply also grew at an average rate of 0.66% per month although with high variability. The kurtosis of 53.1 reveals heavy tails in the distribution of money supply growth and suggests that it is highly responsive to changes in economic activities. The Australian economy also experienced low inflation environment over the same period in which quarterly inflation rate averaged 0.65% or 2.8% annually. Along with low unemployment rate, inflation rate has also been low and kept within 3% target band established by the

Table 2. Descriptive Statistics of the Australian Macroeconomic Announcements and Macroeconomic Surprises.

	Change in Unemployment Rate (%)		Change in Money Supply Growth (%)		Change in Consumer Price Index (%)	
	Actual	Surprise	Actual	Surprise	Actual	Surprise
Mean	−0.0305**	−0.0025	0.6586*	−0.3366**	0.6577*	−0.2578*
Median	−0.0331	0.0103	0.6927	−0.3006	0.5746	−0.2591
Standard deviation	0.1602	0.1629	1.6129	1.6578	0.6553	0.6714
Minimum	−0.4084	−0.4174	−13.7018	−14.8193	−0.4160	−1.5269
Maximum	0.3784	0.4134	3.7004	3.8358	3.7242	2.7998
Skewness	0.1025	−0.0163	−5.8987	−5.4684	2.6306	2.2398
Kurtosis	0.0129	−0.2937	53.0662	49.2803	11.8020	10.4312
Observations	120	120	120	120	40	40

Notes: The table reports summary statistics for the monthly and quarterly percentage changes in news release from January 1995 to January 2007. The announcement surprises are the differences between actual macroeconomic value and the forecasted value based on the ARIMA model.
*, **denote statistical significance at the 1%, 5% levels, respectively.

Reserve Bank. We also find that during this period of largely good economic fundamentals, the announcement surprises from the three news announcements are on average negative, suggesting that the actual data are better than their respective forecasts.

Since economic activities tend to vary widely over business cycles, one primary question of interest in this study is whether the response of swap spreads to changes in macroeconomic fundamentals varies systematically over time. In other words, could the same information be interpreted differently depending on the state of the economy as the news arrives? To test this hypothesis, we first need to classify the level of economic activities into two different states-expansions and contractions over the business cycles.[4]

Burns and Mitchell (1946) define business cycles as "a type of fluctuation found in the aggregate economic activity of nations that organise their work mainly in business enterprises: a cycle consists of expansions occurring at the same time in many economic activities followed by similar general recessions, contractions and revivals which merge in the expansion phase of the next cycle; this sequence of changes is recurrent but not periodic … ."

Following the description of business cycles, we measure expansions and contractions using the local maxima and minima of the sample path of Gross Domestic Product (GDP), the natural measurement of the level of economic activities.[5] With the business cycle reference dates of the Australian Bureau of Statistics (1992), we are able to identify peaks and troughs in Australia's business cycle from 1990 to 2007. We denote the period from trough to peak as expansions and from peak to trough as contractions. Table 3 shows the dates of turning points in the Australian

Table 3. Australian Business Cycle.

Turning Point		Duration in Months	
Peak	Trough	Contraction (peak–trough)	Expansion (trough–peak)
1989.12	1993.02	39	26
1995.04	1997.02	22	40
2000.06	2001.02	8	39
2004.05	2006.02	21	11
2007.01			

Note: This table reports the Australian business cycle from December 1989 to January 2007. There are 116 expansion and 90 contraction months.

business cycles together with the duration of each phase of cycle. As expected, we find that there are more expansions (116 months) than contractions (90 months). The Australian economy had particularly been doing well from 1997 to 2004 during which expansions took place for most of the sample period.

EMPIRICAL MODELS

In this study, we use a univariate exponential GARCH (EGRACH) that proposed by Nelson (1991) to estimate the return volatility for several reasons. Unlike GARCH, the EGARCH variant imposes no positive constraints on the estimated parameters and explicitly accounts for asymmetry common in asset return volatility, thereby avoiding possible misspecification in the volatility process (Glosten, Jagannathan, & Runkle, 1993). In addition, EGARCH allows for a general probability density function (i.e., GED), which nests the normal distribution along with several other possible densities.

In order to capture this effect, we include the news variables in both the mean return and the conditional volatility. In our analysis, we first examine the surprise effects of the news arrivals (i.e., MS, UE, and CPI) on each swap spread change and its conditional volatility over the full sample period, and then investigate the news surprise effects in each state of economy. To remove any serial correlations and sign bias of $z_{i,t}$ in the estimate, we include an MA(q) process for the mean equation and specify the conditional variance as an EGARCH(1, 1) model for the full sample analysis as follows:

$$\Delta Swapsprd_{i,t} = \alpha_{i,c} + \sum_{k=1}^{q} \alpha_{i,k} \in_{i,t-k} + \sum_{N=1}^{4} \mu_{i,N} News_{N,t} + \varepsilon_{i,t} \tag{1}$$

$$\begin{aligned} \ln(h_{i,t}) = {} & \beta_{i,0} + \beta_{i,1} \ln(h_{i,t-1}) + \beta_{i,2} z_{i,t-1} \\ & + \beta_{i,3}\{|z_{i,t-1}| - E(|z_{i,t-1}|)\} + \sum_{N=1}^{4} \gamma_{i,N} News_{N,t} \end{aligned} \tag{2}$$

$$\text{where} \quad \varepsilon_{i,t} = z_{i,t} \sqrt[2]{h_{i,t}} \text{ and } z_{i,t} \sim N(0,1)$$

where $\Delta Swapsprd_{i,t}$ = Swap spread change for maturity i (i = 1, 2, 3, 4, 5, and 6 for 2, 3, 4, 5, 7, and 10-year swaps respectively); $\varepsilon_{i,t}$ = the error term is assumed $\sim(0,\ h_{i,t})$; $h_{i,t}$ = Conditional return volatility for asset i;

and $News_{N,t}$ = the unexpected component of each macroeconomic announcement (N = 1, 2, and 3 for *MS*, *UE*, and *CPI* respectively) as measured by the difference between the announced figures and the expected value forecasted by an ARIMA model. These monthly and quarterly surprise variables are assigned a value of zero for days without the particular macroeconomic announcement and the magnitude of the surprises for days with announcements.

The coefficient μ_i represents the impact of the unexpected component of news on the swap spread i. The coefficient β_1 measures the persistence of the conditional variance. The coefficients β_2 and β_3 represent the impact of the lagged errors on the current conditional variance. A negative β_2 indicates that the negative shocks have a larger effect on the conditional variance, that is, the asymmetric variance effect. Meanwhile, a significant γ_i suggests that the unexpected news ($NEWS_t$) has a direct impact on the conditional variance on the announcement dates.

To test whether the state of economy changes the news announcement effects, we modify the above equations by multiplying the unexpected news $News_{N,t}$ with a dummy variable D_e which denotes the state of the economy.[6] Therefore, the model becomes,

$$\Delta Swapsprd_{i,t} = \alpha_{i,c} + \sum_{k=1}^{q} \alpha_{i,k} \in_{i,t-k} + \sum_{N=1}^{4} \delta_{i,N}(D_e * News_{N,t}) + \varepsilon_{i,t} \quad (3)$$

$$\ln(h_{i,t}) = \beta_{i,0} + \beta_{i,1}\ln(h_{i,t-1}) + \beta_{i,2} z_{i,t-1} + \beta_{i,3}\{|z_{i,t-1}| - E(|z_{i,t-1}|)\} + \sum_{N=1}^{4} \rho_{i,N}(D_e * News_{N,t}) \quad (4)$$

$$\text{where} \quad \varepsilon_{i,t} = z_{i,t}\sqrt[2]{h_{i,t}} \text{ and } z_{i,t} \sim N(0,1)$$

The variable (D_e * $News_{N,t}$) denotes the unexpected news under the contraction or expansion state of the economy. The coefficient δ_i measures the impact of unexpected news on the swap spread i under the contraction state or expansion state of economy. While the coefficient ρ_i measures the impact of unexpected news on the conditional variance under different state of economy. Other variables are as defined in previous Equations. We estimate the parameters of the above equations for each return asset using the quasi maximum likelihood (QML) procedure described in Bollerslev and Wooldridge (1992). Hence the estimate results are consistent and asymptotically normal and efficient.

EMPIRICAL RESULTS

Table 4 reports the full sample results of the effects of news surprises on swap spread changes. Among the three news announcements, we find that only unexpected inflation rate is significant in explaining the swap spread changes across all maturities except 7-year swap. The inverse relationship between inflation surprises and changes in the swap spread indicates that a higher (lower) than expected inflation rate contributes to a reduction (widening) in the swap spreads. The changes of the swap spread however could come from changes in Treasury yield or changes in swap rate. In other words, a reduction of the swap spread may indicate that the swap rate and Treasury yield move in opposite directions, or in the same direction but different magnitudes. Hence, while a higher than expected inflation rate (indicates a strong economic growth) increases inflation premium on interest rate, it also reduces the default risk premium of the swap rate. The decrease in swap spreads during a higher inflation can be explained by using the option pricing model that proposed by Sorensen and Bollier (1994). If the actual inflation rate is higher than the expected inflation rate (indicates future interest rates are expected to rise), then the option to receive fixed is worth less than the option to pay fixed. In this situation, the expected losses from default on a par swap are not symmetric due to the higher default risk exposure in paying fixed and the lower default risk exposure in receiving fixed. The presence of this default risk implies that the payer of fixed may not receive the later (increasing) floating payments. Upon default, these higher floating rates will not be paid, thus leaving the payer of fixed in a more disadvantaged situation. A lower fixed rate coupon will compensate for this risk, causing the swap spread to decrease. On the other hand, if the actual inflation rate is lower than expected (indicates future interest rates are expected to fall), the value of the option to receive fixed will be higher than the value of the option to pay fixed. To compensate the potential default risk from the pay-fixed party, the receive-fixed party will require a higher fixed coupon, hence causing the swap spread to increase (see Fang & Muljono, 2003).

Consistent with previous studies (see Ederington & Lee, 1993; Roley, 1983; Urich & Wachtel, 1981), the 4- and 7-year swap spread change respond negatively to unexpected change in money supply (with coefficient (μ_{MS}) values of -0.0046 and -0.0053 respectively). In their study, Urich and Wachtel (1981) find that interest rate levels have a positive relationship with the unexpected change in money supply. They interpret this as an inflationary effect. That is unexpected change in money supply may exert

Table 4. The Impact of Macroeconomic News Surprises on Australian Interest Rate Swap Spreads: Full Sample.

	2-Year Swap Spread		3-Year Swap Spread		4-Year Swap Spread		5-Year Swap Spread		7-Year Swap Spread		10-Year Swap Spread	
	Coefficient	Standard error	Coefficient	Standard error	Coefficient	Standard error	Coefficient	Standard error	Coefficient	Standard error	Coefficient	Standard error
Panel A: Conditional mean												
α_c	0.0002	0.0003	−0.0001	0.0003	−0.0001	0.0003	0.0002	0.0004	0.0001	0.0003	**0.0006****	0.0003
μ_{MS}	−0.0025	0.0022	−0.0026	0.0016	**−0.0046****	0.0019	−0.0041	0.0062	**−0.0053***	0.0019	−0.002	0.0028
μ_{UE}	0.0081	0.0167	0.0345	0.0447	−0.0047	0.0326	0.0055	0.0133	−0.0152	0.0245	**−0.0306****	0.0148
μ_{CPI}	**−0.0093***	0.0015	**−0.009***	0.0014	**−0.0077****	0.0038	**−0.0051*****	0.0030	−0.0005	0.0031	**−0.0022***	0.0007
AR												
Panel B: Conditional variance												
β_0	**−0.3339***	0.0828	**−0.2837****	0.1421	**−0.4326***	0.1227	**−1.3039****	0.5352	**−0.2269***	0.0715	**−1.4765***	0.2625
β_1	**0.9703***	0.0106	**0.9706***	0.0010	**0.9567***	0.0146	**0.827***	0.0907	**0.9792***	0.0077	**0.8319***	0.0342
β_2	−0.0035	0.0253	−0.0066	0.0442	−0.0101	0.02688	−0.0384	0.0708	0.0288	0.0252	−0.0533	0.0492
β_3	**0.2103***	0.0324	**0.1451***	0.0532	**0.2371***	0.0558	**0.3405***	0.0367	**0.144***	0.0399	**0.5017***	0.0585
γ_{MS}	−0.0421	0.0563	0.0501	0.0692	−0.0401	0.04697	**−0.1572*****	0.0945	0.0563	0.0458	**−0.4259***	0.1067
γ_{UE}	−0.5406	0.8471	2.2499	2.2269	0.1443	0.9756	−3.3473	2.2445	−0.7584	0.681	−1.7572	1.5344
γ_{CPI}	**−0.8468***	0.2775	**−1.2404***	0.3420	−0.3072	0.2571	**−1.4783*****	0.7722	−0.1079	0.203	**−1.572***	0.2631

Notes: This table reports quasi-maximum likelihood (QML) estimate results (models are estimated using Bollerslev–Wooldridge Heteroskedasticity consistent covariance, and the Marquardt optimization algorithm) for the EGARCH (1,1) model of Eq. (1):

$$\Delta Swapsprd_{i,t} = \alpha_{i,c} + \sum_{k=1}^{q} \alpha_{i,k} \in_{i,t-k} + \sum_{N=1}^{4} \mu_{i,N} News_{N,t} + \varepsilon_{i,t}$$

$$\ln(h_{i,t}) = \beta_{i,0} + \beta_{i,1} \ln(h_{i,t-1}) + \beta_{i,2} z_{i,t-1} + \beta_{i,3}\{|z_{i,t-1}| - E(|z_{i,t-1}|)\} + \sum_{N=1}^{4} \gamma_{i,N} News_{N,t}$$

$$\text{where} \quad \varepsilon_{i,t} = z_{i,t} \sqrt[2]{h_{i,t}} \ \text{and} \ z_{i,t} \sim N(0,1)$$

where $\Delta Swapsprd_{i,t}$ is the change in swap spreads, $News_{N,t}$ denotes the surprises of news announcements (N) which are transformed into daily variables by assigning zero for days without the particular news announcement and the values of the surprises for announcement days. q is the number of MA lags required to remove serial correlations. $\varepsilon_{i,t}$ denotes the error term which is assumed to be $\sim(0, h_t)$. $\sqrt{h_t}$ is the conditional volatility of $\Delta Swapsprd_{i,t}$. The sample period is from January 1995 to January 2007.

*, **, and *** indicate statistical significance at the 1%, 5%, and 10% levels, respectively.

an upward pressure on interest rate as the central bank may engage in an open market operation that tightens the supply of reserves to offset the unexpected change. Hence, causing the swap spread change to decrease (as interest rates are expected to rise). The 10-year swap spread change is the only swap that responds negatively and significantly to unanticipated unemployment rate change (with a coefficient (μ_{UE}) value of −0.0306). This suggests that the arrivals of unemployment news have the greatest effect on the long-term interest rate swap spread in both economic and statistical sense.

On the conditional volatility of the swap spread changes, the estimates of the lagged volatility coefficient β_1 are highly statistically significant and fall within the range 0.8270–0.9792. This implies that the swap spread volatilities are highly persistent across all maturities. The asymmetric impact (as measured by β_2) is not significant across all swap maturities which means that negative shocks have greater impact on swap market than the positive shocks is not evident. Finally, the coefficients (β_3) of lagged innovations are positive and statistically significant. In relation to the unanticipated macroeconomic announcements on the conditional volatility of swap spread change, the unanticipated news on inflation rate are found to have negative effects on the conditional volatility of 2-, 3-, 5-, and 10-year swap spread change and the unexpected component of the change in money supply also has a significantly negative effect on the 5- and 10-year conditional volatility of swap spread change. Overall, the results seem to be consistent with Ederington and Lee (1996) and Brenner et al. (2009). Ederington and Lee (1996) show that implied volatility tends to rise in the days before news announcement release. They also find that there is a sharp fall in implied volatilities just after announcements. They argue that the announcement itself helps market to resolve uncertainty. Similarly, Brenner et al. (2009) find that the conditional return volatility rises before a news announcement and then declines on the day of news release. They attribute this volatility behavior to mean reversion in short-term interest rates that may have caused the impact of announcement shock to decrease for long-term bonds.

Further into our analysis, we examine swap spread responses to macroeconomic announcement surprises under different state of economy. Recent studies (see Anderson, Bollerslev, Diebold, & Vega, 2007; Boyd et al., 2005) suggest that the impact of some macroeconomic variables tends to dominate in periods of economic growth while other variables may be more influential in periods of economic slowdowns. Tables 5 and 6 report the impact of macroeconomic surprises on swap spreads during expansions and contractions, respectively.

It is interesting to note that in the economic expansion periods (see Table 5), swap market participants seem to ignore the inflation rate surprises as none of the coefficients of inflation rate surprises (measured by δ_{CPI}) in the mean equation is statistically significant. Other macroeconomic variable like money supply (δ_{MS}) has the same significant effects on swap spread change as discussed in the full sample periods. However, we expect the unemployment shocks have a negative and significant effect on the swap spreads of longer term maturities. This is because market participants are more concern with macroeconomic variables (in this instance the unanticipated unemployment figure) that may signal the end of the expansion period and the arrival of the contraction period. As a result, the growth prospect of the private sector may remain stagnant or decline, hence the possibility of the central bank cut interest rate is highly likely which in turn may affect the swap spreads. Looking at the coefficients of unemployment surprises (measured by δ_{UE}), they are negative but not statistically significant except the 10-year swap spread. These results are consistent with those in Table 4. This suggests that the unemployment surprises have the greatest impact on the long-term swap spreads during the expansion periods.

In contrast to the findings during economic expansions, inflation rate surprises appear to be the most influential news information during contractions. Table 6 shows that swap spread change across all maturity is highly responsive to the CPI surprises. The coefficient δ_{CPI} for inflation rate surprises is negatively significant at the 5% level for all swap spread change. One explanation for the significant relationship during contractions is that swap market participants pay more attention to inflation figure because an increase in inflation (indicates future interest rates are expected to increase) is associated with an improving business condition, which in turn improves credit quality and subsequently causes the swap spread to decline. Unlike during expansions however, news surprises on inflation rate are not important on the swap spread changes. Other macroeconomic surprises have no significant impact on swap spread change except the unexpected money supply has a significant effect on 4-year swap spread change.

Finally, results in Panel B of Tables 5 and 6 show that the macroeconomic shocks in general are negatively related to changes in conditional volatility of the swap spreads, suggesting that these newsworthy announcements tend to reduce uncertainty on the announcement days in the swap market during expansion and contraction periods. While there are some variations on the effects of the news surprises in different phase of the business cycles, the impacts appear to be quite consistent. For example, shocks generated from

Table 5. The Impact of macroeconomic News Surprises on Australian Interest Rate Swap Spreads: Expansion Periods.

	2-Year Swap Spread		3-Year Swap Spread		4-Year Swap Spread		5-Year Swap Spread		7-Year Swap Spread		10-Year Swap Spread	
	Coefficient	Standard error	Coefficient	Standard error	Coefficient	Standard error	Coefficient	Standard error	Coefficient	Standard error	Coefficient	Standard error
Panel A: Conditional mean												
α_c	0.0002	0.0003	0.0002	0.0003	−0.0002	0.0003	0.0004	0.0004	0.0001	0.0003	**0.0006****	0.0003
δ_{MS}	−0.0022	0.0028	−0.0039	0.0041	**−0.0061***	0.0019	−0.0047	0.0035	**−0.0071***	0.0021	−0.0034	0.0034
δ_{UE}	−0.032	0.0202	0.0347	0.0524	−0.0282	0.0356	−0.0068	0.0186	−0.0242	0.0252	**−0.0397****	0.0163
δ_{CPI}	−0.008	0.0067	−0.0024	0.0051	−0.0256	0.0206	0.0031	0.0049	0.0143	0.0093	−0.0053	0.0052
Panel B: Conditional variance												
β_0	**−0.3287***	0.0875	−0.3232	0.1962	**−0.4703***	0.1148	**−0.8179*****	0.4617	**−0.2203***	0.0622	−1.1133	0.2493
β_1	**0.9717***	0.0110	**0.9685***	0.0227	**0.9548***	0.0142	**0.8897***	0.0732	**0.981***	0.0069	**0.8775***	0.0317
β_2	−0.0015	0.0244	−0.0098	0.0413	−0.0149	0.0271	−0.0197	0.0467	0.0234	0.0225	−0.0493	0.0525
β_3	**0.2077***	0.0329	**0.1606****	0.0675	**0.2624***	0.0465	**0.2756***	0.0437	**0.1365***	0.0333	**0.4329***	0.0627
ρ_{MS}	−0.0131	0.0529	0.0587	0.08	−0.0436	0.0483	−0.0593	0.1039	0.0702	0.0451	**−0.2866****	0.1179
ρ_{UE}	0.1673	0.7737	3.14	2.0753	0.6149	0.8542	**−3.2015****	1.5744	−0.0354	0.6238	−1.9174	1.4305
ρ_{CPI}	**−1.1384***	0.3769	**−1.3646***	0.5251	0.4372	0.507	**−2.8977***	1.0708	0.6666	0.3624	**−1.7613***	0.4647

Notes: This table reports quasi-maximum likelihood (QML) estimate results (models are estimated using Bollerslev–Wooldridge Heteroskedasticity consistent covariance, and the Marquardt optimization algorithm) for the EGARCH (1,1) model of Eq. (2):

$$\Delta Swapsprd_{i,t} = \alpha_{i,c} + \sum_{k=1}^{q} \alpha_{i,k} \epsilon_{i,t-k} + \sum_{N=1}^{4} \delta_{i,N}(D_e * News_{N,t}) + \varepsilon_{i,t}$$

$$\ln(h_{i,t}) = \beta_{i,0} + \beta_{i,1}\ln(h_{i,t-1}) + \beta_{i,2}z_{i,t-1} + \beta_{i,3}\{|z_{i,t-1}| - E(|z_{i,t-1}|)\} + \sum_{N=1}^{4} \rho_{i,N}(D_e * News_{N,t})$$

$$\text{where} \quad \varepsilon_{i,t} = z_{i,t}\sqrt[2]{h_{i,t}} \text{ and } z_{i,t} \sim N(0,1)$$

where $\Delta Swapsprd_{i,t}$ is the change in swap spreads. $D_{e,t}$ is a dummy variable takes on a value of 1 during expansions and zero otherwise. $News_{N,t}$ denotes the surprises of news announcements (N) which are transformed into daily variables by assigning zero for days without the particular news announcement and the values of the surprises for announcement days. q is the number of MA lags required to remove serial correlations. ε_t denotes the error term which is assumed to be $\sim(0, h_t)$. $\sqrt{h_t}$ is the conditional volatility of $\Delta Swapsprd_{i,t}$. The sample period is from January 1995 to January 2007. *, **, and *** indicate statistical significance at the 1%, 5%, and 10% levels, respectively.

Table 6. The Impact of Macroeconomic News Surprises on Australian Interest Rate Swap Spreads: Contraction Periods.

	2-Year Swap Spread		3-Year Swap Spread		4-Year Swap Spread		5-Year Swap Spread		7-Year Swap Spread		10-Year Swap Spread	
	Coefficient	Standard error	Coefficient	Standard error	Coefficient	Standard error	Coefficient	Standard error	Coefficient	Standard error	Coefficient	Standard error
Panel A: Conditional mean												
α_c	0.0003	0.0003	0.0001	0.0003	0.0001	0.0002	0.0006	0.0004	0.0001	0.0003	**0.001***	0.0004
δ_{MS}	−0.0016	0.0047	0.0007	0.0041	**0.0105****	0.0051	0.0098	0.0081	0.0016	0.0054	0.0074	0.0129
δ_{UE}	0.0241	0.0316	0.0243	0.0211	0.0286	0.0192	0.0107	0.023	0.0336	0.0384	0.0171	0.0329
δ_{CPI}	**−0.0098***	0.0012	**−0.0092***	0.0022	**−0.0065****	0.0027	**−0.0052****	0.0026	**−0.0044****	0.0021	**−0.0021***	0.0005
Panel B: Conditional variance												
β_0	**−0.4386***	0.1164	**−0.2684*****	0.1400	**−0.3619***	0.1172	**−2.1139****	0.8304	**−0.2433***	0.0624	**−1.4371***	0.2870
β_1	**0.9601***	0.0149	**0.9728***	0.0167	**0.9644***	0.0145	**0.7185***	0.1323	**0.9768***	0.0076	**0.8399***	0.0368
β_2	0.001	0.0269	0.0021	0.0548	−0.01	0.0261	−0.0953	0.0837	0.0232	0.0266	−0.0579	0.0517
β_3	**0.2493***	0.0347	**0.1468***	0.0565	**0.2044***	0.0543	**0.4894***	0.0512	**0.1451***	0.0372	**0.5208***	0.0698
ρ_{MS}	−0.0728	0.2916	0.0407	0.3154	−0.0302	0.4735	**−0.6556*****	0.3566	0.2416	0.2461	**−1.0446***	0.3650
ρ_{UE}	−1.6225	2.4772	−3.4311	2.5848	−0.9855	4.7043	−4.997	3.7028	**−3.7345****	1.8632	**−4.9003*****	2.6643
ρ_{CPI}	**−0.521***	0.2551	**−1.0711***	0.2593	**−0.825***	0.2934	**−1.1029***	0.3669	**−0.5112****	0.2438	**−1.3955***	0.2765

Notes: This table reports quasi-maximum likelihood (QML) estimate results (models are estimated using Bollerslev–Wooldridge Heteroskedasticity consistent covariance, and the Marquardt optimization algorithm) for the EGARCH (1,1) model of Eq. (2):

$$\Delta Swapsprd_{i,t} = \alpha_{i,c} + \sum_{k=1}^{q} \alpha_{i,k} \epsilon_{i,t-k} + \sum_{N=1}^{4} \delta_{i,N}(D_e * News_{N,t}) + \varepsilon_{i,t}$$

$$\ln(h_{i,t}) = \beta_{i,0} + \beta_{i,1}\ln(h_{i,t-1}) + \beta_{i,2}z_{i,t-1} + \beta_{i,3}\{|z_{i,t-1}| - E(|z_{i,t-1}|)\} + \sum_{N=1}^{4} \rho_{i,N}(D_e * News_{N,t})$$

$$\text{where} \quad \varepsilon_{i,t} = z_{i,t}\sqrt[2]{h_{i,t}} \text{ and } z_{i,t} \sim N(0,1)$$

where $\Delta Swapsprd_{i,t}$ is the change in swap spreads. $D_{e,t}$ is a dummy variable takes on a value of 1 during contractions and zero otherwise. $News_{N,t}$ denotes the surprises of news announcements (N) which are transformed into daily variables by assigning zero for days without the particular news announcement and the values of the surprises for announcement days. q is the number of MA lags required to remove serial correlations. ε_t denotes the error term which is assumed to be $\sim (0, h_t)$. $\sqrt{h_t}$ is the conditional volatility of $\Delta Swapsprd_{i,t}$. The sample period is from January 1995 to January 2007.
*, **, and *** indicate statistical significance at the 1%, 5%, and 10% levels, respectively.

inflation rate announcements are generally negatively significant at the 1% level across all maturities in both states of economy. They also tend to dominate other news announcements in the swap market. The shocks from the inflation rate appear to dampen the conditional volatility of the swap spread. On the other hand, the shocks from money supply changes are restricted to the conditional volatility of 10-year swap spread during both expansions and contractions. The effect from the money supply shocks tends to calm down the conditional volatility of the swap spread.

CONCLUSIONS

This study investigates which macroeconomic news announcements are more influential on the behavior of Australian interest rate swap spreads and to the extent that they affect the changes in the swap spread during economic expansions and contractions. Using news releases from money supply growth, unemployment rate, and inflation rate, we find that news information provided by inflation rate announcements is the only important news throughout the business cycles but most dominant during economic contractions. Whilst the unanticipated unemployment rate tends to be more relevant to 10-year swap and the unanticipated change in money supply tends to be more relevant to 4- and 7-year swaps during expansions. Our findings suggest that market participants pay attention to different macroeconomic news announcements depending on the state of the economy. Information revealed by these news releases therefore may vary in their relevance in each phase of the business cycles.

We also find shocks from these news surprises appear to have significant impact on the conditional volatility of the swap spreads during both economic phases. The macroeconomic shocks in general are negatively related to changes in conditional volatility of the swap spreads, suggesting that these newsworthy announcements tend to reduce uncertainty on the news announcement days in the swap market during expansion and contraction periods. While there are some variations on the effects of the news surprises in different phase of the business cycles, the impacts appear to be quite consistent.

NOTES

1. Boyd et al. (2005) examine only the unemployment rate news announcements compared with three news announcements in this study.

2. Fama (1971) first formalized the relationship between information arrival and the price formation process by making use of the efficient market hypothesis to assert that asset prices immediately reach an equilibrium state reflecting the arrival of new information in the marketplace.

3. Previous related studies that also used ARIMA model are Urich and Watchel (1981), Wasserfallen (1988), and Singh (1993).

4. A business cycle is a graphic representation of the fluctuations in the level of economic activity. The curves of the cycle extend over a number of years, fluctuating through periods of expansions and contractions. These fluctuations are the result of changes in the levels of production, spending, and employment. Expansions and contractions were defined as periods of rising and falling levels of economic activity, respectively.

5. The chain volume measure of GDP is used.

6. We define separate state of economy dummy variables for contraction and expansion which each takes on a value of unity on the state of economy to which they are assigned and zero otherwise.

REFERENCES

Almeida, A., Goodhart, C., & Payne, R. (1998). The effects of macroeconomic news on high-frequency exchange rate behaviour. *Journal of Financial and Quantitative Analysis*, *33*, 383–408.

Anderson, T. G., Bollerslev, T., Diebold, F. X., & Vega, C. (2003). Micro effects of macro announcements: Real-time price discovery in foreign exchange. *American Economic Review*, *93*, 38–62.

Anderson, T. G., Bollerslev, T., Diebold, F. X., & Vega, C. (2007). Real-time price discovery in global stock, bond and foreign exchange markets. *Journal of International economics*. *73*, 251–277.

Australian Bureau of Statistics. (1992). The business cycle in Australia: 1959 to 1992. *Australian Economic Indicators*.

Azad, A. S. M. S., Fang, V., & Wickramanayake, J. (2011). Low-frequency volatility of yen interest rate swap market in relation to macroeconomic risk. *International Review of Finance*, *11*, 353–390.

Balduzzi, P., Elton, E., & Green, C. (2001). Economic news and bond prices: Evidence from the U.S. treasury market. *Journal of Financial and Quantitative Analysis*, *36*, 523–543.

Bollerslev, T., Cai, J., & Song, F. M. (2000). Intraday periodicity, long memory volatility, and macroeconomic announcement effects in the U.S. treasury bond market. *Journal of Empirical Finance*, *7*, 37–55.

Bollerslev, T., & Wooldridge, J. M. (1992). Quasi-maximum likelihood estimation and inference in dynamic models with time-varying covariances. *Econometric Reviews*, *11*, 143–172.

Boyd, J. H., Hu, J., & Jagannathan, R. (2005). The stock market's reaction to unemployment news: Why bad news is usually good for stocks. *The Journal of Finance*, *60*, 649–672.

Brenner, M., Pasquariello, P., & Subrahmanyam, M. G. (2009). On the comovement of U.S. financial markets around macroeconomic news announcements. *Journal of Financial and Quantitative Analysis*, *44*, 1265–1289.

Burns, A. F., & Mitchell, W. C. (1946). *Measuring business cycles*. New York, NY: NBER.

Chen, N., Roll, R., & Ross, S. (1986). Economic forces and the stock market. *Journal of Business, 59*, 355–388.

Connolloy, R., & Wang, A. (2003). International equity market co-movements: Economic fundamentals or contagion? *Pacific-Basin Finance Journal, 11*, 23–43.

Duffie, D., Saita, L., & Wang, K. (2007). Multi-period corporate default prediction with stochastic covariates. *Journal of Financial Economics, 83*, 635–665.

Ederington, L. H., & Lee, J. H. (1993). How market process information: News release and volatility. *Journal of Finance, 48*, 1161–1191.

Ederington, L. H., & Lee, J. H. (1996). The creation and resolution of market uncertainty: The impact of information release on implied volatility. *Journal of Financial and Quantitative Analysis, 31*, 513–539.

Ewing, B. T. (2003). The response of the default risk premium to macroeconomic shock. *Quarterly Review of Economic and Finance, 43*, 261–272.

Fama, E. (1971). Risk, return, and equilibrium. *Journal of Political Economy, 79*, 30–55.

Fama, E. F., & French, K. R. (1989). Business conditions and expected returns on stocks and bonds. *Journal of Financial Economics, 25*, 23–49.

Fang, V., Lin, C. T., & Parbhoo, K. M. (2008). Macroeconomic news, business cycles and Australian financial markets. *Asia-Pacific Financial Markets, 15*, 185–207.

Fang, V., & Muljono, R. (2003). An empirical analysis of the Australian dollar swap spreads. *Pacific Basin Finance Journal, 11*, 153–173.

Flannery, M. J., & Protopapadakis, A. (2002). Macroeconomic factors do influence aggregate stock returns. *Review of Financial Studies, 15*, 751–782.

Fleming, M. J., & Remolona, E. M. (1997). What moves the bond market. *Economic Policy Review, 3*, 31–50. (Federal Reserve Bank of New York).

Fornari, F. (2004). Macroeconomic announcements and implied volatilities in swaption markets. *BIS Quarterly Review* (September), 79–86.

Furfine, C. (2001). Do macro announcements still drive the US bond market? *BIS Quarterly Review* (June), 49–57.

Glosten, L. R., Jagannathan, R., & Runkle, D. E. (1993). On the relation between the expected value and the volatility of the nominal excess return on stocks. *Journal of Finance, 48*, 1779–1801.

Green, C. T. (2004). Economic news and the impact of trading on bond prices. *Journal of Finance, 59*, 1201–1233.

Jaffee, D. M. (1975). Cyclical variation in the risk structure of interest rates. *Journal of Monetary Economics, 1*, 309–325.

Nelson, D. B. (1991). Conditional heteroskedasticity in asset returns: A new approach. *Econometrica, 59*(2), 347–370.

Ramchander, S., Simpson, M., & Chaudhry, M. (2005). The influence of macroeconomic news on term and quality spreads. *The Quarterly Review of Economics and Finance, 45*, 84–102.

Ramchander, S., Simpson, M., & Webb, J. (2003). Macroeconomic news and mortgage rates. *Journal of Real Estate Finance and Economics, 27*, 355–377.

Roley, V. V. (1983). The response of short term interest rate to weekly money announcement. *Journal of Money, Credit and Banking, 15*, 334–354.

Simpson, M. W., Ramchander, S., & Chaudhry, M. (2005). The impact of macroeconomic surprises on spot and forward foreign exchange markets. *Journal of International Money and Finance, 24*, 693–718.

Singh, R. A. (1993). Response of stock prices to money supply announcements: Australian evidence. *Accounting and Finance*, 43–59.

Sorensen, E. H., & Bollier, T. F. (1994). Pricing swap default risk. *Financial Analysts Journal*, *50*, 23–33.

Tang, D., & Yan, H. (2006). Macroeconomic conditions, firm characteristics and credit spreads. *Journal of Financial Services Research*, *29*, 177–210.

Urich, T., & Wachtel, P. (1981). Market response to the weekly money supply announcements in the 1970s. *Journal of Finance*, *36*, 1063–1072.

Wasserfallen, W. (1988). Macroeconomic news and the stock market. *Journal of Banking and Finance*, *13*, 613–626.

Wilson, T. C. (1997a). Portfolio credit risk (1). *Risk*, *10*(9), 111–116.

Wilson, T. C. (1997b). Portfolio credit risk (2). *Risk*, *10*(10), 56–61.

THE EVOLUTION OF THE USE OF DERIVATIVES IN SLOVENIAN NON-FINANCIAL COMPANIES

Ales Berk Skok, Igor Loncarski and Matevz Skocir

ABSTRACT

We investigate the evolution of corporate risk management practices in Slovenian non-financial firms in the period 2004–2009 and compare the findings several surveys conducted for other countries. We mail questionaires to non-financial companies, where the target group included non-financial companies listed on Ljubljana Stock Exchange and the largest exporting companies in Slovenia. We find that the current use of derivatives for hedging purposes is still at a lower level than in the majority of developed countries. The great expansion of Slovenian economy in the period 2004–2008, the development of Slovenian financial system, the convergence of Slovenian and EU accounting standards and recent financial crisis did not sufficiently induce Slovenian firms to adopt risk management practices. The most often stated reasons for the low use of derivatives are (1) insufficient risk exposure, (2) problems with the evaluation and monitoring of derivatives and (3) the costs associated with the implementation of derivatives programme. In our opinion, the institutional environment in Slovenia does not induce managers to undertake proper risk management activities. We argue that not only

Derivative Securities Pricing and Modelling
Contemporary Studies in Economic and Financial Analysis, Volume 94, 399–427

ISSN: 1569-3759/doi:10.1108/S1569-3759(2012)0000094019

managers, but also owners and creditors should be more accountable for the decisions they take (or do not take).

Keywords: Risk management; derivatives; survey; Slovenia; international comparison

INTRODUCTION

The development of financial markets and simultaneous introduction of new financial products have caused the substantial expansion in the corporate use of derivatives for hedging purposes. Recent increase in the volatility of financial and commodities markets coupled with macroeconomic instability induced greater concerns about corporate exposures to different risk classes and raised additional interest in corporate risk management activities. Namely, current economic crisis made many financial and non-financial firms report large losses which could have been avoided with the implementation of proper risk management techniques.

Several theoretical studies argue that risk management adds value to the company due to different market imperfections. Smith and Stulz (1985), Froot, Scharfstein, and Stein (1993) and Tufano (1998), for example, argue that corporate risk management enhances the firm value by minimizing the corporate tax burden, reducing the expected costs of financial distress and by improving the corporate financing and investment policy. Moreover, theoretical models propose that the use of derivatives increases with size, the existence of tax losses and the proportion of shares owned by firm's management (Froot et al., 1993; Nance, Smith, & Smithson, 1993; Smith & Stulz, 1985).

The widespread use of derivatives by non-financial firms and the increased complexity of their risk management policies were a motivation for many studies, which examined risk management practices of corporations. More specifically, one strain of literature has focused on the use of derivatives by non-financial firms in different countries and on the impact of institutional environment on risk management practices. See, for example, Bodnar, Hayt, and Marston (1998) for the United States, Bodnar and Gebhardt (1998) for Germany, Alkebäck and Hagelin (1999) for Sweden, Jalilvand and Switzer (2000) for Canada, De Ceuster, Durink, Laveren, and Lodewyckx (2000) for Belgium, Bodnar, De Jong, and Macrae (2003) for the Netherlands, El-Masry (2003) for the United

Kingdom, Bodnar, Consolandi, Gabbi, and Jaiswal-Dale (2008) for Italy and Kapitsinas (2008) for Greece. The main areas that have been covered by the mentioned surveys are (1) the extent of derivatives use in particular risk category, (2) the organization of risk management activity, and (3) control and reporting procedures. The studies document several differences in the intensity of use and in the attitudes towards the use of derivatives between countries. The differences can be attributed to different institutional setting or different size and industry distribution of studied firms in different countries.

A similar research about corporate risk management was conducted among Slovenian non-financial firms in 2004 (see Berk, 2006) and it presented the extent of the use of derivatives and related practices in the risk management process. The results demonstrated that the share of users of derivatives was relatively small compared to the findings for the United States and Germany. Although Slovenian firms used derivatives to hedge specific risks in a similar way as their US and German counterparts, the general conclusion was that Slovenian firms lagged behind German and US peers in many areas of risk management (Berk, 2006).

This chapter provides an insight into the current risk management practices related to the use of derivatives in Slovenian firms, where we mostly focus on the comparison with the findings in 2004. The study examines various questions regarding the use of derivatives, such as (1) which particular financial risks are being managed, (2) which derivatives are used for hedging certain types of risks, (3) how risk management activities are organized within the firm, (4) what are the performance measurement and reporting procedures.

DATA AND METHODOLOGY

Sample Selection

In this study we investigate the progress made in corporate risk management practices since the time last research was conducted in 2004. For this reason, the target group of companies we used for mailing a survey form was very similar to the one used in 2004. The target group included non-financial companies listed on Ljubljana Stock Exchange, which have to meet certain standards regarding the size and transparency of their operations and are thus expected to be the most advanced in the country. In addition, the survey sample included the top exporters, based on the database of the

Chamber of Commerce and Industry of Slovenia. Included are large and medium-sized companies, which earn more than 50% of their revenues abroad. Financial institutions like banks, brokerage houses, finance and insurance companies were excluded as the nature of their activities is different from the other non-financial companies. At the end, the entire target group for mailing consisted of 327 companies. There were 210 companies that were included in the survey sample in 2004 and 117 were new companies (Berk, 2006). After the last round of mailings, the total sample of responses consisted of 51 companies, which makes the response rate equal to 15.6%. The previous survey included 257 companies in the target sample, while the number of answers was 57 and the response rate was 22.2% (Berk, 2006).[1]

For the purpose of comparison, the structure of the questionnaire closely follows that of many foreign surveys on derivatives use. The foreign surveys, selected in comparison with Slovenian two studies, are the study by Bodnar et al. (2003) for Dutch companies, El-Masry (2003) for UK companies, Bodnar et al. (2008) for Italian companies and Kapitsinas (2008) for Greek companies. The main reason for comparing our results with the selected studies from EU countries is to reduce the impact of institutional factors and business environment on the results as much as possible and to increase the comparability of risk management practices among different countries.

Characteristics of the Sample

The companies in the two samples from Slovenian surveys slightly differ in size, measured by total revenues. In the 2009 survey sample 8.3% of the surveyed companies report revenues greater than EUR 500 million, while there were just 3.51% such companies in 2004. On the other side, size group of up to EUR 250 million included 94.74% companies in 2004 but only 77.1% in 2009 (Berk, 2006). The remaining companies were included in the revenue size group from EUR 250 million to EUR 500 million (14.6% in 2009 and 1.75% in 2004).

The industry profile of the survey sample indicates that this study reflects the corporate risk management practices especially for the firms in the manufacturing sector in Slovenia, since this sector is represented by 38 companies (74.5%). There are two companies (3.9%) in the telecommunications and retail and wholesale trade sector, while the remaining five companies (9.8%) were classified into the transportation, energy supply, entertainment and recreation, financial and insurance services and mining and quarrying sectors. Industry distribution of the 2004 survey sample indicates slightly different distribution of companies across industry sectors. The sectors with the highest number of responding firms are manufacturing with 30 companies (52.6%), wholesale and retail trade with five companies (8.8%) and accommodation and food service sector with two companies (3.5%). The remaining five companies (8.8%) were classified in one of the following sectors: construction, transportation, entertainment and recreation, financial and insurance activities, information and communication (Berk, 2006).[2]

Companies were asked to provide some information about their business, financial issues and performance. In 2008, the average revenue for the companies in the sample was EUR 261.76 million (EUR 48.14 million[3]). The average revenues for sample firms in 2004 amounted to EUR 76.7 million (EUR 27.2 million) (Berk, 2006). The structure of revenues and expenses of Slovenian firms indicate quite significant dependence on foreign markets. Around 70% of the responding firms earn more than 50% of their revenues in foreign markets. However, their foreign currency exposure is smaller, since just 17.6% of firms obtain more than 50% of revenues outside the euroarea. On the other hand, the foreign markets are slightly less important for Slovenian firms regarding their imports. In 2008, 27.5% of firms recorded more than 50% of their expenses in foreign markets, while just 7.8% firms incur more than 50% of their expenses outside euro area. The comparison of descriptives shows that international orientation of Slovenian firms has not changed significantly in the period 2004–2008. In 2004, 69% of firms obtained more than 50% of revenues in foreign markets, while 27.3% of firms incurred more than 50% of expenses in foreign markets (Berk, 2006).

Firms in the current survey sample on average earned EUR 5.8 million (EUR 1.1 million) net income in the financial year 2008. The average investments amounted to EUR 20.3 million (EUR 3.1 million) and the average depreciation was equal to EUR 9.4 million (EUR 2.5 million). On average, the debt-to-capital ratio was 50.7% (47.7%), the return on equity 12.1% (6.9%) and the profit margin 6.1% (1.55%).

In the 2009 survey the internal owners are the prevailing interest group in the ownership structure of these firms. They are present in 27 (52.9%) of surveyed firms, while they are the sole owners of ten (19.6%) firms in the sample. The state has a share in the ownership structure of 15 (29.4%) firms, while this share is greater than 50% in four (7.8%) firms. Foreign owners are present in the ownership structure of 13 (25.5%) firms, while they are the sole owners of five (9.8%) firms. The other owners are minority shareholders, privatization funds, holding companies, etc.

RESULTS

The Use of Derivatives

The management of risk exposures with derivative instruments is still relatively poorly developed area in Slovenian firms, since in 2009 share of derivatives users was only 47.1%. The fact that the target sample consisted mainly of large and medium sized companies with significant risk exposures indicates that the derivatives use rate among Slovenian firms is even lower. The research on derivatives use in 2004 revealed 21 users and 36 non-users of derivative securities, making the derivatives use rate equal to 36.8% (Berk, 2006). The share of derivatives users increased in 2009 compared to 2004, but the difference is not statistically significant. *The international comparison of the use of derivatives supports the notion that Slovenia slightly lags behind the more developed countries with advanced financial environments.* The share of derivative users for foreign countries runs up to 81% in Sweden (Pramborg, 2005) with the most frequently observed use rate around 60% (see Fig. 1).

The majority of users in Slovenia introduced derivatives in the period before financial crisis. Moreover, the survey results do not indicate any considerable increase in the intensity of the use among users in the last three years before the survey. The survey results thus do not support the notion that firms were stimulated to increase their hedging activities during financial crisis. Bodnar, Graham, Harvey, and Marston (2011) document that their survey firms increased derivatives activities during the crisis. In the field of foreign exchange risk, there were 62% of firms which increased level of risk management and only 5% which decreased, in the field of interest rate risk, there were 63% of firms which increased level of risk management and only 7% which decreased and in the field of commodity risk, there were 54% of firms which increased level of risk management and only 4% which decreased. There are two possible reasons for such situation in the field of corporate risk management in Slovenia. Firstly, favourable economic conditions before crisis caused a general underestimation of risk exposures and low awareness of their adverse consequences on business operations. And secondly, the role of corporate risk management in some firms is still unclear. It is possible that managers

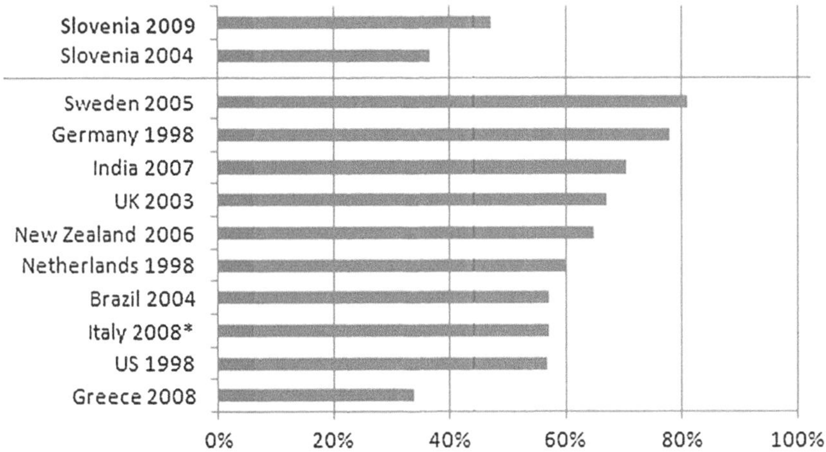

Fig. 1. The Derivatives Use Rate in Selected Countries. *The survey for Italian firms reveals the derivatives use rate for different risk segments. In this figure the derivatives use rate of the highest risk category (foreign exchange risk) is presented. *Source*: Bodnar and Gebhardt (1998); Bodnar et al. (2003); El-Masry (2003); Saito and Schiozer (2005); Pramborg (2005); Naylor and Greenwood (2006); Anand and Kaushik (2007); Bodnar et al. (2008); Kapitsinas (2008); Survey results (2004, 2009).

perceive it as a supplementary activity, which is not on the priority list of activities in crisis times.

The survey results show that the users of derivatives in the current survey sample are larger in size than non users, while the average net income, growth rate of revenues, profit margin, return on equity and debt to capital ratio are not statistically different between users and non users of derivatives (see Table 1). The correlation between the size of the firm and its willingness to hedge risks with derivatives supports the idea of economies of scale associated with the implementation of risk management. On the other hand, the insignificant difference between leverage, profitability and derivatives use could imply the absence of two theoretical motives for risk management, that is the reduction of expected costs of financial distress and improvement of financing and investment policy.

The notion that theoretical motives for corporate risk management do not provide sufficient (endogenous) incentives for Slovenian firms to manage risk was already discussed in the study by Berk Skok and Loncarski (2011). The authors argue that the observed situation in the field of corporate risk management is the result of specific post-transitional legal and business

Table 1. Differences in Financial Performance between the Users and Non Users of Derivatives in 2009.

		Median	Mean	Standard Deviation	Difference in Means
Revenues	Users	190,400,000	486,597,357	785,920,182	−448,859,932***
	Non users	32,766,000	37,737,425	34,568,055	
Net income	Users	2,720,000	10,166,311	35,317,271	−8,298,076
	Non users	326,000	1,868,235	3,634,561	
Growth rate of revenues	Users	11.50%	13.85%	10.05%	23.02%
	Non users	14.00%	36.86%	98.89%	
Profit margin	Users	1.56%	3.09%	3.70%	5.86%
	Non users	1.34%	8.95%	36.53%	
Return on equity	Users	8.42%	11.07%	9.38%	1.79%
	Non users	3.85%	12.86%	53.92%	
Debt to capital	Users	47.24%	49.25%	21.39%	5.12%
	Non users	52.07%	54.37%	17.48%	

Source: Survey results (2009).
*Significant at below 10% level; **significant at below 5% level; ***significant at below 1% level.

environment in Slovenia. Slovenian firms were in the past on average underleveraged and thus the probability for financial distress was much lower. However, in the last few years a lot of firms substantially increased the use of debt, but this obviously has not yet represented an incentive to manage risk. Moreover, relatively small number of Slovenian firms is listed and actively traded, which reduces the shareholders influence and the public interest in the corporate risk management practices.

In addition to the inefficiency of Slovenian equity market, the special corporate governance mechanisms determined by the ownership structure contribute to the relatively poor development of risk management in non-financial firms. A lot of Slovenian firms are owned by large owners, such as in most cases quasi-government funds or privatization-based investment funds. These owners often pursue different goals, such as political influence, consolidation of ownership, extraction of private benefits, etc., which are not consistent with the shareholder value maximization principle (Berk Skok & Loncarski, 2011).*The analysis of the ownership structure of the survey respondents reveals that the government has significantly larger stake in the ownership structure of derivative users than non users,*[4] *while the ownership stake of management and employees is not significantly different between the two groups of comparison.*

Goals and Concerns about the Derivatives Use

In the theoretical literature on corporate risk management the predominant argument for using derivatives is that it represents an efficient way to reduce the volatility of firms' cash flows, which leads to the highest market value of the firm (Froot et al., 1993; Smith & Stulz, 1985, etc.). The examination of the main goals of risk management activity pursued by derivative users in Slovenia reveals that *managing the volatility of firm's cash flows is the most important goal of derivatives use in Slovenian firms, since 47.8% of derivative users consider the goal in that way*. Slightly less derivative users (37.5%) indicate that hedging the value of balance sheet items is the most important goal of their derivatives use, while the other goals are less important.[5] The importance of particular goals of hedging did not change considerably from 2004 except for the hedging balance sheet items, which increased in importance. The firms assigned the highest importance to cash flow hedging in 2004 survey and in comparative foreign surveys as well. However, higher importance of hedging accounting profit in foreign countries (e.g. in Netherlands and Greece) indicates the importance of corporate earnings in reporting the performance results to the public (see Fig. 2).

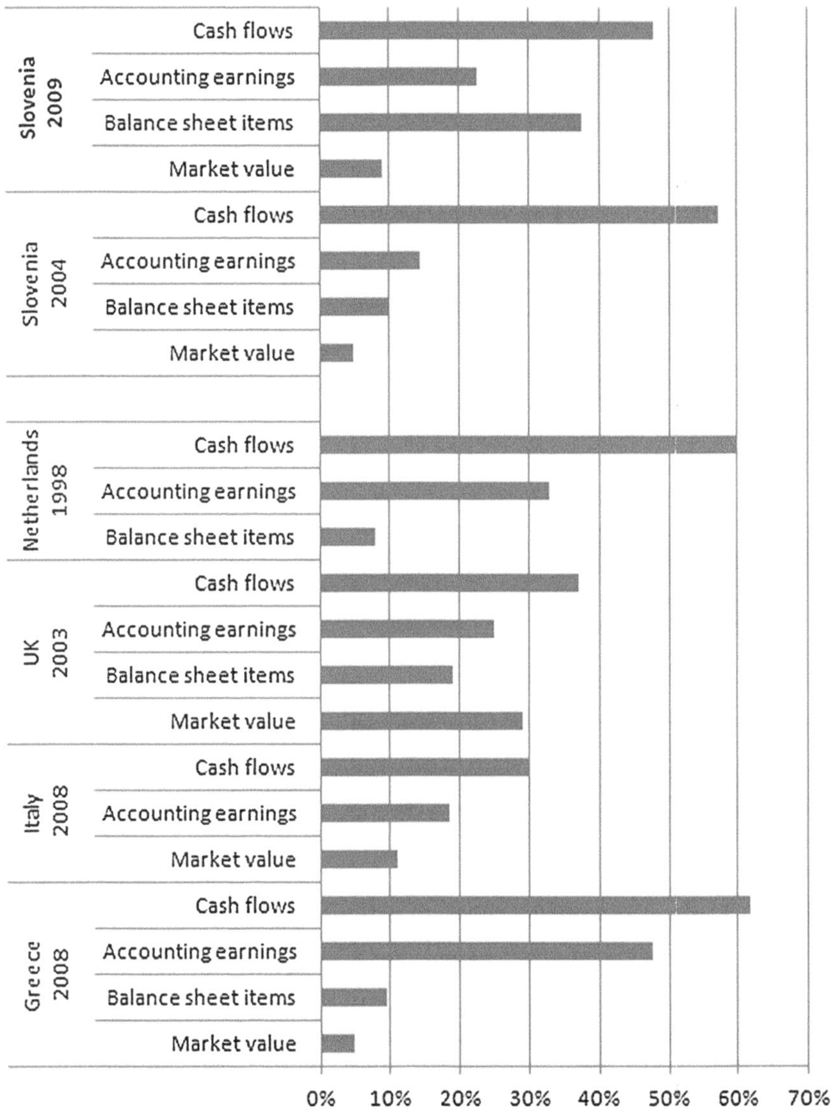

Fig. 2. The Main Goal of Derivatives Use in Slovenia, Netherlands, United Kingdom, Italy and Greece (Percentage of Derivative Users). *Sources*: Bodnar et al. (2003); El-Masry (2003); Bodnar et al. (2008); Kapitsinas (2008); Survey results (2004, 2009).

The implementation of risk management practices involves different concerns regarding the use of derivatives. In both Slovenian surveys firms assigned the highest level of concern to the market risk, which represents the unexpected changes in the price of derivatives. Other important concerns for derivatives use are credit risk (roughly 10% more firms consider credit risk as being of high concern in 2009 compared to 2004), monitoring and evaluation of hedge results and poor liquidity of derivative instruments (see Fig. 3). All these factors are closely related or depend considerably on the development of the derivative market. The liquidity of the market and the assortment of derivatives products have influence on the prices of these instruments. Moreover, these problems with derivatives also induce companies to use other hedging methods, such as operational hedging, financing in foreign currency and others, which can represent a substitute for hedging with derivatives. Taken all together, concerns of Slovenian users of derivatives in 2009 is much more aligned with concerns of foreign users documented by Bodnar et al. (2011) as four highlighted areas of high concerns are market risk (25% of respondents), accounting treatment (18%), counterparty credit risk (15%) and monitoring and evaluating (14%).

The presented concerns about the derivatives use are often among the main reasons that many firms decide not to use these instruments in corporate risk management. The firms that responded negatively on the question about the use of derivatives consider difficult pricing and valuation as the most important reason for not using derivatives, followed by

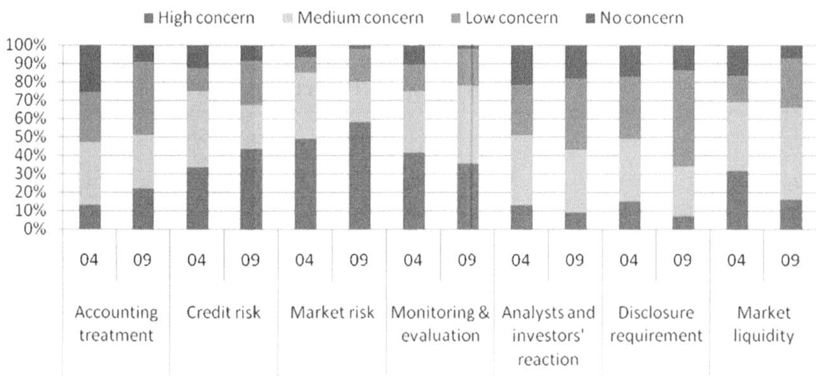

Fig. 3. Concerns Regarding the Derivatives Use in Slovenia, 2004 and 2009 (Percentage of Respondents). *Source*: Survey results (2004, 2009).

insufficient exposure, high cost of hedging programme and use of other methods of hedging (Table 2). *The importance of particular reasons for not using derivatives is slightly different in comparison to the study conducted in 2004, where the most frequently stated reason was insufficient exposure, closely followed by implementation of other methods for reducing risk exposure.* The difficult pricing and valuing of derivatives and costs of hedging programme were slightly less pronounced reasons for not using derivatives in 2004 than in 2009 (Berk, 2006). The international comparison of the main reasons for not using derivatives (Table 2) reveals that Dutch and UK firms consider insufficient exposure as the primary reason for not using derivatives as well (Bodnar et al., 2003; El-Masry, 2003). Moreover, UK firms rank concerns about the perceptions of derivatives use by investors, regulators, analysts or the public and the accounting treatment among the most important reasons for not using derivatives..

Management of Particular Financial Risk Exposures

The Areas of Derivatives Use

The structure of the firm's derivatives portfolio mainly depends on the volatility of particular financial variable and on intensity of the firm's exposure to it. The significant changes in corporate business environment between 2004 and 2009 had an important influence on the need to hedge risk exposures. *However, the survey results do not show that substantial turbulence*

Table 2. The Main Reasons for Not Using Derivatives in Slovenia, Netherlands and United Kingdom (Percentage of Non Users).

	Slovenia 2009	Slovenia 2004	Netherlands 1998	United Kingdom 2003
Insufficient exposure	34,6%	33,3%	67,0%	24,0%
Difficult valuation	34,6%	19,4%	11,0%	12,0%
Costs of hedging	19,2%	11,1%	11,1%	25,0%
Other methods of hedging	15,4%	30,6%	4,0%	12,0%
Public perception	3,8%	5,6%	0,0%	25,0%
Disclosure requirement	0,0%	2,8%	0,0%	22,0%
Accounting treatment	2,8%	0,0%	0,0%	–

Source: Bodnar, De Jong, and Macrae (2003); El-Masry (2003); Survey results (2004, 2009).

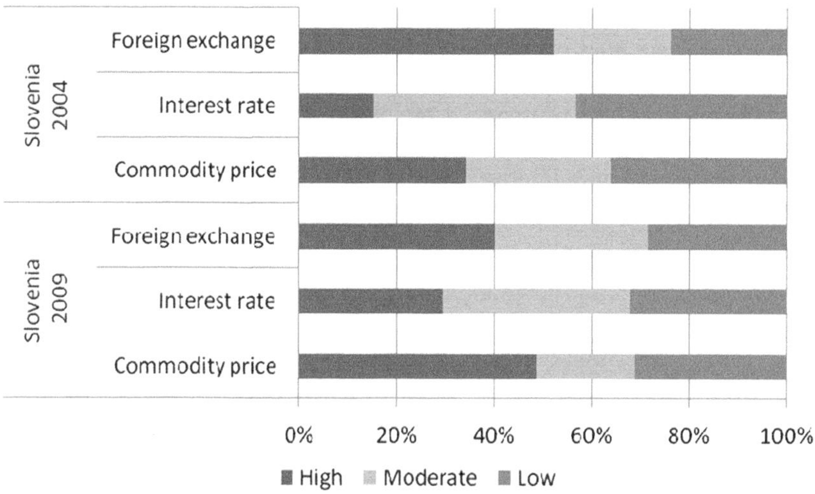

Fig. 4. The Need for Management of Particular Risk with Derivative Instruments in Slovenian Firms in 2004 and 2009 (Percentage of Respondents). *Source*: Survey results (2004, 2009).

in financial markets in the period following the financial and economic crisis significantly changed the corporate need for hedging foreign exchange, interest rate and commodity price risk (see Fig. 4 where types of risk have the same ranking if one considers high and moderate need together). In the 2009 survey, 48.6% of respondents perceive the highest need to manage commodity price risk, 40.0% to manage foreign exchange risk and 29.4% to manage interest rate risk. In 2004, these proportions were 52.1% for foreign exchange risk, 34% for commodity price risk and 15.2% for interest rate risk (Berk, 2006).[6] *This means that relative importance of types of risk according to high needs changed between the two surveys.*

The need for hedging particular risk exposure is one determinant of the actual use of derivatives in particular risk areas. *The use of derivatives for hedging foreign exchange, interest rate and commodity price risk did not significantly change in 2009 compared to 2004. However, the analysis shows that interest rate risk was in 2009 the main area of derivatives use, which is hedged by 79% of derivative users. Foreign exchange risk is hedged by 75% of users and commodity price risk by 63% of users. In 2004, 81% of users hedged foreign exchange risk, while 52.4% hedged interest rate risk and only 33.3% commodity price risk* (Berk, 2006). The interest rate risk is the main risk category hedged by Greek and Italian firms as well (Bodnar et al., 2008;

Kapitsinas, 2008). In United Kingdom and Netherlands, the majority of users (more than 90%) decided to manage foreign exchange risk (Bodnar et al., 2003; El-Masry, 2003). This comparison is presented in the Fig. 5.

The further analysis of financial risk hedging in 2009 reveals that 33.3% of derivative users hedged all three types of risk exposure, 25% hedged foreign exchange and interest rate risk, while 12.5% of users hedged commodity price risk in combination with foreign exchange or interest rate

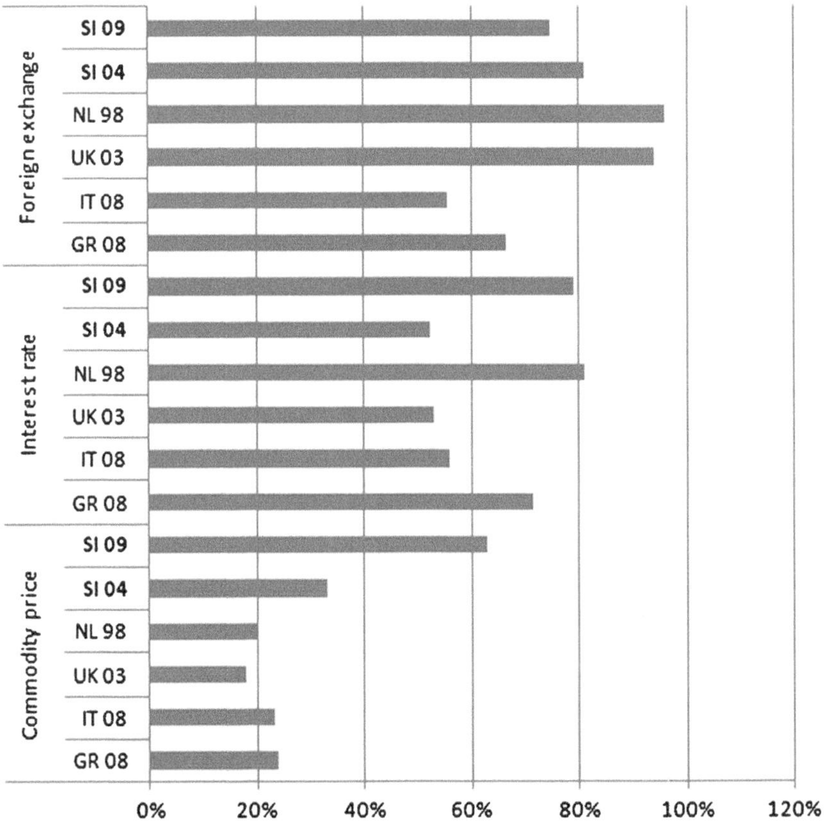

Fig. 5. The Use of Derivatives in Hedging Foreign Exchange, Interest Rate and Commodity Price Risk in Slovenia and Selected Foreign Countries (Percentage of Users). *Source*: Bodnar et al. (2003); El-Masry (2003); Bodnar et al. (2008); Kapitsinas (2008); Survey results (2004, 2009).

risk. Very small number of firms decided to use derivatives to hedge just one type of risk exposure.

The Structure of Derivatives Portfolio

Firms include different types of derivative securities in their hedging portfolio according to the individual characteristics of particular derivative contract. Both Slovenian surveys on derivatives use revealed that the most often used derivative instrument is OTC forward, which was held in the portfolio at 66.6% of derivative users in 2004 and 2009 (see Fig. 6). Slovenian firms also often use OTC swaps in their hedging practices. This type of derivative was used by one half of the derivative users in 2009. The other types of derivatives, held in the portfolio of Slovenian firms, are structured derivatives, futures, exchange options and OTC options. In 2004 the surveyed companies also used hybrid debt, which was not used in 2009 (Berk, 2006).

Foreign Exchange Risk Management

Foreign exchange risk is currently the second most important risk category managed by Slovenian non-financial firms. The management of this risk can be further distinguished into different categories. Table 3 demonstrates that intensity of hedging particular foreign exchange risk exposures decreased in 2009 compared to 2004. The Slovenian firms hedge exposure from anticipated transactions more often than contractual commitments and translation exposure. Namely, 87.5% of foreign exchange derivative users hedged anticipated transactions within one year in 2004, while 75% of users

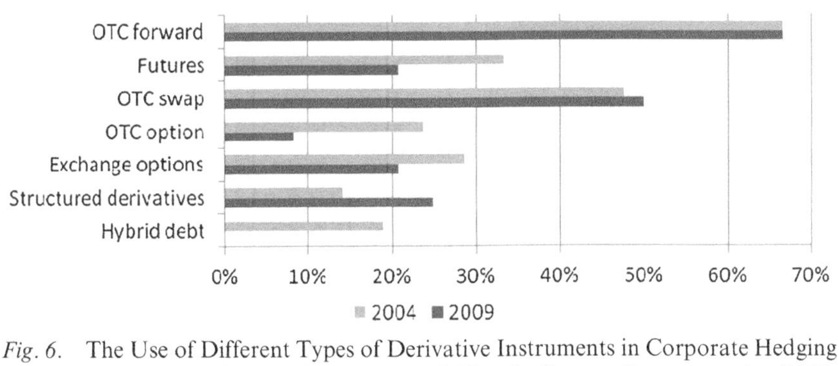

Fig. 6. The Use of Different Types of Derivative Instruments in Corporate Hedging in Slovenia, 2004 and 2009 (Percentage of Users). *Source*: Survey results (2004, 2009).

Table 3. Intensity of Hedging Foreign Exchange Risk Exposure in Slovenia, Netherlands and Greece (Percentage of Foreign Exchange Derivative Users).

	Slovenia 2004		Slovenia 2009		Netherlands 1999		Greece 2008	
	Freq.	Som.	Freq.	Som.	Freq.	Som.	Freq.	Som.
Translation exposure	25.0%	25.0%	15.8%	15.8%	8.0%	14.0%	20.0%	0.0%
Competitive exposure	23.1%	46.2%	22.2%	11.1%	8.0%	36.0%	19.0%	7.0%
Anticipated transactions >1 year	0.0%	53.8%	0.0%	45.0%	8.0%	44.0%	14.3%	35.7%
Anticipated transactions <1 year	50.0%	37.5%	45.0%	30.0%	53.0%	38.0%	58.0%	42.0%
Off balance sheet commitments	46.2%	38.5%	11.8%	11.8%	41.0%	47.0%	21.4%	7.1%
On balance sheet commitments	52.9%	35.3%	47.4%	10.5%	67.0%	24.0%	46.0%	46.9%
Foreign repatriations	6.3%	31.3%	10.0%	10.0%	42.0%	42.0%	28.6%	28.6%

Source: Bodnar et al. (2003); Kapitsinas (2008); Survey results (2004, 2009).

in 2009. In 2004, a majority of users (52.9%) used derivatives to frequently manage on balance sheet commitments, while another 35.3% did so sometimes (Berk, 2006). In 2009, this exposure was managed frequently by 47.4% of users and sometimes by 10.5% of users. The intensity of hedging has decreased for all types of foreign exchange risk exposures in the period 2004–2009.

The comparison of Slovenian and foreign firms' foreign exchange risk management practices reveals quite similar hedging patterns and the preference for hedging short-term currency exposures. Moreover, Slovenian firms more frequently use derivatives to hedge translation exposure than foreign firms, but on the other hand, they use derivatives for hedging of foreign repatriations less intensively than foreign firms.

The theoretical literature proposes the use of derivatives with symmetrical payoff profile (e.g. forwards, futures, etc.) for identifiable firm commitments, whereas for uncertain future cash the use of derivatives with unsymmetrical payoff profile (e.g. options) (Shapiro, 1996). The surveys on derivatives use in selected countries reveal that companies use particular derivative securities for foreign exchange hedging with quite similar intensity. The most often used instruments are forward contracts. In Slovenia, the second and third most important derivatives are exchange options and structured derivatives while the use of other derivatives is less intense (Table 4).

Slovenian firms mostly try to match the maturity of derivative contracts and the maturity of the exposure. Table 5 demonstrates that majority of users (around 75%) hedged the maturity of exposures in 2009 with a slight

Table 4. The Use of Foreign Exchange Derivatives in Slovenia, Netherlands, Italy and Greece (Percentage of Derivative Users).

	Slovenia 2009	Slovenia 2004	Netherlands 1998	Italy 2008	Greece 2008
OTC forward	83.3%	70.6%	77.0%	55.8%	85.7%
Futures	16.7%	11.8%	0.0%	9.9%	14.3%
OTC swap	16.7%	11.8%	0.0%	23.4%	71.3%
OTC option	5.6%	11.8%	2.0%	25.6%	14.3%
Exchange options	22.2%	29.4%	12.0%	4.7%	0.0%
Structured derivatives	22.2%	11.8%	7.0%	18.6%	21.4%
Hybrid debt	0.0%	11.8%	2.0%	9.9%	0.0%

Source: Bodnar et al. (2003); Bodnar, Consolandi, and Gabbi Jaiswal-Dale (2008); Kapitsinas (2008); Survey results (2004, 2009).

Table 5. Hedging Horizon of Slovenian Firms, 2004 and 2009.

		Contractual Commitments	Anticipated Transactions	Competitive Exposure	Foreign Repatriations	Translation of Foreign Accounts
Hedge shorter than the	2004	8.3%	7.1%	10.0%	0.0%	0.0%
maturity of the exposure	2009	14.3%	0.0%	0.0%	25.0%	28.6%
Hedge the same as maturity	2004	58.3%	64.3%	50.0%	33.3%	37.5%
of the exposure	2009	64.3%	83.3%	85.7%	75.0%	71.4%
Hedge longer than the maturity	2004	0.0%	7.1%	10.0%	16.7%	0.0%
of the exposure	2009	14.3%	0.0%	14.3%	0.0%	0.0%
Hedge to the end of budget/fiscal	2004	33.3%	21.4%	30.0%	50.0%	62.5%
year	2009	7.1%	16.7%	0.0%	0.0%	0.0%

Source: Survey results (2004, 2009).

bias towards under hedging the exposures. Hedging the maturity of the exposure was the most important also in 2004 with the difference that more firms decided to over hedge than to under hedge the exposure. In 2009, hedging the exposures to the end of budget/fiscal year was almost negligible.

Interest Rate Risk

The 2009 survey shows that interest rate risk is the most frequently managed risk in Slovenian companies. Fig. 7 displays frequency of use of interest rate derivatives contracts in order to meet four common objectives: to swap from fixed rate debt to floating rate debt, to swap from floating rate debt to fixed rate debt, to fix in advance the spread on new debt and to reduce the costs of future financing. The surveyed Slovenian firms most frequently use floating-to-fixed rate swaps and spread fixing on new debt. Except in the category floating-to-fixed rate swaps, where the use rate increased from 60% to 79% and where in our opinion the far largest change in usage of derivatives within Slovenian companies stems from, intensity of use of interest rate derivatives in general decreased in 2009 compared to 2004.The non-financial firms in Italy, United Kingdom and Greece also the most frequently use derivatives instruments to swap floating interest rate for fixed or to fix the spread on new debt in advance (Bodnar et al., 2008; El-Masry, 2003; Kapitsinas, 2008).

The objectives of interest rate risk management can be achieved with the use of different types of derivatives contracts. The survey results reveal that interest rate swaps are the most suitable instruments for interest rate hedging (see Fig. 8). The relative importance of other derivatives in interest rate risk management has slightly changed in 2009 compared to 2004. Slovenian firms have increased the use of different types of structured derivatives and option contracts. On the other hand, Slovenian firms do not consider hybrid debt as a suitable tool for interest rate hedging anymore.

Commodity Price Risk

In Slovenian companies management of commodity risk is still the weakest area of use of derivatives. However, the 2009 survey results indicate a substantial increase of use of commodity derivatives since 2004 (see Fig. 5) *as well as the need to hedge commodity exposures* (see Fig. 4). At the same time, the relative importance of particular instruments for hedging commodity risk has changed from 2004 to 2009 (see Fig. 9). In 2004, the most often used derivatives were OTC options and swaps (Berk, 2006), while in 2009 almost half of commodity derivative users used forward contracts.

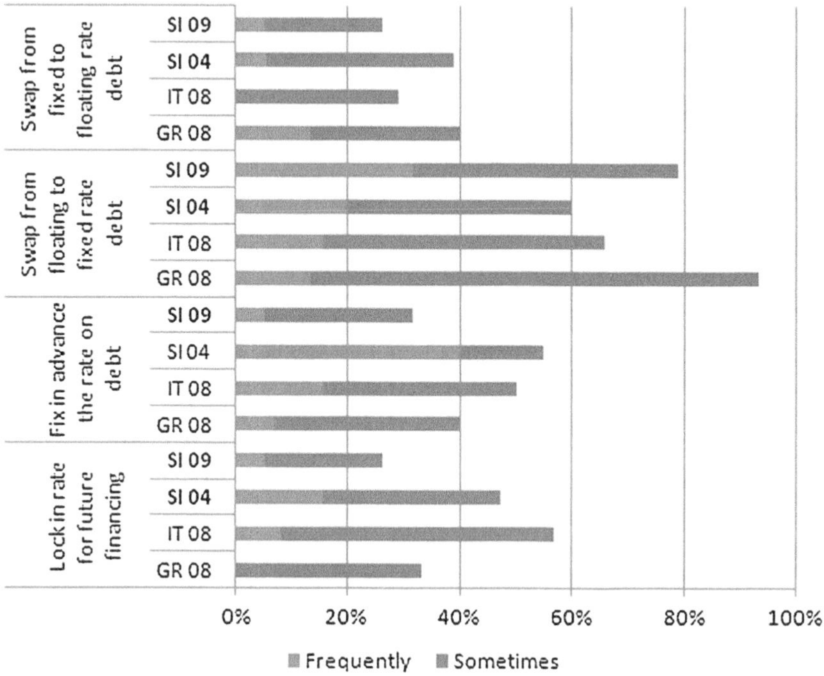

Fig. 7. Frequency of Interest Rate Derivatives Use for Certain Objectives in Slovenia, Italy and Greece. *Source*: Bodnar et al. (2008); Kapitsinas (2008); Survey results (2004, 2009).

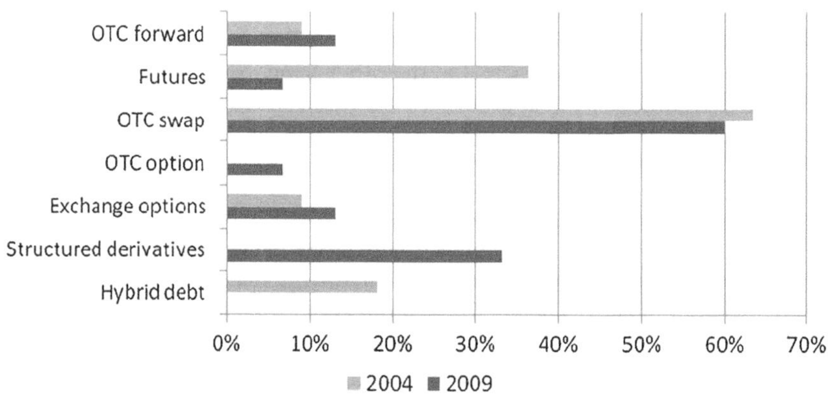

Fig. 8. Preference over Interest Rate Derivatives in Slovenia, 2004 and 2009. *Source*: Survey results (2004, 2009).

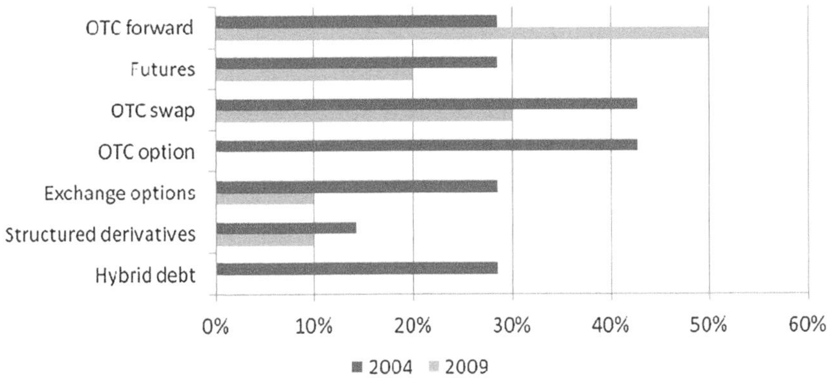

Fig. 9. The Use of Particular Derivatives in Commodity Risk Management in Slovenian Firms in 2004 and 2009. *Source*: Survey results (2004, 2009).

Financial Risk Management Policies

The use of derivative instruments and their trading was relatively weakly organized, reported and regulated in the past. The interest of corporate stakeholders is to establish a systematic approach to corporate hedging and to increase the transparency of derivatives transactions at the firm level (Froot, Scharfstein, & Stein, 1994). Slovenian firms most often decide for centralized organization of risk management activities. This suggests that economies of scale, associated with the number of employees, knowledge, training and others are involved in risk management process. This approach was the most often observed in comparative foreign studies for United Kingdom, Dutch and Greek companies as well (Bodnar et al. 2003; El-Masry, 2003; Kapitsinas, 2008).

Monitoring and Evaluation of Derivatives and the Portfolio

The systematic selection of derivatives and the subsequent monitoring of risk and valuation of a portfolio of derivatives is an important factor for success of the corporate hedging activity. Firms use different methods to evaluate the riskiness of their derivatives transactions or portfolios, such as stress testing, scenario analysis, but value-at-risk (VaR) being the most widespread. The survey results show that Slovenian companies in 2009 lag behind their foreign counterparties in the use of VaR method (see Fig. 10).

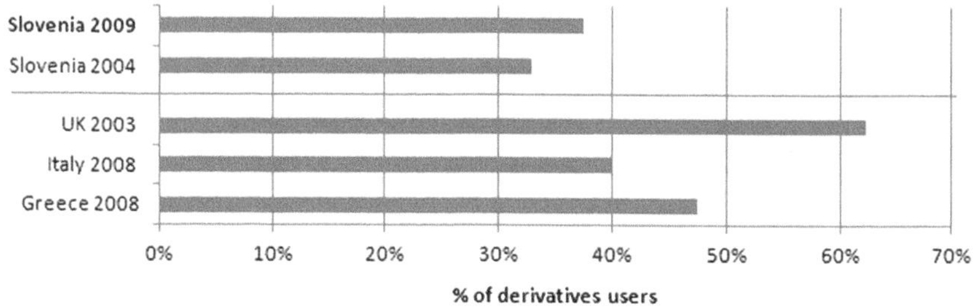

Fig. 10. The Use of Value-at-Risk Method for the Evaluation of the Derivatives' Risk in Slovenia, United Kingdom, Italy and Greece. *Source*: El-Masry (2003); Bodnar et al. (2008); Kapitsinas (2008); Survey results (2004, 2009).

The frequent monitoring and valuation of the firm's derivative positions enable companies to promptly react to adverse market movements or to take advantage of positive market trends. Slovenian companies do not recognize such benefits as *2009 survey results show that almost half of the responding Slovenian firms still don't have scheduled valuation policy and that no progress has been made since 2004* (see Fig. 11). *Moreover, Slovenian firms valued the derivatives portfolio even less frequently in 2009 compared to 2004.* The number of firms, which value their portfolio weekly slightly decreased and the number of firms with valuation policy on monthly or quarterly basis slightly increased in the last period. Percentage of firms valuing portfolio of derivatives at least monthly decreased in 2009 compared to 2004. The majority of foreign firms value their derivatives portfolio on a monthly basis. El-Masry (2003) reported that 50% of the UK firms had this valuation policy in 2003. Kapitsinas (2008) observed high percentage of Greek firms with valuation policy on monthly basis (42.9%) and very low percentage of firms without scheduled policy (9.52%). Bodnar et al. (2011) report that 68% of their non-financial firms use monthly frequency to value their portfolio of derivatives.

In the valuation process the Slovenian firms most often rely on internal valuation or on the original dealer in the derivatives transactions. The in-house software was indicated as the primary source of derivatives evaluation by 46.7% of respondents in 2004 (Berk, 2006) and by 27.3% respondents in 2009. The original dealer was considered as the primary source by 36.7% in 2004 (Berk, 2006) and by 27.3% in 2009.

Best practice suggests that special credit policy defining the lowest acceptable credit rating of a derivative transaction counterparty should be

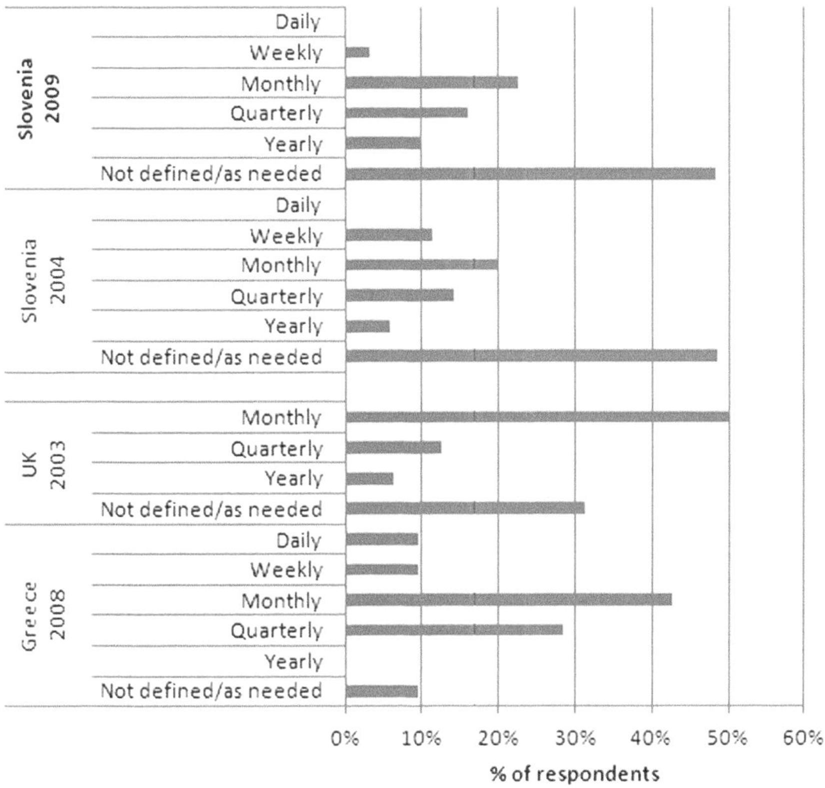

Fig. 11. The Frequency of Valuing the Portfolio of Derivatives in Slovenia, United Kingdom and Greece. *Source*: El-Masry (2003); Kapitsinas (2008); Survey results (2004, 2009).

set. Back in 2004 Slovenian companies did not have well-defined credit policy. The 2009 survey results show that the criteria for the derivative transaction counterparty risk were even less strict compared to 2004 (see Fig. 12). In 2009 *majority of Slovenian firms still did not have established counterparty risk policy and that the percentage of firms in this category increased.* In 2004, 54.1% of derivative users revealed that they did not have predefined counterparty risk policy for derivatives transactions with maturities up to 12 months and 52.9% of them did not have policy for transaction with maturities more than a year (Berk, 2006). In 2009, there were 65.7% and 67.5% of users in these two groups respectively. This negative trend raises doubts about the adequacy of the internal audit that

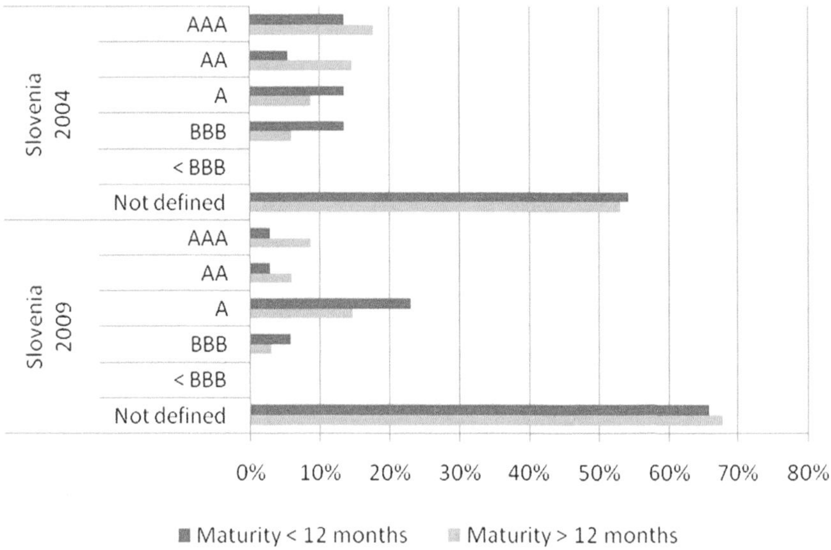

Fig. 12. The Lowest Rate of Counterparty Credit Rating for Derivative Transactions Required by Slovenian Users, 2004 and 2009. *Source*: Survey results (2004, 2009).

firms that do use the derivatives have in place. Moreover, in 2009 majority of firms with established counterparty risk policy required the rating A by the counterparty, while in 2004 they required AAA. The examination of the results of other surveys reveals that foreign firms prefer to implement much more strict rules regarding the counterparty risk. Bodnar et al. (2003) report that only 39% of Dutch firms did not have a policy regarding the counterparty risk, while in Greece this share amounted to around 30%. The majority of users in these two countries preferred the credit rating AA or A by the counterparty (Bodnar et al., 2003; Kapitsinas, 2008).

Corporate Hedging Policy Documentation and Reporting

The increased attention of corporate stakeholders about the use of derivatives in risk management increased the importance of setting a clearly defined documentation and reporting policies. *Slovenian firms still do not assign considerable importance to development of the corporate hedging documentation policy. Namely, share of firms with documented policy about derivatives did not significantly increase from 2004 to 2009.* In 2009 28.6% of firms reported they did not have established documented policy regarding the use of derivatives which was even higher from 34.7% reported back in 2004 (Berk, 2006).Reporting in accordance with IFRS accounting standards obviously did not induce Slovenian firms to implement the corporate hedging documentation policy.

In addition, the survey results do not show that the frequency of reporting of corporate hedging activities has increased in Slovenia from 2004 to 2009.

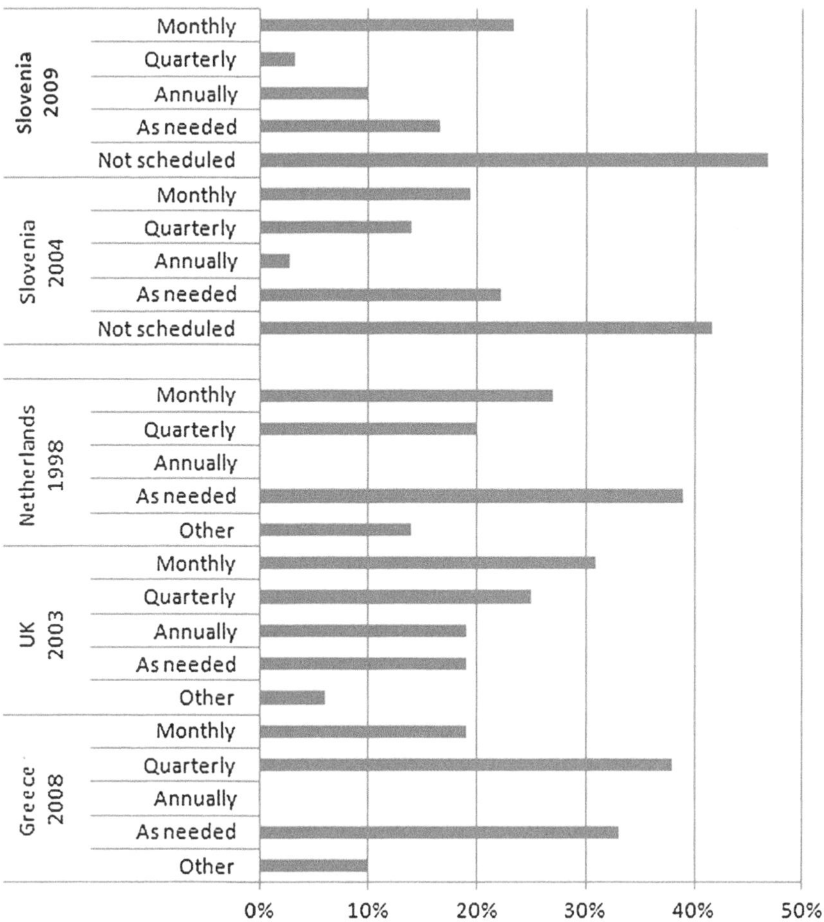

Fig. 13. Frequency of Reporting Derivatives Activity. *Source*: Bodnar et al. (2003); El-Masry (2003); Kapitsinas (2008); Survey results (2004, 2009).

Namely, in 2004 33.3% of responding firms reported their hedging activities at least quarterly, while the share of such firms in 2009 survey amounted only to 26.7%. Furthermore, 41.7% of responding firms did not report their activities at all in 2004 (Berk, 2006). The share of such firms even increased to 46.7% in 2009 (see Fig. 13). With such habits Slovenian companies also lag behind the selected foreign counterparts in the reporting area. Namely, the comparative study for Dutch firms reveals 47% of firms reporting at least quarterly about their hedging practices in 2003 (Bodnar et al., 2003). The share of such firms was 56% in the United Kingdom (El-Masry, 2003) and 57% in Greece (Kapitsinas, 2008).

CONCLUSION

This chapter presents an overview of corporate risk management using derivatives in Slovenia and the progress in this field since previous research conducted in 2004. The 2009 survey results reveal that the overall usage of derivative instruments increased compared to 2004. However, it is surprising that the complexity of the use of derivatives has not changed, given that macroeconomic environment and financial markets have both undergone significant changes. The adoption of Euro in Slovenia in 2007 increased financial stability in the country and lowered the foreign exchange risk exposure for exporters. On the other hand, Slovenian companies have been hit hard by the financial and economic crisis which significantly increased volatilities in financial and commodity markets. It is therefore not surprising that companies decreased the use of derivatives for hedging foreign exchange risk and substantially increased use of interest rate and commodity derivatives.

The use of derivatives is more intense in larger Slovenian firms which can be explained by the most common argument in the literature, that is presence of considerable economies of scale associated with the risk management process. Regarding performance, no clear relation between the extent of use of derivatives and the corporate profitability can be identified. The same holds for the growth in sales, leverage and ownership structure. This indicates that the motives presented in the theoretical literature on corporate risk management are not very explicit in Slovenia.

The 2009 survey reveals that the use of derivatives in Slovenian non-financial firms is still much lower than in the majority of developed countries. In our opinion there are several reasons for this: Firstly, companies in countries with better developed financial markets have longer history of the derivatives use. In Slovenia, the competition in banking sector has increased only recently with the entrance of some foreign banks in Slovenian market, which led to the increase in the number of derivative products offered to non-financial companies. Secondly, the special characteristics of Slovenian post-transitional legal and business environment represent one of the key reasons for the observed differences in corporate derivative practices. Thirdly, relatively small number of firms in Slovenia is listed and actively traded, which reduces the shareholders influence and the public interest in the corporate risk management practices. Moreover, in many public Slovenian firms there is a concentration of ownership (large owners), such are government-owned funds and privatization-based investment funds. These owners often pursue other than traditional value-maximizing goals, such as consolidation of ownership, political goals, etc. In such an environment, the managers do not put enough emphasis on the positive effects of corporate hedging, which results in lower use of derivatives for the purpose of the corporate risk management.

NOTES

1. Response rate in both Slovenian surveys was lower than in the majority of the surveys discussed in the previous chapter, as the latter ranged from 8.59% in the study for Indian companies (Anand & Kaushik, 2007), up to 84.0% in Finnish survey (Hakkarainen, Kasanen, & Puttonen, 1997). The median response rate for these surveys is equal to 34.24%.
2. The comparative foreign survey samples include higher percentage of large companies and they have more equal distribution of firms across different industry classes. In Bodnar et al. (2011) survey includes 47% of firms with revenue higher than USD 500 million.
3. The values in brackets represent the median for selected variable as for skewed distributions the median represent better estimation of the central tendency.
4. The observed correlation between the ownership of government and the use of derivatives must be interpreted with caution, because of the already stated significant impact of the firm size on the use of derivatives.
5. The average importance of presented goals measured on the five level scale (1 – the highest importance, ..., 5 – the lowest) is the following: 2.17 for cash flow hedging, 2.42 for hedging the value of balance sheet items, 3.09 for hedging accounting profit, 3.41 for achieving risk adjusted return, 3.83 to decrease the costs of capital and 4.36 to hedge the market value of the firm.
6. The average rankings of foreign exchange hedging, interest rate hedging and commodity price hedging were 1.72, 2.28 and 2.02, respectively, in 2004 and 1.89, 2.03 and 1.83, respectively, in 2009. Ranking 1 represents the highest and 3 the lowest need to hedge.

REFERENCES

Alkebäck, P., & Hagelin, N. (1999). Derivative usage by nonfinancial firms in Sweden with an international comparison. *Journal of International Financial Management and Accounting*, *10*(2), 105–120.

Anand, M., & Kaushik, K. P. (2007). Management motivations for use of foreign currency derivatives in India. IIML Working Paper Series. Calcutta.

Berk, A. (2006). The use of derivatives in Slovenian non-financial firms: Is financial risk already well managed? *Zbornikradova Ekonomskogfakulteta u Rijeci*, *24*(2), 225–256.

Berk Skok, A., & Loncarski, I. (2011). Are exogenous requirements sufficient enough to induce corporate risk management activities? *Post-Communist Economies*, *23*(1), 119–137.

Bodnar, G. M., Consolandi C., Gabbi, G., & Jaiswal-Dale, A. (2008). *A survey on risk management and usage of derivatives by non-financial Italian firms*. Carefin Research Paper 7, Universitá Bocconi, Milano.

Bodnar, G. M., Hayt, G. S., & Marston, R. C. (1998). 1998 Wharton survey of financial risk management by US non-financial firms. *Financial Management*, *27*(4), 70–91.

Bodnar, G. M., De Jong, A., & Macrae, V. (2003). The impact of institutional differences on derivatives usage: A comparative study of US and Dutch firms. *European Financial Management*, *9*(3), 271–297.

Bodnar, G. M., & Gebhardt, G. (1998). Derivative usage in risk management by US and German non-financial firms: A comparative survey. *Journal of International Financial Management and Accounting*, *10*(3), 153–187.

Bodnar, M. G., Graham, J., Harvey, R. C., & Marston, C. R. (2011). *Managing risk management*. Working Paper (electronic version). Retrieved from http://ssrn.com/abstract=1787144

De Ceuster, M. J. K., Durink, E., Laveren, E., & Lodewyckx, J. (2000). A survey into the use of derivatives by large non-financial firms operating in Belgium. *European Financial Management*, *6*(3), 301–318.

El-Masry, A. (2003). *A survey of derivatives use by UK non-financial companies*. Social Science Research Network, Manchester Business School 455.

Froot, A. K., Scharfstein, S. D., & Stein, C. J. (1993). Risk management: Coordinating corporate investment and financing policies. *Journal of Finance*, *48*(5), 1629–1658.

Froot, A. K., Scharfstein, S. D., & Stein, C. J. (1994). A framework for risk management. *Harvard Business Review*, *72*(6), 91–102.

Hakkarainen, A. N., Kasanen, E., & Puttonen, V. (1997). Interest rate risk management in major Finnish firms. *European Financial Management*, *3*(3), 255–268.

Jalilvand, A., & Switzer, J. (2000). A global perspective on the use of derivatives for corporate risk management decisions. *Managerial Finance*, *6*(3).

Kapitsinas, S. (2008). Derivatives usage in risk management by non-financial firms: Evidence from Greece. *Munich Personal RePEc Archive*, *9*.

Nance, D. R., Smith, C. W., & Smithson, C. W. (1993). On the determinants of corporate hedging. *Journal of Finance*, *48*(1), 267–284.

Naylor, M. J., & Greenwood, R. C. (2006). The characteristics of foreign exchange hedging: A comparative analysis. *Journal of Asia-Pacific Business*, *9*(2), 121–152.

Pramborg, B. (2005). Foreign exchange risk management by Swedish and Korean non-financial firms: A comparative survey. *Pacific-Basin Finance Journal*, *13*, 343–366.

Saito, R., & Schiozer, R. F. (2005). Derivatives usage in risk management by non-financial firms: A comparison between Brazilian and international evidence. Working Paper, Getulio Vargas foundation, Rio de Janeiro.

Shapiro, A. C. (1996). *Multinational financial management* (5th ed). Upper Saddle River, NJ: Prentice Hall.

Smith, C. W., & Stulz, R. M. (1985). The determinants of firms' hedging policies. *Journal of Financial and Quantitative Analysis*, *20*(4), 391–405.

Tufano, P. (1998). Agency cost of corporate risk management. *Financial Management Association*, *27*(1), 67–77.

INDEX